**CONSTITUTIONAL CONVERGENCE IN EAST ASIA**

This comparative study of the constitutional jurisprudence of three East Asian jurisdictions investigates how the rulings of the Constitutional Court of Taiwan, the Constitutional Court of Korea and the Hong Kong Court of Final Appeal have converged. The unique political contexts of all three jurisdictions have led to strong courts using the structured proportionality doctrine and innovative constitutional remedies to address human rights issues. Hong Kong, Taiwan, and South Korea have the only courts in Asia that regularly use a structured four-stage Proportionality Analysis to invalidate laws, and routinely apply innovative constitutional remedies such as Suspension Orders and Remedial Interpretation to rectify constitutionally flawed legislation. This volume explores how judges in these areas are affected by politics within their different constitutional systems. The latest developments in Asian constitutional law are covered, with detailed analysis of key cases.

Po Jen Yap is a Professor of Law at The University of Hong Kong. He is an Advocate and Solicitor of the Supreme Court of Singapore and an Attorney at Law in the State of New York, USA. He is the author of *Constitutional Dialogue in Common Law Asia* (2015) and *Courts and Democracies in Asia* (2017).

Chien-Chih Lin is an Associate Research Professor at Institutum Iurisprudentiae, Academia Sinica (Taiwan). He has published in multiple law journals and edited volumes, including *The Oxford Handbook of Constitutional Law in Asia, American Journal of Comparative Law,* and *International Journal of Constitutional Law.* He is the book review editor of the *International Journal of Constitutional Law.*

COMPARATIVE CONSTITUTIONAL LAW AND POLICY

*Series Editors*

Tom Ginsburg *University of Chicago*
Zachary Elkins *University of Texas at Austin*
Ran Hirschl *University of Toronto*

Comparative constitutional law is an intellectually vibrant field that encompasses an increasingly broad array of approaches and methodologies. This series collects analytically innovative and empirically grounded work from scholars of comparative constitutionalism across academic disciplines. Books in the series include theoretically informed studies of single constitutional jurisdictions, comparative studies of constitutional law and institutions, and edited collections of original essays that respond to challenging theoretical and empirical questions in the field.

*Books in the Series*

*Filtering Populist Claims to Fight Populism: The Italian Case in a Comparative Perspective* Giuseppe Martinico

*Constitutionalism in Context* David S. Law

*The New Fourth Branch: Institutions for Protecting Constitutional Democracy* Mark Tushnet

*The Veil of Participation: Citizens and Political Parties in Constitution-Making Processes* Alexander Hudson

*Towering Judges: A Comparative Study of Constitutional Judges* Edited by Rehan Abeyratne and Iddo Porat

*The Constitution of Arbitration* Victor Ferreres Comella

*Redrafting Constitutions in Democratic Orders: Theoretical and Comparative Perspectives* Edited by Gabriel L. Negretto

*From Parchment to Practice: Implementing New Constitutions* Edited by Tom Ginsburg and Aziz Z. Huq

*The Failure of Popular Constitution Making in Turkey: Regressing Towards Constitutional Autocracy* Edited by Felix Petersen and Zeynep Yanaşmayan

*A Qualified Hope: The Indian Supreme Court and Progressive Social Change* Edited by Gerald N. Rosenberg, Sudhir Krishnaswamy, and Shishir Bail

*Reconstructing Rights: Courts, Parties, and Equality Rights in India, South Africa, and the United States* Stephan Stohler

*Constitutions in Times of Financial Crisis* Edited by Tom Ginsburg, Mark D. Rosen, and Georg Vanberg

*Hybrid Constitutionalism: The Politics of Constitutional Review in the Chinese Special Administrative Regions* Eric C. Ip

*Constitution-Making and Transnational Legal Order* Edited by Tom Ginsburg, Terence C. Halliday, and Gregory Shaffer

*The Invisible Constitution in Comparative Perspective* Edited by Rosalind Dixon and Adrienne Stone

*The Politico-Legal Dynamics of Judicial Review: A Comparative Analysis* Theunis Roux

*Constitutional Courts in Asia: A Comparative Perspective* Edited by Albert H. Y. Chen and Andrew Harding

*Judicial Review in Norway: A Bicentennial Debate* Anine Kierulf

*Constituent Assemblies* Edited by Jon Elster, Roberto Gargarella, Vatsal Naresh, and Bjorn Erik Rasch

*The DNA of Constitutional Justice in Latin America: Politics, Governance, and Judicial Design* Daniel M. Brinks and Abby Blass

*The Adventures of the Constituent Power: Beyond Revolutions?* Andrew Arato

*Canada in the World: Comparative Perspectives on the Canadian Constitution* Edited by Richard Albert and David R. Cameron

*Constitutions, Religion and Politics in Asia: Indonesia, Malaysia and Sri Lanka* Dian A. H. Shah

*Courts and Democracies in Asia* Po Jen Yap

*Proportionality: New Frontiers, New Challenges* Edited by Vicki C. Jackson and Mark Tushnet

*Constituents before Assembly: Participation, Deliberation, and Representation in the Crafting of New Constitutions* Todd A. Eisenstadt, A. Carl LeVan, and Tofigh Maboudi

*Assessing Constitutional Performance* Edited by Tom Ginsburg and Aziz Huq

*Buddhism, Politics and the Limits of Law: The Pyrrhic Constitutionalism of Sri Lanka* Benjamin Schonthal

*Engaging with Social Rights: Procedure, Participation and Democracy in South Africa's Second Wave* Brian Ray

*Constitutional Courts as Mediators: Armed Conflict, Civil-Military Relations, and the Rule of Law in Latin America* Julio Ríos-Figueroa

*Perils of Judicial Self-Government in Transitional Societies* David Kosař

*Making We the People: Democratic Constitutional Founding in Postwar Japan and South Korea* Chaihark Hahm and Sung Ho Kim

*Radical Deprivation on Trial: The Impact of Judicial Activism on Socioeconomic Rights in the Global South* César Rodríguez-Garavito and Diana Rodríguez-Franco

*Unstable Constitutionalism: Law and Politics in South Asia* Edited by Mark Tushnet and Madhav Khosla

*Magna Carta and Its Modern Legacy* Edited by Robert Hazell and James Melton

*Constitutions and Religious Freedom* Frank B. Cross

*International Courts and the Performance of International Agreements: A General Theory with Evidence from the European Union* Clifford J. Carrubba and Matthew J. Gabel

*Reputation and Judicial Tactics: A Theory of National and International Courts* Shai Dothan

*Social Difference and Constitutionalism in Pan-Asia* Edited by Susan H. Williams

*Constitutionalism in Asia in the Early Twenty-First Century* Edited by Albert H. Y. Chen

*Constitutions in Authoritarian Regimes* Edited by Tom Ginsburg and Alberto Simpser

*Presidential Legislation in India: The Law and Practice of Ordinances* Shubhankar Dam

*Social and Political Foundations of Constitutions* Edited by Denis J. Galligan and Mila Versteeg

*Consequential Courts: Judicial Roles in Global Perspective* Edited by Diana Kapiszewski, Gordon Silverstein, and Robert A. Kagan

*Comparative Constitutional Design* Edited by Tom Ginsburg

# Constitutional Convergence in East Asia

**PO JEN YAP**
The University of Hong Kong

**CHIEN-CHIH LIN**
Academia Sinica, Taiwan

CAMBRIDGE
UNIVERSITY PRESS

**CAMBRIDGE**
**UNIVERSITY PRESS**

University Printing House, Cambridge CB2 8BS, United Kingdom

One Liberty Plaza, 20th Floor, New York, NY 10006, USA

477 Williamstown Road, Port Melbourne, VIC 3207, Australia

314–321, 3rd Floor, Plot 3, Splendor Forum, Jasola District Centre, New Delhi – 110025, India

103 Penang Road, #05–06/07, Visioncrest Commercial, Singapore 238467

Cambridge University Press is part of the University of Cambridge.

It furthers the University's mission by disseminating knowledge in the pursuit of education, learning, and research at the highest international levels of excellence.

www.cambridge.org
Information on this title: www.cambridge.org/9781108831178
DOI: 10.1017/9781108923422



First published 2022

*A catalogue record for this publication is available from the British Library.*

*Library of Congress Cataloging-in-Publication Data*
NAMES: Yap, Po Jen, author. | Lin, Chien-Chih (J.S.D.), author.
TITLE: Constitutional convergence in East Asia / Po Jen Yap, The University of Hong Kong; Chien-Chih Lin, Academia Sinica, Taiwan.
DESCRIPTION: Cambridge, United Kingdom ; New York, NY : Cambridge University Press, 2022. | Series: Comparative constitutional law and policy | Includes bibliographical references and index. | Contents: Introduction – Reasons for convergence – Convergence on structured proportionality – Convergence on innovative constitutional remedies – Limits on convergence – Conclusion.
SUBJECTS: LCSH: Constitutional law–East Asia.

ISBN 978-1-108-83117-8 Hardback

# Contents

# Foreword

Comparative constitutional studies has become truly global in the last couple of decades, and there is no region of the world which has escaped scholarly purview. In East Asia, there is now a burgeoning scholarship focused on constitutional developments. This work has significantly enriched our understanding of the region, as well as its importance in the world.

In this insightful, carefully researched, and illuminating volume, two leading young scholars in Asia tackle a new question, namely that of constitutional convergence. Convergence has long fascinated scholars of comparative law and social science, for good reason. Similarity and difference are, of course, at the heart of any comparative enterprise: it is their observation that spurs inquiry into causes and consequences. The first task of the comparativist is descriptive: simply to document similarity and difference, and how they change over time. But the more challenging task is to develop explanation.

Convergence and divergence add temporal and relational dimensions: are the objects of study moving closer together over time, or are they instead moving away from each other? Explaining convergence and divergence is particularly tricky because, to put it simply, things are always in motion. One has to carefully select cases to examine, as well as a time period and scope of the research. Then one must weigh the various forces that cause change over time.

Professors Yap and Lin masterfully use this approach to ask why it is that high courts in some Asian jurisdictions have converged on jurisprudential techniques, while others have not. Their focus is on doctrine and remedy. Using well-selected case studies, they carefully work through the various caselaw to demonstrate a good deal of convergence among Hong Kong, Taiwan and Korea, three liberal jurisdictions in Asia. These are legally dynamic places, which have experienced broader changes in their political and social systems in recent decades. Yap and Lin's framework is rigorous, and well-grounded in the existing literature, but also pushes it forward. The inclusion of a non-democratic case, Hong Kong, helps us see that the primary driving force is not the political character of the regime. Rather, the key qualities seem to be a liberal grounding, along with judges who have the capacity and inclination to advance liberal values.

The result is a significant contribution to our understanding. The study enriches the literature on transnational judicial borrowing, which has been a major issue of debate in comparative constitutional studies. Many judges participate in a kind of transnational conversation in which they share approaches, read each other's cases and wrestle with rationales from other jurisdictions. We have a good deal of normative work debating whether and when judges should look abroad. Some scholars actively advocate convergence as normatively desirable, a position which smacks of high modernism, as if law could be removed from its connection with a broader culture it inhabits. Against this view, some judges reject borrowing entirely, insisting on legally grounded norms that fit in a national context. 'We must never forget', Justice Scalia once wrote in a blistering dissent, 'that it is the Constitution of the United States we are expounding'. Citing the jurisprudence of other countries' courts was anathema to Scalia, and his position evokes the romanticism of the nation-state finding its expression in national law. Yet Scalia's position is enduring, and indeed, in an era of rising nationalism and populism, it may be more powerful than ever.

Using the Asian materials, Yap and Lin demonstrate a kind of middle way between these two positions. Convergence can occur organically, without triggering nationalist backlash. The quality of the decision-making in the cases they study seems to be enriched by convergence, but they also point out its spatial and substantive limits. The result is a wonderful study of analytic approaches in an important part of the world.

Above all, this study marks the maturity of constitutional studies in East Asia. These three jurisdictions with powerful courts, regularly engaged in the issues of the day in their societies, are worthy of more attention outside the region. Scholars interested in convergence and borrowing will of course find much food for thought in this book. And the expertly-executed comparative approach will illuminate the jurisdictions they study, even for those who already know one or the other of them well.

Tom Ginsburg
Leo Spitz Professor of International Law
Ludwig and Hilde Wolf Research Scholar
Professor of Political Science
University of Chicago Law School

# Acknowledgements

We owe a tremendous debt of gratitude to all the comparative constitutional law scholars in our field who have shaped our views over the years. Specifically, we would really like to extend our deepest appreciation to Richard Albert, Cora Chan, Johannes Chan, Wen-Chang Chang, Albert Chen, Sujit Choudhry, Fabian Duessel, Rosalind Dixon, Hualing Fu, James Fowkes, Tom Ginsburg, Michaela Hailbronner, Cheng-Yi Huang, Jau-Yuan Hwang, Samuel Issacharoff, David Landau, David Law, Jaehong Lee, Seokmin Lee, Kent Roach, Yoon Jin Shin, Alec Stone Sweet and Mark Tushnet, who have provided insightful comments on various parts and permutations of this manuscript. They have refined our arguments and saved us from much embarrassment.

Special thanks must also go out to Cheng-Yi Chiang, Monica Li-Ru Hsu, Raphael Leung, Fang-Chen Lo, Kitson Chun-Kit Ng and Diana Siu, all of whom have provided invaluable research assistance and technical support. Joe Ng, our editor at Cambridge University Press, has been an absolute joy to work with, and we are very grateful for his assistance at every stage of this project. This book would not have been completed in time without all their unyielding support.

Parts of Chapter 3 were drawn from Po Jen Yap, 'Proportionality in Asia: Joining the Global Choir' in Po Jen Yap (ed.), *Proportionality in Asia* (Cambridge University Press 2020) and Chien-Chih Lin, 'Proportionality in Taiwan' in Po Jen Yap (ed) *Proportionality in Asia* (Cambridge University Press 2020). Parts of Chapter 4 were drawn from Po Jen Yap, 'Remedial Discretion and Dilemmas in Asia' (2019) 69 *University of Toronto Law Journal* 84 – reprinted with permission from University of Toronto Press (https://utpjournals.press), DOI: 10.3138/utlj.69.s1.004 © University of Toronto Press 2019.

This research project has been generously supported by the Hong Kong Research Grants Council's General Research Fund Project No. 17600417.

# Abbreviations

| | |
|---|---|
| BORO | Bill of Rights Ordinance |
| CCP | Chinese Communist Party |
| CEEO | Chief Executive Election Ordinance |
| CRI | Constitutional Research Institute |
| CSSA | Comprehensive Social Security Assistance Scheme |
| DJP | Democratic Justice Party |
| DLP | Democratic Liberal Party |
| DPJ | Democratic Party of Japan |
| DPP | Democratic Progressive Party |
| DUP | Democratic United Party |
| ECICO | Elections (Corrupt and Illegal Conduct) Ordinance |
| FC | Functional Constituencies |
| GC | Geographical Constituencies |
| GFCC | German Federal Constitutional Court |
| GNP | Grand National Party |
| HKCA | Hong Kong Court of Appeal |
| HKCFA | Hong Kong Court of Final Appeal |
| HKCFI | Hong Kong Court of First Instance |
| HKSAR | Hong Kong Special Administrative Region |
| ICCPR | International Covenant on Civil and Political Rights |
| JFBA | Japan Federation of Bar Association |
| JORC | Judicial Officers Recommendation Commission |
| JSC | Supreme Court of Japan |
| KCC | Constitutional Court of Korea |
| KMT | Kuomintang |
| LDP | Liberal Democratic Party |
| LegCo | Legislative Council |
| MDP | Millennium Democratic Party |
| MMM | Mixed Member Majoritarian |

| | |
|---|---|
| NCNP | National Congress for New Politics |
| NKP | New Korea Party |
| NPCSC | Standing Committee of the National People's Congress |
| NPJ | Non-Permanent Judge |
| NSL | National Security Law |
| OWP | One Way Permit |
| PA | Proportionality Analysis |
| PFCR | Prohibition on Face Covering Regulation |
| PFP | People First Party |
| POO | Public Order Ordinance |
| PPD | Party for Peace and Democracy |
| RI | Remedial Interpretation |
| ROC | Republic of China |
| SJ | Secretary for Justice |
| SNTV | Single Non-transferrable Vote |
| SO | Suspension Order |
| SP | Structured Proportionality |
| TCC | Constitutional Court of Taiwan |
| UFP | United Future Party |
| UKSC | Supreme Court of the United Kingdom |
| UNDP | United New Democratic Party |
| UPP | United Progressive Party |

# 1

# Introduction

With the advent of globalization and the ubiquity of modern technology, the world has become highly-networked, increasingly interdependent, and a seamless transnational flow of commodities and capital is gradually erasing national boundaries.[1] These technological, economic and political developments have also generated endogenous and exogenous changes in domestic legal orders, such that independent states are slowly but inexorably converging on a swathe of rules, which regularly include policies on trade, labour, the environment and consumer safety standards.[2]

Constitutional ideas are not immune from this globalizing force. Mark Tushnet has projected that constitutional systems all over the world would 'inevitably' converge 'in their structures and in their protections of fundamental human rights'.[3] There are multiple pathways to such constitutional convergence. The changes can arise exogenously, for example when new constitutions are imposed by foreign powers on domestic states,[4] or when countries are coerced into accepting constitutional change in exchange for economic or military aid.[5] Other changes can be

[1] Robert O. Keohane, *Power and Governance in a Partially Globalized World* (Routledge 2002); Manfred Steger, 'Political Ideologies in the Age of Globalization' in Michael Freeden, Lyman Tower Sargent, and Marc Stears (eds), *The Oxford Handbook of Political Ideologies* (Oxford University Press 2013) 214–231.

[2] Daniel W. Drezner, 'Globalization and Policy Convergence' (2001) 3 *International Studies Review* 53, 53; Beth A. Simmons and Zachary Elkins, 'The Globalization of Liberalization: Policy Diffusion in the International Political Economy' (2004) 98 *American Political Science Review* 171, 171–172.

[3] Mark Tushnet, 'The Inevitable Globalization of Constitutional Law' (2009) 49 *Virginia Journal of International Law* 985, 987. See also Cheryl Saunders, 'Transplants in Public Law' in Mark Elliott, Jason N. E. Varubas and Shona Wilson Stark (eds), *The Unity of Public Law?* (Hart 2018); Wen-Chen Chang and Jiunn-Rong Yeh, 'Internationalization of Constitutional Law' in Michel Rosenfeld and András Sajó (eds), *The Oxford Handbook of Comparative Constitutional Law* (Oxford University Press 2012).

[4] Richard Albert, Xenophon Contiades and Alkmene Fotiadou (eds), *The Law and Legitimacy of Imposed Constitutions* (Routledge 2018).

[5] Ryan Goodman and Derek Jinks, 'How to Influence States: Socialization and International Human Rights Law' (2004) 54 *Duke Law Journal* 621; Rosalind Dixon and Eric A. Posner, 'The Limits of Constitutional Convergence' (2011) 11 *Chicago Journal of International Law* 399, 414–417; Benedict Goderis and Mila Versteeg, 'Transnational Constitutionalism: A Conceptual Framework' in Denis

endogenous. David Law has contended that global investment and migratory patterns can positively impact human rights insofar as states intentionally 'race to the top' in the protection of property and human rights, so as to attract the best talents and businesses from around the world to relocate to their shores.[6] Even as states converge as they compete for financial and human capital, states also converge as they borrow constitutional materials from one another.[7] While constitutional borrowing does not preclude the possibility of local adaption and adjustment, Sujit Choudhry is right to recast this 'borrowing' phenomenon as a migration of constitutional ideas, as this 'migration' metaphor explicitly welcomes a wider range of uses for comparative materials and encompasses a broader range of relationships that arise between the movement of constitutional ideas and recipient jurisdictions.[8] Specifically, this migration-driven constitutional convergence can result from the political branches of government relying on foreign materials when they entrench[9] or amend[10] a constitution. But convergence may also occur as a result of domestic judges consulting and incorporating comparative legal materials when they interpret their local constitutions.[11]

It is this latter type of migration-driven constitutional convergence that this book will examine closely. Specifically, we will explain and explore how the constitutional jurisprudence in three East Asian democracies – Taiwan, South Korea and Hong Kong – are aligning as a consequence of domestic judicial construction and practice.

Vicki Jackson has argued that courts can converge on both outcomes and judicial methodology.[12] As we will argue in this book, both forms of constitutional convergence are indeed occurring in Taiwan, South Korea and Hong Kong. Convergence, of course, does not mean complete coincidence or uniformity.[13] But it is striking that within Asia, these three jurisdictions have the most liberal courts that have in recent

J. Galligan and Mila Versteeg (eds), *Social and Political Functions of Constitutions* (Cambridge University Press 2013) 106–112.

6 David S. Law, 'Globalization and the Future of Constitutional Rights' (2008) 102 *Northwestern University Law Review* 1277; David S. Law and Mila Versteeg, 'The Evolution and Ideology of Global Constitutionalism' (2011) 99 *California Law Review* 1163, 1175–1176.

7 See D.M. Davis, 'Constitutional Borrowing: The Influence of Legal Culture and Local History in the Recognition of Comparative Influence' (2003) 1 *International Journal of Constitutional Law* 181, 189–194.

8 See Sujit Choudhry, 'Migration as a New Metaphor in Comparative Constitutional Law' in Sujit Choudhry (ed.), *The Migration of Constitutional Ideas* (Cambridge University Press 2009) 21.

9 Gregory Shaffer, Tom Ginsburg and Terence C. Halliday (eds), *Constitution-Making and Transnational Legal Order* (Cambridge University Press 2019).

10 Richard Albert, *Constitutional Amendments: Making, Breaking, and Changing Constitutions* (Oxford University Press 2019).

11 Mark Tushnet, 'The Possibilities of Comparative Constitutional Law' (1999) 108 *Yale Law Journal* 1225; Sujit Choudhry, 'Globalization in Search of Justification: Toward a Theory of Comparative Constitutional Interpretation' (1999) 74 *Indiana Law Journal* 819.

12 Vicki Jackson, *Constitutional Engagement in a Transnational Era* (Oxford University Press 2010) 42.

13 Tushnet (n. 3) 987.

years ruled in favour of progressive causes, for example gay marriage,[14] transsexual marriage[15] and abortion rights.[16]

What is equally significant, in our view, is not just the convergence on constitutional outcomes, but also how the courts of final resort in all three jurisdictions have achieved 'methodological convergence'.[17] The Constitutional Court of Taiwan (TCC), the Constitutional Court of Korea (KCC), and the Hong Kong Court of Final Appeal (HKCFA) have converged on the use of Structured Proportionality[18] (SP) in rights-adjudication, and they have also converged on the use of innovative judge-made constitutional remedies,[19] which either delay or expedite the legal consequences that generally follow from the judicial declaration of an unconstitutional practice. It bears emphasizing that the judiciaries in Taiwan, South Korea and Hong Kong are the *only* Asian courts that apply Structured Proportionality regularly and reason through this structured, judge-made doctrinal framework sequentially.[20] Notably, they are also the only courts in Asia that routinely apply both Suspension Orders to delay the invalidation of an unconstitutional practice and Remedial Interpretation to rewrite an otherwise unconstitutional law.[21]

14 J.Y. Interpretation No. 748 (2017) (Constitutional Court of Taiwan), available at http://cons.judicial.gov.tw/jcc/en-us/jep03/show?expno=748, accessed 8 May 2021.

15 W v. *Registrar of Marriages* [2013] 16 HKCFAR 112 (Hong Kong Court of Final Appeal).

16 *Case on the Crime of Abortion*, 2017Hun-Ba127 (11 April 2019) (Constitutional Court of Korea).

17 Jackson (n. 12) 42.

18 See Chapter 3, this volume.

19 See Chapter 4, this volume.

20 In *Navtej Singh Johar* v. *Union of India 2018 Indlaw SC* 786 the Supreme Court of India on 6 September 2018 relied on the Proportionality Analysis (PA) to invalidate an archaic statutory provision that criminalized same-sex consensual intercourse. While the Court did not explicitly reference a structured and sequential PA, different judges relied on different sub-limbs of PA for their decisions. A few weeks later, the Supreme Court for the first time in *Justice K. S. Puttaswamy (Retired)* v. *Union of India 2018 Indlaw* SC 898 formulated a structured four-stage SP in the following terms: '1. A law interfering with fundamental rights must be in pursuance of a legitimate state aim; 2. The justification for rights-infringing measures that interfere with or limit the exercise of fundamental rights and liberties must be based on the existence of a rational connection between those measures, the situation in fact and the object sought to be achieved; 3. The measures must be necessary to achieve the object and must not infringe rights to an extent greater than is necessary to fulfil the aim; 4. Restrictions must not only serve a legitimate purposes; they must also be necessary to protect them.' In that case, the Indian Supreme Court invalidated various governmental rules, which mandated that every bank account in India had to be linked to the individual's unique digital identification number or the account would be frozen, on the basis that the measures were a disproportionate violation of the person's constitutional right to property. This four-stage SP has not been cited by subsequent panels of the Indian Supreme Court and it is thus unclear whether this case marked the dawn of SP in India or was merely an anomaly.

21 The Constitutional Court of Indonesia used to apply both constitutional remedies too, but Suspension Orders have fallen out of favour with the Court, as the government routinely dragged its feet on complying with a delayed remedy. The Court now prefers to apply a Remedial Interpretation of an impugned law that provides the assurance of an immediate remedy that comes into effect when the judicial declaration is made. See Fritz Edward Siregar, 'Pragmatism and the Use of Suspension Orders by Indonesia's Constitutional Court' in Po Jen Yap (ed.) *Constitutional Remedies in Asia* (Routledge 2019) 73–74.

## REASONS FOR CONVERGENCE

We should stress at the outset that the TCC, the KCC, and the HKCFA are not *deliberately* converging their constitutional jurisprudence with one another. The three courts seldom look to – let alone explicitly cite – one another's precedents. For the TCC and the KCC, German law is the most persuasive foreign legal source;[22] for the HKCFA, Anglo-Canadian constitutional precedents are the overseas caselaw that are most routinely referenced and endorsed.[23] But insofar as Germany and Canada/United Kingdom have converged on Structured Proportionality[24] and these novel constitutional remedies,[25] and so far as the TCC or the KCC adopts German jurisprudence (explicitly or covertly) and the HKCFA endorses Anglo-Canadian precedents, the three Asian jurisdictions are *indirectly* converging on liberal Western constitutional norms. Moreover, the three East Asian courts are converging on these liberal Western constitutional practices by overturning domestic laws and imposing independent constraint on state power.

There are two inter-related institutional reasons for this 'judicialization'[26] of public law norms, which promotes this constitutional convergence within East Asia. First, judicialization in East Asia is fostered by a fragmentation of power within the political branches of government,[27] which hampers the ability of the government of the day to pursue a unified legislative agenda efficaciously. Taiwan and South Korea are classic Asian paradigms of dynamic democracies.[28] In a dynamic democracy, the ruling party's control of state affairs is temporary, as competing parties regularly take turn in office. With the absence of a semi-permanent government, the judiciary enjoys more space to determine policy outcomes, as rival factions in the political branches are less likely to collaborate actively to overrule

22 David S. Law, 'Judicial Comparativism and Judicial Diplomacy' (2015) 163 *University of Pennsylvania Law Review* 927, 963 and 979.

23 Ibid. 989.

24 BVerfGE 7, 377 (1958) (German Federal Constitutional Court); *R* v. *Oakes* [1986] 1 SCR 103 (Supreme Court of Canada); *De Freitas* v. *Permanent Secretary of Ministry of Agriculture, Fisheries, Lands and Housing* [1999] 1 AC 69 (Privy Council).

25 For examples on Remedial Interpretation of legislation, see *Ghaidan* v. *Godin-Mendoza* [2004] 2 AC 557 (UK House of Lords); *Schachter* v. *Canada* [1992] 2 SCR 679, 93 DLR (4th) 1 (Supreme Court of Canada); BVerfGE 2, 266 (1953) (German Federal Constitutional Court). For examples on Suspension Orders, see BVerfGE 33, 303 (1972) (German Federal Constitutional Court) and *Reference Re Manitoba Language Rights* [1985] 1 S.C.R. 721 (Supreme Court of Canada).

26 C. Neal Tate and Torbjorn Vallinder (eds), *The Global Expansion of Judicial Power* (New York University Press 1997); Alec Stone Sweet, *Governing with Judges: Constitutional Politics in Europe* (Oxford University Press 2000) 12–20; Ran Hirschl, *Towards Juristocracy* (Harvard University Press 2004) 211; Doreen Lustig and J. H. H. Weiler, 'Judicial Review in the Contemporary World – Retrospective and Prospective' (2018) 16 *International Journal of Constitutional* Law 315.

27 C. Neal Tate, 'Why the Expansion of Judicial Power' in C. Neal Tate and Torbjorn Vallinder (eds) *The Global Expansion of Judicial Power* (New York University Press 1995) 30; John Ferejohn, 'Judicializing Politics, Politicizing Law' (2002) 65 *Law & Contemporary Problems* 41, 59.

28 Po Jen Yap, *Courts and Democracies in Asia* (Cambridge University Press 2017) 94–124.

or punish the courts – especially since constitutional review by an independent branch of government provides a form of insurance for political parties when fortunes turn.[29] Insulated from political backlash, these courts have more opportunities and policy space to independently adopt Western constitutional practices that are inconsistent with the legislative/ regulatory status quo.

While political power is most fragmented in a competitive democracy, this fragmentation can even occur in some authoritarian democracies. Hong Kong is one such example. Notably, the Chief Executive – head of the Hong Kong Special Administrative Region (HKSAR) government – is not drawn from any political party, and there has never been a dominant political party in control of the Legislative Council since the establishment of the HKSAR in 1997. Therefore, the Chief Executive has to regularly rely on the legislative support of multiple political parties, independents and corporate representatives before any legislation in Hong Kong can be passed.[30] While the government can easily whip up support for laws that China considers imperative, pro-Beijing lawmakers are frequently not on the same page vis-à-vis socio-political or economic reforms that are not core concerns of the communist regime.[31] In such circumstances, the local lawmakers would break ranks with the HKSAR government to cater to their own constituents. In essence, the absence of a unitary government in Hong Kong provides the courts with the policy space to determine substantive outcomes in a range of constitutional issues where the pro-Beijing parties themselves are divided, and the transaction costs for overriding the courts are simply too prohibitive.[32]

Second, judicialization is facilitated by an independent judiciary.[33] Judges are empowered and protected when their ex ante and ex post autonomy are secured

[29] Tom Ginsburg, *Judicial Review in New Democracies: Constitutional Courts in Asian Cases* (Cambridge University Press 2003) 25.

[30] Brian Fong, 'Executive-Legislative Disconnection in Post-colonial Hong Kong' (2014) 1 *China Perspectives* 5, 12.

[31] The now-aborted extradition bill is a prime example. In 2019, the Hong Kong Chief Executive attempted to pass a deeply unpopular law that would have allowed the local government to extradite persons in Hong Kong to Mainland China to face trial for crimes allegedly committed in the latter territory. Notably, this controversial bill was conceived by the Chief Executive alone and was not a directive from China. Beijing-friendly lawmakers in Hong Kong who represented the business sectors had deep reservations about the law as the business sectors had significant financial dealings in the Mainland, and many Beijing-friendly lawmakers even publicly opposed its passage. The bill was eventually suspended after over a million people took to the streets to voice their disapproval, and the bill was eventually formally withdrawn. Tony Cheung and Joyce Ng, 'Extradition Bill Protests: Why Have Hong Kong's Business Elite and Tycoons Abandoned Carrie Lam?' (*South China Morning Post*, 23 July 2019), available at www.scmp.com/news/hong-kong/politics/article/3019441/extradition-bill-protests-why-have-hong-kongs-business, accessed 8 May 2021.

[32] Eric C. Ip, *Hybrid Constitutionalism: The Politics of Constitutional Review in the Chinese Special Administrative Regions* (Cambridge University Press–2019) 175–192.

[33] Roderick A. Macdonald and Hoi Kong, 'Judicial Independence as a Constitutional Virtue' in Michel Rosenfeld and András Sajó (eds), *The Oxford Handbook of Comparative Constitutional Law* (Oxford University Press 2012) 831–858.

from a singular dominant external actor.[34] Where politicians have a significant role in the judicial appointment process, they will always seek to elevate judicial candidates who reflect their political views.[35] But in a dynamic democracy where political power routinely rotates between rivalling parties, different legislative factions will have their turn in picking judges, which will lead to ideological diversity on the bench. And the judges elevated to their courts of final resort will not be beholden or accountable to one political party. This is so in Taiwan and South Korea. But ex ante judicial autonomy can also be established in authoritarian democracies where politicians do not have a *de facto* major role in the appointment of judges. In Hong Kong, judges are in substance selected[36] by the nine-member Judicial Officers Recommendation Commission (JORC) chaired by the Chief Justice, and the JORC primarily comprises judges and lawyers. And it is the Chief Justice – and not politicians – who shapes the membership of his HKCFA and even the specific panels that hear the appeals. Furthermore, in Taiwan, South Korea and Hong Kong, ex post judicial autonomy is also secured insofar as the judges on their courts of final resort are protected from arbitrary removal while they hold office.[37] It is important to note that none of the top judges in any of the three jurisdictions has ever been impeached, nor has any top judge been compelled to resign. Ex ante and ex post judicial autonomy are interdependent and conjunctively enhance judicial power.

Aside from these institutional variables that facilitate the rise of a strong judiciary, for a liberal court to be established, liberal judges must have the opportunity to get appointed, and they must *desire* liberal outcomes and *choose* to pursue them.[38] Judges cherish their reputation.[39] But in autocratic regimes, courts can only please their primary audience – the ruling government – for their institutional survival

34 Daniel M. Brinks and Abby Blass, 'Rethinking Judicial Empowerment: The New Foundations of Constitutional Justice' (2017) 15 *International Journal of Constitutional Law* 296, 299. See also Mark Tushnet, 'Preserving Judicial Independence in Dominant Party States' (2015) 60 *New York School Law Review* 107, 111–114.

35 Robert Dahl, 'Decision-Making in a Democracy: The Supreme Court as a National Policy-Maker' (1957) 6 *Journal of Public Law* 279; Jeffrey A. Segal and Harold J. Spaeth, *The Supreme Court and the Attitudinal Model Revisited* (Cambridge University Press 2002); Benjamin Alarie and Andrew J. Green, *Commitment and Cooperation in High Courts: A Cross Country Examination of Institutional Constraints on Judges* (Oxford University Press 2017) 83.

36 Formally, all judges in Hong Kong are appointed by the Chief Executive of the HKSAR on the recommendation of the JORC. Judicial appointments to the HKCFA, in addition, must be endorsed by the Legislative Council. See Articles 88 and 90 of the Hong Kong Basic Law. But, in practice, the Chief Executive has appointed every JORC recommendation and the Legislative Council has endorsed every HKCFA appointment. See Chapter 2 for a full discussion.

37 Article 81 of the Constitution of the Republic of China (Taiwan); Article 8 of the Constitutional Court Act (Korea); Article 89 of the Hong Kong Basic Law.

38 Lee Epstein and Jack Knight, *The Choices Justices Make* (CQ Press 1998) 22–36.

39 Nuno Garoupa and Tom Ginsburg, *Judicial Reputation: A Comparative Theory* (University of Chicago Press, 2015).

hinges on this.[40] On the other hand, where the government is divided, and judges are protected from political reprisal, they can 'engage in self presentation to other audiences whose esteem is important to them',[41] for example the public, lawyers, academia, the international community and luminary judges from other leading courts of final resort. Hong Kong, Taiwan and South Korea have the most liberal courts in Asia precisely because of the political fragmentation in their constitutional systems, and the insulation of their judges from the control of one dominant party in government, which allow for independent liberal judges to be regularly appointed to the highest court. And these liberal judges in turn can hand down liberal rulings when they have a majority. Such independent liberal judges in East Asia can therefore forge a 'constitutional identity'[42] for their jurisdiction that deviates from the status quo imposed by their governments.[43] For Hong Kong, liberal-minded judges would turn to human rights standards established in England and Canada to advance their progressive causes, while the Korean and Taiwanese Constitutional Courts would seek assistance from German law. The judicial endorsement of foreign precedents from 'high prestige courts and countries'[44] that have deep historical legal ties[45] to their jurisdictions in fact bolsters the legitimacy of the Courts' use of these decisions. In this way, the judges can parry off insinuations that they are merely foisting their own personal vision upon society, but are instead converging their Asian practices with the established norms of exalted, modern states in the West that their own legal systems are modelled after.

40 Tamir Moustafa and Tom Ginsburg, 'Introduction: The Functions of Courts in Authoritarian Politics' in Tom Ginsburg and Tamir Moustafa (eds), *Rule by Law* (Cambridge University Press 2008) 14–21.

41 Lawrence Baum, *Judges and Their Audiences: A Perspective on Judicial Behaviour* (Princeton University Press 2008) 4.

42 Gary Jeffrey Jacobsohn, *Constitutional Identity* (Harvard University Press 2010); See also Ran Hirschl, *Comparative Law Matters: The Renaissance of Comparative Constitutional Law* (Oxford University Press 2014) 41–43.

43 Lustig and Weiler (n. 26) 365–369.

44 Law (n. 22) 1000. See also Cheryl Saunders, 'Judicial Engagement' in Rosalind Dixon and Tom Ginsburg (eds), *Comparative Constitutional Law in Asia* (Edward Elgar 2012) 80, 87.

45 In Taiwan, core legislation such as the Civil Code and the Criminal Code was based on the German equivalent when the Republic of China was established in 1911 and German law remains influential in Taiwan today. See Chang-fa Lo, 'Taiwan: External Influences mixed with Traditional Elements to Form Its Unique Legal System' in E. Ann Black and Gary F. Bell (eds), *Law and Legal Institutions of Asia* (Cambridge University Press 2011). Similarly, when the Republic of Korea was founded in 1948, its Civil Code and Criminal Code were modelled after the German equivalents and the current Korean Constitutional Court is also modelled after the German Federal Constitutional Court. See Chongko Choi, 'On the Reception of Western Law in Korea' (1981) 9 *Korean Journal of Comparative Law* 141, 164–165; Paul Kichyun Ryu, 'The New Korean Criminal Code of October 3, 1953. An Analysis of Ideologies Embedded in It' (1957) 48 *Journal of Criminal Law, Criminology, and Police Science* 275. China only regained sovereignty over Hong Kong from the British in 1997 and the operative Hong Kong Basic Law (Articles 8 and 84) expressly authorizes the continued application of the common law within the territory.

## CONVERGENCE ON STRUCTURED PROPORTIONALITY

In the aftermath of the Second World War, a 'post-war paradigm'[46] of domestic constitutional law emerged, with legislatures around the world adopting a domestic charter of rights and empowering their courts to independently determine whether state limitations on these rights are demonstrably justified, and to invalidate those laws that are not.[47] The Proportionality Analysis (PA) – in its various forms and configurations – developed as the umbrella term used to reference the different ways judges weight the relative importance of state interests and evaluate the extent to which this conflict can be minimized by a more careful choice of legislative means that is less injurious to the individual.[48]

While PA may have originated from Germany,[49] it has not remained a European product. PA has been locally transplanted across Anglophone nations (for example, Canada and New Zealand), mixed legal systems that are rooted in the common law (for example, Israel and South Africa) and even parts of Latin America and Asia.[50] In view of PA's ubiquity, it is now widely viewed as a 'general principle of constitutional governance',[51] an embodiment of 'generic constitutional law'[52] and even celebrated as the 'ultimate rule of law'.[53]

Strong courts around the world generally apply a more structured version of PA.[54] Typically, this Structured Proportionality (SP) has four cumulative steps. When applying SP, the courts would ensure that (i) the state is pursuing a legitimate aim; (ii) the governmental measure undertaken is rationally connected to the stated policy objectives; (iii) the right-derogation is no more than necessary to achieve those stated goals and (iv) the regulatory measure is proportionate *stricto sensu*; that is, there is a fair balance struck between the rights of the individual and the interests

46 Lorraine E. Weinrib, 'The Post-War Paradigm and American Exceptionalism' in Sujit Choudhry (ed.), *The Migration of Constitutional Ideas* (Cambridge University Press 2006) 84.

47 See Alec Stone Sweet and Jud Mathews, 'Proportionality Balancing and Global Constitutionalism' (2008) 47 *Columbia Journal of Transnational Law* 72.

48 David S. Law, 'Generic Constitutional Law' (2005) 89 *Minnesota Law Review* 652, 702; Alec Stone Sweet and Jud Mathews, *Proportionality Balancing and Constitutional Governance* (Oxford University Press 2019).

49 Dieter Grimm, 'Proportionality in Canadian and German Constitutional Jurisprudence' (2007) 57 *University of Toronto Law Journal* 383, 384–385; Andrej Lang, 'Proportionality Analysis by the German Federal Constitutional Court' in Mordechai Kremnitzer, Talya Steiner and Andrej Lang (eds), *Proportionality in Action: Comparative and Empirical Perspectives on the Judicial Practice* (Cambridge University Press 2020) 22, 23.

50 Po Jen Yap (ed), *Proportionality in Asia* (Cambridge University Press 2020) 3.

51 Stone Sweet and Mathews (n. 47) 194.

52 Law (n. 48).

53 David Beatty, *The Ultimate Rule of Law* (Oxford University Press 2005).

54 The Supreme Court of the United States of America and the High Court of Australia are notable courts that do not apply SP. See Vicki Jackson, 'Constitutional Law in an Age of Proportionality' (2015) 124 *Yale Law Journal* 3094; Jeremy Kirk, 'Constitutional Guarantees, Characterization and the Concept of Proportionality' (1997) 21 *Melbourne University Law Review* 1, 63.

of the community such that the consequences of the law are not unacceptably harsh on the individual.

Within Asia, Taiwan, South Korea and Hong Kong are exceptional insofar as their courts are the *only* ones that have converged on the use of SP. Their judges reason through the four SP stages sequentially and harness SP to overturn state action regularly.

Notably, SP is a judicial construct in all three East Asian democracies. The Hong Kong Basic Law does not even include a general limitation clause for rights. While the Constitutions of Taiwan[55] and South Korea[56] both have one, many of the doctrinal SP steps their Constitutional Courts apply are not found in these clauses, and the relevant clauses also do not give any guidance on the standard of review judges should adopt, let alone authorize judges to *re-balance* legislative policy determinations. Notably, in Hong Kong, when the four-stage SP was first endorsed, the HKCFA not only relied on caselaw from Canada and the United Kingdom, it also referenced the writings of Dieter Grimm and Aharon Barak.[57] The KCC has also consulted German precedent when it applied the balancing test of SP.[58]

In its early permutations, PA in each jurisdiction was unstructured and was deployed only to uphold state action.[59] But as power fragmented across the political branches of government, and/or courts gained confidence over time, the judges inserted more structure into PA, gravitated toward a 'highly intrusive standard of review',[60] and began using SP to void legislation. The fragmentation of power within the political branches of government and the protection of courts from punishment is central to the rise of SP.

For all three courts, Stage 1 of SP – the legitimacy test – is rarely deployed to void legislation. But where it is, the laws void under Stage 1 usually pertain to

55 Article 23 of the Constitution of the Republic of China reads: 'All the freedoms and rights enumerated . . . shall not be restricted by law except such as may be necessary to prevent infringement upon the freedoms of other persons, to avert an imminent crisis, to maintain social order or to advance public welfare.'

56 Article 37(2) of the Constitution of the Republic of Korea reads: 'The freedoms and rights of citizens may be restricted by Act only when necessary for national security, the maintenance of law and order or for public welfare. Even when such restriction is imposed, no essential aspect of the freedom or right shall be violated.'

57 *Hysan Development* v. *Town Planning Board* [2016] 19 HKCFAR 372 (Hong Kong Court of Final Appeal).

58 *Cumulative Taxation of Income from Assets of Spouses Case*, 2001Hun-Ba82 (29 August 2002) (Constitutional Court of Korea). See also Yoon Jin Shin, 'Proportionality in South Korea' in Po Jen Yap (ed), *Proportionality in Asia* (Cambridge University Press 2020) 83 (arguing that SP in South Korea 'was imported from Germany').

59 J.Y. Interpretation No. 414 (1996) (Constitutional Court of Taiwan), available at http://cons.judicial.gov.tw/jcc/en-us/jep03/show?expno=414, accessed 8 May 2021; *Case on Constitutional Complaint for Judicial Scrivener Law*, 88Hun-Ma1 (17 March 1989) (Constitutional Court of Korea); *HKSAR* v. *Ng Kung Siu* [1999] 2 HKCFAR 442 (Hong Kong Court of Final Appeal).

60 Stone Sweet and Mathews (n. 47) 4.

anachronistic legislation that is patriarchal[61] or heterosexist.[62] Therefore, Stage 1 of SP provides judges in all three courts with the opportunity to reshape the jurisdiction's constitutional culture, pursue progressive causes and make society more inclusive. Stage 2 of SP requires the governmental measure to have a 'rational connection'[63] to the legislative aims or for the means chosen to be 'appropriate'.[64] Usually a low threshold for the government to overcome, in exceptional circumstances, Stage 2 has extraordinary bite. Hong Kong rules limiting social welfare payments to its Permanent Residents,[65] Taiwan legislation imposing interest payments on penalty surcharges for unpaid taxes,[66] and South Korean anti-trust regulations on news conglomerates[67] were all void for failing Stage 2, even though these invalidated rules all concern socio-economic policies that traditionally attract judicial deference. Furthermore, Stage 2 has been deployed in pursuit of progressive human rights causes opposed by their governments: ending indefinite detention of undocumented migrants in Taiwan,[68] decriminalizing adultery in South Korea,[69] and granting expatriates in same-sex marriages the same right to spousal visas as heterosexual married couples in Hong Kong.[70] The Courts most frequently use Stage 3 of SP – the necessity test – to overturn the legislative status quo, as it allows the judiciary to point to reasonable but unexplored policy alternatives that would have been just as effective. Recently, the KCC deployed Stage 3 to invalidate the virtually blanket ban on abortions in South Korea.[71] With this progressive ruling, South Korean women, vis-à-vis their counterparts in Taiwan[72] and Hong Kong,[73] will be able to exercise a comparable right to their bodily autonomy. Stage 4 of SP requires courts to openly re-calibrate the legislative balance struck by the government, and all three courts have sparingly invalidated laws on this ground, but it is

61 *Case on Same Surname-Same Origin Marriage Ban*, 95Hun-Ka6 (16 July 1997) (Constitutional Court of Korea); *Case on House Hold Head System*, 2001Hun-Ka9 (3 February 2005) (Constitutional Court of Korea); *Case on Sexual Intercourse under Pretense of Marriage Case*, 2008Hun-Ba58, 2009Hun-Ba191 (consolidated) (26 November 2009) (Constitutional Court of Korea).

62 *Secretary for Justice* v. *Yau Yuk Lung* [2007] 10 HKCFAR 335 (Hong Kong Court of Final Appeal).

63 *Hysan Development* v. *Town Planning Board* [2016] 19 HKCFAR 372 (Hong Kong Court of Final Appeal). J.Y. Interpretation No. 746 (Taiwan) (2017) (Constitutional Court of Taiwan), available at http://cons.judicial.gov.tw/jcc/en-us/jep03/show?expno=746, accessed 8 May 2021.

64 *Case on School Site Acquisition Charge*, 2003Hun-Ka20 (31 March 2005) (Constitutional Court of Korea).

65 *Kong Yunming* v. *Director of Social Welfare* [2013] 16 HKCFAR 950 (Hong Kong Court of Final Appeal).

66 J.Y. Interpretation No. 746 (Taiwan) (2017) (Constitutional Court of Taiwan), available at http://cons.judicial.gov.tw/jcc/en-us/jep03/show?expno=746, accessed 8 May 2021.

67 *The Newspaper Act Case*, 2005Hun-Ma165 (26 July 2006) (Constitutional Court of Korea).

68 J.Y. Interpretation No. 710 (Taiwan) (2013) (Constitutional Court of Taiwan), at [3], available at http://cons.judicial.gov.tw/jcc/en-us/jep03/show?expno=710, accessed 8 May 2021.

69 *Adultery Case*, 2009Hun-Ba17 (26 February 2015) (Constitutional Court of Korea).

70 *QT* v. *Director of Immigration* [2018] HKCFA 28 (Hong Kong Court of Final Appeal).

71 *Case on the Crime of Abortion*, 2017Hun-Ba127 (11 April 2019) (Constitutional Court of Korea).

72 Paragraph 1, Article 9 of the Genetic Health Act (Taiwan).

73 Section 47A of the Offences against the Person Ordinance (Cap 212).

notable that the KCC and TCC have used this ground to assess the proportionality of statutory *minimum* sentences imposed on a variety of penal offences.[74] In Chapter 3, on SP, we will survey the full gamut of constitutional law in these three East Asian democracies, for example free speech,[75] freedom of assembly,[76] criminal due process,[77] prisoners' rights,[78] the right to work,[79] sexual autonomy[80] and the right to property,[81] to underscore the extraordinary convergence in these jurisdictions.

But we must emphasize at the outset that the judicial deployment of SP *in itself* does not guarantee policy uniformity across all three jurisdictions. Convergence does not mean homogeneity.[82] For example, using SP, the TCC has scuttled the government's plans to fingerprint all its citizens,[83] while the KCC has condoned this

74 *Request for Constitutional Review of Article 53 Section 1 of the Military Criminal Act*, 2006Hun-Ka13 (29 November 2007) (Constitutional Court of Korea); J.Y. Interpretation No. 669 (Taiwan) (2009) (Constitutional Court of Taiwan), at [2], available at http://cons.judicial.gov.tw/jcc/en-us/jep03/show?expno=669, accessed 8 May 2021.

75 *Prohibition of Medical Advertisement of the Medical Service Act Case*, 2003Hun-Ka3 (27 October 2005) (Constitutional Court of Korea); *Kwok Hay Kwong* v. *Medical Council of Hong Kong* [2008] 3 HKLRD 524 (Hong Kong Court of Appeal).

76 J.Y. Interpretation No. 445 (1998) (Constitutional Court of Taiwan), available at http://cons.judicial.gov.tw/jcc/en-us/jep03/show?expno=445, accessed 8 May 2021; *Case on the Ban on Outdoor Assemblies within 100m of the National Assembly Building*, 2013Hun-Ba322, 2016Hun-Ba354, 2017Hun-Ba360, 398, 471, 2018Hun-Ka3, 4, 9 (consolidated) (31 May 2018) (Constitutional Court of Korea).

77 J.Y. Interpretation No. 669 (2009) (Constitutional Court of Taiwan), available at; *Request for Constitutional Review of Article 53 Section 1 of the Military Criminal Act*, 2006Hun-Ka13 (29 November 2007) (Constitutional Court of Korea).

78 *Restriction on Right to Vote of Prisoners and Probationers with Suspended Sentence*, 2012Hun-Ma409, 510, 2013Hun-Ma167 (consolidated) (28 January 2014; *Chan Kin Sum* v. *Secretary of Justice* [2009] 2 HKLRD 166 (Hong Kong Court of First Instance).

79 J.Y. Interpretation No. 649 (2008) (Constitutional Court of Taiwan), available at http://cons.judicial.gov.tw/jcc/en-us/jep03/show?expno=649, accessed 8 May 2021; *Case on the Monopoly of Massage Therapists by Visually Impaired Persons*, 2003Hun-Ma715, 2006Hun-Ma368 (25 May 2006) (Constitutional Court of Korea).

80 *Adultery Case*, 2009Hun-Ba17 (26 February 2015) (Constitutional Court of Korea); J.Y. Interpretation No. 791 (2020) (Constitutional Court of Taiwan), available at https://cons.judicial.gov.tw/jcc/zh-tw/jep03/show?expno=791, accessed 8 May 2021.

81 J.Y. Interpretation No. 580 (2004) (Constitutional Court of Taiwan), available at http://cons.judicial.gov.tw/jcc/en-us/jep03/show?expno=580, accessed 8 May 2021; *Hysan Development* v. *Town Planning Board* [2016] 19 HKCFAR 372 (Hong Kong Court of Final Appeal); *Imposing School Site Acquisition Charge on Purchaser of Housing Units from Developer Case*, 2003Hun-Ka20 (31 March 2005) (Constitutional Court of Korea).

82 See also Jacco Bomhoff, *Balancing Constitutional Rights: The Origins and Meanings of Postwar Legal Discourse* (Cambridge University Press 2013) (arguing that judicial balancing in Germany and the United States does not mean the same thing).

83 J.Y. Interpretation No. 603 (2005) (Constitutional Court of Taiwan), available at http://cons.judicial.gov.tw/jcc/en-us/jep03/show?expno=603, accessed 8 May 2021.

governmental practice.[84] The KCC[85] is also less enlightened on gay rights than its Taiwanese[86] or Hong Kong[87] counterparts. But Chapter 3 will definitively show that the said convergence in these three East Asian democracies far exceeds the divergence.

Naturally, we should stress herein that we are *not* arguing that convergence on the use of SP will *automatically* lead to a convergence on more liberal outcomes. Methodological convergence on SP does *not guarantee* substantive convergence. But what SP does – and successfully so – is to provide judges with a standardized and sequenced doctrinal template with which to scrutinize governmental derogation on rights,[88] such that the courts have a legal basis to overturn state action if they so *choose*. Furthermore, the doctrinal acceptance of SP – as opposed to a deferential standard of review – in these East Asian democracies holds the promise and increases the probability of a more rights-friendly outcome, because judges now have recourse to a *heightened* standard of review to evaluate the constitutionality of governmental action. It is therefore no coincidence that with the availability and use of SP, Taiwan, South Korea and Hong Kong have the most progressive and consequential courts in Asia. Conservative courts – like the courts of Singapore – will always reject SP because the use of SP will require them to sequentially scrutinize whether the impugned law is legitimate, suitable, necessary and balanced; and conservative courts will take pains to avoid this. A deferential standard of review over governmental action will allow the judges to uphold the impugned law more easily and quickly.[89] In short, a court that chooses only to use a deferential standard of review will never be a liberal one.[90] But courts that adopt SP have the highest chance of reaching liberal results when liberal judges are on the bench. Political scientists have argued that judges apply a deferential standard of review when their extra-legal preferences are for deference, and a more robust standard of review when their extra-legal preferences are for judicial intervention.[91] We do not disagree with this. Our point herein is only that when SP is on the table, liberal judges can use this

84 *Case on Putting Ten Fingerprints on Application for Issuance of Resident Registration Certificate*, 2011Hun-Ma731 (28 May 2015) (Constitutional Court of Korea).

85 *Case on the Constitutional Complaint against Article 92-5 of the Former Military Criminal Act Which Prescribes Punishment by Imprisonment for 'Other Indecent Conduct'* 2012Hun-Ba258 (28 July 2016) (Constitutional Court of Korea).

86 J.Y. Interpretation No. 748 (Taiwan) (2017) (Constitutional Court of Taiwan), available at http://cons.judicial.gov.tw/jcc/en-us/jep03/show?expno=748, accessed 8 May 2021.

87 *Leung Chun Kwong* v. *Secretary for the Civil Service* [2019] HKCFA 19 (Hong Kong Court of Final Appeal).

88 Jackson (n. 54), 3094, 3142.

89 Po Jen Yap, *Constitutional Dialogue in Common Law Asia* (Oxford University Press 2015).

90 Po Jen Yap, 'Proportionality in Asia: Joining the Global Choir' in Po Jen Yap (ed.), *Proportionality in Asia* (Cambridge University Press 2020) 9–18.

91 Frank B. Cross, *Decision Making in the U.S. Courts of Appeals* (Stanford University Press 2007) 53; Segal and Spaeth (n. 35) 86–97.

doctrinal tool when they so choose. But courts without SP lack the same legal infrastructure for regular judicial intervention to subvert pre-existing law.

## CONVERGENCE ON INNOVATIVE CONSTITUTIONAL REMEDIES

Where courts are empowered to review the constitutionality of legislation, the standard practice is for the judiciary to invalidate the law, when it is deemed unconstitutional, to the extent of its inconsistency. The unconstitutional law is also invalidated immediately and the courts would leave it to the legislature to introduce remedial legislation post-invalidation.

However, with the rise of the modern state, and the realist swing towards remedial discretion, both common law and civil law courts have implemented innovative constitutional remedies that complement the power to declare legislative actions incompatible with their respective bills of rights.[92] One such remedial innovation relates to the court's power to interpret legislation in a rights-compatible way.[93] In essence, this interpretive power creates 'a practical power of law reform (in substance, a legislative power)'[94] for the judiciary. In tandem with this power of Remedial Interpretation (RI) courts have also issued Suspension Orders. In such instances, the impugned law is deemed to be unconstitutional, but the judiciary delays this declaration, usually with a fixed deadline, so that the legislature is given time to pass corrective legislation.[95]

Notably, in Asia, the courts in Taiwan, South Korea and Hong Kong are the *only* ones that regularly rely on *both* RI and Suspension Orders to rectify constitutionally flawed legislation. Furthermore, neither remedy is expressly authorized by legislation or their respective Constitutions. These novel remedies were wholly created by their top judges. The HKCFA referenced the Supreme Court of Canada when the former first created its Suspension Order.[96] English law was cited when the HKCFA first used RI on an impugned law.[97] When a Suspension Order – known in Korea as

92 Kent Roach, 'Dialogic Remedies' (2019) 17 *International Journal of Constitutional Law* 860; Stephen Gardbaum, 'What Makes for More or Less Powerful Constitutional Courts?' (2018) 29 *Duke Journal of Comparative & International Law* 1, 16–17.

93 *Ghaidan* v. *Godin-Mendoza* [2004] 2 AC 557 (UK House of Lords); *Schachter* v. *Canada* [1992] 2 SCR 679, 93 DLR (4th) 1 (Supreme Court of Canada); BVerfGE 2, 266 (1953) (German Federal Constitutional Court).

94 Philip Sales and Richard Ekins, 'Rights-Consistent Interpretation under the Human Rights Act 1998' (2011) 127 *Law Quarterly Review* 217, 224.

95 BVerfGE 33, 303 (1972) (German Federal Constitutional Court); *Reference Re Manitoba Language Rights* [1985] 1 S.C.R. 721 (Supreme Court of Canada).

96 *Koo Sze Yiu* v. *Chief Executive of HKSAR* [2006] 9 HKCFAR 441 (Hong Kong Court of Final Appeal).

97 *HKSAR* v. *Lam Kwong Wai* [2006] 9 HKCFAR 574 (Hong Kong Court of Final Appeal) [77].

a decision of incompatibility[98] or non-conformity[99] ruling – was first issued by the KCC, the Court referred to German law for this.[100] Similarly, when the KCC first applied RI – known in South Korea as a decision of limited[101] or conditional[102] constitutionality/unconstitutionality – German law was relied on.[103] The judicial use of both remedial techniques was heavily criticized by the dissent in the two Korean decisions as, according to the dissent, Germany had statutory authorization for these remedial measures,[104] while the KCC was only empowered to hand down a 'decision of unconstitutionality'.[105]

With the convergence on the enforcement of these innovative constitutional remedies, these three courts have delayed or expedited the legal consequences that generally follow from the judicial declaration of an unconstitutional practice, thereby blurring the traditional distinction between adjudication and legislation.

The judicial use of a Suspension Order is most defensible when there is a range of constitutional options that could be implemented in light of the court's ruling,[106] such that due deference is paid to the primacy of the legislature's law-making role when lawmakers are granted the space and time to make the initial determination on how best to discharge their constitutional responsibility among the competing policy options available.[107] Such judicial orders are dialogic, as the court initiates the conversation when it accepts the rights claims advanced by the litigants, but parliament completes the conversation when it decides how best to complement and implement the judicial ruling.[108] While both the South Korean[109] and Hong Kong[110] courts deemed the blanket ban on prisoner voting incompatible with their Constitutions, both courts issued a Suspension Order and neither court dictated to

98 Dong-Heub Lee, 'Development and Current Situation of the Constitutional Adjudication in Korea' (2012) 53(2) *Seoul Law Journal* 1.

99 The Constitutional Court of Korea, *Thirty Years of the Constitutional Court of Korea* (The Constitutional Court of Korea 2018) 125.

100 *National Assembly Candidacy Deposit Case*, 88Hun-Ka6 (8 September 1989) (Constitutional Court of Korea).

101 The Constitutional Court of Korea, *Twenty Years of the Constitutional Court of Korea* (The Constitutional Court of Korea 2008) 101; Jong Ik Chon, 'Effect of Constitutional Review on the Legislature and the Executive Branch for Last 25 Years in Korea' (2015) *Journal of Korean Law* 131, 139.

102 The Constitutional Court of Korea (n. 99).

103 *Inheritance Tax Act Case*, 89Hun-Ma38 (21 July 1989) (Constitutional Court of Korea).

104 Article 31(2) of the Federal Constitutional Court Act (Germany) reads: '... if the Federal Constitutional Court declares a law to be compatible or incompatible with the Basic Law or if it voids the law...'.

105 See Articles 45 and 47 of the Constitutional Court Act (South Korea).

106 See Kent Roach, 'Remedial Consensus and Dialogue under the Charter: General Declarations and Delayed Declarations of Invalidity' (2002) 35 *UBC Law Review* 211, 212; Yap (n. 89).

107 See Bruce Ryder, 'Suspending the Charter' (2003) 21 *Supreme Court Law Review* (2d) 267, 285.

108 Roach (n. 92).

109 *Restriction on Right to Vote of Prisoners and Probationers with Suspended Sentence*, 2012Hun-Ma409 (28 January 2014) (Constitutional Court of Korea).

110 *Chan Kin Sum* v. *Secretary of Justice* [2009] 2 HKLRD 166 (Hong Kong Court of First Instance).

the lawmakers the details of an acceptable legislative sequel. In the end, the Hong Kong Legislative Council decided to give every prisoner the vote, while the South Korean National Assembly decided to limit this to prisoners sentenced to less than one year of imprisonment.[111]

The use of such Suspension Orders is not without its critics. Robert Leckey has warned that the increased use of delayed remedies harms individual rights-bearers, as the latter may be victorious in court but deprived of a remedy until corrective legislation is enacted, if at all.[112] While Leckey's concerns over the over-use of delayed remedies are valid, in Taiwan, South Korea, and Hong Kong, the uncertainties associated with the application of Suspension Orders have been mitigated by the courts. These Asian judges are more 'experimentalist'[113] and they have *converged* in adding significant 'bite' to their delayed declarations of invalidity such that the government is incentivized to comply with the court's ruling, or judicial safeguards are put in place to mitigate any legislative or executive delinquency.

In South Korea, since 1993,[114] the KCC has used a variant of this Suspension Order, which is termed a 'simple'[115] decision of non-conformity. When this 'simple' decision of non-conformity is issued, the government is prohibited from enforcing the unconstitutional legislation pending its review, and there is 'an immediate suspension of the underlying proceeding [in the lower courts] that gave rise to the constitutional challenge'.[116] On the other hand, in Hong Kong, the HKCFA has determined that the government is not shielded from any legal liability incurred if the latter abuses its authority while the delayed declaration of invalidity is in effect.[117] Furthermore, in both Taiwan and Hong Kong, the courts have coupled their use of a delayed declaration of invalidity with a remedial reading-in proviso that takes effect automatically, in the event of any legislative default, upon the expiry of the suspension period. In *W (2013)*,[118] the HKCFA ruled that it was unconstitutional to prohibit a post-operative male-to-female transsexual from marrying in the capacity of her acquired gender. While a delayed declaration of invalidity was issued that gave the Hong Kong legislature one year to reform this area of law, the Court also decided that upon the expiry of the 12-month suspension period and in the absence of any

111 Article 18(1)[2] of the Public Official Election Act; Article 43(2) of the Criminal Act.

112 Robert Leckey, 'The Harms of Remedial Discretion' (2016) 14 *International Journal of Constitutional Law* 584, 591.

113 See also Charles F. Sabel and William H. Simon, 'Destabilization Rights: How Public Law Litigation Succeeds' (2004) 117 *Harvard Law Review* 1016, 1019.

114 *Prohibition of Labor Dispute by the Public Sector Laborers Case*, 88Hun-Ma5 (11 March 1993) (Constitutional Court of Korea).

115 The Constitutional Court of Korea (n. 101) 165.

116 Ibid. 166.

117 *Koo Sze Yiu* v. *Chief Executive of HKSAR* [2006] 9 HKCFAR 441 (Hong Kong Court of Final Appeal).

118 W v. *Registrar of Marriages* [2013] 16 HKCFAR 112 (Hong Kong Court of Final Appeal).

legislative intervention, the post-operative male-to-female transsexual person would be automatically recognized as a woman for the purposes of marriage in Hong Kong.[119] In the same vein, when the TCC in 2017 declared that the nation's ban on same-sex marriage was unconstitutional, it gave the legislature two years to remedy this legislative exclusion, but if the Legislative Yuan defaulted after the deadline, the Court held that same-sex couples would be entitled to 'apply for marriage registration to the authorities in charge of household registration ... and [they] shall be accorded the status of a legally-recognized couple'.[120] Furthermore, the Constitutional Courts and Taiwan and Korea have even issued interim remedial readings of the impugned law pending legislative review.[121]

On the other hand, an RI of an impugned law – whereby the courts read in words or read down the legal effect of statutory language, without resorting to an outright invalidation – is often defended on the basis that the legislature would prefer 'its legislative provision to have a valid, even if reduced, operation than to have no operation at all, so long as the valid operation is not fundamentally or essentially different from what it enacted'.[122] Unlike a typical canon of constitutional avoidance, which allows a court to adopt an interpretation of a statute that is constitutionally less problematic when there are 'two equally plausible'[123] readings of the legislation, an RI of the impugned law goes even further: even if the statutory language is clear, the judiciary will read lengthy phrases and even sentences into the impugned legislation, so as to make it constitutionally compliant. In *Yeung May Wan (2005)*,[124] the HKCFA held that police powers must be 'construed consistently with [Hong Kong's] constitutional guarantees against arbitrary arrest';[125] and hence the impugned statutory provision that permitted a police officer to apprehend a person 'who he reasonably believes will be charged' must be read down to mean

119 At the end of the suspension period, the Hong Kong Legislative Council refused to pass any remedial legislation to expressly allow transsexual persons to marry in their acquired gender; but the Registrar of Marriages, following the HKCFA ruling in W, has now permitted all post-operative male-to-female transsexual persons to marry pursuant to the judicially imposed remedial interpretation of the pre-existing matrimonial legislation.

120 J.Y. Interpretation No. 748 (2017) (Constitutional Court of Taiwan), at [17], available at http://cons.judicial.gov.tw/jcc/en-us/jep03/show?expno=748, accessed 8 May 2021. See also Ming-Sung Kuo and Hui-Wen Chen, 'The Brown Moment in Taiwan: Making Sense of the Law and Politics of the Taiwanese Same-Sex Marriage Case in a Comparative Light' (2017) 31 *Columbia Journal of Asian Law* 72. In 2019, the Legislative Yuan passed a law conferring matrimonial rights on same-sex couples. See The Enforcement Act of Judicial Yuan Interpretation No. 748 (2019) (Taiwan), available at https://law.moj.gov.tw/LawClass/LawAll.aspx?pcode=B0000008, accessed 8 May 2021.

121 J.Y. Interpretation No. 755 (2017) (Constitutional Court of Taiwan), available at http://cons.judicial.gov.tw/jcc/en-us/jep03/show?expno=755, accessed 8 May 2021; *Case on Search by Arrest Warrant of Dwellings other than the suspect's*, 2015Hun-Ba370 (26 April 2018) (Constitutional Court of Korea) (Official English Summary).

122 *Lam Kwong Wai* (n. 97).

123 For an American example, see *Salinas* v. *United States* 522 U.S. 52, 59–60 (1997).

124 *Yeung May Wan* v. *HKSAR* [2005] 8 HKCFAR (Hong Kong Court of Final Appeal).

125 Ibid. [66].

'who he reasonably believes will be charged *on the basis of a reasonable suspicion that the arrested person is guilty of the offence to be charged*.'[126] In the same vein, the TCC has read down the punitive effects of a draconian law that criminalized defamation; while the constitutionality of the impugned law was upheld, the TCC determined that where the accused has 'no way of showing the truthfulness of the statement, the court must find the accused not guilty when the evidence proffered for the court's review shows that the accused has reasonable grounds to believe that the statement was true at the moment of dissemination'.[127] As for South Korea, RI – termed 'a decision of limited constitutionality'[128] – was first applied in July 1989 when the KCC declared that a tax law, which required beneficial owners of real property to also hold the registered title,[129] was *constitutional* if it was interpreted to exempt beneficial owners who did not hold the registered title for legitimate non-tax evasion purposes.[130] Subsequently, in 1991, the KCC issued its first decision of limited unconstitutionality.[131] The judicial power to award 'suitable measures to restore the injured party's fame'[132] was deemed *unconstitutional* if it was interpreted to include a power to compel the defendant to apologize to the plaintiff. (The regulatory breadth of a comparable law in Taiwan was also narrowed by the TCC.[133]) The KCC has acknowledged that in substance both 'modified'[134] rulings are the same and have equal binding force.[135]

Such 'strained interpretation'[136] of impugned legislative provisions creates a legislative power for the judiciary, but where the requisite changes needed to the law do not require the government to deliberate over a range of complex polycentric policy alternatives, such piecemeal reforms writ small undertaken by the judges themselves may also be more expedient and effective, especially if there are more important items on the legislative agenda.

Furthermore, all three courts have converged in using RI when an open invalidation of the impugned law would trigger governmental disquiet or public backlash. By incrementally modifying the text of the law on its own, instead of openly deeming the legislation in question unconstitutional, the court diffuses potential

126 Ibid.

127 J.Y. Interpretation No. 509 (Taiwan) (2000) (Constitutional Court of Taiwan), at [2], available at http://cons.judicial.gov.tw/jcc/en-us/jep03/show?expno=509, accessed 8 May 2021.

128 Constitutional Court of Korea (n. 101) 167.

129 Article 32-2(1) of the Inheritance Tax Act (South Korea).

130 *Inheritance Tax Act Case*, 89Hun-Ma38 (21 July 1989) (Constitutional Court of Korea).

131 *Notice of Apology Case*, 89Hun-Ma160 (1 April 1991) (Constitutional Court of Korea).

132 Article 764 of the Civil Act reads: 'The court may, on the application of the injured party, order the person who has impaired another's fame to take suitable measures to restore the injured party's fame, either in lieu of, or together with damages.'

133 J.Y. Interpretation No. 656 (Taiwan) (2009) (Constitutional Court of Taiwan), at [3], available at http://cons.judicial.gov.tw/jcc/en-us/jep03/show?expno=656, accessed 8 May 2021.

134 The Constitutional Court of Korea (n. 101) 163.

135 Ibid. 224.

136 *Lam Kwong Wai* (n. 97).

political opposition, while quietly adjusting the operational meaning of the flawed statute to achieve greater constitutional compliance. When the TCC was confronted with a challenge to the constitutionality of a legislative provision that imposed strict liability on any person who publishes any information in any medium which may induce a person to engage in sexual activity with a child/ juvenile,[137] the Court was hard-pressed to uphold this dragnet law. Therefore, on its own initiative, the Court decided to read-in a new defence into the legislation: any information distributed by [the accused] which '*neither contains child or juvenile sexual transaction nor is intended to induce children or juveniles to engage in sexual transaction and necessary precautionary measures have been taken to limit the recipients of such information to those who are eighteen years of age or older*'[138] would not violate the statute in question. Similarly, in view of the country's long-standing tensions with North Korea, the KCC was understandably reluctant to openly invalidate legislation pertaining to national security. So instead, vague and overbroad penal provisions, which criminally sanctioned any person who praised or sympathized with the activities of anti-government organizations, were read down such that the law would only apply if '*national security and the basic order of free democracy*''[139] was threatened. Draconian laws that punish the unauthorised dissemination of all military secrets were also judicially confined to classified materials that, if disclosed, would '*pose a clear threat to national security*'.[140] Such constitutional avoidance seeks to preserve the Court's reputation and institutional capital, as judges 'effectively re-write laws while pretending to exercise restraint'.[141] Similarly, in Hong Kong, an administrative by-law that imposed a blanket prohibition on all signs and messages, including signs or messages on a person's clothing in the public gallery of the Legislative Council, was read down by the HKCFA, such that the impugned by-law would only apply to '*conduct which amounts to behaving in a disorderly manner.*'[142] Notably, the HKCFA did so by adopting a statutory construction that conflicted with the plain meaning of the law, while still claiming fidelity to the legislature's intent. Unlike an express declaration of unconstitutionality, such judicial acts of 'passive avoidance'[143] allow the HKCFA to spearhead constitutional

137 J.Y. Interpretation No. 623 (Taiwan) (2007) (Constitutional Court of Taiwan), at [4], available at http://cons.judicial.gov.tw/jcc/en-us/jep03/show?expno=623, accessed 8 May 2021.

138 Ibid.

139 *Praising and Encouraging under National Security Act Case*, 89Hun-Ka113 (2 April 1990) (Constitutional Court of Korea); The Constitutional Court of Korea (n. 101) 214. See also Chaihark Hahm, 'Human Rights in Korea' in Randall Peerenboom, Carole J. Peterson and Albert H. Y. Chen (eds), *Human Rights in Asia: A Comparative Legal Study of Twelve Asian Jurisdictions, France and the USA* (Routledge 2006) 265, 279–280.

140 *Military Secret Leakage Case*, 89Hun-Ka104 (25 February 1992) (Constitutional Court of Korea).

141 Eric S. Fish, 'Constitutional Avoidance as Interpretation and as Remedy' (2015–2016) 114 *Michigan Law Review* 1275, 1315.

142 *HKSAR* v. *Fong Kwok Shan Christine* [2017] 20 HKCFAR 425 (Hong Kong Court of Final Appeal) [107].

143 Anita S. Krishnakumar, 'Passive Avoidance' (2019) 71 *Stanford Law Review* 513, 569.

change on the stealth, thereby avoiding public disquiet that the Court is now expressly condoning chaos.

But there are of course differences in how the three East Asian courts apply these innovative remedies, which we will explore. Specifically, the main differences pertain to the judicial use of Suspension Orders. In Hong Kong, a Suspension Order is always accompanied with a fixed deadline for legislative compliance,[144] and occasionally the Court imposes a remedial reading-in proviso that takes effect automatically if there is no remedial law at the end of the suspension period.[145] The latter remedy also exists in Taiwan,[146] but not South Korea. Unlike Hong Kong, in South Korea and Taiwan, their Constitutional Courts have also issued Suspension Orders – albeit occasionally – that do *not* impose a deadline for legislative compliance.[147] Furthermore, in Taiwan and South Korea, their Courts have even issued interim remedial readings of the impugned law pending legislative review.[148] This has not happened in Hong Kong. But we must not miss the forest for the trees. The indisputable fact remains that Hong Kong, Taiwan and South Korea are the only jurisdictions in Asia with courts that have converged on the regular and routine use of Suspension Orders and Remedial Interpretation when engaging in constitutional adjudication.

## LIMITS ON CONVERGENCE

But there are limits to this constitutional convergence. The three courts will *not* converge on electoral reform and matters impacting national security. While Taiwan and South Korea are dynamic democracies, where competing political parties take turn in office, Hong Kong is a sub-unit of communist China. And China will not tolerate any judicial attempts to remove the Central Government's relentless chokehold on the city. Therefore, the pursuit of major electoral systemic changes, personnel changes adverse to China's core interests, or challenges that are perceived to undermine national security or sovereignty are simply off-limits to the Hong Kong judiciary.

144 *Koo Sze Yiu* v. *Chief Executive of HKSAR* [2006] 9 HKCFAR 441 (Hong Kong Court of Final Appeal).

145 W v. *Registrar of Marriages* [2013] 16 HKCFAR 112 (Hong Kong Court of Final Appeal).

146 J.Y. Interpretation No. 748 (2017) (Constitutional Court of Taiwan), available at http://cons.judicial.gov.tw/jcc/en-us/jep03/show?expno=748, accessed 8 May 2021.

147 *Case on the House Head System*, 2001Hun-Ga9, 10, 11, 12, 13, 14, 15 and 2004Hun-Ga5 (consolidated) (3 February 2005) (Constitutional Court of Korea); J.Y. Interpretation No. 601 (2005) (Constitutional Court of Taiwan), available at http://cons.judicial.gov.tw/jcc/en-us/jep03/show?expno=601, accessed 8 May 2021.

148 J.Y. Interpretation No. 755 (2017) (Constitutional Court of Taiwan), available at http://cons.judicial.gov.tw/jcc/en-us/jep03/show?expno=755, accessed 8 May 2021; *Case on Search by Arrest Warrant of Dwellings other than the suspect's*, 2015Hun-Ba370 (26 April 2018) (Constitutional Court of Korea) (Official English Summary).

There is a symbiotic relationship between a country's state of democratization and the long-term sustainability of the power that its judges can wield in generating electoral change.[149]

While China will acquiesce to the HKCFA's efforts to advance human rights protection in Hong Kong, the Central Government will not allow the local courts to usher in democratic reform that threatens its rule. The Standing Committee of the National People's Congress is empowered to overturn every constitutional decision issued by the Hong Kong courts,[150] and the former in fact did so in the very first constitutional decision handed down by the HKCFA that it took issue with.[151] With the Standing Committee of the National People's Congress (NPCSC)'s plenary power to interpret the Basic Law hanging like the sword of Damocles over Hong Kong, the HKCFA implicitly understands that its ability to generate significant changes in other areas of constitutional law is contingent on its genuflection to Beijing on the communist regime's core concerns.

As China's authoritarian impulses intensify under President Xi Jinping,[152] the Hong Kong judiciary has also increasingly toed the party line on democratic change. In 2017, the HKCFA for the first time announced that 'electoral laws involve political or policy considerations, [and therefore] a wider margin of appreciation ought generally to be accorded'[153] to the government. With this pronouncement, the HKCFA sounded the death knell for the constitutional review of electoral law.[154] Furthermore, the Hong Kong courts have also proceeded to oust duly elected pro-democracy lawmakers from office[155] and bar pro-Hong Kong independence candidates from running for office.[156]

149 Po Jen Yap, *Courts and Democracies in Asia* (Cambridge University Press 2017).

150 Article 158(1) of the Hong Kong Basic Law reads: 'The power of interpretation of this Law shall be vested in the Standing Committee of the National People's Congress.'

151 In 1999, the NPCSC issued its First Interpretation under the Hong Kong Basic Law and overruled the HKCFA's decision in *Ng Ka Ling* v. *Director of Immigration* [1999] 2 HKCFAR 4, which exempted Mainland children born to Hong Kong Permanent Residents from obtaining the requisite immigration permits before they could acquire the right of abode in Hong Kong.

152 Cora Chan, 'Thirty Years from Tiananmen: China, Hong Kong, and the Ongoing Experiment to Preserve Liberal Values in an Authoritarian State' (2019) *International Journal of Constitutional Law* 439.

153 *Kwok Cheuk Kin* v. *Secretary for Constitutional and Mainland Affairs* [2017] 20 HKCFAR 353 (Hong Kong Court of Final Appeal) [42].

154 Previously, the Hong Kong judiciary was willing to and had successfully ushered in modest changes to Hong Kong's restrictive electoral regime by extending voting rights writ small to non-indigenous villagers [*Secretary for Justice* v. *Chan Wah* [2000] 3 HKCFAR 459 (Hong Kong Court of Final Appeal)]; disenfranchised prisoners [*Chan Kin Sum* v. *Secretary for Justice* [2009] 2 HKLRD 166 (Hong Kong Court of First Instance)]; and allowing those who had been convicted of minor offences pending appeal to stand for elections [*Wong Hin Wai* v. *Secretary for Justice* [2012] 4 HKLRD 170 (Hong Kong Court of First Instance)].

155 *Chief Executive of the Hong Kong Special Administrative Region* v. *President of the Legislative Council* [2017] 1 HKLRD 460 (Hong Kong Court of Appeal); *Yau Wai Ching and Chief Executive of HKSAR* [2017] 20 HKCFAR 390 (Hong Kong Court of Final Appeal).

156 *Chan Ho Tin* v. *Lo Ying Ki Alan* [2018] HKCFI 345 (Hong Kong Court of First Instance).

In June 2020, the NPCSC annexed a new national security legislation to the city's Basic Law. Secession, subversion of state power and collusion with foreign governments, are now criminal offences, and offenders may face up to life imprisonment for grave violations. Notably, while Hong Kong courts have been conferred jurisdiction to adjudicate most cases brought under this law, and local criminal law procedures and human rights safeguards would continue to apply, in serious cases where foreign governments are involved or the Hong Kong government is unable to enforce the law effectively, the Chinese procuratorate and courts are legally empowered to take over. The Chief Executive of Hong Kong – in consultation with the Chief Justice – will decide on the list of judges who will hear these national security cases, but it is important to note that all these national security judges will only be drawn from the pool of pre-existing Hong Kong judges.[157] As of 1 May 2021, no one has been extradited to China to face trial under the National Security Law (NSL), but 54 people have been charged under this law. 47 of those persons charged under the NSL are pro-democracy activists who had organized an informal election primary to field candidates who can win seats in the Legislative Council election, and subsequently block the passage of the government's budget, thereby forcing the Chief Executive's resignation.[158] But it is important to note that the Hong Kong judiciary has emphasized that *only* common law principles – and not Mainland Chinese legal doctrines – will be used to interpret the NSL.[159] We will fully examine the details and implications of this NSL on Hong Kong in Chapter 5.

In contrast, in dynamic democracies where political power is diffused among competing political parties and branches of government, the empowered courts have facilitated their nations' democratic transformation by making both micro and macro systemic changes to enhance the fairness of voting procedures and electoral institutions. These 'consequential'[160] courts are able to directly address institutional failures in the political system, including, but not limited to, the anti-competitive 'rules of engagement [enacted] to protect established powers from the risk of successful challenge'.[161]

Vis-à-vis Taiwan, the TCC has chastised the nation's President for concurrently appointing his Vice-President as Premier;[162] successfully invalidated constitutional

157 Article 44 of the Law of the People's Republic of China on Safeguarding National Security in the Hong Kong Special Administrative Region.

158 Austin Ramzy and Tiffany May, 'Hong Kong Charges 47 Democracy Supporters With Violating Security Law' (*New York Times*, 28 February 2021), available at www.nytimes.com/2021/02/28/world/asia/hong-kong-security-law-arrests.html.

159 *Tong Ying Kit* v. *HKSAR* [2020] HKCFI 2133 (Hong Kong Court of First Instance) [49].

160 See Diana Kapiszewski, Gordon Silverstein and Robert A. Kagan (eds), *Consequential Courts: Judicial Roles in Global Perspective* (Cambridge University Press 2013).

161 Samuel Issacharoff and Richard H. Pildes, 'Politics as Markets: Partisan Lockups of the Democratic Process' (1997–1998) 50 *Stanford Law Review* 643, 646.

162 J.Y. Interpretation No. 419 (Taiwan) (1996) (Constitutional Court of Taiwan), at [14], available at http://cons.judicial.gov.tw/jcc/en-us/jep03/show?expno=419, accessed 8 May 2021.

amendments that attempted to extend the term of existing National Assembly[163] delegates;[164] and authorized state prosecutors to collect incriminating evidence against President Chen Shui-bian while he was in office, which could be used against him after his presidential term concluded.[165]

Similarly, in South Korea, the KCC has been able to mitigate the effects of systemic political barriers erected by lawmakers to preserve incumbency: prohibitive deposits for National Assembly[166] and presidential[167] elections, gerrymandering of electoral constituencies[168] and disenfranchisement of small political parties.[169] A particularly significant decision was handed down in 2001 when the Constitutional Court mandated that each voter be allowed to cast two votes in the National Assembly election: one for his or her preferred individual candidate in the electoral district and the other for the preferred political party that would field the proportional representative in the national legislature.[170] (Prior to the 2004 National Assembly election, a voter could only vote for the district representative and proportional representative seats were allocated in proportion to the votes the political parties received in the electoral districts.) Most fascinatingly, the KCC in 2017 unanimously removed President Park Geun-hye – the nation's top leader – from office on the basis that the President had unlawfully allowed her close confidante to intervene in state affairs for over three years.[171]

## CONCLUSION

This book seeks to provide important insights into why and how the constitutional jurisprudence in East Asia converges. Chapter 2 begins by explaining why this

163 Prior to its abolition in 2005, the National Assembly in Taiwan was the branch of government that was vested with the power to amend the Constitution. The power to amend the Constitution is now vested in the Legislative Yuan.

164 J.Y. Interpretation No. 499 (Taiwan) (2000) (Constitutional Court of Taiwan), at [12], available at http://cons.judicial.gov.tw/jcc/en-us/jep03/show?expno=499, accessed 8 May 2021.

165 J.Y. Interpretation No. 627 (Taiwan) (2007) (Constitutional Court of Taiwan), at [4], available at http://cons.judicial.gov.tw/jcc/en-us/jep03/show?expno=627, accessed 8 May 2021. After President Chen left office in 2008, he was convicted of various corruption and money laundering offences, and he has been sentenced to 11 years imprisonment.

166 *One-Person One-Vote Case*, 2000Hun-Ma91, etc. (consolidated) (19 July 2001) (Constitutional Court of Korea).

167 *Deposit Money in Presidential Elections Case*, 2007Hun-Ma1024 (27 November 2008) (Constitutional Court of Korea).

168 *Case on Standard for Population Disparity allowed in Division of Electoral District*, 2013Hun-Ma781, 2014 Hun-Ma53 (consolidated) (30 October 2014) (Constitutional Court of Korea).

169 *Case on Prohibition of Using the Name of a Political Party whose Registration has been cancelled*, 2012Hun-Ma431, 2012Hun-Ka19 (consolidated) (28 January 2014) (Constitutional Court of Korea).

170 *One-Person One-Vote Case*, 2000Hun-Ma91, etc. (consolidated) (19 July 2001) (Constitutional Court of Korea). See also Chon (n. 101) 157.

171 *Impeachment of the President (Park Geun-hye)*, 2016Hun-Na1 (10 March 2017) (Constitutional Court of Korea).

convergence in Taiwan, South Korea and Hong Kong is occurring. For each of the three jurisdictions, this chapter will closely explore how power in the political branches of government is fragmented, and how its highest court of final resort is insulated from legislative/executive control. With these institutional variables in place, liberal judges can get appointed to the highest court, and these judges can intentionally build their respective Court's institutional capability in selected Western law and use these foreign liberal precedents to subvert local legislation. To underscore our point, this Chapter will also examine Japan. Like Taiwan, South Korea and Hong Kong, Japan is one of the world's most advanced economies. But unlike its East Asian brethren, Japan has been ruled – almost continuously[172] – by a monolithic centre-right party (Liberal Democratic Party (LDP)) since 1955, and this *singular* dominant party has been able to stack the nation's highest court with its ideological allies on a *regular* and *uninterrupted* basis.[173] Therefore, while the TCC, KCC and HKCFA have been able to acquire policy space to independently adopt Western constitutional practices that are inconsistent with pre-existing law, the Supreme Court of Japan has largely been a handmaiden of the dominant ruling regime and has affirmed the constitutionality of almost every impugned legislation.[174]

Notably, while Japan's LDP has practically controlled Japan for almost seven decades and is merely maintaining the status quo vis-à-vis its judiciary, any Chinese intervention in Hong Kong's judicial operations would unsettle the 'One Country, Two Systems' political status quo. Vis-à-vis social and political institutions, 'once a country or region has started down a track, the costs of reversal are very high. There will be other choice points, but the entrenchments of certain institutional arrangements obstruct an easy reversal of the initial choice'.[175] In Hong Kong, the people and foreign investors are accustomed to a legal system based on a liberal common law framework. It will be prohibitively costly for Beijing to subvert Hong Kong's legal system, since confidence in Hong Kong's stability is crucial to maintaining the city as a gateway for foreign financial capital to invest in China.[176] Furthermore, Chinese State Owned Enterprises controlled by the Communist Party rely on Hong Kong to raise capital for its own political and economic ambitions.[177] Therefore, unlike the LDP's overwhelming and uninterrupted control over the Japanese

172 The LDP has been ousted from power only twice and briefly: 1993–1994 and 2009–2012.

173 David S. Law, 'Why Has Judicial Review Failed in Japan?' (2011) 88 *Washington University Law Review* 1425; David S. Law, 'The Anatomy of a Conservative Court: Judicial Review in Japan' (2009) 87 *Texas Law Review* 1545.

174 Shigenori Matsui, *The Constitution of Japan: A Contextual Analysis* (Hart 2011).

175 Margaret Levi, 'A Model, a Method, and a Map' in Mark Irving Lichbach and Alan S. Zuckerman (eds), *Comparative Politics* (Cambridge University Press 2002) 19, 28.

176 Anton Malkin and Yu-wai Vic Li, 'You Can Check in Anytime You like, but You Can Never Leave' in Ka Zeng (ed), *Handbook on the International Political Economy of China* (Edward Elgar 2019) 170, 171–186.

177 Ibid. 172.

Supreme Court, China can and will only interfere with the Hong Kong judiciary when Beijing's core interests in Hong Kong are at stake.

Chapter 3 will continue by exploring how the three courts have converged on Structured Proportionality (SP) and examine common themes on how SP is practised across the three jurisdictions. Chapter 4 will analyse the courts' convergence on two innovative constitutional remedies – the Suspension Order and the Remedial Interpretation of legislation – that allow the courts to either postpone or expedite the legal consequences that generally follow from a judicial declaration of an unconstitutional practice. Finally, Chapter 5 concludes by addressing the limits of this constitutional convergence. Hong Kong is a sub-unit of communist China, and, while it remains so, the courts will have no role in making major electoral changes or impeding Beijing's sovereignty over the city. On the other hand, in the dynamic democracies of Taiwan and South Korea, where there is an absence of a singular hegemonic political player, the courts have been able to significantly reshape their political environment and contribute to democratic politics.

Courts are political institutions.[178] And judges do not operate in an institutional or ideological vacuum, as they are shaped by the social, political and economic struggles that take place within their political systems.[179] Where the strategic environment confers a 'zone of discretion'[180] on the courts, the judges can construct a constitutional identity for their jurisdiction distinct from their government's vision, and redefine the polity's place in the world.[181] And this constitutional convergence in East Asia will endure so long as the political system in each jurisdiction remains fragmented, the courts continue to be independent *and* judges choose to align their local jurisprudence with Western human rights law.

[178] Ran Hirschl, 'The Judicialization of Politics' in Keith Whittington, R. Daniel Keleman and Gregory Caldeira (eds), *The Oxford Handbook of Law and Politics* (Oxford University Press 2010) 134.

[179] Ibid.

[180] Alec Stone Sweet, 'Constitutions and Judicial Power' in Daniele Caramani (ed.), *Comparative Politics* (Oxford University Press 2008) 228.

[181] Ran Hirschl, *Comparative Matters: The Renaissance of Comparative Constitutional Law* (Oxford University Press 2014) 41–43.

# 2

# Reasons for Convergence

## INTRODUCTION

In this Chapter, we explain why the constitutional jurisprudence of the Constitutional Court of Taiwan (TCC), the Constitutional Court of Korea (KCC) and the Hong Kong Court of Final Appeal (HKCFA) are converging. It is important to emphasize at the outset that the three courts are not *intentionally* aligning with one another. The three courts rarely look to – let alone cite – one another's precedents. For the TCC and the KCC, Germany is the foreign jurisdiction most considered by both courts;[1] for the HKCFA, Anglo-Canadian constitutional caselaw is the most persuasive.[2] But insofar as Germany and Canada/United Kingdom have converged on Structured Proportionality[3] and innovative constitutional remedies,[4] and so far as the TCC or the KCC adopts these German precedents (openly or behind the scenes) and the HKCFA endorses Anglo-Canadian caselaw, the three Asian jurisdictions are *indirectly* converging with one another in the practice of Western liberal constitutional norms.

The real question is why these Asian courts of final resort are able to *independently* embrace liberal Western constitutional practices, which are regularly *inconsistent* with the conservative norms pursued by their local legislatures. This expansion of judicial power in East Asia, whereby courts emerge as independent constraints on governmental authority, is not just a regional trend but part of a global

[1] David S. Law, 'Judicial Comparativism and Judicial Diplomacy' (2015) 163 *University of Pennsylvania Law Review* 927, 963, 979.

[2] Ibid. 989.

[3] BVerfGE 7, 377 (1958) (German Federal Constitutional Court); *R.* v. *Oakes* [1986] 1 SCR 103 (Supreme Court of Canada); *De Freitas* v. *Permanent Secretary of Ministry of Agriculture, Fisheries, Lands and Housing* [1999] 1 AC 69 (Privy Council).

[4] For examples on Remedial Interpretation of legislation, see *Ghaidan* v. *Godin-Mendoza* [2004] 2 AC 557 (UK House of Lords); *Schachter* v. *Canada* [1992] 2 SCR 679, 93 DLR (4th) 1 (Supreme Court of Canada); BVerfGE 2, 266 (1953) (German Federal Constitutional Court). For examples on Suspension Orders, see BVerfGE 33, 303 (1972) (German Federal Constitutional Court) and *Reference Re Manitoba Language Rights* [1985] 1 S.C.R. 721 (Supreme Court of Canada).

phenomenon.[5] In this Chapter, we offer two overlapping institutional explanations for the 'judicialisation'[6] of public law norms, which fosters this constitutional convergence within East Asia. In tandem with these institutional variables, we will also explain how the top judges in these three Asian courts intentionally use selected Western law to pursue their liberal agenda.

First, judicialization is facilitated by a fragmentation of power within the political branches,[7] which limits the capacity of a singular party/coalition to doggedly pursue a unified agenda effectively. Governments in authoritarian regimes can easily coordinate across state institutions and impose discipline on all the political actors.[8] Courts operating in such a political environment can rarely deviate from the legislative status quo without being punished or overruled.[9] But in a dynamic democracy, for which Taiwan and South Korea are classic Asian examples,[10] political power regularly rotates between competing parties, and the courts in turn have more space to determine policy outcomes as active cooperation between rival factions in the legislature to overrule the judiciary occurs less frequently, especially since constitutional review by an independent branch of government provides a form of insurance for political parties when fortunes turn.[11] In such circumstances, the courts have more opportunities and political space to independently impose Western constitutional norms that are contrary to the legislative status quo.

While political power is most fragmented in a competitive democracy, this fragmentation can even occur in some authoritarian democracies. Hong Kong is one such example. As the Chief Executive – head of the Hong Kong Special Administrative Region (HKSAR) government – is not inducted from any political party, and with the presence of multiple political parties, independents, and corporate representatives in the Legislative Council, the HKSAR government has to constantly broker conflicting interests between competing political forces when it

5 Alec Stone Sweet, *Governing with Judges: Constitutional Politics in Europe* (Oxford University Press 2000); Tom Ginsburg, *Judicial Review in New Democracies: Constitutional Courts in Asian Cases* (Cambridge University Press 2003); Ran Hirschl, *Towards Juristocracy* (Harvard University Press 2004); Björn Dressel (ed.), *Judicialization of Politics in Asia* (Routledge 2012); Po Jen Yap, *Courts and Democracies in Asia* (Cambridge University Press 2017); Albert H. Y. Chen and Andrew Harding (eds), *Constitutional Courts in Asia: A Comparative Perspective* (Cambridge University Press 2018).

6 Alec Stone Sweet (n. 5) 12–20; Ran Hirschl (n. 5) 211; Doreen Lustig and J. H. H. Weiler, 'Judicial Review in the Contemporary World – Retrospective and Prospective' (2018) 16 *International Journal of Constitutional Law* 315.

7 John Ferejohn, 'Judicializing Politics, Politicizing Law' (2002) 65 *Law & Contemporary Problems* 41, 59.

8 Tom Ginsburg and Alberto Simpser (eds), *Constitutions in Authoritarian Regimes* (Cambridge University Press 2014).

9 Tom Ginsburg and Tamir Moustafa (eds), *Rule by Law: The Politics of Courts in Authoritarian Regimes* (Cambridge University Press 2008); Po Jen Yap, *Constitutional Dialogue in Common Law Asia* (Oxford University Press 2015).

10 Yap (n. 5) 94–124.

11 Ginsburg (n. 5) 25.

seeks to pass legislation.[12] While the government can easily whip up support for legislation that Beijing considers imperative, the pro-Beijing[13] lawmakers' interests often deviate from the local government's agenda on socio-political issues that are not crucial to Beijing. In such instances, these local lawmakers would break ranks with the HKSAR government to cater to their own constituents. In essence, a divided government in Hong Kong provides the judiciary with the policy space to determine substantive outcomes in a host of constitutional issues, without risking overrides from the political branches.

Second, judicialization is facilitated by an independent judiciary. Judges are empowered when their ex ante and ex post autonomy are secured from a single dominant outside actor.[14] Daniel M. Brinks and Abby Blass define ex ante autonomy as the court's freedom from 'control from an identifiable faction or interest outside the court before the judges are seated"[15] and ex post autonomy refers to the judges' freedom from political pressure by an identifiable faction or interest after they are appointed.[16]

Where politicians have a significant role in the judicial appointment process, they will always seek to appoint judges who share their political ideology.[17] Where the same political party has a monopoly over the appointment process, it can continuously feed like-minded judicial agents into the constitutional system, as is the case in Japan.[18] Such judges become regime allies.[19] But in a competitive democracy where political power regularly rotates between rivalling parties, different factions will have their turn in the appointment process and the bench will be politically more diverse. And the judges appointed to their highest courts will not be beholden or accountable to a singular political party. We observe this in South Korea and Taiwan. But ex ante judicial autonomy can also be secured in authoritarian democracies where politicians do not have a *de facto* significant role in the judicial appointment process.

12 Brian Fong, 'Executive-Legislative Disconnection in Post-colonial Hong Kong' (2014) 1 *China Perspectives* 5, 12.

13 Pro-Beijing lawmakers in the Legislative Council include both fiscally-conservative business elites and socialist leftists.

14 Daniel M. Brinks and Abby Blass, 'Rethinking Judicial Empowerment: The New Foundations of Constitutional Justice' (2017) 15 *International Journal of Constitutional Law* 296, 299. See also Mark Tushnet, 'Preserving Judicial Independence in Dominant Party States' (2015) 60 *New York School Law Review* 107, 111–114.

15 Brinks and Blass (n. 14) 307.

16 Ibid.

17 Robert Dahl, 'Decision-Making in a Democracy: The Supreme Court as a National Policy-Maker' (1957) 6 *Journal of Public Law* 279; Jeffrey A. Segal and Harold J. Spaeth, *The Supreme Court and the Attitudinal Model Revisited* (Cambridge University Press 2002); Benjamin Alarie and Andrew J. Green, *Commitment and Cooperation in High Courts: A Cross Country Examination of Institutional Constraints on Judges* (Oxford University Press 2017) 83.

18 See David S. Law, 'Why Has Judicial Review Failed in Japan?' (2011) 88 *Washington University Law Review* 1425; David S. Law, 'The Anatomy of a Conservative Court: Judicial Review in Japan' (2009) 87 *Texas Law Review* 1545.

19 Brinks and Blass (n. 14) 301.

The less influence the political branches of government wield over judicial appointments, the less control they have over the shaping of judges in their image.[20] In Hong Kong, where judges are *in substance* chosen[21] by the nine-member Judicial Officers Recommendation Commission (JORC) chaired by the Chief Justice, and primarily comprising judges and lawyers, the Chief Justice has great latitude in shaping the composition of the bench, especially the crucial HKCFA. In practice, all members of the HKCFA are promoted from the Court of Appeal, and all Court of Appeal judges are drawn from the Court of First Instance. Therefore, the Chief Justice who commands the entire Hong Kong judiciary occupies the vantage spot to recruit, assess and promote his preferred candidates through the ranks. Furthermore, in Taiwan, South Korea and Hong Kong, ex post judicial autonomy is also secured insofar as the judges on their highest courts are protected from arbitrary removal during their term in office.[22] It is noteworthy that the impeachment procedure has never been used against their top judges in any of the three jurisdictions, nor has any top judge been forced to resign. Notably, empirical research has also demonstrated that the rules governing the selection and removal of judges are the only de jure protections that enhance judicial independence in practice and they operate conjunctively.[23]

In this Chapter, vis-à-vis Taiwan, South Korea and Hong Kong, we will explore how power is fragmented within their respective political branches of government, and analyse the extent to which their top courts enjoy ex ante and ex post autonomy. Both variables are interdependent, and, in tandem, enhance judicial power. To underscore our point, we will also examine Japan. Like Taiwan, South Korea and Hong Kong, Japan is one of the world's most advanced economies. But unlike its East Asian brethren, Japan has been ruled – almost uninterrupted – by a monolithic centre-right party (the Liberal Democratic Party) since 1955, and this *singular* dominant party has been able to stack the nation's highest court with its ideological allies on a *regular* and *continuous* basis. Therefore, while the TCC, KCC, and HKCFA have been able to acquire political space to independently impose Western constitutional norms that are inconsistent with the pre-existing legislative status quo, the Supreme Court of Japan has largely been a handmaiden of the dominant ruling

20 The Supreme Court of India is a striking example of how a court has completely sidelined the political branches of government in the judicial appointment process and usurped the power to renew its membership. In *Supreme Court Advocates-on-Record Association* v. *Union of India* [2016] 5 SCC 1, the Indian Supreme Court invalidated a constitutional amendment that created a six-member National Judicial Appointments Commission, and restored the prior judge-led collegium system where the judges themselves had near-complete control over the Supreme Court appointment process.

21 Formally, all judges in Hong Kong are appointed by the Chief Executive of the HKSAR on the recommendation of the JORC. See Article 88 of the Hong Kong Basic Law.

22 Article 81 of the Constitution of the Republic of China (Taiwan); Article 8 of the Constitutional Court Act (South Korea); Article 89 of the Hong Kong Basic Law.

23 James Melton and Tom Ginsburg, 'Does De Jure Judicial Independence Really Matter? A Re-evaluation of Explanations for Judicial Independence' (2014) 2 *Journal of Law and Courts* 187.

regime and has upheld the constitutionality of almost every piece of legislation that comes its way. While these institutional variables facilitate the exercise of strong judicial review, the judges themselves must desire such liberal outcomes. When judicial appointments and removals are not controlled by a singular dominant party in government, liberal judges can be appointed to the highest courts over time and pursue their agenda on the bench. This Chapter concludes by looking at how the judges in the three courts intentionally build institutional capability in comparative law from selected Western countries and explains why they use foreign legal precedents from these 'high-prestige courts and countries'[24] to subvert local legislation.

## TAIWAN'S POLITICAL SYSTEM AND ITS CONSTITUTIONAL COURT

Taiwan – officially termed the Republic of China (ROC) – is currently governed under an amended version of the ROC Constitution,[25] which was first enacted by the Kuomintang (KMT) in Mainland China in 1946 when the country was in the midst of a civil war between the KMT and the Chinese Communist Party (CCP).[26] As war waged on, the KMT passed the Temporary Provisions Effective During the Period of Communist Rebellion,[27] which suspended the Constitution and granted the President extensive emergency powers in 1948. Subsequently, martial law was declared in May 1949 and the KMT suspended all national elections.[28] Following the KMT's defeat on the Mainland, Chiang Kai-shek and his regime retreated to Taiwan in December 1949. Martial law was imposed across Taiwan, and all political parties save the KMT were banned. Autocratic rule persisted in Taiwan for decades until 1979 when the United States severed formal diplomatic relations with the latter. With the loss of its most important foreign ally, the KMT regime was forced to shore up its legitimacy by holding local elections.[29] Members from the KMT's long-time nemesis, *Tangwai* – the term literally means 'outside the party' – founded the Democratic Progressive Party (DPP) in 1986, one year before the ban on political parties was lifted. With the end of martial law rule in 1987 and the repeal of the

24 Law (n. 1) 1000.

25 The Constitution of the Republic of China (1947) (Taiwan), available at https://english.president.gov.tw/Page/94, accessed 9 May 2021.

26 Chien-Chih Lin, 'Constitutions and Courts in Chinese Authoritarian Regimes: China and Pre-Democratic Taiwan in Comparison' (2016) 14 *International Journal of Constitutional Law* 351, 355.

27 Temporary Provisions Effective during the Period of Communist Rebellion (1991) (Taiwan), available at https://law.moj.gov.tw/LawClass/LawAll.aspx?pcode=A0000005, accessed 9 May 2021.

28 Lin (n. 26) 365.

29 翁岳生：'台灣法治的發展 The Development of Rule of Law in Taiwan' (2017) 6 馬漢寶講座論文彙編 Herbert Han-Pao Ma Distinguished Lectureship 97, 125.

Temporary Provisions in 1991,[30] the wave of democracy finally reached Taiwanese shores.

The President of Taiwan currently serves a four-year term and is limited to two terms.[31] Since the direct election of President Lee Teng-hui (KMT) in 1996, the presidency has rotated between the KMT and the DPP three times: in 2000 (President Chen Shui-bian, DPP), in 2008 (President Ma Ying-jeou, KMT) and in 2016 (President Tsai Ing-wen, DPP). It would appear that the Taiwanese regularly vote for change after one party has been in power for two consecutive terms.

The Legislative Yuan – the legislature in Taiwan – is divided into two main ideological camps. There is the centre-right pan-blue camp comprising the KMT, the New Party (founded in 1993) and the People First Party (PFP) (founded in 2000); and the centre-left pan-green camp compromising the DPP, Taiwan Solidarity Union (founded in 2001), and the New Power Party (founded in 2015). The pan-blue camp typically supports the one-China policy, while the pan-green camp generally seeks independence for Taiwan.[32] Members in the pan-blue camp are typically also social and fiscal conservatives, while the pan-green camp is relatively more liberal on social and economic issues. Unlike the Presidency, the DPP was unable to seize control of the legislature until 2016. But this does not mean that the KMT had monopoly over the legislative agenda when it also controlled the Presidency. During President Lee's term in office (1988–2000),[33] even though his KMT party had a majority in the Legislative Yuan, there were deep factions within his own party, which led to 18 KMT legislators splintering away in 2000 to form the People First Party.

Power was even more fragmented when President Chen (2000–2008) was in office, as his DPP party never gained majority control of the legislature over the entire course of his Presidency. While President Chen's election marked a milestone in Taiwan's democratic development, as the KMT lost control of the Presidency for the first time in the nation's history, a divided government meant that legislative bills were regularly stalled and the legislative agendas of both parties were regularly thwarted. In fact, the passage rate of laws fell from 73 per cent (February 1999–May 2000) to a low of 39 per cent (May 2000–January 2002).[34]

30 Chien-Chih Lin, 'Survival of the Fittest (?): The Endurance of the ROC Constitution and the Constitution of Japan' (2014) 62 *American Journal of Comparative Law* 775, 782.

31 Paragraph 6 Article 2 of the Additional Articles of the Constitution of the Republic of China (Taiwan).

32 Shing-yuan Sheng and Hsiao-chuan (Mandy) Liao, 'Issues, Political Cleavages, and Party Competition in Taiwan' in Christopher H. Achen and T. Y. Wang (eds), *The Taiwan Voter* (University of Michigan Press 2017) 98, 123–127.

33 Before 1996, President Lee was elected by the National Assembly. He became the first popularly elected President in Taiwan in 1996.

34 Shing-Yuan Sheng 盛杏湲, '立法機關與行政機關在立法過程中的影響力: 一致政府與分立政府的比較 The Influence of the Legislative Branch and the Executive Branch in the Process of Lawmaking: A Comparison of the Unified and Divided Governments' (2003) 7(2) 台灣政治學刊 *Taiwan Political Science Review* 51, 86.

In the 2001 legislative election, the DPP took 40 per cent of the seats (87 out of 225 seats), followed by the KMT (30 per cent, 68 out of 225) and the People First Party (20 per cent, 46 out of 225).[35] While the DPP was the largest party in the legislature, the pan-blue camp (the KMT, the People First Party and the PFP) had control. Nevertheless, the PFP, a splinter group from the KMT, did not always cooperate with the KMT in light of their past acrimonious history. The composition of the legislature basically remained unchanged during President Chen's second term from 2004 to 2008, with the DPP occupying a plurality (89 out of 225), rather than a majority, of the legislative seats in the 2004 legislative election.[36]

In 2008, Ma Ying-jeou from the KMT was elected President. His KMT party also gained control of the Legislative Yuan by winning 81 legislative seats out of 113 seats.[37] In contrast, the DPP retained merely 27 seats.[38] But President Ma's political power waned in his second term. In September 2013, a serious conflict broke out between President Ma and Wang Jin-pyng, a KMT member and President of the Legislative Yuan. Ma expelled Wang from the KMT because the former believed that Wang had pressured state prosecutors not to institute proceedings against the DPP party whip, Ker Chien-ming, for criminal breach of trust. Wang immediately sought an injunction to suspend the expulsion and simultaneously challenged the legality of his party expulsion in the Taipei District Court. In 2014, the courts ruled in Wang's favour, and he remained as the President of the Legislative Yuan until his term expired in 2016. But because of this saga between the Taiwanese President and the influential President of the legislature, Ma was no longer able to rely on his own party's support for the rest of his term.[39]

Following President Ma's eight-year rule, Tsai Ing-wen from the DPP was elected President and her party also wrested control of the Legislative Yuan in 2016, a first in

35 Central Election Commission, 'The Fifth-Term Legislative Election: Seats for Each Political Party', available at https://db.cec.gov.tw/histMain.jsp?voteSel=20011201A2 (in Chinese), accessed 8 July 2019. For an English summary, see Central Election Commission, '2001 Legislator Election', available at www.cec.gov.tw/english/cms/le/24839, accessed 8 July 2019.

36 Central Election Commission, 'The Sixth-Term Legislative Election: Seats for Each Political Party', available at https://db.cec.gov.tw/histMain.jsp?voteSel=20041201A2 (in Chinese), accessed 8 July 2019. For an English summary, see Central Election Commission, '2004 Legislator Election', available at www.cec.gov.tw/english/cms/le/24840, accessed 8 July 2019.

37 Central Election Commission, 'The Seventh-Term Legislative Election: Seats for Each Political Party', available at https://db.cec.gov.tw/histMain.jsp?voteSel=20080101A2 (in Chinese), accessed 8 July 2019. For an English summary, see Central Election Commission, '2008 Legislator Election', available at www.cec.gov.tw/english/cms/le/24841, accessed 8 July 2019. In 2005, a constitutional amendment was passed to reduce the number of legislative seats from 225 to 113. See Paragraph 1, Article 4 of the Additional Articles of the Constitution of the Republic of China (Taiwan).

38 Central Election Commission, 'The Seventh-Term Legislative Election: Seats for Each Political Party', available at https://db.cec.gov.tw/histMain.jsp?voteSel=20080101A2 (in Chinese), accessed 8 July 2019. For an English summary, see Central Election Commission, '2008 Legislator Election', available at www.cec.gov.tw/english/cms/le/24841, accessed 8 July 2019.

39 Dafydd Fell, *Government and Politics in Taiwan* (Routledge 2018) 110–112.

the nation's history. Although the DPP controlled both branches of government, the DPP was not a monolithic party. There are many factions (the working class, human rights activists and pro-independence advocates) co-existing within the DPP[40]; they are united primarily by their opposition to the KMT's autocracy, but they divide along other ideological lines. Same-sex marriage is one such example. While President Tsai supports same-sex marriage, her own party whip Ker Chien-ming and other Christian DPP legislators had deep reservations.[41] Furthermore, DPP supporters are mainly from Southern Taiwan,[42] where residents hold strongly to their traditional values. In 2020, Tsai won a second term, and the DPP retained a majority in the Legislative Yuan by winning 61 of 113 seats.[43] The KMT remained the main opposition party, with 38 seats.[44]

In short, political power in Taiwan is deeply fragmented. Competing political parties regularly take turns to occupy the Presidency, and there are intra-party conflicts that make it impossible for any singular political faction to pursue a unified agenda even when the same party occupies both the Presidency and the legislature. This fragmentation of political power in turn empowers the TCC to assert its independence without risking significant political reprisal.

The TCC comprises 15 Justices, including the President and the Vice President of the Judicial Yuan. All the Justices are nominated by the President of Taiwan and have to be approved by the Legislative Yuan.[45] When there is a pending vacancy, the President of Taiwan will form a judicial recommendation committee. This committee is chaired by the Vice President of Taiwan and comprises six or seven members. Other members would usually include former Chief Justices and former associate Justices of the TCC. To qualify as a TCC Justice, one has to be a career judge, a prosecutor, a lawyer or a professor, and there is a cap on the number of Justices that can be appointed from each category.[46] After deliberation, the committee will provide a short-list of candidates to the President of Taiwan, and s/he in practice will choose the nominee from this pool.[47]

40 Ibid. 112–113, 204, 211.

41 For the legislators' religious belief and their attitudes towards same-sex marriage, see Pridewatch Taiwan, 'The Attitudes of the Ninth-Term Legislators toward Same-Sex Marriage', available at https://pridewatch.tw/beta/9th-legislators, accessed 24 July 2019.

42 Chia-hung Tsai, 'Who Is the Taiwan Voter?' in Christopher H. Achen and T. Y. Wang (eds), *The Taiwan Voter* (University of Michigan Press 2017) 26, 30–31.

43 Central Election Commission, 'The Tenth-Term Legislative Election: Seats for Each Political Party', available at https://db.cec.gov.tw/histMain.jsp?voteSel=20200101A2 (in Chinese), accessed 17 March 2020. For an English summary, see Central Election Commission, '2020 Legislator Election', available at www.cec.gov.tw/english/cms/le/32472, accessed 17 March 2020.

44 Ibid.

45 Paragraph 1, Article 5 of the Additional Articles of the Constitution of the Republic of China (Taiwan).

46 Paragraphs 1 and 2, Article 4 of the Judicial Yuan Organization Act.

47 We would like to thank Professor Yueh-sheng Weng, who has served as the President of the Judicial Yuan and Chief Justice, and participated on multiple occasions in the recommendation committee.

After the judicial candidate is nominated by the President, the Legislative Yuan will evaluate the candidate. The candidate's political ideology and character would usually be the focal point of this examination. When the President's party is in control of the Legislature Yuan, the candidate usually sails through the confirmation process. But when President Chen (DPP) was in office, the KMT-controlled legislature vetoed four of his candidates for purely partisan reasons.[48]

Post-appointment, the Justices serve a non-renewable[49] term of eight years, except for the President and the Vice President, whose term is not constitutionally guaranteed.[50] Typically, every President and Vice President of the TCC will resign out of courtesy to allow an incoming President of Taiwan choose new leaders for the Court, unless their nation's elected President asks them to stay on. Before 2003, the Justices served a renewable term of nine years. With the introduction of a non-renewable term, sitting Justices no longer have incentives to rule in favour of the ruling party in exchange for reappointment. The short term of eight years also allows the membership of the TCC to be regularly refreshed, and no single political party can effectively control the Constitutional Court for a long time should political power alternate regularly.[51] Moreover, the Judicial Yuan controls its own budget, which is subject to legislative audit but immune from executive intervention.[52]

TCC Justices can only be removed, suspended or have their salaries reduced for cause.[53] Specifically, a sitting Justice can be suspended from office by the President of Taiwan for incapacity[54] or removed from office for a prison conviction,[55] but only upon the written request of at least 10 TCC Justices. Alternatively, TCC Justices can

48 Jiunn-rong Yeh, 'Politicization of Constitutional Courts in Asia: Institutional Features, Contexts and Legitimacy' in Henbning Glaser (ed.), *Constitutional Jurisprudence: Function, Impact and Challenges* (Nomos Verlagsgesellschaft 2016) 215, 219–220.

49 Note that a TCC Justice can return to the bench as its Chief Justice after serving as an Associate Justice. Hsu Tzong-Li was appointed Chief Justice of the TCC in 2016, even though he completed his term as an Associate Justice in 2011.

50 Paragraph 2, Article 5 of the Additional Articles of the Constitution of the Republic of China (Taiwan).

51 For example, after President Ma assumed office in 2008 he appointed five Justices in 2009, two in 2010, four in 2011 and another four in 2015. Similarly, President Tsai of the DPP appointed seven Justices in 2017 and four in 2019. Therefore, President Ma's KMT-appointed bench was swiftly replaced by a DPP-appointed bench.

52 Paragraph 6, Article 5 of the Additional Articles of the Constitution of the Republic of China (Taiwan).

53 Article 81 of the Constitution of the Republic of China (Taiwan) reads: '... No judge shall be removed from office unless he has been found guilty of a criminal offense or subjected to disciplinary measure, or declared to be under interdiction. No judge shall, except in accordance with law, be suspended or transferred or have his salary reduced.'

54 Article 43 of the Judges Act.

55 Article 42 of the Judges Act.

also be impeached[56] by the Control Yuan[57] – Taiwan's ombudsman – for ethical violations[58] or if they are in dereliction of their duties.[59] Their impeachment would be adjudicated by the Court of the Judiciary staffed with judges on the Supreme Court and Supreme Administrative Court.[60] But, to date, no Justice has ever been suspended, impeached or removed from office.

In addition to these institutional protections that enhance judicial independence, the TCC has also endeavoured to gain public support because 'public support for courts is a bulwark of judicial independence'.[61] One strategy the TCC uses to enhance its popularity relates to how it modifies the legal effect of its decision. As a general rule, when the TCC strikes down a law, the law is only invalidated prospectively.[62] This ruling will not benefit the petitioners, as the impugned law would be deemed constitutional at the time it was applied by the lower courts to the petitioners. To address this problem, the TCC has ruled that if a law challenged by the citizenry has been declared unconstitutional, that petitioner may return to the ordinary courts and ask for a retrial or an extraordinary appeal.[63] This equally applies when the TCC issues a delayed declaration of invalidity.[64]

Political fragmentation in the different branches of government has also empowered the courts. Between 2000 and 2008, the DPP controlled the presidency while the pan-blue camp, headed by the KMT, controlled the legislature. Notably, in response to the TCC's decision[65] to invalidate statutory provisions passed by the KMT-controlled Legislative Yuan, which had created a special commission to launch criminal prosecutions and revoke judicial findings relating to the assassination attempts on President Chen,[66] the KMT decided to exact revenge on the Court. Specifically, the Legislative Yuan voted to withhold bonuses from the TCC

56 Article 99 of the Constitution of the Republic of China (Taiwan).

57 Paragraph 1, Article 90 of the Constitution of the Republic of China (Taiwan) reads: 'The Control Yuan shall be the highest control body of the State and shall exercise the powers of impeachment, censure and audit . . .'.

58 Articles 15 and 18 of the Judges Act.

59 Article 30 of the Judges Act.

60 Paragraph 2, Article 48 of the Judges Act.

61 R. Daniel Kelemen, 'The Political Foundations of Judicial Independence in the European Union' (2012) 19 *Journal of European Public Policy* 43, 45. For similar argument, see Georg Vanberg, 'Establishing Judicial Independence in West Germany' (2000) 32 *Comparative Politics* 333, 348; Bernd Hayo and Stefan Voigt, 'Explaining de facto judicial independence' (2007) 27 *International Review of Law and Economics* 269, 284.

62 J.Y. Interpretation No. 592 (Taiwan) (2005) (Constitutional Court of Taiwan), available at http://cons.judicial.gov.tw/jcc/en-us/jep03/show?expno=592, accessed 9 May 2021.

63 J.Y. Interpretation No. 185 (Taiwan) (1984) (Constitutional Court of Taiwan), available at http://cons.judicial.gov.tw/jcc/en-us/jep03/show?expno=185, accessed 9 May 2021.

64 J.Y. Interpretation No. 725 (Taiwan) (2014) (Constitutional Court of Taiwan), available at http://cons.judicial.gov.tw/jcc/en-us/jep03/show?expno=725, accessed 9 May 2021.

65 J.Y. Interpretation No. 585 (Taiwan) (2004) (Constitutional Court of Taiwan), available at http://cons.judicial.gov.tw/jcc/en-us/jep03/show?expno=585, accessed 9 May 2021.

66 A gunman attempted to assassinate both President Chen Shui-bian and Vice President Annette Lu when they were campaigning on 19 March 2004, the eve of Taiwan's presidential election. Because

Justices. Out-voted by the KMT in the legislature, the DPP legislators petitioned the TCC directly, arguing that the Constitution forbade the reduction of the Justices' salaries.[67] Notably in Taiwan, with at least the support of one-third of the lawmakers, minority legislators can directly petition the TCC on the constitutionality of any issues 'governing their [legislative] functions and duties'[68] and seek judicial intervention. With the assistance of these minority legislators, the TCC asserted in Interpretation No. 601 (2005) that 'judicial independence would be in jeopardy if judges did not have any guarantee of their remuneration'[69] and declared the withholding of the judicial bonus unconstitutional. By relying on a legislative minority to bring the petition before the Court, the TCC had the opportunity to defend its independence.[70]

In an important empirical study, Nuno Garoupa, Veronica Grembi and Shirley Ching-ping Lin argued that they found no evidence of partisan voting on the TCC.[71] Their explanation for this non-partisanship is that 'the Taiwanese Grand Justices needed to assert their independence from the other branches of government and gain credible reputations in order to maximize their influence'.[72] While we agree with their basic premise that the TCC seeks to enhance its reputation, we must emphasize that this does not mean that there is no ideological difference between Justices confirmed by different political parties. Their study suffers from one major limitation: all the cases in their dataset (1988–2008) were decided by Justices who were confirmed by a KMT-controlled legislature. Notably, the KMT-controlled legislature rejected four candidates nominated by President Chen (from the DPP) for purely partisan reasons in 2007.[73] Therefore, it is clear at least to the lawmakers that the Justices' political ideology matters and makes a difference.

both of them suffered only minor injuries, and as Chen and Lu eventually won the 2004 presidential election with a razor-thin margin, many KMT members believed that Chen orchestrated the shooting in order to gain sympathy votes in a tight presidential race. What is more puzzling is that the assassin committed suicide ten days after the shooting and the Prosecutor General in Taiwan decided to close the case after the former's death. This event has been termed the '319 Shooting' in Taiwan. The KMT wanted to prove that the assassination attempt was a political stunt engineered by President Chen and created the Special Commission on the Investigation of the Truth in Respect of the 319 Shooting to investigate the controversy.

67 Article 81 of the Constitution of the Republic of China (Taiwan) reads: '. . . No judge shall, except in accordance with law, be suspended or transferred or have his salary reduced.'

68 Section 3, Paragraph 1, Article 5 of the Constitutional Interpretation Procedure Act.

69 J.Y. Interpretation No. 601 (Taiwan) (2005) (Constitutional Court of Taiwan), at [23], available at http://cons.judicial.gov.tw/jcc/en-us/jep03/show?expno=601, accessed 9 May 2021.

70 In 2018, the Legislative Yuan passed the Constitutional Litigation Act, which will allow one-fourth of lawmakers to petition the TCC directly after it takes effect in 2022. Notably, the Constitutional Litigation Act was drafted by the Judicial Yuan, and was crafted by the judiciary to strengthen its hand by reducing the number of legislators needed to bring a petition before the TCC.

71 Nuno Garoupa, Veronica Grembi and Shirley Ching-ping Lin, 'Explaining Constitutional Review in New Democracies: The Case of Taiwan' (2011) 20 *Pacific Rim Law and Policy Journal* 1, 37.

72 Ibid. 35.

73 Alison Hsiao, 'Legislature Approves Judicial Nominees' (*Taipei Times*, 26 October 2016), available at www.taipeitimes.com/News/front/archives/2016/10/26/2003657934, accessed 10 July 2019.

Furthermore, KMT appointees are generally more deferential to governmental exercise of state power. Between 2008 and 2016, after the KMT controlled both the Presidency and the legislature, and President Ma (KMT) had the opportunity to replace all of President Chen (DPP)'s judges, the TCC over the course of President Ma's presidency became a 'nominal'[74] constitutional player in Taiwan politics. On the other hand, the DPP-appointed Justices are widely perceived to be more liberal and activist;[75] and they overwhelmingly voted to scuttle the government's plan to fingerprint every citizen in Interpretation No. 603 (2005),[76] legalized same-sex marriage in Interpretation No. 748 (2017)[77] and decriminalized adultery in Interpretation No. 791 (2020).[78]

Finally, the TCC rulings are binding on all institutions and persons in Taiwan,[79] and they can only be overruled by the TCC itself or through a constitutional amendment. But, since 2005, a constitutional amendment requires the consent of three-fourths of the legislators and must be approved in a national referendum by a majority of all eligible voters in Taiwan – an excruciatingly high threshold that makes it practically impossible to amend any part of the Constitution.[80] Notably, there has been no constitutional amendment in Taiwan since 2005. Furthermore, even a constitutional amendment may not work, as the TCC has even asserted the power to invalidate any constitutional amendment that violates 'the constitutional order of liberal democracy'.[81] In this sense, the TCC is now truly supreme.

74 Ming-Sung Kuo, 'Moving towards a Nominal Constitutional Court: Critical Reflections on the Shift from Judicial Activism to Constitutional Irrelevance in Taiwan's Constitutional Politics' (2016) 25 *Pacific Rim Law & Policy Journal* 597, 603.

75 Hou Po-Ching, 'Tsai Nominates Four Justices, and the Liberals Will Dominate the TCC' (*The Storm Media*, 6 June 2019), available at www.storm.mg/article/1358276?srcid=73746f726d2e6d675f636466343439623336234346266633_1562740515, accessed 10 July 2019.

76 J.Y. Interpretation No. 603 (2005) (Constitutional Court of Taiwan), at [13], available at http://cons.judicial.gov.tw/jcc/en-us/jep03/show?expno=603, accessed 9 May 2021.

77 J.Y. Interpretation No. 748 (2017) (Constitutional Court of Taiwan), at [16], available at http://cons.judicial.gov.tw/jcc/en-us/jep03/show?expno=748, accessed 9 May 2021.

78 J.Y. Interpretation No. 791 (2020) (Constitutional Court of Taiwan), at [29], available at https://cons.judicial.gov.tw/jcc/zh-tw/jep03/show?expno=791, accessed 9 May 2021.

79 J.Y. Interpretation No. 185 (1984) (Constitutional Court of Taiwan), at [1], available at http://cons.judicial.gov.tw/jcc/en-us/jep03/show?expno=185, accessed 9 May 2021.

80 Article 12 of the Additional Articles of the Constitution of the Republic of China reads: 'Amendment of the Constitution shall be initiated upon the proposal of one-fourth of the total members of the Legislative Yuan, passed by at least three-fourths of the members present at a meeting attended by at least three-fourths of the total members of the Legislative Yuan, and sanctioned by electors in the free area of the Republic of China at a referendum held upon expiration of a six-month period of public announcement of the proposal, wherein the number of valid votes in favor exceeds one-half of the total number of electors.'

81 J.Y. Interpretation No. 499 (2000) (Constitutional Court of Taiwan), at [12], available at http://cons.judicial.gov.tw/jcc/en-us/jep03/show?expno=499, accessed 9 May 2021. In this case, delegates on the National Assembly, which was the legislative body exclusively responsible for the passage of constitutional amendments prior to 2005, had attempted to extend their existing term of office by over two years when they revised the Constitution in 1999. The TCC invalidated the 1999 constitutional amendments on both procedural and substantive grounds. In 2014, in Interpretation No. 721 (2014),

## SOUTH KOREA'S POLITICAL SYSTEM AND ITS CONSTITUTIONAL COURT

The passage of the operative Constitution of the Republic of Korea in 1987 ushered in the establishment of the current Sixth Republic,[82] which was the culmination of the democratization movement that had demanded political change since South Korea's last military regime took power in 1979.[83]

Unlike Taiwan, South Korea post-democratization did not experience a phase with a dominant party in control of government. Political power in South Korea is so fragmented that post-1987, the President's party rarely controls the National Assembly, and, even then, never for long. Weak political parties have been a cardinal feature of South Korea's modern electoral scene. Political parties are largely instruments of their powerful leaders with strong regional appeal and these parties continuously split, merge or reconfigure as their party bosses leave the political stage.[84] For instance, the Democratic Justice Party (DJP) – the country's leading right-wing party in 1987 – became the Democratic Liberal Party (DLP) in 1990,[85] the New Korea Party in 1996,[86] the Grand National Party (GNP) in 1997,[87] the Saenuri Party in 2012[88] and finally the Liberty Korea Party in 2017.[89] This cycle of party mergers and breakups is not unique to the DLP and its successors. In the same vein, the DLP's main nemesis, the Democratic Party, fragmented and was reconfigured multiple times before it reverted to its current incarnation as the Democratic

this power to invalidate unconstitutional constitutional amendments was re-affirmed. See J.Y. Interpretation No. 721 (2014) (Constitutional Court of Taiwan), at [1], available at http://cons.judicial.gov.tw/jcc/en-us/jep03/show?expno=721, accessed 9 May 2021.

82 Korea has had six Republics since its independence in 1945. Only the 2nd Republic, which existed for less than one year between 1960 and 1961, and the current 6th Republic have been democracies. See Ginsburg (n. 5) 208–209.

83 Tom Ginsburg, 'Constitutional Courts in East Asia: Understanding Variation' (2008) 3 *Journal of Comparative Law* 80, 85. See also James M. West and Dae-Kyu Yoon, 'The Constitutional Court of the Republic of Korea: Transforming the Jurisprudence of the Vortex?' (1992) 40 *American Journal of Comparative Law* 73.

84 Byung-Kook Kim, 'Party Politics in South Korea's Democracy: The Crisis of Success' in Larry Diamond and Byung-Kook Kim (eds), *Consolidating Democracy in South Korea* (Lynne Rienner Publishers 2000) 53–60; Yoonkyung Lee, 'Political Parties' in Chung-in Moon and M. Jae Moon (eds), *Routledge Handbook of Korean Politics and Public Administration* (Routledge 2020) 77, 82–83. It should be noted that this regional cleavage has waned since 2000. See Wook Kim, 'Political Polarization: Regionalism, Ideology, and Generational Changes' in Chung-in Moon and M. Jae Moon (eds), *Routledge Handbook of Korean Politics and Public Administration* (Routledge 2020) 112, 117–118.

85 Jiyoon Kim, 'The Party System in Korea and Identity Politics' in Larry Diamond and Gi-Wook Shin (eds), *New Challenges for Maturing Democracies in Korea and Taiwan* (Stanford University Press 2014) 76; Lee (n. 84) 84.

86 Youngmi Kim, *The Politics of Coalition in Korea* (Routledge 2011) 45; Lee (n. 84) 84.

87 Kim (n. 85); Lee (n. 84) 84.

88 Ibid.

89 Uk Heo and Seongyi Yun, 'South Korea in 2017: Presidential Impeachment and Security Volatility' (2018) 58 *Asian Survey* 65, 66; Lee (n. 84) 84.

Party of Korea in 2015 once again.[90] The Liberty Korea Party and its predecessors appeal to social and fiscal conservatives while the Democratic Party and its predecessors are more liberal.[91]

The President of South Korea can only serve a single five-year term.[92] The National Assembly is the unicameral national legislature and legislators serve a renewable four-year term.[93] South Korea's first President after democratization in 1987 was Roh Tae-Woo and his DJP only took 125 (out of the 299) seats in the 1988 National Assembly election.[94] The Party for Peace and Democracy (PPD, or Peace Democratic Party), the party founded by Kim Dae-jung in October 1987,[95] came in second with 70 seats,[96] and the PPD transformed into the Democratic Party in 1991.[97]

Even after President Roh merged the DJP with other small political parties to form the DLP in 1990, this new party was only able to win 149 of the 299 seats in the 1992 legislative election.[98] Meanwhile, the Democratic Party – the main opposition party – was the second largest party with 97 seats.[99] The President's party was the largest one in the legislature, but it did not control a majority of the seats. Roh's political successor, Kim Young-sam, was elected President in 1992, but his DLP party only had plurality control of the National Assembly. In September 1995, the Democratic Party reconfigured as the National Congress for New Politics (NCNP), and the DLP became the New Korea Party (NKP) in February 1996.[100]

Real party turnover finally took place when Kim Dae-jung of the NCNP – Roh's primary political rival – was elected President in December 1997. When President Kim Dae-jung was sworn in, his party did not have majority control of the National Assembly, and President Kim had to govern by forming a coalition with smaller parties.[101] But the NCNP, which reconfigured as the Millennium Democratic Party (MDP) in January 2000,[102] lost a significant number of seats in the legislative election held in April 2000. The Grand National Party (GNP), which was rebranded

90 Lee (n. 84) 84.
91 Kim 'Political Polarization' (n. 84) 118–121.
92 Article 70 of the Constitution of the Republic of Korea.
93 Article 42 of the Constitution of the Republic of Korea.
94 The National Assembly of the Republic of Korea, 'Past Parties', available at http://korea.assembly.go.kr/int/past_03.jsp, accessed 19 July 2019.
95 Kim (n 85) 77.
96 The National Assembly of the Republic of Korea, 'Past Parties', available at http://korea.assembly.go.kr/int/past_03.jsp, accessed 19 July 2019.
97 Kim (n. 85).
98 The National Assembly of the Republic of Korea, 'Past Parties', available at http://korea.assembly.go.kr/int/past_03.jsp, accessed 19 July 2019.
99 Ibid.
100 Kim (n. 86).
101 Chan Wook Park, 'The National Assembly in Democratized Korea' in Zheng Yongnian, Lye Liang Fook, and Wilhelm Hofmeister (eds), *Parliaments in Asia* (Routledge 2014) 185, 192.
102 Aurel Croissant, 'Electoral Politics in South Korea' in Aurel Croissant (ed.), *Electoral Politics in Southeast and East Asia* (Friedrich-Ebert-Stiftung 2002) 251.

from the NKP in November 1997,[103] emerged as the greatest victor, winning 133 out of 273 seats.[104] With a minority government in the legislature, President Kim had to govern once again by allying with smaller parties throughout his term.

The MDP's Roh Moo-hyun, a minister in Kim Dae-jung's administration, assumed the Presidency in early 2003, and the MDP was the second largest party in the National Assembly. Due to a factional struggle, President Roh and a pro-Roh faction within the MDP soon splintered away to found the Uri Party in November 2003,[105] which became the third largest political party in the National Assembly. On the other hand, Roh's political rivals, which included the GNP and the MDP, occupied more than 80 per cent [106] of the seats in the National Assembly. Roh's political enemies tried to impeach him for alleged electoral violations in 2003 and the President was suspended pending a decision from the Constitutional Court. In the midst of this chaos, Roh's Uri Party surprisingly won 152 (out of 299) seats[107] in the 2004 legislative election, and the Constitutional Court also restored Roh to office shortly after that. But Roh soon lost his majority, as his lawmakers either defected or were removed.[108] Those defectors came together as the United New Democratic Party (UNDP) in August 2007 and the Uri Party also dissolved in the same month.[109]

GNP's Lee Myung-bak won the Presidency in 2007 and his party also controlled a slim majority of 153 out of 300 seats in the National Assembly after the 2008 legislative election.[110] The UNDP reconfigured multiple times and became the Democratic Party in 2008[111] and then the Democratic United Party (DUP) in 2011.[112] The GNP rebranded itself as the Saenuri Party in 2012[113] and the latter retained 152 out of 300 seats in the 2012 legislative election.[114]

The Saenuri Party, with Park Geun-hye at the helm, retained the Presidency in 2012. Its main nemesis, the DUP, reconfigured multiple times and became the Democratic Party of Korea (Minjoo Party of Korea) once again in 2015.[115] In the

103 Ibid.

104 The National Assembly of the Republic of Korea, 'Past Parties', available at http://korea.assembly.go.kr/int/past_03.jsp, accessed 19 July 2019.

105 Kim (n. 86) 154.

106 Park (n. 101) 194.

107 The National Assembly of the Republic of Korea, 'Past Parties', available at http://korea.assembly.go.kr/int/past_03.jsp, accessed 19 July 2019.

108 Park (n. 101) 194.

109 Ibid.

110 The National Assembly of the Republic of Korea, 'Past Parties' http://korea.assembly.go.kr/int/past_03.jsp, accessed 3 August 2019.

111 Uk Heo, 'What Delays Democratic Consolidation in South Korea' (2013) 44 *Korea Observer* 569, 580.

112 Ibid.

113 Kim (n. 85).

114 The National Assembly of the Republic of Korea, 'Past Parties', available at http://korea.assembly.go.kr/int/past_03.jsp, accessed 3 August 2019.

115 Lee (n. 84) 84.

April 2016 legislative election, the Democratic Party of Korea became the largest party in the National Assembly, occupying 123 out of 300 seats in the National Assembly.[116] President Park's woes worsened when she was embroiled in an influence-peddling scandal. A bipartisan National Assembly filed a motion for her impeachment in December 2016, and she was removed from office by the Constitutional Court in 2017. Park's fall led to the Democratic Party's Moon Jae-in wresting control of the Presidency in the election held that year. In January 2020, the right-wing conservative parties merged to become the United Future Party (UFP),[117] but this alliance was not sufficient to prevent Moon's Democratic Party and its satellite party (Together Citizens' Party/Platform Party) from securing a landslide victory in the 2020 legislative election. Moon and his affiliates now control 180 out of 300 seats of the National Assembly,[118] while the UFP and its allies retained only 103 seats.[119]

South Korea's weak party system is a consequence of its culture of personality-driven politics.[120] When a key personality is weakened, and there are defections, political parties dissolve and power fragments.

The KCC – established only in 1988[121] and unhampered by past institutional and bureaucratic baggage – benefitted from South Korea's weak party system as it asserted itself to become a major player in the country's constitutional politics. There are nine Justices on the KCC and they are appointed in accordance to what has been termed the 'representative model':[122] each branch of government – the Supreme Court, the National Assembly, and the President of South Korea – gets to nominate three Justices.[123] In practice, the three nominees proposed by the National Assembly, and the three nominees put forward by the Chief Justice of

116 Hyung-A. Kim, 'President Roh Moo-Hyun's Last Interview and the Roh Moo-Hyun Phenomenon in South Korea' (2017) 47 *Journal of Contemporary Asia* 273, 279.

117 Ser Myo-Ja, 'United Future Party Launches After Merger' (*Korea JoongAng Daily*, 20 January 20, 2020), available at https://koreajoongangdaily.joins.com/news/article/article.aspx?aid=3073936, accessed 30 April 2020.

118 Kim Soo-yeon, '(6th LD) Ruling Party Wins Landslide Victory in Parliamentary Elections Amid Pandemic' (*Yonhap News Agency*, 16 April 2020), available at https://en.yna.co.kr/view/AEN20200415005856315, accessed 28 April 2020.

119 Ibid.

120 Kim (n. 85) 75.

121 A Constitutional Committee existed formally in the 4th and 5th Republic, but it was never called upon by the Supreme Court to exercise its constitutional powers during this period. See Ginsburg (n. 5) 212–213.

122 Tom Ginsburg, 'Economic Analysis and the Design of Constitutional Courts' (2002) 3 *Theoretical Inquiries in Law* 49, 67.

123 Article 111(2) & (3) of the Constitution of the Republic of Korea reads: '(2) The Constitutional Court shall be composed of nine Justices qualified to be court judges, and they shall be appointed by the President. (3) Among the Justices referred to in paragraph (2), three shall be appointed from persons selected by the National Assembly, and three appointed from persons nominated by the Chief Justice of the Supreme Court.'

the Supreme Court, are always appointed by the President.[124] For the position of KCC President, the South Korean President gets to nominate the candidate, when there is a vacancy, but the candidate must also be approved by the National Assembly.[125] For the President's other nominees, they do not require legislative approval, but a 'personnel hearing'[126] before the National Assembly is held upon request.

In reality, the President of South Korea can control the appointment of four to five Justices because there is an unwritten norm that allows the main minority party in the legislature to nominate at least one Justice for the three spots allocated to the National Assembly.[127] Take the composition of the KCC as it stood in October 2020 as an example: three Justices were selected by President Moon Jae-in[128] – one by the former Chief Justice of the Supreme Court[129] (who was former President Lee

124 See Joon Seok Hong, 'Signaling the Turn: The Supermajority Requirement and Judicial Power on the Constitutional Court of Korea' (2019) 67 *American Journal of Comparative Law* 177, 185.

125 Article 111 (4) of the Constitution of the Republic of Korea. Notably, the President of South Korea does not always get his preferred President for the KCC approved. In 2006, President Roh's nomination of Jeon Hyo-sook as the KCC President was heavily criticized because she was a sitting KCC Justice and merely resigned so that the President could reappoint her as the Court's President. Her nomination was eventually withdrawn. In the same vein, in 2017, President Moon's nomination of Kim Yi-Su as the KCC President was rejected by the National Assembly as he was a sitting KCC Justice. See The Constitutional Court of Korea, *Thirty Years of the Constitutional Court of Korea* (The Constitutional Court of Korea 2018) 110.

126 See Article 65-2 of the National Assembly Act. But note that Article 46-3(1)[2] of the National Assembly Act only requires an approval bill for Constitutional Court Justices nominated by the National Assembly, but not those Justices nominated by the President or the Supreme Court. For the candidates nominated by the President or the Chief Justice of the Supreme Court, the National Assembly will send its findings after the personnel hearing to the relevant public official who nominated the judicial candidate. See The Constitutional Court of Korea, *Thirty Years of the Constitutional Court of Korea* (Constitutional Court of Korea 2018) 112–113. See also Association of Asian Constitutional Courts and Equivalent Institutions Secretariat for Research and Development, *Jurisdictions and Organization of AACC Members* (AACC SRD & Constitutional Court of Korea 2018) 109. For examples where President Moon appointed KCC Justices notwithstanding legislative opposition, see Yonhap, 'Moon Appoints Two Disputed Justices' (*The Korea Times*, 19 April 2019), available at www.koreatimes.co.kr/www/nation/2019/04/113_267446.html?fbclid=IwAR1AyTuAEzYeikwF33YGWJRU3ULor2EIioBO9wUEO8bCtXK1e-lTndKxQfk, accessed 7 January 2020.

127 Ginsburg (n. 5) 221. Given that the President of South Korea also nominates the Chief Justice of the Supreme Court (if a vacancy arises), who in turn can choose up to three Justices, some scholars have suggested that the President of South Korea can directly or indirectly influence the appointment of up to six KCC Justices. See Hong (n. 124). Some scholars have noted that that a party can appoint up to eight Justices when the President and the majority party in the National Assembly are from the same political party. See Jeon, Jeong-hyun, 'Political Functions and Dilemma of the Korean Constitutional Court' (2016) 47 *Korea Observer* 461, 482.

128 Yonhap News, 'President Designates New Chief of Constitutional Court' (*Yonhap News Agency*, 29 August 2018), available at https://en.yna.co.kr/view/AEN20180829010100315, accessed 7 January 2020; Yonhap News, 'President Nominates Two New Constitutional Court Justices' (*Yonhap News Agency*, 20 March 2019), available at https://en.yna.co.kr/view/AEN20190320006700315, accessed 7 January 2020.

129 KBS World, 'New Constitutional Court Justice Lee Seon-ae Takes Office' (*KBS World*, 29 March 2017), available at http://world.kbs.co.kr/service/news_view.htm?lang=e&Seq_Code=126304, accessed 7 January 2020.

Myung-bak's appointee); two by the current Chief Justice of the Supreme Court (appointed by President Moon);[130] one by Moon's Democratic Party of Korea,[131] which occupied a majority in the National Assembly; one by the Liberty Korea Party[132] (known as the Saenuri Party before February 2017), the second largest party in the National Assembly; and the last Justice by the third largest party, the Bareunmirae Party,[133] founded in 2018.[134]

This diversity of the KCC reflects the political fragmentation in South Korea and this actually strengthens judicial independence, as every major political party knows it has allies on the bench. Furthermore, each KCC Justice does not serve for very long, which reduces the incentives on the government of the day to punish the Court since all the judges can be replaced quickly. While each KCC Justice formally serves a *renewable* term of six years,[135] which undercuts judicial independence, in practice only two Justices out of 55 have ever been reappointed, and none after 1994.[136] Because the chances of re-appointment are now very slim, Justices are no longer constrained by the need to rule in a way that will secure them a second term. Given that no political party can control either the National Assembly or the presidency for long, and since all the KCC Justices serve such short terms, all the major political parties have some stake in preserving judicial independence, especially as these parties will have the opportunity to appoint their preferred Justices soon enough. Notably, every President of South Korea post-democratization, except Lee Myung-bak,[137] has even been able to appoint his or her own KCC President to lead the Court. With judicial terms that are non-renewable in practice, and a high turnover rate on the KCC, judicial independence is enhanced as the judges are freed from ruling with an eye on reappointment, and the political branches have less incentive to punish the Court for a decision they dislike. Therefore, even though a KCC Justice can be removed from office

130 Lee Suh-yoon, 'South Korean Constitutional Court to Undergo Liberal Shift' (*The Korea Times*, 26 August 2018), available at www.koreatimes.co.kr/www/nation/2018/08/356_254310.html, accessed 7 January 2020.

131 Shim Kyu-Seok, 'Moon Taps Liberal to Lead Constitutional Court' (*Korea JoongAng Daily*, 31 August 2018), available at http://koreajoongangdaily.joins.com/news/article/article.aspx?aid=3052579, accessed 7 January 2020.

132 Ock Hyun-ju, '[Feature] Liberal Constitutional Court Triggers Hopes, Concerns' (*The Korea Herald*, 8 May 2019). Available at www.koreaherald.com/view.php?ud=20190507000668, accessed 7 January 2020.

133 Lee Suh-yoon, 'Constitutional Court Paralyzed in Partisan Feud' (*The Korea Times*, 2 October 2018), available at www.koreatimes.co.kr/www/nation/2018/10/356_256270.html, accessed 7 January 2020.

134 The National Assembly of the Republic of Korea, 'Past Parties', available at http://korea.assembly.go.kr/int/past_03.jsp, accessed 3 August 2019.

135 Article 112(1) of the Constitution of the Republic of Korea.

136 Justice Kim Moon-hee served on the bench from September 1988 to September 2000 and Justice Kim Chin-woo served from September 1988 to January 1997. See The Constitutional Court of Korea (n. 125) 36.

137 The Constitutional Court of Korea (n. 125) 108–109.

by a majority vote in the National Assembly[138] for violating 'the Constitution or statutes in the course of execution of his or her duties',[139] no such attempts have ever been made.

Finally, a KCC decision can only be overruled by a future KCC panel or overturned with a constitutional amendment. But any such constitutional amendment must be approved by the National Assembly and endorsed by a majority of all votes cast in a national referendum.[140] It is noteworthy that South Korea has never amended its Constitution post-democratization and the KCC is now the final arbiter of all constitutional controversies in the country.

## HONG KONG'S POLITICAL SYSTEM AND ITS COURT OF FINAL APPEAL

The Hong Kong Special Administrative Region (HKSAR) was established in 1997 after Britain returned its former colony to the People's Republic of China. The head of the HKSAR government – the Chief Executive (CE) – is currently elected by an Election Committee composed of only 1,200 members.[141] From the upcoming 2022 CE election onwards, the CE will be elected by a committee of 1500 members.[142] With this change, Beijing added Hong Kong representatives of China's national organizations to and removed elected Hong Kong district councillors[143] from the Committee, thereby extending its control over the CE selection.

[138] Article 65 (2) of the Constitution of the Republic of Korea reads: 'A motion for impeachment . . . may be proposed by one third or more of the total members of the National Assembly, and shall require a concurrent vote of a majority of the total members of the National Assembly for passage.'

[139] Article 48 [2] of the Constitutional Court Act.

[140] Article 130(2) of the Constitution of the Republic of Korea reads: 'The proposed amendments to the Constitution shall be submitted to a national referendum not later than thirty days after passage by the National Assembly, and shall be determined by more than one half of all votes cast by more than one half of voters eligible to vote in elections for members of the National Assembly.'

[141] Three hundred members are fielded from each of the following four sectors: (1) the industrial, commercial and financial sectors, (2) the professions, (3) labour, social services, religious and other sectors; and (4) members of the Legislative Council, representatives of district-based organizations, Hong Kong deputies to the National People's Congress and representatives of Hong Kong members of the National Committee of the Chinese People's Political Consultative Conference. See *Amendment to Annex I to the Basic Law of the Hong Kong Special Administrative Region of the People's Republic of China Concerning the Method for the Selection of the Chief Executive of the Hong Kong Special Administrative Region* (Approved at the Sixteenth Session of the Standing Committee of the Eleventh National People's Congress on 28 August 2010).

[142] Section 2 of the Annex I to the Basic Law of the Hong Kong Special Administrative Region of the People's Republic of China Concerning the Method for the Selection of the Chief Executive of the Hong Kong Special Administrative Region, available at www.xinhuanet.com/english/download/2021-3-30/AnnexI.pdf, accessed 20 May 2021.

[143] District Councillors advise the government on municipal affairs and undertake community projects. In the 2019 District Council elections, pro-democracy councillors won in a landslide and captured 17 out of 18 District Councils in Hong Kong. But for the 2021 electoral change, this win would have given the pro-democracy bloc 117 seats in the 1200-member Chief Executive Election Committee.

An overwhelming majority of the Election Committee members are pro-Beijing, thereby ensuring that only a pro-Beijing candidate can be selected as Chief Executive.[144] But as the Chief Executive cannot be a member of any political party,[145] he or she lacks a strong party base to turn to for political support. To date, all Chief Executives have been former civil servants or businessmen. The Chief Executive is assisted by a ministerial team that he or she appoints, and these ministers, known as Principal Officials, are in charge of various portfolios such as Justice, Finance and Home Affairs.[146] Most Principal Officials, past and present, do not have any party affiliations,[147] such that executive power is not generally shared with the pro-Beijing parties in the legislature to foster better ties.

The Hong Kong Legislative Council is a unicameral body. Prior to the 2021 electoral revamp, it was composed of 70 members[148] elected via two different electoral methods. 35 seats in the Legislative Council were constituted via universal suffrage in Geographical Constituencies (GC) elections.[149] But proportional representation was used in the allocation of these GC electoral seats, which meant that no single political party could win a majority of those seats.[150] The pro-Beijing coalition within the legislature had instead splintered off into smaller political parties and independents, leading to fragmentation within the governing coalition.[151] Notably, in 2019, the Democratic Alliance for the Betterment and Progress of Hong Kong – the largest pro-Beijing party in Hong Kong – only had 13 seats in the Legislative Council.[152]

The other 35 seats in the Legislative Council were constituted via Functional Constituencies (FC), a system in which the right to vote depends upon a person's membership or registration in a recognized social, economic, industrial,

144 Simon Young and Richard Cullen, *Electing Hong Kong's Chief Executive* (Hong Kong University Press 2010) 79, 91.

145 Section 31 of the Chief Executive Election Ordinance (Cap 569) (Hong Kong).

146 Yap (n. 9) 37–38.

147 Brian C. H. Fong, 'Executive-Legislative Disconnection in the HKSAR: Uneasy Partnership between Chief Executives and Pro-Government Parties, 1997–2016' in Brian C. H. Fong and Tai-lok Lui (eds), *Hong Kong 20 Years after the Handover: Emerging Social and Institutional Fractures After* 1997 (Palgrave Macmillan 2018) 45, 59.

148 See Annex 2 of the Hong Kong Basic Law, as amended in 2010.

149 Ibid.

150 See Elaine Chan and Rowena Kwok, 'Democratization in Turmoil? Elections in Hong Kong' (1999) 8(20) *Journal of Contemporary China* 47, 56; Maurice Duverger, *Political Parties*, vol. 2 (Methuen 1954) 248–249; Stephen Gardbaum, 'Political Parties, Voting Systems, and the Separation of Powers' (2017) 65 *American Journal of Comparative Law* 229, 247.

151 Ngok Ma, 'From Executive Dominance to Fragmented Authority: An Institutional and Political Analysis' in Brian C. H. Fong and Tai-lok Lui (eds), *Hong Kong 20 Years After the Handover: Emerging Social and Institutional Fractures After* 1997 (Palgrave Macmillan 2018) 21, 31.

152 Democratic Alliance for the Betterment and Progress of Hong Kong, 'Legislative Councillors' (Democratic Alliance for the Betterment and Progress of Hong Kong n.d.), available at www.eng.dab.org.hk/dab-people/councillors/legislative-councillors/, accessed 16 April 2019.

commercial, political advisory or professional body represented in the legislature.[153] In many of these FCs, for example Insurance, Transport, Finance, Labour, it is not the individuals working in these professions who are eligible to vote. Instead, it is only the recognized corporate bodies operating in these professions that can vote. Most elected corporate representatives in the FCs are pro-business and therefore, within the Hong Kong context, also pro-Beijing. However, each elected corporate representative in the Legislative Council is only electorally accountable to his or her respective FC sectoral constituents, and as the FC caters to a very narrow political base of sectoral interests, FC politicians are unlikely to compromise with the local government when their FCs' interests are directly affected by pending legislation.

This political set-up was part of the Chinese government's original design. Beijing did not want to see the emergence of a powerful Chief Executive or a strong governing party, with deep socio-political roots in Hong Kong, which could resist its control.[154] But the unintended consequence of this deliberate fragmentation of political power was legislative grid-lock.

While the pro-Beijing coalition in the Legislative Council will be united in defending the Chinese Central Government's core interests in Hong Kong, these lawmakers do not owe their political allegiance to the Chief Executive of the HKSAR or a singular political party in Hong Kong. On issues not fundamental to Beijing, these lawmakers would break ranks with the local government to accommodate their own constituents. Notably, between 1998 and 2016, the Government's average legislative success rate stood at 56.29 per cent – undoubtedly a low level for a semi-democracy – with 39.84 per cent of all legislative initiatives originally scheduled in the annual Legislative Programme shelved as a result of opposition from defiant parliamentarians, including those belonging to the pro-Beijing coalition.[155] Legislative work also grinded to a halt between 2019 and 2020 as a result of filibustering and fights within the Legislative Council.[156]

In 2021, Beijing foisted a new electoral map on Hong Kong. The Legislative Council will be expanded to 90 members, but GC and FC seats will be slashed to

153 For a critique of the FC system, see Simon Young and Anthony Law, 'Privileged to Vote: Inequalities and Anomalies of the FC System' in Christine Loh (ed.), *Functional Constituencies: A Unique Feature of the Hong Kong Legislative Council* (Hong Kong University Press 2007).

154 Ngok Ma, *Political Development in Hong Kong: The State, Political Society and Civil Society* (Hong Kong University Press 2007) 141.

155 Brian C. H. Fong, 'Executive-Legislative Disconnection in the HKSAR: Uneasy Partnership Between Chief Executives and Pro-Government Parties, 1997–2016' in Brian C. H. Fong and Tai-lok Lui (eds), *Hong Kong 20 Years After the Handover: Emerging Social and Institutional Fractures After 1997* (Palgrave Macmillan 2018) 45, 55; Richard Cullen, *Hong Kong Constitutionalism: The British Legacy and the Chinese Future* (Routledge 2020) 109–111.

156 SCMP Editorial, 'The Public Will Suffer if Legco Row Drags on' (*South China Morning Post*, 18 April 2020), available at www.scmp.com/comment/opinion/article/3080554/public-will-suffer-if-legco-row-drags, accessed 20 May 2021.

20 and 30 seats respectively.[157] 40 new seats will now be reserved for members chosen by the Election Committee of the Chief Executive. All candidates must be pre-vetted by a Candidate Eligibility Review Committee Law – staffed by senior government officials – to ensure that prospective lawmakers would abide by the Basic Law. All these measures were introduced by Beijing to ensure that only "patriots" would govern Hong Kong.[158]

While these legislative reforms will end the filibustering, fights, and Beijing's perception of foreign interference in the Legislative Council, these changes may not lead to unified policy making. After all, the trade-based FCs accountable to narrow sectoral interests are retained, and one additional veto player is added to the legislative mix – the Election Committee of the CE. What these changes do is to entrench Beijing's domination in the Legislative Council, but they do not resolve intra-party division. Trade unionists and tycoons still co-exist uneasily in the Legislative Council, as do nationalists and conglomerates who want Hong Kong to remain attractive to international investors. They may all be Beijing loyalists but their conflicting socio-economic visions and contrasting policy prescriptions will not be easily bridged. Notably, a new well-financed pro-Beijing party has emerged in Hong Kong – the Bauhinia Party which is run by Western-educated Mainland Chinese business-friendly bankers – to contest the upcoming legislative election, and its entry into the political scene may cut into the electoral haul of pre-existing pro-Beijing parties.

On the other hand, the Hong Kong judiciary enjoys significant autonomy from the local government. The Chief Justice and the Permanent Judges on the HKCFA have security of tenure until they are 65.[159] They can only be removed for cause, and only by the Chief Executive upon a recommendation by an independent tribunal and the Legislative Council's endorsement of the removal.[160] To date, no attempts have ever been made to impeach any HKCFA judge. Notably, the HKSAR has had three Chief Justices, and the first two were both appointed at a relatively young age, which gave each of them a long runway to shape the bench for over a decade. (Chief Justice Andrew Li was appointed when he was only 49. Chief Justice Geoffrey Ma assumed leadership of the HKCFA when he was 54. The third incumbent Chief Justice Andrew Cheung was appointed in 2021 when he was 59.)

157 Section 1 of the Annex II to the Basic Law of the Hong Kong Special Administrative Region of the People's Republic of China Concerning the Method for the Formation of the Legislative Council of the Hong Kong Special Administrative Region and Its Voting Procedures, available at www.xinhuanet.com/english/download/2021-3-30/AnnexII.pdf, accessed 20 May 2021.

158 Jeff Li, 'Hong Kong: China Limits Parliament to "Patriots"' (*BBC*, 30 March, 2021), available at www.bbc.com/news/world-asia-china-56560829, accessed 20 May 2021.

159 Section 14(11) of the Hong Kong Court of Final Appeal Ordinance (Cap 484) (Hong Kong). After a Permanent Judge reaches the age of 65, his or her term may be extended for not more than two periods of three years. Section 14(2) of the Hong Kong Court of Final Appeal Ordinance (Cap 484) (Hong Kong).

160 Articles 89 and 90 of the Hong Kong Basic Law.

The Chief Justice shapes the bench in two main ways. The first relates to judicial appointments. The Basic Law provides that judges in Hong Kong are appointed by the Chief Executive, on the recommendation of the JORC.[161] Judicial appointments to the HKCFA, in addition, must be endorsed by the Legislative Council.[162] But, in practice, the Chief Executive has appointed every candidate the JORC recommends and the Legislative Council has endorsed his or her every HKCFA appointment.[163] More importantly, to date, the government has not interfered in the appointment of any judge in Hong Kong,[164] save the input of the government appointees on the JORC. Therefore, *in substance*, the Chief Justice who chairs the nine-member JORC has great latitude in shaping the composition of the bench, especially the crucial HKCFA. Typically, the JORC comprises the Chief Justice, two judges appointed by him, the Chairman of the Bar Association, the President of the Law Society, the Secretary for Justice and three lay persons appointed by the Chief Executive.[165] The presence of the Secretary for Justice and the government appointees on the JORC would impose ex ante constraints on the Chief Justice to choose to pursue candidates who are perceived by the HKSAR government to be in the political mainstream. But as all Permanent Judges of the HKCFA are in practice promoted from the Court of Appeal, and all Court of Appeal judges are drawn from the Court of First Instance, the Chief Justice who commands the entire Hong Kong judiciary occupies the vantage spot to recruit, evaluate and expedite the promotion of his preferred candidates through the ranks. The lay persons on the JORC, whose memberships are refreshed regularly, are usually drawn from academia (law excluded) and the corporate world, and they would simply not have the in-depth knowledge of the Hong Kong judiciary to independently determine which Court of Appeal judges deserve promotion to the HKCFA. The Secretary for Justice (SJ) – typically a barrister – only serves for a term conterminous with the Chief Executive[166] who appoints him or her, and returns to private practice thereafter. Unless the Chief Justice is seeking to promote an individual the government deems politically controversial, the SJ too will be hard-pressed to openly block the promotion of the appellate judges the former wants, especially if the SJ will appear once again as mere counsel before these judges in a few years. Therefore, so long as the

161 Article 88 of the Hong Kong Basic Law.

162 Article 90 of the Hong Kong Basic Law.

163 Albert H. Y. Chen and P. Y. Lo, 'Hong Kong's Judiciary under One Country, Two Systems' in H. P. Lee and Marilyn Pittard (eds), *Asia Pacific Judiciaries: Independence, Impartiality and Integrity* (Cambridge University Press 2018) 145.

164 Farewell Sitting for the Honourable Mr Justice Chan PJ (18 October 2013) (2013) 16 HKCFAR 1012, 1019.

165 The Government of Hong Kong Special Administrative Region, 'Judicial Officers Recommendation Commission', available at www.info.gov.hk/gia/general/202101/08/P2021010800299.htm, accessed 19 May 2021.

166 Article 46 of the Hong Kong Basic Law provides that the Chief Executive of the HKSAR may serve no more than two consecutive five-year terms. To date, no Chief Executive has been able to complete two full terms and all SJs have only served between five to eight years in office.

Chief Justice does not seek to promote any controversial personalities, he will in all probability get his preferred nominees approved. Furthermore, if the Permanent Judge, whom the Chief Justice is seeking to appoint, is 65 years old or older, the Chief Justice is not even statutorily required to consult the JORC; the Chief Justice alone decides, subject to the Chief Executive's formal approval.[167] Rather extraordinarily, in Hong Kong, a departing/retiring Chief Justice also chairs the JORC that selects his successor. Therefore, this allows the incumbent to pick a successor that is acceptable to Beijing but who will also not overturn his legacy.[168]

Second, the Chief Justice shapes the bench by determining the composition of the HKCFA panels.[169] The HKCFA hears substantive appeals in panels of five judges.[170] Typically, this will include the Chief Justice, the three Permanent Judges of the HKCFA, and an overseas Non-Permanent Judge (NPJ).[171] The overseas NPJ judges have included concurrent or retired judges from the highest courts in Australia, Canada, the United Kingdom and New Zealand.[172] Notably, the Chief Justice alone decides which NPJ hears a particular case;[173] and of all the HKCFA cases heard to date, overseas NPJs have only dissented on *three* occasions,[174] and never once in a constitutional law dispute. But this is *not* to say that the overseas NPJs merely rubber-stamp the HKCFA's preferred policy agenda. It is just that the chances of an eminent Anglo-Canadian jurist voting against a majority of the HKCFA, when the latter wants to *align* itself with liberal Western constitutional practices, are practically nil. (Overseas NPJs might not accord the same level of deference to the local judges if the HKCFA was seeking to *depart* from established Western conceptions of human rights.) And if a liberal-leaning Chief Justice chooses his NPJ for every constitutional law dispute strategically, he can almost be assured of one reliable vote in his favour every time and he would merely need to convince one more colleague to join him to gain a majority. And insofar as the

167 Section 14(2)(b) of the Hong Kong Court of Final Appeal Ordinance (Cap 484).

168 Gary Cheung, 'Hong Kong's Next Chief Justice: Call to Cast the Net Wider, Consider Top Legal Brains Who Are Not Sitting Judges' *South China Morning Post* (Hong Kong, 11 November 2019), available at www.scmp.com/news/hong-kong/politics/article/3037058/hong-kongs-next-chief-justice-call-cast-net-wider-consider, accessed 2 January 2020.

169 Sections 16(1), (2), (4) of the Hong Kong Court of Final Appeal Ordinance (Cap 484). Simon N. M. Young, Antonio Da Roza and Yash Ghai, 'Role of the Chief Justice' in Simon N.M. Young, Antonio Da Roza and Yash Ghai (eds), *Hong Kong's Court of Final Appeal: The Development of the Law in China's Hong Kong* (Cambridge University Press 2014) 230.

170 Section 16(3) of the Hong Kong Court of Final Appeal Ordinance (Cap 484) (Hong Kong).

171 Article 82 of the Hong Kong Basic Law provides: 'The power of final adjudication of the Hong Kong Special Administrative Region shall be vested in the Court of Final Appeal of the Region, which may as required invite judges from other common law jurisdictions to sit on the Court of Final Appeal.'

172 Hong Kong Court of Final Appeal, 'Hong Kong Non-Permanent Judges', available at www.hkcfa.hk/en/about/who/judges/npjs/index.html, accessed 3 August 2019.

173 Young, Da Roza, and Ghai (n. 169) 230.

174 The three cases are: *The Bank of East Asia Ltd* v. *Tsien Wui Marble Factory Ltd* [1999] 2 HKCFAR 349; *Next Magazine Publishing Ltd* v. *Ma Ching Fat* [2003] 6 HKCFAR 63; *Hong Kong Electric Co Ltd* v. *Commissioner of Rating and Valuation (No 3)* [2012] 15 HKCFAR 1.

Chief Justice gets to fill Permanent Judge vacancies on the HKCFA, he can promote ideological allies to the highest court to vote alongside him.[175] Notably, the HKSAR's first Chief Justice – Andrew Li – had *never* dissented in the 13 years he served at the helm of the HKCFA. The second Chief Justice, Geoffrey Ma, who has led the HKCFA since 2010, has found himself in the minority only *once*.[176] The third and incumbent Chief Justice, Andrew Cheung, assumed office in 2021 and has not dissented to date.

Even for local cases adjudicated under the National Security Law (NSL) enacted in June 2020, the Chief Executive of Hong Kong – in consultation with the Chief Justice – will decide on the list of judges who will hear these national security cases, but it is important to note that all these national security judges will only be appointed from the pool of *pre-existing* Hong Kong judges.[177] Judges who are foreign nationals, including overseas NPJs, are still eligible to hear these cases. As of 1 May 2021, 54 people have been charged under the NSL. 47 of the people charged were pro-democracy activists who, prior the 2021 election revamp, had organized an informal election primary to field candidates who can win seats in the Legislative Council and subsequently block the passage of the government's budget, thereby forcing the CE's resignation.[178] But it is important to note that, the Hong Kong judiciary has emphasized that *only* common law principles – and not Mainland Chinese legal doctrines – will be used to interpret the NSL.[179]

The HKCFA is not omnipotent, as the Standing Committee of the National People's Congress (NPCSC) in Beijing is empowered under the Basic Law to overrule any constitutional decision of the HKCFA by a Legislative Interpretation.[180] In fact, the NPCSC chastised the HKCFA by overturning its very *first* constitutional decision handed down post-handover.[181] But this is not to say that the courts are politically irrelevant in Hong Kong's constitutional landscape. The Hong Kong judiciary has built up a history of invalidating legislation since the Bill of

175 CJ Andrew Li and CJ Geoffrey Ma each had the opportunity to fill at least two Permanent Judge positions on the HKCFA.

176 *T* v. *Commissioner of Police* [2014] 17 HKCFAR 593.

177 Article 44 of the Law of the People's Republic of China on Safeguarding National Security in the Hong Kong Special Administrative Region.

178 Austin Ramzy and Tiffany May, 'Hong Kong Charges 47 Democracy Supporters With Violating Security Law' (*The New York Times*, 28 February 2021), available at www.nytimes.com/2021/02/28/world/asia/hong-kong-security-law-arrests.html, accessed 20 May 2021.

179 *Tong Ying Kit* v. *HKSAR* [2020] HKCFI 2133 (Hong Kong Court of First Instance) [49].

180 Article 158 of the Hong Kong Basic Law reads: 'When the Standing Committee makes an interpretation of the provisions concerned, the courts of the Region, in applying those provisions, shall follow the interpretation of the Standing Committee.'

181 On 26 June 1999, the NPCSC issued its First Interpretation under the Basic Law and overruled the CFA's decision in *Ng Ka Ling* v. *Director of Immigration* [1999] 2 HKCFAR 4 that exempted Mainland children born to Hong Kong Permanent Residents from obtaining the requisite immigration permits before they could acquire the right of abode in Hong Kong.

Rights Ordinance was enacted in the territory in 1991.[182] Like all political practices, judicial practices are path-dependent,[183] such that Hong Kong judges can appeal to history and *stare decisis* for continuing the practice of enforcing human rights against the Hong Kong government.[184] Furthermore, Beijing cannot and will not reverse every decision by the HKCFA, as it does not want to appear to be rescinding from its commitment to allow the HKSAR to 'exercise a high degree of autonomy and enjoy… independent judicial power',[185] which would adversely impact on Hong Kong's long-term viability as an international financial centre and China's own long-term goal of re-unifying Taiwan.

The HKSAR government is similarly unable to reverse with ease adverse constitutional decisions handed down by the courts. For the FC electoral seats, the individual legislators are only accountable electorally to the voters in their specific sectoral constituencies; for the GC seats, the use of proportional representation in the pre-2021 electoral system has led to the electoral success of multiple small parties and individual lawmakers.[186] As the Chief Executive is not drawn from any political party, and with the presence of multiple political parties, independents and FC representatives, and now Election Committee members in the Legislative Council, the HKSAR government has to constantly broker different interests among competing political forces when it seeks to pass legislation.[187] While this is not difficult

[182] Yash Ghai, 'Sentinels of Liberty or Sheep in Woolf's Clothing? Judicial Politics and the Hong Kong Bill of Rights' (1997) 60 *Modern Law Review* 459.

[183] Alec Stone Sweet, 'Path Dependence, Precedent, and Judicial Power' in Martin Shapiro and Alec Stone Sweet, *On Law, Politics, and Judicialization* (Oxford University Press 2002) 112.

[184] Article 8 of the Hong Kong Basic Law reads: 'The laws previously in force in Hong Kong, that is, the common law, rules of equity, ordinances, subordinate legislation and customary law shall be maintained, except for any that contravene this Law, and subject to any amendment by the legislature of the Hong Kong Special Administrative Region.' Article 39 of the Hong Kong Basic Law reads: 'The provisions of the International Covenant on Civil and Political Rights, the International Covenant on Economic, Social and Cultural Rights, and international labour conventions as applied to Hong Kong shall remain in force and shall be implemented through the laws of the Hong Kong Special Administrative Region.'

[185] Article 2 of the Hong Kong Basic Law.

[186] Siu-kai Lau, 'Hong Kong's Partial Democracy under Stress' in Yue-man Yeung (ed.), *New Challenges for Development and Modernisation* (The Chinese University of Hong Kong Press 2002) 186.

[187] The now-aborted extradition bill is a prime example. In 2019, the Chief Executive attempted to pass a controversial law that would allow persons in Hong Kong to be extradited to face trial in Mainland China. Notably, this controversial bill was conceived by the Chief Executive alone and was not a directive from China. Beijing-friendly lawmakers in Hong Kong who represented the business sectors had deep reservations about the law and many even openly opposed its passage. The bill was eventually suspended when over a million people took to the streets to voice their disapproval. Tony Cheung and Joyce Ng, 'Extradition Bill Protests: Why Have Hong Kong's Business Elite and Tycoons Abandoned Carrie Lam?' *South China Morning Post* (Hong Kong, 23 July 2019), available at www.scmp.com/news/hong-kong/politics/article/3019441/extradition-bill-protests-why-have-hong-kongs-business, accessed 2 August 2019. See also C. L. Lim, 'The Hong Kong Extradition Bill' (2020) *Law Quarterly Review* 19–23. See also Richard Cullen, *Hong Kong Constitutionalism: The British Legacy and the Chinese Future* (Routledge 2020) 131–136.

when the government is whipping up support for legislation that Beijing considers imperative, the pro-Beijing lawmakers' interests often diverge from the HKSAR government on issues that are not fundamental to Beijing. In such cases, these lawmakers would break ranks with the local government to accommodate their own constituents. This fragile coalition between the HKSAR executive government and the pro-Beijing lawmakers therefore limits the former's ability to command a legislative majority on *non-core* socio-political issues; and the political impasse in turn provides the Hong Kong judiciary with significant discretion to rule against the government and draw Hong Kong's constitutional jurisprudence into convergence with the West.

## JAPAN'S POLITICAL SYSTEM AND ITS SUPREME COURT

Turning to Japan, another advanced economy in East Asia, a different constitutional picture emerges precisely because political power is consolidated within one single political party – the Liberal Democratic Party – and because of its longevity in power, the LDP has been able to shape the ideological composition of the Supreme Court of Japan (JSC) by controlling appointments to the JSC.

Formally, judicial independence in Japan is constitutionally guaranteed.[188] While a Japanese Supreme Court (JSC) judge can be dismissed by voters at the polls,[189] in practice, this has never happened.[190] This public recall of judges only takes place every ten years,[191] and a JSC judge never stays long enough on the Court to face *repeated* public judgment – a typical JSC judge is appointed when he or she is 64 years old[192] and has to retire at 70, the statutory age of retirement for JSC

188 Article 76 of the Constitution of Japan reads: 'The whole judicial power is vested in a Supreme Court and in such inferior courts as are established by law. No extraordinary tribunal shall be established, nor shall any organ or agency of the Executive be given final judicial power. All judges shall be independent in the exercise of their conscience and shall be bound only by this Constitution and the laws.'

189 Article 79 of the Constitution of Japan reads: 'The appointment of the judges of the Supreme Court shall be reviewed by the people at the first general election of members of the House of Representatives following their appointment, and shall be reviewed again at the first general election of members of the House of Representatives after a lapse of ten (10) years, and in the same manner thereafter. In cases mentioned in the foregoing paragraph, when the majority of the voters favours the dismissal of a judge, he shall be dismissed.'

190 Shigenori Matsui, *The Constitution of Japan: A Contextual Analysis* (Hart 2011) 124.

191 See Article 79 of the Constitution of Japan.

192 J. Mark Ramseyer and Eric B. Rasmusen, *Measuring Judicial Independence: The Political Economy of Judging in Japan* (Chicago University Press 2003); Yasuo Hasebe, 'The Supreme Court of Japan A Judicial Court, Not Necessarily a Constitutional Court' in Albert H. Y. Chen and Andrew Harding (eds), *Constitutional Courts in Asia: A Comparative Perspective* (Cambridge University Press 2018) 290.

judges.[193] Furthermore, no JSC judge has to date been impeached and removed for misconduct,[194] a separate mechanism for removal.[195]

Notwithstanding these formal protections that secure judicial autonomy, the JSC remains one of the most conservative courts, empowered with constitutional review, in Asia. Notably, since its establishment in 1947, the JSC has only declared statutory provisions unconstitutional on ten occasions.[196]

The dismal constitutional record of the JSC is typical of courts operating in dominant-party democracies where judges often do little to countermand the dominant government's hegemony.[197] As David S. Law puts it, a court that co-exists for decades with the same conservative ruling party is likely to behave conservatively.[198] The anaemic nature of the JSC's constitutional jurisprudence is merely symptomatic of the country's structural constitutional malaise.

Japan has been ruled by the centre-right LDP almost continuously since the party's formation in 1955. The LDP has been ousted from power only twice, and briefly too: 1993–1994 and 2009–2012. Its resilience rests on the party's ability to institutionalize a clientelist network that allows the dominant incumbent government to use state resources to continuously reward loyal voters. LDP national-level politicians maintain *koenkai* (person support organizations), staffed with local politicians and business luminaries who monitor and solicit votes on their behalf, and these local politicians/businesses are rewarded or punished on the basis of voter turnout and support.[199] Targeted large-scale land improvement and public work

193 Article 50 of the Court Act (Japan).

194 Norikazu Kawagishi, 'Towards a More Responsive Judiciary: Courts and Judicial Power in Japan' in Jiunn-rong Yeh and Wen-Chen Chang (eds), *Asian Courts in Context* (Cambridge University Press 2015) 101.

195 Articles 64 read with 78 of the Constitution of Japan.

196 Saikō saibansho [Sup Ct], grand bench, 4 April 1973, 27:3 Keishu 265 (Parricide Case); Saikō saibansho [Sup Ct], grand bench, 30 April 1975, 29:4 Minshu 572 (Pharmaceutical Act Case); Saikō saibansho [Sup Ct], grand bench, 14 April 1976, 30:3 Minshu 223 (Malapportionment Case I); Saikō saibansho [Sup Ct], grand bench, 17 July 1985, 39:5 Minshu 1100 (Malapportionment Case II); Saikō saibansho [Sup Ct], grand bench, 22 April 1987, 41:3 Minshu 408 (Forest Act Case); Saikō saibansho [Sup Ct], grand bench, 11 September 2002, 56:7 Minshu 1439 (Postal Act Case); Saikō saibansho [Sup Ct], grand bench, 14 September 2005, 59:7 Minshu 2087 (Overseas Voters Case); Saikō saibansho [Sup Ct], grand bench, 4 June 2008, 62:6 Minshu 1367 (Illegitimate Children Nationality Discrimination Case) (together with Saikō saibansho [Sup Ct], grand bench, 4 June 2008, 228 Shumin 101): Saikō saibansho [Sup Ct], grand bench, 4 September 2013, 67:6 Minshu 1320 (Illegitimate Children Succession Discrimination Case); Saikō saibansho [Sup Ct], grand bench, 16 December 2015, 69:8 Minshu 2427 (Remarriage Waiting Period Case).

197 Yap (n. 9) 78.

198 Law 'Why Has Judicial Review Failed in Japan?' (n. 18) 1445.

199 Ethan Scheiner, *Democracy without Competition in Japan: Opposition Failure in a One Party Dominant State* (Cambridge University Press 2006) 71–75. See also Steven R. Reed 'The Liberal Democratic Party: An Explanation of Its Successes and Failures' in Robert Pekkanen (ed.), *Critical Readings on the Liberal Democratic Party in Japan* volume 4 (Brill 2018) 1339; Kōji Nakakita, *The Liberal Democratic Party of Japan: The Realities of Power* (Routledge 2020) 163–180.

grants are regularly awarded to sectoral regions that regularly vote LDP.[200] These clientelist practices are most prevalent in rural Japan, which makes up a third of the country's electoral map.[201]

And precisely because of its longevity in power, the LDP has been able to continuously stack the JSC with 'ideologically reliable agents'[202] who could not be easily replaced by the opposition during their very brief stints in power.

There are 15 Justices on the JSC, including the Chief Justice. The current practice is for career judges to take six seats on the JSC. Of the remaining nine appointees, there would be two public prosecutors, two government officials, four practising lawyers, and one academic.[203] Notably, career judges only reach the Supreme Court after a lifetime of ideological screening. The Chief Justice along with the General Secretariat – the administrative arm of the Supreme Court – oversees the appointment, reappointment, training, assignment, promotion and remuneration of the lower court judges.[204] Furthermore, the Secretariat is empowered to assign subordinate court judges to judicial posts all over the country every three years.[205] Lower court judges who hand down liberal decisions or belong to leftist human rights groups, for example the Young Lawyers Guild, are 'banished' to the hinterlands and have their illustrious careers short-circuited,[206] while promising conservative ones are given plum posts and promoted through the ranks.[207]

John O. Haley agrees that the JSC is conservative, but he argues that it is conservative *not* because the appointment process is politicized by the LDP, but because judges in Japan 'share the prevailing communitarian orientation of their society'[208] and do not seek to be agents of social change. Others take the view that the Chief Justice and the Secretariat, in view of LDP's sheer political dominance in Japan, are simply nominating judges that the LDP leaders themselves would have approved if the government had to make the choices for themselves,[209] so as to avoid an embarrassing public veto by the Prime Minister. This latter hypothesis has now been confirmed by new revelations of how JSC judges are appointed. While custom suggests that the Prime Minister always approves the candidates the Chief Justice

200 Ibid. 72–73.
201 Ibid. 5.
202 Law, 'The Anatomy of a Conservative Court' (n. 18) 1545.
203 Kawagishi (n. 194) 94.
204 David M. O'Brien and Yasuo Ohkoshi 'Stifling Judicial Independence from within: The Japanese Judiciary' in Peter H. Russell and David M. O'Brien (eds), *Judicial Independence in the Age of Democracy: Critical Perspectives from around the World* (University of Virginia Press 2001) 44–45.
205 Ramseyer and Rasmusen (n. 192) 10.
206 Ibid. 19–24.
207 Ibid.
208 John O. Haley, 'Constitutional Adjudication in Japan: Context, Structure, and Values' (2011) 88 *Washington Law Review* 1467, 1491.
209 Frank K. Upham, 'Political Lackeys or Faithful Public Servants? Two Views of the Japanese Judiciary' (2005) 30 *Law & Social Inquiry* 421, 445.

formally recommends to fill vacant career judge positions on the JSC,[210] negotiations over judicial appointees are conducted between the Japanese Cabinet and the Chief Justice behind the scenes,[211] and a consensus is reached prior to the formal recommendation. The Japanese Cabinet has an even freer hand in filling appointments from the government bureaus and the Prosecutors Office; the latter notably reports to the Minister of Justice.[212] In short, an LDP government would have significant control over the appointment of at least ten judges, a majority on the JSC. Furthermore, while the Japan Federation of Bar Association (JFBA) gets to recommend four practising lawyers, it is widely believed that the JFBA lost one spot – it used to have five seats on the JSC – due to the liberal tilt of the Tokyo Bar Association,[213] one of Japan's five major local bar associations involved in the judicial selection. While the JSC has never directly interfered in the process by which JFBA's nominees are selected, there are ex ante incentives for the JFBA to choose candidates who are acceptable to the Chief Justice.[214]

Even after the JSC judges are appointed, less pliant ones can be reined in. In the late 1960s, the JSC, under the influence of Justice Jiro Tanaka, handed down a pair of pro-labour constitutional decisions that riled the conservative LDP government.[215] In the *All Postal Workers, Tokyo Central Post Office Case*,[216] a blanket ban on public corporation employees going on strike was read down by the JSC to only prohibit violent or prolonged strikes. This liberal ruling was extended to local public employees.[217] Tanaka, who was expected to be the next Chief Justice, was bypassed and the Chief Justice position eventually went to Kazuto Ishida, a conservative LDP ally.[218] These pro-union decisions were soon gutted by Chief Justice Ishida and subsequent appointees to the JSC.[219]

210 Shigenori Matsui, 'Why Is the Japanese Supreme Court so Conservative?' (2011) 88 *Washington University Law Review* 1375, 1405; John O. Haley, 'The Japanese Judiciary: Maintaining Integrity, Autonomy, and the Public Trust' in Daniel H. Foote (ed.), *Law in Japan: A Turning Point* (University of Washington Press 2008) 109.

211 Law, 'The Anatomy of a Conservative Court' (n. 18) 1550–1551; Tokiyasu Fujita, *Saikousai kaisouroku (Memoirs of the Supreme Court)* (Yuhikaku Publishing 2012).

212 The Japanese Cabinet directly picks the JSC seats 'reserved' for bureaucrats and the Chief Justice rubber-stamps the Ministry of Justice's choices for seats allocated to the Prosecutors Office. See Law, 'The Anatomy of a Conservative Court' (n. 18) 1565, 1571–1572.

213 Ibid. 1570–1571.

214 Ibid. 1568.

215 Saiko Saibansho [Sup. Ct.] 26 October 1966, 20 Saiko Saibansho keiji hanreishu [Keishu] 901 (grand bench); Saiko Saibansho [Sup. Ct.] 2 April 1969, 23 Saiko Saibansho keiji hanreishu [Keishu] 305 (grand bench).

216 Saiko Saibansho [Sup. Ct.] 26 October 1966, 20 Saiko Saibansho keiji hanreishu [Keishu] 901 (grand bench).

217 Saiko Saibansho [Sup. Ct.] 2 April 1969, 23 Saiko Saibansho keiji hanreishu [Keishu] 305 (grand bench). See Matsui (n. 190) 227–228.

218 Masaki Abe, 'The Internal Control of a Bureaucratic Judiciary: The Case of Japan' (1995) 23 *International Journal of the Sociology of Law* 303, 316; Law, 'The Anatomy of a Conservative Court' (n. 18) 1592–1593.

219 Saiko Saibansho [Sup. Ct.] 25 April 1973, 27 Saiko Saibansho keiji hanreishu [Keishu] 547 (grand bench); See Matsui (n. 210) 1403–1404.

In light of the power concentrated in the hands of the Chief Justice over judicial promotions and assignments, it is unsurprising that the LDP would be very deliberate about this appointment. The LDP government anticipated a massive electoral defeat in the 2009 general election and strategically appointed Hironobu Takesaki as Chief Justice in late 2008. This was a notable break from tradition, as Takesaki was not even a member of the JSC at the time of his appointment and he was young enough to serve over five years as Chief Justice,[220] such that he could outlast a single-term, non-LDP government. (The LDP, as expected, lost the 2009 general election, but the opposition Democratic Party of Japan (DPJ) government only lasted three years, and the LDP was returned to power in 2012.) Notably, Japan's Chief Justices typically serve between two and four years before reaching the mandatory retirement age.[221] This way, the LDP government can keep their Chief Justice on a tight leash and replace him quickly. The brevity of the Japanese Chief Justice's term stands in sharp contrast with Hong Kong's. The last two Chief Justices of Hong Kong have been able to leave their mark on the bench precisely because they were able to shape it over the course of a decade at its helm. Furthermore, while the Japanese Chief Justice is picked by the country's premier, in Hong Kong it is the departing Chief Justice who also chairs the Judicial Officers Recommendation Commission that picks the succeeding Chief Justice. So that allows for the incumbent Hong Kong Chief Justice to pick a successor who is acceptable to Beijing, but who will also not subvert his legacy. The presence of the Non-Permanent Judges (at least one in a panel of five judges) drawn from the top courts of the United Kingdom, Canada and Australia on the HKCFA – for example, legal giants like former Canadian Chief Justice Beverley McLachlin, former Australian Chief Justice Robert French and former United Kingdom Supreme Court Presidents Lord Neuberger of Abbotsbury and Lady Hale of Richmond, also impose a constraining force on the Hong Kong judiciary.

To compound problems for the JSC, the Court has a crushing workload. On average, the JSC decides over 6,000 cases a year.[222] In contrast, the HKCFA – also a court of final resort with general jurisdiction – disposes of fewer than 40 substantive appeals a year.[223] (The KCC determines about 385 cases on the merits annually,[224] and the TCC on average decides 15 cases a year.[225]) While disputes are typically

220 See Law 'Why Has Judicial Review Failed in Japan?' (n. 18) 1461–1462.

221 Ibid. 1462.

222 The JSC decided 4,595 civil/administrative cases and 2,092 criminal cases in 2019. Supreme Court of Japan, 'Publications: Statistics', available at www.courts.go.jp/english/vc-files/courts-en/file/2019_STATISTICAL_TABLES.pdf, accessed 23 September 2020.

223 Hong Kong Judiciary, 'Hong Kong Judiciary Annual Report 2019', available at www.judiciary.hk/en/publications/annu_rept_2019r/eng/caseload_fa.html, accessed 14 August 2020.

224 Constitutional Court of Korea, 'Caseload Statistics', available at http://english.ccourt.go.kr/cckhome/eng/decisions/caseLoadStatic/caseLoadStatic.do, accessed 14 August 2020.

225 Constitutional Court, Judicial Yuan, ROC, 'Statistics', available at https://cons.judicial.gov.tw/jcc/Uploads/files/108%E5%B9%B4%E5%A0%B1%E8%A1%A8.pdf, accessed 14 August 2020.

resolved by the JSC in one of its three Petty Benches, composed of five justices each, any statutory provision or administrative regulation can only be declared unconstitutional by its Full (Grand) Bench.[226] The sheer volume of decisions that the JSC has to make daily would make it impossible for it to overturn prior precedents regularly, especially since a Full (Grand) Bench is required whenever a declaration of unconstitutionality could potentially be issued. The limited capacity of the JSC therefore impacts the substance of constitutional law, as capacity constraints impose strong pressure on its judges to *not* revisit prior determinations made by other governmental actors or past benches.[227]

With judges who are practically pre-vetted by the *same* party for decades, a Court that is so pressed for time, and regular openings on the JSC that allow for ideological drifts to be quickly corrected, it is unsurprising that the Supreme Court has been a marginal constitutional player in Japan. And it is precisely because of these institutional and political variables that impact the JSC's behaviour that its performance is so distinctive and divergent from its counterparts operating in other East Asian democracies.

## COMPARATIVE LAW AND JUDICIAL CHOICES

Political fragmentation reduces the capability of politicians to interfere in judicial decision-making, as the dispersion of power makes it more difficult for incumbents to rally political support for the curtailing of judicial autonomy. The less concentrated governmental power is, the higher the 'transaction costs'[228] of overruling judges, as the consent of more political players is required to overturn the courts. Courts enjoy the greatest policy space where political power is 'least concentrated and most contested'.[229] Furthermore, where judicial appointments are not in the hands of the political branches (as we see in Hong Kong) or where competing political parties take turns in office (as is the case in Taiwan and South Korea), and

226 Article 10 of the Court Act reads: 'Regulations of the Supreme Court shall determine which cases are to be handled by full bench and which by petty bench; provided, however, that in the following instances, a petty bench may not give a judicial decision (i) Cases in which a determination is to be made on the constitutionality of law, order, rule, or disposition, based on the argument by a party (except the cases where the opinion is the same as that of the judicial decision previously rendered through the full bench in which the constitutionality of act, order, rule, or disposition is recognized). (ii) Cases other than those referred to in the preceding item when any law, order, rule, or disposition is to be decided as unconstitutional. (iii) Cases where an opinion concerning interpretation and application of the Constitution or of any other laws and regulations is contrary to that of a judicial decision previously rendered by the Supreme Court.'

227 See also Andrew B. Coan, 'Judicial Capacity and the Substance of Constitutional Law' (2012) 122 *Yale Law Journal* 422.

228 Eric C. Ip, *Hybrid Constitutionalism: The Politics of Constitutional Review in the Chinese Special Administrative Regions* (Cambridge University Press 2019) 38–48.

229 Stephen Gardbaum, 'What Makes for More or Less Powerful Constitutional Courts?' (2018) 29 *Duke Journal of Comparative and International Law* 1, 27.

judges enjoy a full panoply of institutional protections that secure its ex post autonomy, no single party will have the ability to shape the bench in its image for an extended period. In turn, independent judges can regularly pursue a policy agenda that deviates from the legislative status quo.

Aside from these institutional variables that foster the judicialization of state governance, for a liberal court to be established, those judges sitting on the respective courts of final resort must desire liberal outcomes and choose to achieve them.[230] Judges value their reputations.[231] But in authoritarian regimes, judges can only cater to their primary audience – the political branches of government – for their institutional survival hinges on this.[232] On the other hand, where political power is fragmented, and judges are insulated from political retaliation, they can 'engage in self presentation to other audiences whose esteem is important to them',[233] for example the public, lawyers, academia, the international community and eminent foreign judges in other reputable courts of final resort. In Asia, Hong Kong, Taiwan and South Korea have the most liberal courts precisely because of this fragmentation of political power, and judicial independence from a singular dominant ruling party in government, which allows for liberal judges to be regularly elevated to the highest court. And these liberal judges in turn can hand down liberal rulings when they secure a majority on the bench. Such independent judges in East Asia can therefore forge a 'constitutional identity'[234] for their jurisdiction that subverts the legislative status quo.[235]

As Jacco Bomhoff argues, judges invoke legal arguments that are acceptable to the community they live in[236] and they have some degree of choice in this regard.[237] Judges on the highest courts can choose from a range of precedents and even overrule/disregard precedents they do not like.[238] Judicial choices are shaped by the values judges hold, and these values serve as motivational goals and guide behaviour.[239] In Hong Kong, liberal judges in pursuit of progressive causes would turn to human rights standards established in England (which regularly tracks European Court of Human Rights jurisprudence) and Canada to advance their agenda. Notably, the Hong Kong Basic Law expressly authorizes its judges to 'refer to precedents of other common law

230 Lee Epstein and Jack Knight, *The Choices Justices Make* (CQ Press 1998) 22–36.

231 Nuno Garoupa and Tom Ginsburg, *Judicial Reputation: A Comparative Theory* (University of Chicago Press 2015).

232 Ginsburg and Moustafa (n. 9); Yap (n. 9).

233 Lawrence Baum, *Judges and Their Audiences: A Perspective on Judicial Behaviour* (Princeton 2008) 4.

234 Gary Jeffrey Jacobsohn, *Constitutional Identity* (Harvard University Press 2010); See also Ran Hirschl, *Comparative Law Matters: The Renaissance of Comparative Constitutional Law* (Oxford University Press 2014) 41–43.

235 Lustig and Weiler (n. 6) 365–369.

236 Jacco Bomhoff, *Balancing Constitutional Rights: The Origins and Meanings of Postwar Legal Discourse* (Cambridge University Press 2013) 22.

237 Ibid. 23.

238 Segal and Spaeth (n. 17) 288–311.

239 Rachel Cahill-O'Callaghan, *Values in the Supreme Court: Decisions, Division and Diversity* (Hart 2020) 5.

jurisdictions'[240] and by a convention created by the Chief Justice, at least one out of five judges siting on any substantive appeal before the HKCFA will *always* be an overseas judge from Australia, Canada, New Zealand or the United Kingdom.[241] Out of 13 overseas NPJs currently serving on the HKCFA, nine are retired or current judges from the UK Supreme Court.[242] To date, all the current and retired Permanent Judges, save three,[243] on the HKCFA have received their legal education *exclusively* in England. In fact, the first two Hong Kong Chief Justices were British Citizens and they only renounced their foreign allegiance prior to taking office.[244] Before announcing in October 2019 that he would retire in January 2021, Chief Justice Geoffrey Ma picked liberal stalwarts Lady Hale and Beverley McLachlin to join the HKCFA as NPJs, and he rostered them specifically for upcoming blockbuster human rights cases.[245] For McLachlin NPJ's first trip to Hong Kong, she was tasked to decide on whether the Hong Kong Bill of Rights Ordinance prohibits human trafficking.[246] In an extra-judicial address delivered in September 2019, the Chief Justice even emphasized that the Hong Kong Basic Law not only sets out relevant constitutional rights, it 'introduces applicable international standards in relation to such rights'[247] and, according to him, this explains why 'reference [by the HKCFA] is frequently made to decisions of the European Court of Human Rights on comparable provisions to those rights contained in the [Hong Kong] Bill of Rights'.[248]

For Taiwan, the drafting of its original Constitution and the Additional Articles of the Constitution inserted post-democratization were substantially influenced by Germany. So were major pieces of legislation such as the Civil Code and

240 Article 84 of the Hong Kong Basic Law.

241 Justice Joseph Fok PJ, 'Judges from Other Common law jurisdictions in the Hong Kong Court of Final Appeal' (International Bar Association Annual Conference, Seoul, 24 September 2019, at [14]), available at www.hkcfa.hk/filemanager/speech/en/upload/2237/IBA%20Seoul%20-%20Global%20Justice%20and%20Globetrotting%20Judges.pdf, accessed 2 January 2020.

242 Hong Kong Court of Final Appeal, 'Hong Kong Non-Permanent Judges', available at www.hkcfa.hk/en/about/who/judges/npjs/index.html, accessed 2 January 2020.

243 Of all the Permanent Judges who have ever served on the HKCFA, only Patrick Chan, Andrew Cheung, and Johnson Lam have never studied law in England.

244 Chief Justice Andrew Li only renounced his British citizenship prior to his appointment as Chief Justice, while Chief Justice Geoffrey Ma only renounced his British citizenship prior to his appointment as Chief Judge of the High Court of the HKSAR. Article 90 of the Basic Law only imposes a Chinese citizenship requirement on the two abovementioned judicial posts.

245 For Lady Hale NPJ's maiden case in Hong Kong, she was originally picked by the Chief Justice to sit on a landmark gender discrimination constitutional challenge, but this case has been re-rostered because of COVID-19 and the corresponding impact on border controls.

246 *ZN* v. *Secretary for Justice* [2019] HKCFA 53 (Hong Kong Court of Final Appeal). In this case, the HKCFA unanimously ruled that the Hong Kong Bill of Rights 'may... prohibit human trafficking for the purposes of slavery' [80(1)] but left this issue open for determination in a future case.

247 Chief Justice Geoffrey Ma, 'Hong Kong and the Rule of Law: Is It Tangible?' (International Bar Association Annual Conference, Seoul, 24 September 2019, [7]), available at www.hkcfa.hk/filemanager/speech/en/upload/2242/2019.09.24%20-%20International%20Bar%20Association%20Annual%20Conference%202019%20(Seoul,%20Korea)%20(Final).pdf, accessed 2 January 2020.

248 Ibid.

Criminal Code.[249] Post-democratization, there were more judges appointed to the TCC with doctorates from German law schools than local ones. Out of 57 TCC Justices who were appointed after 1987 – the year martial law was lifted – 37 of them have doctoral degrees in law, and, of the 37 judges, 18 did their doctoral work in Germany and only 7 in Taiwan. America is a distant second, with 8 Justices completing their doctoral programs in the United States. As for the current bench, 9 out of 15 have doctoral degrees, and 5 of them have doctoral degrees from Germany. Of the 4 Chief Justices who have served after the country democratized, 2 of them have German doctorates. These German-trained Justices are deeply influenced by German constitutional jurisprudence, and they in turn influence their colleagues. Perhaps the most influential constitutional law jurist of them all is former Chief Justice Yueh-Sheng Weng (President of the Judicial Yuan from 1999 to 2003, Chief Justice[250] from 2003 to 2007) who graduated from the University of Heidelberg, and who has mentored many of the sitting Justices on the TCC today. It is therefore no coincidence that Germany is the most cited foreign legal source in Taiwan.[251] Like the Supreme Court of Israel, TCC judges' preference for Western law reflects the 'state's desire to be included in the liberal-democratic club of nations'.[252] The TCC judges want to redeem the Court's past as a rubber-stamp for the martial law government,[253] and also seek to chart a rights-culture distinct from China, which still claims the territory as its own.[254] Therefore, this identity concern is arguably the key determinant in the judicial choices vis-à-vis foreign references.[255] Take Interpretation No. 371 (1995)[256] as an example. In this landmark decision, the TCC ruled that lower courts could directly petition the Court on constitutional issues, even though there was no statutory or constitutional

249 Chang-fa Lo, 'Taiwan: External Influences mixed with Traditional Elements to Form Its Unique Legal System' in E. Ann Black and Gary F. Bell (eds), *Law and Legal Institutions of Asia* (Cambridge University Press 2011).

250 Before 2003, there was no official 'Chief Justice' in Taiwan. The president of the Judicial Yuan is the head of the judiciary. He is responsible for all administrative issues relating to the operations of the Judicial Yuan but he is *not* a Justice on the Taiwanese Constitutional Court. Since 2003, the president of the Judicial Yuan has served concurrently as a Justice of the Taiwan Constitutional Court and is normally called the Chief Justice of Taiwan.

251 Wen-Chen Chang and Jiunn-Rong Yeh, 'Judges as Discursive Agent: The Use of Foreign Precedents by the Constitutional Court of Taiwan' in Tania Groppi and Marie-Claire Ponthoreau (eds), *The Use of Foreign Precedents by Constitutional Judges* (Hart 2013) 382.

252 Ran Hirschl, *Comparative Matters: The Renaissance of Comparative Constitutional Law* (OUP 2014) 23.

253 Jiunn-rong Yeh and Wen-Chen Chang, 'An Evolving Court with Changing Functions: The Constitutional Court and Judicial Review in Taiwan' in Albert H. Y. Chen and Andrew Harding (eds), *Constitutional Courts in Asia* (Cambridge University Press 2018) 121–123.

254 林建志, '迎接司法國的到來 Towards Juristocracy?' (2019) 48 國立臺灣大學法學論叢 *National Taiwan University Law Journal* 873, 905–906.

255 Hirschl (n. 252) 76.

256 J.Y. Interpretation No. 371 (1995) (Constitutional Court of Taiwan), available at http://cons.judicial.gov.tw/jcc/en-us/jep03/show?expno=371, accessed 9 May 2021.

authorization for this innovation. In essence, the TCC did so by imitating the judicial review system in Germany. Tom Ginsburg has argued that this judicial borrowing 'shows the particular importance of Germany as a reference point for Taiwan law'[257] because the TCC wants to make Taiwan more similar to Germany and other modern countries that observe the rule of law.[258]

In South Korea, its Constitution and major legislation are also substantially influenced by the German equivalents.[259] More importantly, the Constitutional Court has intentionally routinized and institutionalized foreign legal research, with a special focus on German and American law.[260] Within the KCC, there are only two country-specific foreign Constitution Study Societies: the American and German ones.[261] In short, it has been intentionally building its capability in selected Western law. Not only does the Court hire full-time Constitutional Researchers, whose *main* duty is to assist the Court on *foreign* legal research, the KCC is the *only* court in Asia that has established a Constitutional Research Institute (CRI) whose *primary* task is to engage in comparative constitutional scholarship and to investigate the work of other leading Constitutional Courts around the world, of which the *Bundesverfassungsgericht* is the frontrunner.[262] Notwithstanding Korea's historical ties with Japan, insider sources in the Court have revealed that the KCC's reliance on Japanese law has diminished precisely because the JSC is perceived by judges to be too conservative.[263] The KCC's first President, Kyu-Kwang Cho, had relied heavily on German precedents[264] when the Court was first established in 1988, and this judicial reliance on Germany 'has continued to be a hallmark of the Constitutional Court'.[265] According to many Korean judges and scholars, the German Constitutional Court system and its constitutional jurisprudence is regarded as 'an advanced role model in general'[266] for local emulation. The CRI, set up only in 2011, has furthered the Court's goal of leveraging on foreign law by pursuing research projects that complement the Court's adjudicatory case-load. Some of the significant recent major research projects completed by the CRI all

257 Ginsburg (n. 5) 139.

258 Ibid.

259 Yoon Jin Shin, 'Cosmopolitanising Rights Practice: The Case of South Korea' in Takao Suami, Anne Peers, Dimitri Vanoverbeke and Mattias Kumm (eds), *Global Constitutionalism from European and East Asian Perspectives* (Cambridge University Press 2018) 256.

260 Law (n. 1) 962.

261 The Constitutional Court of Korea (n. 125) 103.

262 Seokmin Lee and Fabian Duessel, 'Researching Korean Constitutional Law and the Constitutional Court of Korea' (2016) 16 *Journal of Korean Law* 265, 282–283; cf. Kang-Kook Lee, 'The Past and Future of Constitutional Adjudication in Korea' in Laurent Mayali and John Yoo (eds), *Current Issues in Korean Law* (The Robbins Collection 2014) 1, 10.

263 Law (n. 1) 963.

264 Chan Jin Kim, 'Constitutional Review in Korea' (2006) 34 *Korean Journal of International & Comparative Law* 29, 86.

265 Ibid.

266 Shin (n. 259).

relate to German law and these projects are as follows: in 2019: 'Judicial Review of Statutes and Transitional Arrangements by the German Federal Constitutional Court'; in 2018: 'Balancing and the Principle of Proportionality', 'Abstract Review of Statutes by the German Federal Constitutional Court', and 'General Equality Review in the Federal Constitutional Court of Germany'; in 2017: 'Studies on Disputes among Agencies and Governments in Germany' and 'Diversity of Public Broadcasting in Germany'; in 2016: 'Study on Bundesrat of Germany under the German Constitution', 'Process of Handling Wrongdoings of the Former Regime after Reunification of Germany', 'Control of Administrative Legislation by German Federal Parliament (*Bundestag*)', and 'Laws and Statutes: Germany'.[267]

The judicial use of imported precedents from 'high-prestige courts and countries'[268] that have strong historical legal ties[269] – Germany for Taiwan and Korea, and the English Commonwealth for Hong Kong – to their jurisdictions in fact enhances the legitimacy of the Courts' decisions, especially when they are subverting local legislation. David Law has termed this the 'circumvention hypothesis':[270] judges use prestigious foreign law as legal support to circumvent and overcome domestic law. In adopting these foreign practices, judges can deflect accusations that they are imposing their personal whims, and argue instead that they are aligning their jurisdictions' retrograde Asian practices with the established norms of exalted, successful states in the West. In this way, the strategic use of prestigious foreign law can help promote public acceptance of the Courts' decisions.

267 Constitutional Court of Korea, Constitutional Research Institute, CRI Brochure, available at http://ri.ccourt.go.kr/eng/, accessed 3 January 2020.

268 Law (n. 1) 1000.

269 For Taiwan, important laws such as the Civil Code and the Criminal Code were based on their German equivalents when the Republic of China was founded in 1911 and German law remains influential in Taiwan today. See Lo (n. 249); similarly, when the Republic of Korea was founded in 1948, its Civil Code and Criminal Code were modelled after their German equivalents and the current Korean Constitutional Court is also modelled after the German Federal Constitutional Court. See Chongko Choi, 'On the Reception of Western Law in Korea' (1981) 9 *Korean Journal of Comparative Law* 141, 164–165; Paul Kichyun Ryu, 'The New Korean Criminal Code of October 3, 1953. An Analysis of Ideologies Embedded in It' (1957) 48 *Journal of Criminal Law, Criminology, and Police Science* 275. Hong Kong was a British colony until 1997 and the Hong Kong Basic Law (Articles 8 and 84) expressly authorizes the continued use of the common law and common law precedents.

270 Law (n. 1) 1000.

# 3

# Convergence on Structured Proportionality

## INTRODUCTION

We live in an age of balancing[1] – an era where national courts around the world are empowered to independently determine whether their legislatures' limitations on rights are demonstrably and reasonably justified, and to invalidate those laws that are not.[2] Proportionality Analysis (PA) – in its varying manifestations and permutations – has emerged as the umbrella term used to reference the different ways judges weight conflicting interests and evaluate the extent to which the conflict may be minimized by a more careful choice of means.[3]

With its genesis in German law,[4] PA has diffused globally across civil and common law Europe to the Anglophone nations of Canada, and New Zealand, mixed legal systems that are rooted in the common law (for example, Israel and South Africa), and even parts of Latin America and Asia.[5] In view of PA's prevalence, it is now widely regarded as 'generic constitutional law,'[6] or even the 'ultimate rule of law'.[7]

Proponents of PA have defended this judicial practice on various inter-related grounds. PA instantiates a new constitutional 'culture of justification'[8] whereby

1 Vicki Jackson, 'Constitutional Law in an Age of Proportionality' 124 (2015) *Yale Law Journal* 3094.

2 See Alec Stone Sweet and Jud Mathews, 'Proportionality Balancing and Global Constitutionalism' (2008) 47 *Columbia Journal of Transnational Law* 72.

3 David S. Law, 'Generic Constitutional Law' (2005) 89 *Minnesota Law Review* 652, 702; Stone Sweet and Mathews (n. 2).

4 Dieter Grimm, 'Proportionality in Canadian and German Constitutional Jurisprudence' (2007) 57 *University of Toronto Law Journal* 383, 384–385.

5 Alec Stone Sweet and Jud Mathews, *Proportionality Balancing and Constitutional Governance* (Oxford University Press 2019); Po Jen Yap (ed), *Proportionality in Asia* (Cambridge University Press 2020).

6 Law (n. 3).

7 David Beatty, *The Ultimate Rule of Law* (Oxford University Press 2005).

8 Moshe Cohen-Eliya and Iddo Porat, *Proportionality and Constitutional Culture* (Cambridge University Press 2013) 111.

legislatures are required to defend the 'cogency and persuasiveness'[9] of their actions before the courts. The judicial use of PA corrects 'political market failures'[10] that occur when the legislative process intentionally or inadvertently neglects minority interests.[11] Legal principles – enshrined as rights – are norms that require optimization to the 'greatest extent possible given the legal and factual possibilities',[12] and judges can resolve conflicting principles using PA in a principled and objective way.[13] PA renders rights-adjudication more effective as it introduces a 'highly intrusive standard of judicial review',[14] while mitigating the two-against-one – the neutral judge declares a winner in adjudication and takes a side against the losing party – dilemma in constitutional adjudication, as it allows the court to state that 'it took every pain to minimize the negative consequences of its ruling for the losing party or interests'.[15]

Notwithstanding PA's ubiquity, only jurisdictions that hew to German law or Anglo-Canadian rights jurisprudence apply a particularly structured version of PA. Typically, this Structured Proportionality (SP) has four cumulative steps. When applying SP, the judiciary would ensure that (1) the state is pursuing a legitimate objective; (2) the governmental measure undertaken is rationally connected to the stated policy objective; (3) the right-derogation is no more than necessary to achieve those stated goals; and (4) the regulatory measure is proportionate *stricto sensu*, i.e. there is a fair balance struck between the rights of the individual and the interests of the community such that the consequences of the law are not unacceptably harsh on the individual. In view of the Constitutional Court of Taiwan (TCC) and the Constitutional Court of Korea (KCC)'s heavy reliance on German law, and the Hong Kong Court of Final Appeal (HKCFA)'s frequent usage of Anglo-Canadian constitutional jurisprudence, it is unsurprising that all three jurisdictions have also converged on the use of SP. Within Asia, since Taiwan, South Korea and Hong Kong are the *only* jurisdictions that heavily rely on German or Anglo-Canadian constitutional jurisprudence, it is no coincidence that they are also the *only* Asian jurisdictions where this four-stage SP is consistently applied and the courts reason through this structured doctrinal framework sequentially.[16]

9 Ibid. 112.

10 Niels Petersen, *Proportionality and Judicial Activism: Fundamental Rights Adjudication in Canada, Germany and South Africa* (Cambridge University Press 2017) 181.

11 Ibid. 182.

12 Robert Alexy, *A Theory of Constitutional Rights* (Julian Rivers tr, Oxford University Press 2002) 47; Aharon Barak, *Proportionality: Constitutional Rights and their Limitations* (Cambridge University Press 2012) 237.

13 Alexy (n. 12) 16–18; Barak (n. 12) 542–545.

14 Stone Sweet and Mathews (n. 5) 31.

15 Stone Sweet and Mathews (n. 2) 96.

16 In *Navtej Singh Johar* v. *Union of India* [2018] Indlaw SC 786 the Supreme Court of India on 6 September 2018 relied on the Proportionality Analysis (PA) to invalidate an archaic piece of legislation that criminalized same-sex consensual intercourse. While the Court did not explicitly reference a structured and sequential PA, different judges relied on different sub-limbs of PA for their

Naturally, PA (or SP) is not without its sceptics and their criticisms usually come in two forms. The first form, commonly termed the '*internal* critique of balancing',[17] questions whether incommensurable interests can be identified, valued and compared.[18] Afonso da Silva has since provided a robust reply to this 'incommensurability' objection. According to him, the presence of incommensurable values does not preclude the possibility of balancing rights; on the contrary, weighting rights is a procedure that increases comparability among principles.[19] Where two constitutional interests collide, even though these values may be incommensurable, courts may establish a relation of precedence between them such that judges can 'compare the numerous possibilities of protecting and realising such rights in a concrete situation and to weigh among them'.[20] Therefore, proportionality is not about courts deciding between the protection of a constitutional right and the advancement of legitimate state goals in the abstract. Instead, balancing is about comparing and considering trade-offs in concrete situations such that rational choices can be made between possible alternatives.

Grégoire Webber, in contrast, advances a more refined version of this incommensurability objection. While Webber maintains that constitutional rights are incommensurable and cannot be weighted in the technical sense, he accepts that a reasoned choice can be made between competing trade-offs.[21] But for Webber,

decisions. A few weeks later, the Supreme Court for the first time in *Justice K. S. Puttaswamy (Retired)* v. *Union of India* [2018] Indlaw SC 898 formulated a structured four-stage SP in the following terms: '1. A law interfering with fundamental rights must be in pursuance of a legitimate state aim; 2. The justification for rights-infringing measures that interfere with or limit the exercise of fundamental rights and liberties must be based on the existence of a rational connection between those measures, the situation in fact and the object sought to be achieved; 3. The measures must be necessary to achieve the object and must not infringe rights to an extent greater than is necessary to fulfil the aim; 4. Restrictions must not only serve a legitimate purposes; they must also be necessary to protect them.' In that case, the Indian Supreme Court invalidated various governmental rules, which mandated that every bank account in India had to be linked to the individual's unique digital identification number or the account would be frozen, on the basis that the measures were a disproportionate violation of the person's constitutional right to property. Since then, no other governmental rule has been invalidated for failing this four-stage SP, so it is unclear whether this case marked the dawn of SP in India or whether it is merely an anomaly. In *Anuradha Bhasin* v. *Union of India* [2020] Indlaw SC 21, the Indian Supreme Court ruled that the indefinite suspension of Internet services in Kashmir failed SP and was impermissible under the Temporary Suspension of Telecom Services (Public Emergency or Public Service) Rules, 2017. One should note that only governmental acts were quashed herein, and no legal rule was invalidated.

17 T. Alexander Aleinikoff, 'Constitutional Law in the Age of Balancing' (1987) 96 *Yale Law Journal* 943, 972.

18 Stavros Tsakyrakis, 'Proportionality: An Assault on Human Rights?' (2009) 7 *International Journal of Constitutional Law* 468. See also Francisco J. Urbina, 'Incommensurability and Balancing' (2015) 35 *Oxford Journal of Legal Studies* 575; Francisco J. Urbina, *A Critique of Proportionality and Balancing* (Cambridge University Press 2017).

19 Virgílio Afonso da Silva, 'Comparing the Incommensurable: Constitutional Principles, Balancing and Rational Decision' (2011) 31 *Oxford Journal of Legal Studies* 273, 276.

20 Ibid. 286.

21 Grégoire Webber, *The Negotiable Constitution* (Cambridge University Press 2009) 98–99.

rights are constituted by their limitation, after one takes into account all the moral-political reasons that bear on what the right requires, and in a democracy it is for the *legislature* to articulate the contours and limits of such rights.[22] Therefore, the role of the judiciary in a democracy is not to assess the proportionality of legislative action but to overturn laws only when the limitation of a right adopted by the legislature falls outside the range of reasonable disagreement which animates democratic debate,[23] i.e. when the legislature has made a mistake that is so clear that it is not open to rational question.[24] In essence, Webber's real objection to proportionality is not *internal* to PA, that is, whether PA can be used to choose between competing legislative trade-offs, but is an *external* critique of proportionality: why should the judiciary have the right to recalibrate the competing rights and interests at stake after the legislature – the elected representatives of the people – has already openly debated and determined the appropriate balance?[25] One must note that this line of argument is not an argument against PA per se; it is in essence an argument against the judicial review of legislation in general. After all, whenever courts invalidate a statute passed by Parliament, regardless of whether this is a consequence of PA or categorical judicial rules, judges are supplanting the legislative will and enforcing individual rights at a higher premium. In essence, Webber engages in double-speak; while he speaks of a 'negotiable constitution',[26] what he wants is to practically divest the judiciary of its power to protect individual rights from majoritarian will.[27]

While Webber argues that PA goes too far in usurping legislative authority, Yun-Chien Chang and Xin Dai believe that PA simply does not go far enough. They advocate for judges to adopt a 'full-blown cost-benefit calculus'[28] with 'no fixed sequential structure',[29] in lieu of PA. While Chang and Dai rightly point out that PA is an 'incomplete and under-inclusive cost-benefit analysis',[30] they fail to explain why judges – without economic training – should be the ones to *mimic* the economic decisional processes of the political branches. And their analysis fails to factor in the *costs* inflicted on the court's *legitimacy* if judges *openly* arrogate to the court itself the power to *duplicate* the government's work. Doctrine is a myth, but it

22 Ibid. 10.
23 Ibid. 210.
24 James B. Thayer, 'The Origin and Scope of the American Doctrine of Constitutional Law' (1893) 7 *Harvard Law Review* 129, 144.
25 Aleinikoff (n. 17) 984–985.
26 Webber (n. 21).
27 Aharon Barak, 'Proportionality (2)' in Michel Rosenfeld and András Sajo (eds), *The Oxford Handbook of Comparative Constitutional Law* (Oxford University Press 2012) 738, 752.
28 Yun-Chien Chang and Xin Dai, 'The Limited Usefulness of the Proportionality Principle' *International Journal of Constitutional Law* (forthcoming).
29 Ibid.
30 Ibid.

is a useful one. When judges 'hide their policy behaviour in legal doctrine',[31] they can deflect the accusations of judicial activism that Webber and his acolytes charge.[32] SP is a doctrinal construction and an analytical procedure.[33] Its structured nature and analytical procedure help counsel sequence their arguments and courts frame their decisions,[34] thereby providing a stable defined *legal* infrastructure for rights-contestation to be conducted.[35] In short, the *sequential structured* test that SP entails provides a law-like safe harbour for judicial policy-making; a full blown *unstructured* cost benefit analysis does not. SP creates a 'judicially manageable standard'[36] for courts to apply. Furthermore, insofar as judges dispense with Stages 3 or 4 of SP, when the government fails to discharge its burden under Stages 1 and 2, this judicial economy actually enhances decisional efficiency and conserves political capital. This is a virtue not a vice, as Chang and Dai have charged.[37]

Furthermore, SP also provides the forum for a constitutional dialogue on rights to take place between courts and lawmakers.[38] Through SP, courts do not simply veto legislative action. Instead, legislatures are invited by courts to improve on their statutory product. Even if the original law was invalidated because it was in pursuit of nefarious goals, lawmakers can return and defend a similar law so long as the legislative sequel is in pursuit of a legitimate objective the second time round. Laws that do not achieve the very goals they seek to achieve can be re-tweaked so that there is now a fit between the legislation and its goals. Where there are less restrictive means to pursue these same statutory aims, lawmakers can simply pursue the less draconian legislative option on their second attempt. Moreover, integrated within SP is a margin of appreciation that courts afford the first-instance decisions of the legislature/executive, in view of the relative informational or institutional advantages the latter have over certain policy issues, for example national security and resource allocation.

While the rise of SP is often a natural consequence of legislators *creating* trustee courts to superintend a rights-based constitution,[39] this is not the *only* way SP is birthed. While the KCC was conceived as a trustee court, the HKCFA and the TCC were not. As we have discussed in Chapter 2, both the Hong Kong and Korean courts were originally established for dominant-party regimes. Such autocratic

31 Alec Stone Sweet, 'Path Dependence, Precedent, and Judicial Power' in Martin Shapiro and Alec Stone Sweet, *On Law, Politics, and Judicialization* (Oxford University Press 2002) 112, 128.

32 See also Stone Sweet and Mathews (n. 5) 38.

33 Stone Sweet and Mathews (n. 2) 74–76.

34 Ibid. 88–89.

35 Jackson (n. 1) 3142.

36 Richard H. Fallon, 'Judicially Manageable Standards and Constitutional Meaning' (2006) 119 *Harvard Law Review* 1275.

37 Chang and Dai (n. 28) (arguing that 'when courts skip one or more tests, proportionality analysis would become not as transparent and disciplined as claimed').

38 Stone Sweet and Mathews (n. 5); Jackson (n. 1) 3144; Kent Roach, *Supreme Court on Trial: Judicial Activism or Democratic Dialogue* (Irwin Law 2016) 393.

39 Stone Sweet and Mathews (n. 5) 20–24.

regimes were in no danger of losing power and were thus not seeking to insure against a pending political loss,[40] and had little intention of ceding policy control to the courts. But over time, as power fragmented across separate political institutions and governments became divided, these Asian judges gained policy discretion to independently converge their constitutional jurisprudence with the West and impose tangible costs on their government without being overruled or punished.[41] SP, then, develops over time as the doctrine of choice for this new judicial endeavour or adventure.

Part 1 of this chapter traces the development of SP in Taiwan, and examines how the TCC relies on each Stage of SP to invalidate legislation. Parts 2 and 3 focus on the development and enforcement of SP in South Korea and Hong Kong respectively. This chapter concludes by exploring common themes on the judicial enforcement of SP in these three Asian jurisdictions.

## PART 1: TAIWAN

### DEVELOPMENT OF SP

In Taiwan, Article 23 of the Constitution of the Republic of China provides the textual mandate for the judicial use of SP: 'All the freedoms and rights enumerated ... shall not be restricted by law except such as may be necessary to prevent infringement upon the freedoms of other persons, to avert an imminent crisis, to maintain social order or to advance public welfare.'[42] Although the term 'proportionality' is not explicitly mentioned in the Constitution, the four goals identified in the said Article have been judicially recognized as the grounds for which the government may rely on to restrict constitutional rights. Furthermore, the TCC has relied on the word 'necessary' in Article 23 as the textual basis for applying the necessity test of SP.

The TCC invoked Article 23 for the first time in Interpretation No. 105 (1964), which concerned the licensing regime of publications. In this case, the Court had to address the constitutionality of Articles 40 and 41 of the Publication Act[43] which authorized the Government Information Office and the Executive Yuan to revoke the license of any publisher who committed sedition, treason and offences against public morality. As Taiwan was under martial law rule then, the TCC unsurprisingly upheld the constitutionality of these impugned provisions. In a tersely-reasoned judgment, the Court asserted that these legislative provisions were necessary restrictions on free speech, especially since the Constitution did not expressly

40 For an insurance theory of judicial review, see Tom Ginsburg, *Judicial Review in New Democracies: Constitutional Courts in Asian Cases* (Cambridge University Press 2003).

41 Po Jen Yap, *Courts and Democracies in Asia* (Cambridge University Press 2017) 3.

42 Article 23 of the Constitution of the Republic of China (1947).

43 The Publication Act was completely repealed in 1999.

limit the penalties the government may impose on unlawful publications, and aggrieved applicants could always challenge the legality of specific decisions taken under administrative law.[44] Similarly, in Interpretation No. 194 (1985), the TCC upheld the constitutionality of the mandatory death penalty[45] on the basis that this punitive punishment was necessary as the nation was combating the threat of communism.[46] It is evident that when the nation was under martial law and in the early stages of democratization, the TCC was reluctant to antagonize the political branches. Hence, the government's aims were always deemed legitimate and the necessity test had no bite at all.

But over time, as Taiwan's political transition to a fully-fledged democracy gained momentum, the TCC started to flex its muscles, and invoked Article 23 as a constitutional mandate for all state action to satisfy PA. In Interpretation No. 414 (1996), the TCC expressly used the term 'proportionality' for the first time when assessing the constitutionality of legislation. Specifically, the issue was whether advertisements for medicine could be pre-vetted by the government before they could be broadcast on television. Paragraph 1, Article 66[47] of the Pharmaceutical Affairs Act provided that pharmaceutical manufacturers had to submit their advertisements to the health authority for approval before they were aired. After recognizing that it was important for the state to protect public health and ensure the accuracy of drug commercials, the TCC upheld the regulation as proportionate without further elaboration.[48]

It was not until Interpretation No. 445 (1998) that the TCC first annulled a law using PA. In this case, the Court addressed a legislative blanket ban on all outdoor assemblies and parades that advocated communism or the partition of the country.[49] Herein, the TCC held that the government could not prohibit any assembly or parade that did not 'pose any clear and present danger to social order or public

[44] J.Y. Interpretation No. 105 (1964) (Constitutional Court of Taiwan), at [1], available at http://cons.judicial.gov.tw/jcc/en-us/jep03/show?expno=105, accessed 9 May 2021.

[45] Paragraph 1, Article 5 of the Drug Control Act during the Period for Suppression of the Communist Rebellion read: 'The death penalty will be imposed on those who sell, traffic, and manufacture illegal drugs.'

[46] J.Y. Interpretation No. 194 (1985) (Constitutional Court of Taiwan), at [1], available at http://cons.judicial.gov.tw/jcc/en-us/jep03/show?expno=194, accessed 9 May 2021.

[47] Paragraph 1, Article 66 of the Pharmaceutical Affairs Act reads: 'For publishing or broadcasting medicament advertisement, pharmaceutical firms shall, before publishing or broadcasting, submit all texts, drawings or pictures constituting an advertisement to the central or municipal competent health authority for approval...'.

[48] J.Y. Interpretation No. 414 (1996) (Constitutional Court of Taiwan), at [2], available at http://cons.judicial.gov.tw/jcc/en-us/jep03/show?expno=414, accessed 9 May 2021.

[49] Article 11 of the Assembly and Parade Act read: 'Applications for outdoor assemblies or parades shall be approved except for one of the following conditions: 1. Violating the provision of Article 4 ...' And Article 4 read: 'Communism or secession shall not be asserted in any assembly or parade.'

interests'.[50] Therefore, the blanket ban on all such parades was deemed disproportionate and unnecessary.

While the term 'proportionality' was used in several cases after Interpretation No. 445 (1998), the TCC only in Interpretation No. 476 (1999) elaborated on the legal sub-tests that now constitute SP. In this case, the Justices once again confronted the legislative imposition of the mandatory death penalty for drug offences. While the constitutionality of the death penalty was upheld again, the TCC this time in 1999 determined that PA in Taiwan had three sub-tests: 'due purposes, necessary means, and proper restrictions'.[51] Notably, the TCC did not include the suitability test, the second prong of SP as commonly used today. This omission was odd, especially since several Justices serving on the bench then had German doctorates in law. Furthermore, it was unclear whether the 'proper restrictions' limb had replaced the German 'balancing' sub-test that the TCC has applied since 1997.[52]

This three-stage SP did not last long, as the TCC soon inserted the suitability test into Taiwan's SP in Interpretation No. 542 (2002). In this case, an administrative ordinance, which required residents living at the reservoir catchment area to be relocated, was upheld as proportionate.[53] Furthermore, the TCC applied proportionality *stricto sensu* (or balancing) in lieu of the ambiguous 'proper restriction' test, and ruled that the legislative means (relocation) was proportional to the ends (the protection of water resources). The four-pronged PA is henceforth complete and remains the conventional mode of SP analysis in Taiwan today.

In applying SP, the TCC has also tiered the levels of scrutiny in socio-economic cases, which echoes the German Federal Constitutional Court (GFCC)'s ruling in the *Apotheken-Urteil* (Pharmacy Case) concerning the freedom to work.[54]

50 J.Y. Interpretation No. 445 (1998) (Constitutional Court of Taiwan), at [10], available at http://cons.judicial.gov.tw/jcc/en-us/jep03/show?expno=445, accessed 9 May 2021.

51 J.Y. Interpretation No. 476 (1999) (Constitutional Court of Taiwan), at [1], available at http://cons.judicial.gov.tw/jcc/en-us/jep03/show?expno=476, accessed 9 May 2021.

52 It should be noted that the TCC invoked the balancing test for the first time in Interpretation No. 428 (1997). In this case, Article 25 of the Act Governing the Administration of Post Offices stipulated that the Chunghwa Post Company, run by the government, was not liable for the damages to any registered mails. The TCC upheld the provision, arguing that the law had taken 'into consideration the balance among such factors as the fees charged, the nature of the services, the operating cost, and the degree of injury to the interest of the people.' J.Y. Interpretation No. 428 (1997) (Constitutional Court of Taiwan), at [2], available at http://cons.judicial.gov.tw/jcc/en-us/jep03/show?expno=428, accessed 9 May 2021.

53 J.Y. Interpretation No. 542 (2002) (Constitutional Court of Taiwan), at [2], available at http://cons.judicial.gov.tw/jcc/en-us/jep03/show?expno=542, accessed 9 May 2021.

54 BVerfGE 7, 377 (1958) (German Federal Constitutional Court). In this case, a Bavarian law prohibited the establishment of a new pharmacy unless the new pharmacy would be economically viable and would not threaten the survival of other neighbouring pharmacies. The issue was whether this law violated Paragraph 1, Article 12 of the German Basic Law, which protects occupational freedom, and the German Federal Constitutional Court herein ruled against the state government. For an English translation of this decision, see Jürgen Bröhmer, Gisela Elsner, Clauspeter Hill and

In Interpretation No. 584 (2004), the TCC had to decide whether a person could be statutorily barred from driving a taxi if he had previously committed a serious offence.[55] The TCC first acknowledged that this legislative provision was a serious restriction on the petitioner's occupational freedom, as it permanently barred him from working as a taxi driver. But the Court went on to emphasize that 'The Constitution permits, however, different degrees of liberalness and strictness with respect to restraints to be imposed on the freedom of occupation.'[56] In addition, the TCC differentiated 'objective' restrictions on occupational freedom from those pertaining to 'subjective eligibility'.[57] The latter eligibility requirements refer to restrictions that can be overcome by personal effort.[58] The TCC eventually agreed with the government that there was no less restrictive way to protect the safety of passengers and that the restriction was proportional to the interests achieved because other alternatives, such as tracking these cars electronically, were simply impractical.[59] In the same vein, in Interpretation No. 767 (2018), the TCC opined that the Ministry of Health and Welfare was more qualified than the judiciary to determine who can recover for injuries suffered as a consequence of the side effects of certain medication.[60] As such compensation schemes relate to social welfare policy and the allocation of limited state resources,[61] the TCC decided that the legislature should have more discretion in determining the terms of eligibility and the quantum of compensation.

Interestingly, the TCC does not apply SP on equal protection. Instead, for such cases, the TCC uses the tiered standard of review applicable in the United States[62]

Marc Spitzkatz (eds), 70 *Years German Basic Law: The German Constitution and Its Court* (Konrad-Adenauer-Stiftung e.V., 2019) 852–865.

55 Paragraph 1, Article 37 of the Road Traffic Management and Penalty Act reads: 'A person who committed an offense of manslaughter, snatching, forcible seizing of another person's belongings, robbery, intimidation for the purpose of gaining property, kidnapping for ransom or an offence of interference with sexual freedom … shall be ineligible for registration as a [taxi] driver.'

56 J.Y. Interpretation No. 584 (2004) (Constitutional Court of Taiwan), at [1], available at http://cons.judicial.gov.tw/jcc/en-us/jep03/show?expno=584, accessed 9 May 2021.

57 Ibid. This distinction is modelled on reasoning in the German *Pharmacy* case. See Niels Petersen, 'The German Constitutional Court and Legislative Capture' (2014) 12 *International Journal of Constitutional Law* 650, 665 (discussing the 'subjective access requirements' and 'objective access requirements').

58 J.Y. Interpretation No. 584 (2004) (Constitutional Court of Taiwan), at [1], available at http://cons.judicial.gov.tw/jcc/en-us/jep03/show?expno=584, accessed 9 May 2021.

59 Ibid. [2].

60 J.Y. Interpretation No. 767 (2018) (Constitutional Court of Taiwan), at [5], available at http://cons.judicial.gov.tw/jcc/zh-tw/jep03/show?expno=767, accessed 9 May 2021.

61 Ibid. [6].

62 See Jau-Yuan Hwang 黃昭元, '大法官解釋審查標準之發展(1996~2011): 比例原則的繼受與在地化 Development of Standards of Review by the Constitutional Court from 1996 to 2011: Reception and Localization of the Proportionality Principle' (2013) 42 國立臺灣大學法學論叢 *National Taiwan University Law Journal* 215, 241 (in Chinese).

and would also investigate whether an impugned law targets a 'discrete and insular minority',[63] which in Taiwan includes homosexuals.[64]

## STAGE 1: LEGITIMATE/COMPELLING PUBLIC INTEREST

To date, the TCC has invalidated laws using PA in 49 cases. While an impugned law may fail more than one stage of PA, a law has failed Stage 1, that is, the law serves no legitimate interest, in only three decisions. These three decisions will be explored in turn.

In Interpretation No. 603 (2005),[65] the TCC invalidated Paragraphs 2[66] and 3,[67] Article 8 of the Household Registration Act, which compelled all persons to be fingerprinted before they could receive their national identity cards. Notably, the TCC determined that the law failed PA *inter alia* because the legislative purpose for fingerprinting all citizens was not specified.[68]

Next, in Interpretation No. 744 (2017), the TCC invalidated Paragraph 2, Article 24[69] of the Cosmetic Hygiene and Safety Act, which required all cosmetic advertisements to be pre-approved by the government. Interestingly, the TCC held that this

[63] J.Y. Interpretation No. 748 (2017) (Constitutional Court of Taiwan), at [15], available at http://cons.judicial.gov.tw/jcc/en-us/jep03/show?expno=748. This term is borrowed from Footnote 4 of *United States* v. *Carolene Products* Company, 304 U.S. 144 [1938]: 'There may be narrower scope for operation of the presumption of constitutionality when legislation appears on its face to be within a specific prohibition of the Constitution, such as those of the first ten amendments, which are deemed equally specific when held to be embraced within the Fourteenth … It is unnecessary to consider now whether legislation which restricts those political processes which can ordinarily be expected to bring about repeal of undesirable legislation, is to be subjected to more exacting judicial scrutiny under the general prohibitions of the Fourteenth Amendment than are most other types of legislation … Nor need we inquire whether similar considerations enter into the review of statutes directed at particular religious … or national … or racial minorities …; whether prejudice against discrete and insular minorities may be a special condition, which tends seriously to curtail the operation of those political processes ordinarily to be relied upon to protect minorities, and which may call for a correspondingly more searching judicial inquiry … (citation omitted).'

[64] J.Y. Interpretation No. 748 (2017) (Constitutional Court of Taiwan), at [15], available at http://cons.judicial.gov.tw/jcc/en-us/jep03/show?expno=748, accessed 9 May 2021.

[65] J.Y. Interpretation No. 603 (2005) (Constitutional Court of Taiwan), at [12], available at http://cons.judicial.gov.tw/jcc/en-us/jep03/show?expno=603, accessed 9 May 2021.

[66] Paragraph 2, Article 8 of the Household Registration Act read: 'While applying for a ROC identity card pursuant to the preceding paragraph, the applicant shall be fingerprinted for record keeping; provided that no national who is under fourteen years of age will be fingerprinted until he or she reaches fourteen years of age, at which time he or she shall then be fingerprinted for record keeping.'

[67] Paragraph 3, Article 8 read: 'No ROC identity card will be issued unless the applicant is fingerprinted pursuant to the preceding paragraph.'

[68] In contrast, the KCC has upheld a comparable legislation that requires all persons to be fingerprinted before they receive their Resident Registration Certificates from the government. See *Case on Putting Ten Fingerprints on Application for Issuance of Resident Registration Certificate*, 2011Hun-Ma731 (28 May 2015) (Constitutional Court of Korea).

[69] Paragraph 2, Article 24 of the Cosmetic Hygiene and Safety Act read: 'Before publishing or broadcasting any advertisement, the cosmetic firm shall first submit [the content of the advertisement] to the health authority of the central government or that of a special municipality for approval …'

law did not seek to prevent any 'direct, immediate, and irreparable harms'[70] to consumers and did not serve any 'compelling public interests',[71] and therefore failed the legitimacy test. This ruling is particularly remarkable because it involved commercial speech, which is traditionally less protected in Taiwan.

Finally, in Interpretation No. 766 (2018), the TCC was confronted with the constitutionality of Article 18-1 of the National Pension Act, which provided that pension payments to eligible applicants would only commence from the month their application was approved, and not from the month the applicant became eligible.[72] The government defended the law on the basis that it was costly and time-consuming to ascertain the exact dates on which the applicants qualified for their pension. Nevertheless, the TCC ruled, *inter alia*, that Article 18-1 of the National Pension Act failed the legitimacy test because administrative expediency was not an important public interest[73] and the disputed provision was nullified with immediate effect.[74] In December 2019, the law was amended to allow eligible applicants to be paid retrospectively.[75]

Two out of the three aforementioned decisions were issued in the past few years. Previously, the TCC only required the government's goals to be legitimate.[76] Nowadays, the TCC would require the authorities to demonstrate that the impugned law serve 'important public interests',[77] or even 'compelling public interests'.[78] It is noteworthy that all the laws struck down under Stage 1 also fail other stages of SP as well.[79] In theory, the TCC does not have to examine whether

70 J.Y. Interpretation No. 744 (2017) (Constitutional Court of Taiwan), at [4], available at http://cons.judicial.gov.tw/jcc/en-us/jep03/show?expno=744, accessed 9 May 2021.

71 Ibid.

72 'The insurance benefits under this Act ... will be issued monthly starting from the month of the application approved to the month of pension termination or death of insured person.'

73 J.Y. Interpretation No. 766 (2018) (Constitutional Court of Taiwan), at [5], available at http://cons.judicial.gov.tw/jcc/en-us/jep03/show?expno=766, accessed 9 May 2021.

74 Ibid. [6].

75 Paragraph 2, Article 18-1 of the National Pension Act reads: 'The beneficiary of survivor's pension don't submit application on the month they qualify for the benefits, the insurer should compensate the benefits retroactively to those who are entitled to trace back to five years before they submitted the application. However, for the part which has been claimed by other beneficiary is not included.'

76 J.Y. Interpretation No. 584 (2004) (Constitutional Court of Taiwan), at [2], available at http://cons.judicial.gov.tw/jcc/en-us/jep03/show?expno=584, accessed 9 May 2021.

77 J.Y. Interpretation No. 603 (2005) (Constitutional Court of Taiwan), at [12], available at http://cons.judicial.gov.tw/jcc/en-us/jep03/show?expno=603, accessed 9 May 2021; J.Y. Interpretation No. 766 (2018) (Constitutional Court of Taiwan), at [5], available at http://cons.judicial.gov.tw/jcc/en-us/jep03/show?expno=766, accessed 9 May 2021.

78 J.Y. Interpretation No. 744 (2017) (Constitutional Court of Taiwan), at [4], available at http://cons.judicial.gov.tw/jcc/zh-tw/jep03/show?expno=744, accessed 9 May 2021.

79 For example, in J.Y. Interpretation No. 603 (2005) (Constitutional Court of Taiwan), the TCC also held at [12] that 'even assuming that this need [to fingerprint all citizens] may exist in the future, and this means can help to achieve the purposes listed, mandatory collection and storage of fingerprint information for all citizens above the age of fourteen, ex ante, and requiring all citizens to bear the risks of an ambiguous statutory authorization as well as potential breaches of information go beyond

an impugned law survives other SP stages, once the law fails Stage 1. But in practice, the TCC has never relied on the legitimacy test exclusively to strike down a law, which may suggest that the TCC is unwilling to override the government unless the law poses multiple problems.

## STAGE 2: RATIONAL CONNECTION

To date, the TCC has only ruled against the government at Stage 2 – the suitability test – in eight cases. One such example is Interpretation No. 580 (2004), which interestingly concerned property rights, and not the usual civil-political rights. The law at issue was the 37.5 per cent Arable Rent Reduction Act, which sought to provide assistance to small-time farmers as the agriculture sector in Taiwan modernizes. Specifically, Paragraph 3, Article 19 of the Act[80] required the lessor (usually the landlord), when repossessing his farmland at the end of the lease, to compensate the lessee a sum equal to a third of the land value. The legislature's aim herein was to encourage the expansion of family farms by incentivizing the efficient utilization of the owner's land.[81] Nevertheless, as the TCC rightly pointed out, the impugned provision imposed an additional cost on the lessor's property right, and therefore discouraged, rather than encouraged, the lessor to expand the farmland. Moreover, there were already other statutory provisions in place to help small-time farmers. For instance, Paragraph 1, Article 19[82] of the same Act stipulates that the lessors could not take back their lands if they were unable to cultivate the land themselves or if the lessees needed the land to feed their families. Therefore, Paragraph 3, Article 19 of the Act did not serve the legislative aim and was void.

In Interpretation No. 710 (2013), the TCC was confronted with a constitutional challenge against the Act Governing Relations between Peoples from the Taiwan Area and the Mainland Area, which mandated the detention and speedy repatriation of Chinese people who had no permission to enter Taiwan. Paragraph 2, Article 18 of the Act provided that prior to deportation, the authorities were empowered to

what is necessary. The benefits are clearly outweighed by the costs, which does not conform to the principle of proportionality'.

80 Paragraph 3, Article 19 of the 37.5 per cent Arable Rent Reduction Act read: 'If the lessor retrieves the farm land ... the provisions of Paragraph 2 of Article 17 shall, mutatis mutandis, apply for the compensation of the lessee.' Paragraph 2, Article 17 provides that, *inter alia*, 'the lessor shall compensate the lessee ... The amount equivalent to one third of the difference between the publicly [a]nnounced current land value at the time of the termination of lease contract and the anticipated land value increment tax.'

81 J.Y. Interpretation No. 580 (2004) (Constitutional Court of Taiwan), at [5], available at http://cons.judicial.gov.tw/jcc/en-us/jep03/show?expno=580, accessed 9 May 2021.

82 Paragraph 1, Article 19 of the 37.5 per cent Arable Rent Reduction Act reads: 'When the lease contract expires, the lessor shall not retrieve his farm land for self-cultivation if one of the following conditions applies: 1. The lessor cannot cultivate by himself; 2. All the lessor's current income can maintain his family's subsistence; 3. The lessee will lose the subsistence to maintain his family if the lessor retrieves the leased farm land.'

detain the would-be deportees. While the TCC accepted that it was reasonable to temporarily detain any person from China subject to a valid removal order, Paragraph 2, Article 18[83] failed to specify how long this temporary detention could be. As the absence of a cap on the length of detention could lead to indefinite detention, the TCC ruled that this provision contradicted the legislative goal of ensuring speedy repatriation of deportees, and therefore failed Stage 2.[84] Consequently, the TCC issued a Suspension Order that gave the legislature two years to fix the law, and the revised law in 2015 now provides that these detentions can no longer exceed 150 days.[85]

There has been only one case in which the TCC relied on the suitability test *exclusively* to strike down a legislative provision: Interpretation No. 746 (2017). In Taiwan, taxpayers who failed to pay estate and gift taxes on time would face a penalty, that is, the 'failure-to-pay' surcharges. On top of that, Paragraph 2, Article 51 of the Estate and Gift Tax Act[86] also imposed interests not only on the unpaid taxes but also on that penalty. At the outset, the TCC accepted that tax legislation should be determined by the political branches of government legislature, in view of their financial expertise,[87] and the Court's role was only to ensure there was a rational connection between the legislative means and ends.[88] Nevertheless, the TCC held that the imposition of interests on the penalty charges – and not just the unpaid taxes – would 'doubl[e] the amount of the damages arising from the late payment of taxes, for which there exists no rational basis between the means and the end'.[89] The law was therefore declared unconstitutional and void.

## STAGE 3: LEAST RESTRICTIVE MEANS

The TCC invalidates legislation most frequently at Stage 3 of SP: the necessity test. At this time of writing, the TCC has ruled against the government at this Stage in 35 out of 49 cases in which the disputed laws were invalidated.

Interpretation No. 445 (1998) is one such iconic case. As discussed above, this was the first case in which the TCC used PA to invalidate legislation. In this case, Section 1, Article 11 of the Assembly and Parade Act provided that prior approval for a

83 Paragraph 2, Article 18 of the Act Governing Relations between Peoples from the Taiwan Area and the Mainland Area read: 'Any people from the Mainland Area specified in the preceding paragraph may be temporarily detained prior to enforced deportation…'.

84 J.Y. Interpretation No. 710 (2013) (Constitutional Court of Taiwan), at [3], available at http://cons.judicial.gov.tw/jcc/en-us/jep03/show?expno=710, accessed 9 May 2021.

85 Paragraph 9, Article 18-1 of the Act Governing Relations between Peoples from the Taiwan Area and the Mainland Area.

86 Paragraph 2, Article 51 of the Estate and Gift Tax Act read: 'Interests for the taxes payable and failure-to-pay surcharge … shall accrue daily at the interest rate for one-year term deposit…'.

87 J.Y. Interpretation No. 746 (2017) (Constitutional Court of Taiwan), at [3], available at http://cons.judicial.gov.tw/jcc/en-us/jep03/show?expno=746, accessed 9 May 2021.

88 Ibid.

89 Ibid. [11].

public assembly or parade would not be granted if communism or secession would be advocated at the proposed assembly/parade.[90] The government asserted that this provision was consistent with protecting democratic values enshrined in the Constitution.[91] But the TCC held that any such regulation should 'strike a proper balance between freedom of expression and the societal interests affected, and the regulation should be done by the least restrictive means'.[92] In light of this requirement, the TCC ruled that this content-based regulation could not pass Stage 3 for two reasons. First, insofar as there is a constitutional mandate to protect democratic values, the Constitution already grants the TCC power to dissolve unconstitutional political parties.[93] Therefore, there was no further need to restrict anti-democratic speech unless this involved active plots to sabotage the government or partition the country.[94] Second, the police already possessed additional statutory powers to warn, stop or disperse assemblies and parades if any such danger arose when the parade was ongoing.[95] It was therefore unnecessary to muzzle civil society simply on the basis of one's political belief.[96]

Section 3 of Article 11 of the same Act also stipulated that the approval for notified assemblies would not be granted if there was a 'likelihood that public safety or freedom will be jeopardized, or there will be serious damage to property.' The TCC also ruled that this provision was unnecessary for two reasons. First, the Criminal Code could be used against those who seriously endanger public safety or property rights and the Social Order Maintenance Act could address minor disturbances to social order. Second, the police were also statutorily empowered to stop such assemblies and parades if the above risks materialized when the parade was ongoing.[97] Hence, Section 3 could not survive the necessity test either.[98] It should

90 Article 11 of the Assembly and Parade Act read: 'Applications for outdoor assemblies or parades shall be approved except for one of the following conditions: 1. Violating the provision of Article 4 . . .'. And Article 4 read: 'Communism or secession shall not be asserted in any assembly or parade.'

91 Section 5, Article 5 of Additional Articles of the Constitution of the Republic of China reads: 'A political party shall be considered unconstitutional if its goals or activities endanger the existence of the Republic of China or the nation's free and democratic constitutional order.'

92 J.Y. Interpretation No. 445 (1998) (Constitutional Court of Taiwan), at [8], available at http://cons.judicial.gov.tw/jcc/en-us/jep03/show?expno=445, accessed 9 May 2021.

93 Section 4, Article 5 of Additional Articles of the Constitution of the Republic of China reads: 'The grand justices of the Judicial Yuan shall . . . adjudicate matters relating to . . . the dissolution of unconstitutional political parties.'

94 J.Y. Interpretation No. 445 (1998) (Constitutional Court of Taiwan), at [10], available at http://cons.judicial.gov.tw/jcc/en-us/jep03/show?expno=445, accessed 9 May 2021.

95 Article 25 of the Assembly and Parade Act reads: 'The competent authority may warn, stop, or order to dismiss under one of the following circumstances: . . . Any behaviour exhibiting in the course of the assembly or parade . . . turned out to be against the laws.'

96 J.Y. Interpretation No. 445 (1998) (Constitutional Court of Taiwan), at [10], available at http://cons.judicial.gov.tw/jcc/en-us/jep03/show?expno=445, accessed 9 May 2021.

97 Ibid. [12].

98 Advocacy for communism or for the partition of the national territory is no longer a valid ground for prohibiting outdoor assemblies and parades. Approval for public assemblies will be granted unless there is 'sufficiently obvious evidence' that other people's lives, liberties, and properties will be

be noted that the TCC herein did not categorically reject the constitutionality of prior restraints on the freedom of assemblies,[99] and this actually planted the seed for another landmark Constitutional Court litigation.

In Interpretation No. 718 (2014), the TCC had to determine whether urgent and spontaneous assemblies and parades could be exempted from the approval requirement laid out in Paragraph 1, Article 8 of the Assembly and Parade Act.[100] Notably, the dispute herein arose from the Wild Strawberry student protests against the controversial visit by Chen Yunlin, China's President of the Association for Relations Across the Taiwan Straits, to Taiwan in 2008.[101] Previously, in Interpretation No. 445, the TCC actually upheld the constitutionality of prior restraints on public assemblies as an 'outdoor assembly or parade inevitably will affect public peace and safety, traffic order, quality of residence, or environmental sanitation'.[102] Now, in Interpretation No. 718 (2014), the TCC was ready to revise its stance, and the Court ruled herein that urgent and spontaneous assemblies should be exempted from the pre-approval requirement. First, such assemblies and parades, by their very nature are urgent, and would not serve their purpose unless held immediately.[103] Second, there was sometimes no convener or organizer for such demonstrations, and therefore it was impossible for an organizer to apply for the said approval. Third, the legislature could adopt alternative means to achieve the same goals, though the TCC did not spell out what these options would be.[104] On the basis of these three grounds, the pre-approval requirement for urgent and spontaneous demonstrations failed the necessity test. Hence, the TCC declared that, *inter alia*, Paragraph 1, Article 8 was unconstitutional insofar as it curtailed urgent and spontaneous assemblies, and this restriction would lose legal effect on 1 January 2015. As of October 2020, the government has not revised the impugned Article, but urgent and spontaneous assemblies and parades are now exempted from the operation of the law.

damaged. Section 3, Article 11 of the revised Assembly and Parade Act reads: 'Applications for outdoor assemblies or parades shall be approved except for one of the following conditions: . . . 3. Sufficiently obvious evidence suggesting that it is likely to be harmful to the people's lives, bodies, freedom or cause major damages to people's properties.'

99 J.Y. Interpretation No. 445 (1998) (Constitutional Court of Taiwan), at [8], available at http://cons.judicial.gov.tw/jcc/en-us/jep03/show?expno=445, accessed 9 May 2021.

100 Paragraph 1, Article 8 of the Assembly and Parade Act reads: 'For outdoor assemblies and parades, a permit shall be applied for with the competent authority except in the following conditions: 1. Assemblies or parades held in compliance with laws and regulations. 2. Academic, arts and literature, tourism, sports competitions or other similar activities. 3. Religious and folklore activities, weddings, funerals, celebrations, or festivities.'

101 See Dafydd Fell, 'Social Movements in Taiwan after 2008' in Dafydd Fell (ed), *Taiwan's Social Movements under Ma Ying-jeou* (Routledge 2017) 5.

102 J.Y. Interpretation No. 445 (1998) (Constitutional Court of Taiwan), at [8], available at http://cons.judicial.gov.tw/jcc/en-us/jep03/show?expno=445, accessed 9 May 2021.

103 J.Y. Interpretation No. 718 (2014) (Constitutional Court of Taiwan), at [2], available at http://cons.judicial.gov.tw/jcc/en-us/jep03/show?expno=718, accessed 9 May 2021.

104 Ibid.

Subsequently, in Interpretation No. 654 (2009), a law that authorized prison authorities to record the conversations between counsel and their clients in custody[105] was deemed unconstitutional, as this surveillance impeded their free and unrestricted communication in preparation for trial. The TCC ruled that the impugned provision granted the detention facility personnel a blanket authorization for surveillance, regardless of whether this was necessary to address any security concerns.[106] Therefore, the TCC declared the provision unconstitutional but suspended this declaration of invalidity until 1 May 2009. The revised law now provides that the prison officers can watch over, but not listen in on, any conversations between attorneys and their clients in custody.[107]

The TCC has been equally rigorous in enforcing the constitutional right to work.[108] In Interpretation No. 702 (2012),[109] a ban on the rehiring of teachers who had engaged in conduct 'inconsistent with teachers' morals and dignity'[110] was invalidated, as a lifetime ban was deemed too harsh and deprived the errant teachers of any opportunity to repent.[111] The government was ordered to revise the law within one year, and the new law passed in 2013 now provides that teachers who have been dismissed can be re-appointed four years after their dismissal, so long as their grounds for dismissal did not involve sexual assault, sexual harassment or sexual bullying.[112]

In the same vein, the TCC in Interpretation No. 749 (2017) was confronted with the constitutionality of Paragraph 3, Article 37 of the Road Traffic Management and Penalty Act, which prohibited persons with certain types of criminal record from

105 Paragraph 3, Article 23 of the Detention Act read: 'When a counsel visits an accused in custody, the visitation shall be under surveillance pursuant to Paragraph 2 of the same Article.' And the Paragraph 2 of the same Article reads: 'Officials of the detention house shall supervise the visitation when it is granted.'

106 J.Y. Interpretation No. 654 (2009) (Constitutional Court of Taiwan), at [2], available at http://cons.judicial.gov.tw/jcc/en-us/jep03/show?expno=654, accessed 9 May 2021. The KCC invalidated comparable Korean legislation: See *Interference with Attorney Visits Case*, 91Hun-Ma111 (28 January 1992) (Constitutional Court of Korea).

107 Paragraph 1, Article 23-1 of the Detention Act.

108 Article 15 of the Constitution of the Republic of China (Taiwan) reads: 'The right of existence, the right of work, and the right of property shall be guaranteed to the people.'

109 J.Y. Interpretation No. 702 (2012) (Constitutional Court of Taiwan), at [6], available at http://cons.judicial.gov.tw/jcc/en-us/jep03/show?expno=702, accessed 9 May 2021.

110 Paragraph 3, Article 14 of the Teachers' Act read: 'A teacher to whom any of the circumstances set out in Subparagraphs 1 to 12 of Paragraph 1 . . . may not be re-employed as a teacher.' And the ground for dismissal provided in Subparagraph 6, Paragraph 1 relates to conduct that is 'inconsistent with teachers' morals and dignity.'

111 J.Y. Interpretation No. 702 (2012) (Constitutional Court of Taiwan), at [6], available at http://cons.judicial.gov.tw/jcc/en-us/jep03/show?expno=702, accessed 9 May 2021.

112 Paragraph 6, Article 14 of the Teachers' Act reads: 'With the exception of anyone who has committed a sexual assault; sexual harassment, or sexual bullying . . . any teacher who . . . was . . . dismissed or did not have their appointment renewed, may be re-employed as a teacher after at least four years from the date of effect of their dismissal or the non-renewal.'

working as taxi drivers.[113] While the TCC agreed that the legislature, in the interests of passenger safety, could legitimately exclude those with past violent criminal convictions from this business,[114] it pointed out that many of the crimes listed in Paragraph 3 bore no relation to passenger safety.[115] Moreover, the impugned provision did not take into account the offender's motive, whether the offender was paroled, the offender's contrition post-offence, etc. Therefore, the TCC ruled that this provision constituted an excessive restriction on the constitutional right to work.[116]

## STAGE 4: BALANCING

As Stage 4 of SP – the balancing test – often requires courts to engage openly in policy-making by evaluating 'the counterfactual considerations of the relative harms and benefits'[117] of any impugned law, the TCC has understandably shied away from striking down legislation on this ground. In fact, to date, it has only done so in eight cases, out of over 120 decisions in which it has invoked PA.

Interpretation No. 487 (1999) is the first case in which the TCC ruled against the government at Stage 4. Specifically, Section 2, Article 2 of the Law of Compensation for Wrongful Detentions and Executions provided that persons who had been detained but thereafter not prosecuted or acquitted at trial could not seek compensation from the government if their alleged wrongful conduct had been 'in violation of the public order or morality'. In response, the TCC determined *inter alia* that the statutory exclusion of persons, whose physical freedom had been gravely restrained,

113 Paragraph 3, Article 37 of the Road Traffic Management and Penalty Act read: 'Should a taxi driver commit crimes involving larceny, fraud, theft, obstruction of freedom . . . his/her business registration certificate shall be suspended. Any driver who has been convicted by a court and sentenced to prison, his/her business registration certificate shall be cancelled and his/her driver license shall be revoked.'

114 It should be noted that in Interpretation No. 584 the Court upheld as necessary Article 37, Paragraph 1 of the same Road Traffic Management and Penalty Act, which provided that any person convicted of serious crimes, such as homicide, robbery, kidnapping and so on, shall be prohibited from applying for a taxi driver licence.

115 J.Y. Interpretation No. 749 (2017) (Constitutional Court of Taiwan), at [10], available at http://cons.judicial.gov.tw/jcc/en-us/jep03/show?expno=749, accessed 9 May 2021. Examples raised by the TCC include Paragraph 2 Article 320 of the Criminal Code's (listed in the Criminal Code's Chapter on Larceny), which pertains to the unlawful occupation of another person's real property, and Article 307 of the Criminal Code (listed in the Criminal Code's Chapter on 'Obstructions of Freedom'), which pertains to unlawful searches by law enforcement officials.

116 The legislature revised the disputed provision in 2019 and the new legislative provision excludes crimes that have no relation to passenger safety. See Paragraph 3, Article 37 of the Road Traffic Management and Penalty Act (2019), available at https://law.moj.gov.tw/ENG/LawClass/LawAll.aspx?pcode=K0040012, accessed 9 May 2021.

117 Stone Sweet and Mathews (n. 5) 47.

from compensation simply because their behaviour had violated social order and morality was disproportionate, and therefore unconstitutional.[118]

Another iconic case is Interpretation No. 649 (2008), which addressed the constitutionality of a law that only allowed visually-impaired persons to work as massage therapists.[119] Even persons with other types of disability were excluded from the massage industry. While the TCC recognized that the provision of job opportunities to the blind served an important interest, it ruled that this monopoly had not advanced the economic conditions of the visually impaired in any significant way, but had also harmed the job prospects of the visually unimpaired, including other disabled persons excluded from this affirmative action.[120] Therefore, the right to work of the visually unimpaired and the consumers' interest in having access to a competitive massage market outweighed the state interest in protecting the visually impaired.[121] The law was declared unconstitutional, but the TCC suspended this declaration for three years[122] so that the legislature could have more time to deliberate on a more tailored legislation. Interestingly, the legislature basically chose to do nothing and the law ceased to have effect in 2011.

Subsequently, in Interpretation No. 712 (2013) – another ground-breaking decision – the TCC invalidated a law that barred Taiwanese parents with children from adopting children of their own spouses from China.[123] This law was passed to prevent people from China from abusing the adoption system to become Taiwanese and therefore harming social stability and national security. In principle, the TCC accepted that on foreign affairs and national security, the Court should not interfere with the government's determination unless there were 'glaring and grave mistakes'.[124] Nevertheless, the TCC ruled that that this blanket ban excessively and disproportionately affected a couple's marital happiness and family harmony, as well as the physical and mental well-being of Chinese children with ties in Taiwan.[125]

118 J.Y. Interpretation No. 487 (1999) (Constitutional Court of Taiwan), at [3], available at http://cons.judicial.gov.tw/jcc/en-us/jep03/show?expno=487, accessed 9 May 2021.

119 Paragraph 1, Article 46 of the Physically and Mentally Disabled Citizens Protection Act read: 'Anyone other than the seeing (visual acuity functions) disabled may not be engaged in massage industry.'

120 J.Y. Interpretation No. 649 (2008) (Constitutional Court of Taiwan), at [3], available at http://cons.judicial.gov.tw/jcc/en-us/jep03/show?expno=649, accessed 9 May 2021.

121 Ibid. [5].

122 The Korean Constitutional Court confronted this same issue in 2006 and reached a similar decision, as we will discuss. See Constitutional Court of Korea, 2003Hun-Ma 715 (2006) (Constitutional Court of Korea).

123 Article 65 of the Act Governing Relations between the People of the Taiwan Area and the Mainland Area read: 'Where any of the people of the Taiwan Area adopts any of the people of the Mainland Area, a court shall not approve such adoption ... in the following situations ... :1. Where any of the adoptive parents already has a child or an adopted child.'

124 J.Y. Interpretation No. 712 (2013) (Constitutional Court of Taiwan), at [3], available at http://cons.judicial.gov.tw/jcc/en-us/jep03/show?expno=712, accessed 9 May 2021.

125 Ibid. [5].

Furthermore, in a few cases, the TCC invalidated the impugned legislation *exclusively* at Stage 4, and these concern penal punishments that were deemed too draconian. In Interpretation No. 641 (2008), the TCC invalidated a law that imposed a fine of NT $2000 (roughly USD 65) on every bottle of rice wine sold above its original listed price.[126] While the TCC accepted that this provision was 'a necessary measure when there were no other effective methods to prevent price hikes and maintain the rice wine supply',[127] the law failed Stage 4 as a uniform fine of NT $2000 per bottle, regardless of the number of bottles sold above market value, could be 'patently severe'[128] in certain cases. Therefore, the legislature should place a cap on the fine that could be levied.[129]

Similarly, in Interpretation No. 669 (2009), the TCC was confronted with the constitutionality of Paragraph 1, Article 8 of the Firearms, Knives and Other Weaponry Control Act,[130] which prohibited the manufacture and sale of a variety of guns, including air guns. While the TCC accepted that the law was necessary to protect citizens' life, liberty and property,[131] the TCC ruled that the imposition of a mandatory *minimum* of five years imprisonment was an 'overly severe punishment and a disproportion between offence and penalty is created',[132] as not all air guns have the same capacity to cause serious harm. Therefore, where air guns were concerned, the law was unconstitutional insofar as 'no parole of sentence or substitution of fine is available'.[133] In 2011, the government added a statutory clause that grants the trial judge the discretion to reduce the sentences for minor infractions of air gun offences.[134]

In 2020, the TCC ruled on the statutory provision that imposed a minimum of five years' imprisonment on all offenders convicted of cultivating marijuana in

126 Article 21 of the Cigarette and Alcohol Tax Law read: 'Rice wine sold exclusively by the Cigarette and Alcohol Public Distribution Bureau before this Law came into effect shall be sold according to the original sales price. Anyone who sells rice wine at a price higher than the original sales price shall be fined NT $2000 per bottle of rice wine sold.'

127 J.Y. Interpretation No. 641 (2008) (Constitutional Court of Taiwan), at [3], available at http://cons.judicial.gov.tw/jcc/en-us/jep03/show?expno=641, accessed 9 May 2021.

128 Ibid. [4].

129 In 2008, the Legislative Yuan revised the law and capped the fine. Article 21 of the Tobacco and Alcohol Tax Act now reads: '... If the selling price of the aforementioned rice spirits is higher than the regulated price, the vendor shall be fined from 1 to 3 times the amount of the excess of the regulated price.'

130 Paragraph 1, Article 8 of the Controlling Guns, Ammunition and Knives Act reads: 'Any person who manufactures, sells, traffics without permission pen guns, gas guns, anesthetic guns, hunting rifles, air-propelled guns ... that can emit metals or bullets and are capable of causing personal injuries or death, is punishable with life-imprisonment or no less than 5 years of imprisonment...'.

131 J.Y. Interpretation No. 669 (2009) (Constitutional Court of Taiwan), at [2], available at http://cons.judicial.gov.tw/jcc/en-us/jep03/show?expno=669, accessed 9 May 2021.

132 Ibid. [3].

133 Ibid.

134 Paragraph 6, Article 8 of the Controlling Guns, Ammunition and Knives Act reads: 'If the offenses relating to air guns prescribed in paragraphs 1, 2 and 4 are slight, the sentence against the offenders may be reduced.'

Interpretation No. 790 (2020).[135] While the TCC acknowledged that the disputed provision protected public health, an important public interest,[136] the Court held that the statutory minimum of five years' imprisonment would be too draconian in cases where the offender only cultivated a small amount for personal use.[137] The TCC gave the legislature one year to pass remedial legislation and if the legislature fails to comply, the lower courts may halve the punishment when necessary.[138]

Finally, the TCC also decriminalized adultery in Interpretation No. 791 (2020).[139] While the Court accepted that criminal sanctions might deter infidelity between spouses and this was therefore not completely unsuitable[140] for achieving the ends of upholding familial harmony, the TCC decided that this impugned provision failed the balancing test of SP.[141] On one hand, the TCC contended that adultery had little to do with public interest, as it merely involved consensual sexual intercourse between two adults. On the other hand, the investigation, prosecution and trial of a person for adultery would significantly impact their sexual autonomy, which is closely related to a person's human dignity and freedom of personality.[142] Therefore, the costs inflicted by the criminalization of adultery outweighed the benefits.

## PART 2: SOUTH KOREA

### DEVELOPMENT OF SP

Like Taiwan, the Korean Constitution has a general limitation clause that applies to all constitutional rights. Specifically, Article 37(2) of the Korean Constitution provides: 'The freedoms and rights of citizens may be restricted by Act only when necessary for national security, the maintenance of law and order or for public

135 Paragraph 2, Article 12 of the Narcotics Hazard Prevention Act reads: 'Persons convicted of cultivating Cannabis with intentions to supply for manufacturing narcotics shall be punished with a minimum five-year fixed-term imprisonment, and may be fined no more than five million New Taiwan dollars.'

136 J.Y. Interpretation No. 790 (2020) (Constitutional Court of Taiwan), at [10], available at http://cons.judicial.gov.tw/jcc/zh-tw/jep03/show?expno=790, accessed 9 May 2021.

137 Ibid. [11].

138 Ibid.

139 J.Y. Interpretation No. 791 (2020) (Constitutional Court of Taiwan), available at https://cons.judicial.gov.tw/jcc/zh-tw/jep03/show?expno=791, accessed 9 May 2021.

140 Ibid. [30]. In contrast, the KCC decided that the criminalization of adultery failed Stage 2 of SP and did not elaborate on Stage 4. See the KCC's ruling in *Adultery Case*, 2009Hun-Ba17 (26 February 2015) (Constitutional Court of Korea). According to the KCC, the adultery law not only did not help spouses reconcile, it often tore families apart instead. Moreover, no empirical evidence proved that criminalizing adultery would deter infidelity or that its decriminalization would increase divorce rates.

141 J.Y. Interpretation No. 791 (2020) (Constitutional Court of Taiwan), at [32], available at https://cons.judicial.gov.tw/jcc/zh-tw/jep03/show?expno=791, accessed 9 May 2021.

142 Ibid.

welfare. Even when such restriction is imposed, no essential aspect of the freedom or right shall be violated.'

After commencing operations in 1988, the KCC in March 1989 determined for the first time that statutory restrictions on constitutional rights had to comply with the 'principle of proportionality', which is synonymously and interchangeably referred to as the 'prohibition against excessive restriction'.[143] However, in that case, while the KCC upheld the constitutionality of qualification rules for judicial scriveners, it did not articulate any sub-tests for PA.[144] This state of affairs did not persist for long. In December 1989, the KCC endorsed a four-stage SP: When restricting rights, the government has to (1) pursue a legitimate aim; (2) the means chosen by the state must be appropriate; (3) the government must have chosen the least restrictive means of restricting rights and (4) there must be a balance struck between public interest gains and the loss to individual rights.[145] In September 1990, the KCC relied on the fourstage SP to strike down legislation for the first time in the country's history.[146]

While the KCC treats SP as the 'unified standard'[147] for all rights-derogations to be judicially examined, the Court also affords a margin of discretion to lawmakers when applying SP. Like the HKCFA and the TCC, the KCC accords a significant margin of discretion to the legislature on the enforcement of socio-economic rights. For example, when upholding the constitutionality of the National Insurance Act, which mandated all (public and private) hospitals to provide the requisite national healthcare benefits to all persons in need as stipulated under the Act, the KCC determined that the legislature's 'formative power in enacting socio-economic law'[148] should only be reversed if the assessment was 'clearly erroneous'.[149] Similarly, the KCC is highly deferential to the government in cases implicating national security.[150]

143 *Case on Constitutional Complaint for Judicial Scrivener Law*, 88Hun-Ma1 (17 March 1989) (Constitutional Court of Korea).

144 Ibid.

145 *Land Transaction Licensing Case*, 88Hun-Ka13 (22 December 1989) (Constitutional Court of Korea). On the facts, the KCC upheld a law that required land transactions within selected restricted areas to be approved by the provincial government prior to sale.

146 89Hun-Ka95 (3 September 1990) (Constitutional Court of Korea). On the facts, a tax law was invalidated on the basis that it prioritized the state's tax claim over the proprietary rights of a mortgagee, even if the mortgage was registered before the tax payment was due. See Yoon Jin Shin, 'Proportionality in South Korea: Contextualizing the Cosmopolitan Rights Grammar' in Po Jen Yap (ed), *Proportionality in Asia* (Cambridge University Press 2020) 87.

147 The Constitutional Court of Korea, *The First Ten Years of the Korean Constitutional Court* (The Constitutional Court of 2001) 125.

148 *Case on the Compulsory Designation of Medical Care Institutions*, 99Hun-Ba76 (31 October 2002) (Constitutional Court of Korea) (Official English Summary).

149 Ibid.

150 *Praising and Encouraging under National Security Act Case*, 89Hun-Ka113 (2 April 1990) (Constitutional Court of Korea); *Dissolution of the Unified Progressive Party*, 2013Hun-Da1 (19 December 2014) (Constitutional Court of Korea).

## STAGE 1: LEGITIMATE AIM

Like the HKCFA and TCC, the KCC rarely vetoes legislation on the basis that the legislative purpose is illegitimate or invalid. But the Court has done so on three occasions where the National Assembly has failed to revise centuries-old feudal laws that ossified patriarchy in Korean society.

In July 1997, the KCC declared that an archaic law, which prohibited Koreans with the same family names and lineal origins from marrying one another, no longer served any legitimate purpose.[151] This law applied regardless of the degree of consanguinity between the couple and it only applied to *patrilineal* blood-ties. The KCC noted that there was no scientific or medical evidence for this law, and the feudal Confucian tradition it sought to preserve was no longer constitutionally sustainable. A suspended declaration of invalidity, known as a declaration of non-conformity in South Korea, was issued and the legislature was given 18 months to draft a remedial legislation. Notably, the National Assembly only revised the law in 2005 to prohibit marriages between blood relatives within eight degrees of consanguinity,[152] although the original blanket ban was lifted in practice before that.

The KCC in 2005 also upended a patriarchal law that subordinated a woman to her father, husband (if she were married) or son (if her husband was deceased).[153] Even if a couple divorced and the woman raised their child on her own, that child would still be registered to the ex-husband's household. The KCC determined that this chauvinistic family system, based on Confucian tradition which centred on male linage, could no longer serve as a legitimate objective that the state could defend under its constitutional duty to preserve the country's cultural heritage.[154] Therefore, the impugned discriminatory provisions were declared incompatible with the constitutional right to sex equality.[155] The National Assembly has since repealed all the impugned provisions, save one. The child would still have to assume the father's family name, unless the couple agreed otherwise at the time of the marriage[156] or if the courts authorized the change of surname.[157]

151 *Case on Same Surname-Same Origin Marriage Ban*, 95Hun-Ka6 (16 July 1997) (Constitutional Court of Korea).

152 Article 809(1) of the Civil Act.

153 *Case on House Hold Head System*, 2001Hun-Ka9 (3 February 2005) (Constitutional Court of Korea).

154 Article 9 of the Constitution of the Republic of Korea reads: 'The State shall strive to sustain and develop the cultural heritage and to enhance national culture.'

155 Article 36(1) of the Constitution of the Republic of Korea reads: 'Marriage and family life shall be entered into and sustained on the basis of individual dignity and equality of the sexes, and the State shall do everything in its power to achieve that goal.'

156 Article 781(1) of the Civil Act.

157 Article 781(6) of the Civil Act.

Finally, the KCC struck down a paternalistic criminal law provision that imposed criminal sanctions on any man who induced a female to have sex with him by pretending he would marry her.[158] More significantly, the TCC ruled that this law served no legitimate state interest and failed Stage 1 of SP.[159] According to the KCC, a man's sexual relationship with an adult woman is entirely a private affair, so long as no coercion or violence is involved, especially since pre-marital sex is not a crime in Korea. Moreover, the KCC determined that this impugned provision purported to protect women but was in effect imposing a 'sexual ideology based on patriarchy and moralism',[160] as women 'prone to an obscene act'[161] were statutorily excluded from the law's protection. Furthermore, by portraying women as immature and incapable of making voluntary sexual decisions, this penal law also infringed upon a woman's dignity and right to self-determination.

## STAGE 2: APPROPRIATENESS OF MEANS

Stage 2 of SP herein requires the legislature to have chosen 'appropriate means' to pursue the legislative purpose in question. Notably, Stage 2 of SP has more 'bite' in South Korea, as the KCC not only examines whether the legislation will *achieve* the goal in question; it will further examine whether the means chosen is 'appropriate'. Laws are invalidated in South Korea under Stage 2 of SP when the legislature has failed to consider other relevant factors when crafting the impugned statutory measures.

In 2005, the KCC invalidated a 'school site acquisition charge' that a city government had imposed on housing developers.[162] On the facts, housing developers who were purchasing land to build housing projects with more than 300 units had to pay a charge that would be used to finance the increased demand for schools in that area. Housing developments with less than 300 units were exempted from the tax. By focusing only on the number of units, without taking into account the size of each unit, the type of housing development or the purchasing power of the targeted end-buyers, the Constitutional Court determined that this tax classification was 'not an appropriate means of achieving the legislative purpose'.[163] Notably, a week *before*

158 Article 304 of the Criminal Act read: 'A person who induces a female who is not prone to an obscene act into sexual intercourse under pretence of marriage or through other fraudulent means, shall be punished by imprisonment for not more than two years or by a fine not exceeding five million won.'

159 *Case on Sexual Intercourse under Pretence of Marriage Case*, 2008Hun-Ba58, 2009Hun-Ba191 (consolidated) (26 November 2009) (Constitutional Court of Korea).

160 Ibid. (Official English Summary).

161 Article 304 of the Criminal Act.

162 *Imposing School Site Acquisition Charge on Purchaser of Housing Units from Developer Case*, 2003Hun-Ka20 (31 March 2005) (Constitutional Court of Korea).

163 Ibid. (Official English Summary).

the KCC decision was handed down, the impugned law had already been revised to exempt housing projects forcibly relocated by the government, rental apartments and housing projects that would not involve an increased demand for schools, etc. from the tax.[164]

The KCC, in 2006, invalidated Article 17 of the Newspapers Act, which determined the status of the newspaper's 'market domination' – for the purpose of antitrust compliance – purely on the basis of the periodical's circulation.[165] While the Act served a legitimate aim of 'guaranteeing the diversity of newspapers',[166] the KCC determined that the means chosen was inappropriate for achieving those ends: the KCC decided that the newspapers' market share could not be solely determined by its circulation and the government should also look at the newspapers' sales volume, advertisement volume and the number of subscribers. Furthermore, it was equally inappropriate to place a general-interest daily in the same market as one that published daily news on specialized topics.[167] The abovementioned impugned regulation was removed when the Act was substantially revised and renamed in 2009.[168] In 2015, the KCC decriminalized adultery[169] on the basis of Stage 2 of SP. While the KCC accepted that the law was intended to promote 'marital fidelity'[170] and a 'good sexual culture' – both legitimate state interests – this use of the criminal law was inappropriate to achieve the aforementioned two goals. As observed by the KCC, the use of the criminal law to enforce marital fidelity not only did not help spouses reconcile, its use often tore families apart as this provision had largely become a means for spousal blackmail. The KCC also noted that there was no empirical evidence to show that criminalizing adultery would deter infidelity or that its decriminalization would increase divorce rates.[171] Therefore, the KCC ruled that this provision unconstitutionally violated a person's privacy and right of sexual self-determination.[172]

164 The Constitutional Court of Korea, *Thirty Years of the Constitutional Court of Korea* (The Constitutional Court of Korea 2018) 391–393.

165 *The Newspaper Act Case*, 2005Hun-Ma165 (26 July 2006) (Constitutional Court of Korea).

166 The Constitutional Court of Korea (n. 164) 227.

167 Ibid.

168 The *Act on the Guarantee of Freedom and Functions of Newspapers* was substantially revised and renamed the *Act on the Promotion of Newspapers*.

169 Article 241 of the Criminal Act read: '(1) A married person who commits adultery shall be punished by imprisonment for not more than two years ... (2) The crime in the preceding section shall be prosecuted only upon the accusation of the victimized spouse. If the victimized spouse condones or pardons the adultery, accusation can no longer be made.'

170 *Adultery Case*, 2009Hun-Ba17 (26 February 2015) (Constitutional Court of Korea).

171 Ibid. (Official English Translation).

172 It is noteworthy that adultery has also been decriminalized in Taiwan in 2020. See J.Y. Interpretation No. 791 (2020) (Constitutional Court of Taiwan), available at https://cons.judicial.gov.tw/jcc/zh-tw/jep03/show?expno=791, accessed 9 May 2021.

## STAGE 3: LEAST RESTRICTIVE MEANS

Like the HKCFA and the TCC, the KCC most frequently strikes down an impugned law on the basis of the necessity test. In South Korea, to survive Stage 3, the legislation must be the 'least restrictive means'[173] to accomplish state interests. Nevertheless, on issues where the courts would accord greater deference to the political branches, the KCC would only examine whether the restriction is within the 'the necessary scope to fulfil the legislative purpose',[174] and not whether the restriction is the least restrictive possible.

In 1991, the KCC had to determine whether the courts could compel the defendant to issue a public apology if he or she was found liable for defamation.[175] Specifically, the KCC ruled that in order to restore the reputation of the victim, the defendant could be ordered to publish the verdict in multiple newspapers and it was thus an 'excessive and unnecessary restriction'[176] of the defendant's freedom of conscience[177] to further require a state-coerced public apology. Therefore, the impugned law was ruled unconstitutional insofar as the courts could compel the defendant to issue a public apology to restore the victim's reputation.[178]

Like the TCC, the KCC has also invalidated a raft of laws that restricted the citizenry's right to assemble freely. In 2003, the KCC declared Article 11(1) of the Assembly and Demonstration Act[179] unconstitutional insofar as it prohibited any demonstration within 100 metres of foreign embassies. While the KCC accepted that it was legitimate for the government to secure 'the function of the diplomatic institutions and the protection of the safety of the official diplomatic facilities',[180] the

173 Shin (n. 146).

174 *Prohibition of Medical Advertisement of the Medical Service Act Case*, 2003Hun-Ka3 (27 October 2005) (Constitutional Court of Korea). See also Shin (n. 146).

175 Article 764 of the Civil Act read: 'The court may, on the application of the injured party, order the person who has impaired another's fame to take suitable measures to restore the injured party's fame, either in lieu of, or together with damages.'

176 *Notice of Apology Case*, 89Hun-Ma160 (1 April 1991) (Constitutional Court of Korea).

177 Article 19 of the Constitution of the Republic of Korea (South Korea) (1987).

178 On the other hand, in Interpretation No. 656 (2009), the TCC ruled that it was constitutional for a court to compel the defendant to issue a public apology if this option was necessary to restore the reputation of the defamed, provided that judges had taken into consideration the severity of the reputational harm, the identity of parties, and the offender's economic status. For a comparison of both decisions, see Jiunn-rong Yeh, 'Court-Ordered Apology: The Function of Courts in the Construction of Society, Culture and the Law' in Jiunn-rong Yeh (ed), *The Functional Transformation of Courts: Taiwan and Korea in Comparison* (National Taiwan University Press 2015) 21, 29–36.

179 Article 11(1) of the Assembly and Demonstration Act read: 'No person may hold any assembly or demonstration at any place within one hundred meters from the borderline of the following office buildings or residences: … (1) The National Assembly building, each level of courts, the Constitutional Court, the foreign diplomatic missions in Korea; …'

180 *Prohibition of Assembly in the Vicinity of Diplomatic Institutions*, 2000Hun-Ba67 (30 October 2003) (Constitutional Court of Korea). For a more detailed discussion, see Chaihark Hahm, 'Human Rights in Korea' in Randall Peerenboom, Carole J. Peterson, and Albert H. Y. Chen (eds), *Human*

Court ruled that a complete ban of any assembly near diplomatic institutions violated the Constitution in three circumstances: when the demonstration was not targeting the embassies; when the size of an assembly was relatively small; and when an assembly was held on days the embassy was closed.[181] In 2004, the National Assembly revised Article 11 and allowed assemblies in the vicinity of embassies in the following situations: when the assembly is not targeted at the diplomatic offices or residences of heads of diplomatic missions;[182] when the assembly would not escalate into a large-scale one;[183] and when the assembly takes place on days diplomatic offices are closed.[184]

Notably, the same Article 11(1) also prohibited any demonstration within 100 metres of the National Assembly, and this restriction was also declared excessive in May 2018. In the KCC's view, the National Assembly was tasked with the 'role of "gathering public opinion", [and] the necessity to protect the National Assembly from unreasonable duress ... should ... be limited to protection from potential physical duress or harm against National Assembly members and from the risk of threats against entry into, or the safety of, National Assembly facilities.'[185] Therefore, this law was excessively restrictive insofar as it barred small-scale assemblies and demonstrations held on public holidays. The KCC herein issued a delayed declaration of invalidity and the legislature was given until the end of 2019 to revise the impugned law.[186] In the same vein, laws that prohibited all demonstrations within 100 metres of the courts[187] and the Prime Minister's residence[188] were deemed excessive, and the government was given until 31 December 2019 to pass remedial legislation.[189]

Like the HKCFA and the TCC, the KCC has also upended socio-economic policies using Stage 3 of SP. In 2000, the KCC struck down Article 3 of the Act on the Establishment and Operation of Private Teaching Institutes,[190] which in essence limited students' rights to receive extra-curricular lessons only from university

*Rights in Asia: A Comparative Legal Study of Twelve Asian Jurisdictions, France and the USA* (Routledge 2006) 265, 283–284.

181 Ibid. (Official English Translation).

182 Article 11 [4] (a) of the Assembly and Demonstration Act.

183 Article 11 [4] (b) of the Assembly and Demonstration Act.

184 Article 11 [4] (c) of the Assembly and Demonstration Act.

185 *Case on the Ban on Outdoor Assemblies within 100m of the National Assembly Building*, 2013Hun-Ba322, 2016Hun-Ba354, 2017Hun-Ba360, 398, 471, 2018Hun-Ka3, 4, 9 (consolidated) (31 May 2018) (Constitutional Court of Korea).

186 The National Assembly revised the impugned provision on 9 June 2020.

187 *Case on Banning Outdoor Assembly in the Vicinity of All Levels of Courts*, 2018Hun-Ba137 (26 July 2018) (Constitutional Court of Korea).

188 *Case on Banning Assembly near Official Residence of the Prime Minister*, 2015Hun-Ka28, 2016Hun-Ka5 (consolidated) (28 June 2018) (Constitutional Court of Korea).

189 The National Assembly revised the impugned provision on 9 June 2020.

190 Article 3 of the Act on the Establishment and Operation of Private Teaching Institutes read: 'No person shall provide extracurricular lessons. Provided that this shall not apply where he falls under each of the following subparagraphs: 1. Where he teaches ... at a private teaching institute or

students or through registered private teaching institutes where prices were monitored by the government. While the KCC accepted that the government was entitled to prevent 'high expenditure extracurricular lessons and ... lessen ... parents' burden in private education due to over-heated competition',[191] the disputed law was not the least restrictive means of achieving those goals. Many forms of extra-curricular lessons were unrelated to academic subjects, but such activities were also subject to the ban; students were also barred from taking private lessons from their neighbours or relatives – activities that were typically not 'high-expenditure' or posed social problems for the government.

In 2005, the KCC struck down Article 46(3) of the Medical Service Act,[192] which practically banned all medical advertisements.[193] While the KCC accepted that the law sought to protect consumers by preventing unfair market practices and prohibiting fraudulent/ deceptive advertisements, the Court pointed out that consumers equally needed accurate information to evaluate the performance of medical personnel and procedures, which was barred by the legislative prohibition. Moreover, there were other pre-existing laws, such as the Fair Advertisement Act, the Consumer Protection Act and the Monopoly Regulation and Fair Trade Act, which could address the government's purported legislative goals. Therefore, Article 46(3) excessively violated freedom of speech and was declared unconstitutional.[194]

teaching school; 2. Where he teaches persons ... at a private teaching institute. 3. Where a student (including graduate student) enrolled in a university, college ... teaches.'

191 *Case on Banning Assembly near Official Residence of the Prime Minister*, 2015Hun-Ka28, 2016Hun-Ka5 (consolidated) (28 June 2018) (Constitutional Court of Korea) (Official English Summary).

192 Article 46(3) of the Medical Service Act read: 'No person shall advertise the function, method of medical examination and treatment or of assistance in child delivery, or remedial results of a specific medical institution or specific medical person, by means of mass advertisement, suggestive description, photos, printed matters, broadcasts, or designs, etc.'

193 *Prohibition of Medical Advertisement of the Medical Service Act Case*, 2003Hun-Ka3 (27 October 2005) (Constitutional Court of Korea).

194 The Medical Services Act has been revised many times since this decision and the impugned law now takes the form of Article 56(3) of the Medical Service Act: '(1) No person who is not the founder of a medical institution, the head of a medical institution, or medical personnel ... shall run an advertisement for medical services ... (2) No medical personnel, etc. shall run any of the following advertisements of medical services: 1. Advertisement of new medical technology without undergoing the evaluation ...; 2. Advertisement including contents that are likely to mislead consumers about the effect of medical treatment ...; 3. Advertisement indicating a false fact; 4. Advertisement with any content that compares with a function or treatment method of any other medical personnel, etc.; 5. Advertisement with any content that defames any other medical personnel, etc.; 6. Advertisement with any content that directly exposes medical treatment ...; 7. Advertisement in which any important information ... is omitted; 8. Advertisement that exaggerates an objective fact; 9. Advertisement that expresses a legally groundless qualification or name; 10. Advertisement that shows its contents in the form of a news article or expert opinion using a newspaper, broadcasting medium, magazine, or any other medium ...; (3) No medical advertisement shall be run in any of the following methods: 1. Broadcasting ... 2. Other methods prescribed by Presidential Decree ... (4) Matters necessary for medical advertisements ... shall be prescribed by Presidential Decree...'.

The KCC, as did its Taiwan counterpart,[195] ruled in 2006 that it was disproportionate to grant the visiually impaired an exclusive monopoly in the massage industry.[196] Unlike Taiwan, this restriction was passed not by legislation, but was implemented by an administrative rule. Notably, six judges determined that the impugned rule was not authorized by its enabling legislation, Article 61(4) of the Medical Service Act,[197] but five judges[198] further held that a complete prohibition against all non-visually-impaired persons working as masseurs was excessive and failed SP.[199] In response, the National Assembly amended the Medical Service Act to expressly prohibit non-visiually-impaired persons from working as massage therapists,[200] and the KCC subsequently caved and accepted that the 'massage practice is almost the only occupation [the blind] can normally engage in';[201] and such legislation would be constitutional.[202]

In 2008, the KCC was confronted with a law[203] that banned doctors from disclosing the sex of a foetus to the child's family, including the mother.[204] While the KCC accepted that the legislature had a legitimate purpose of preventing 'sex-selective abortions and to protect the foetus's right to life',[205] the KCC ruled that this blanket restriction was excessive, as sex-selective abortions were no longer prevalent

195 J.Y. Interpretation No. 649 (2008) (Constitutional Court of Taiwan), available at http://cons.judicial.gov.tw/jcc/en-us/jep03/show?expno=649, accessed 9 May 2021.

196 *Case on the Monopoly of Massage Therapists by Visually Impaired Persons*, 2003Hun-Ma715, 2006Hun-Ma368 (25 May 2006) (Constitutional Court of Korea).

197 Article 61(4) of the Medical Service Act read: 'Matters necessary for accreditation of massagists, limit of their service and criteria for facilities in massage treatment houses or massage parlors, etc. shall be determined by the Ordinance of the Ministry of Health and Welfare.'

198 In the KCC, six votes are required to render a law unconstitutional. Article 23(2) of the Constitutional Court Act of South Korea reads: 'The Full Bench shall make a decision on a case by the majority vote of Justices participating in the final review: Provided that a vote of six or more Justices is required in any of the following cases: 1. Where it decides to rule a statute unconstitutional, sustain impeachment, dissolve a political party, or uphold a constitutional complaint; and 2. Where it overrules the Constitutional Court's precedent on interpretation and application of the Constitution or statutes.'

199 *Case on the Monopoly of Massage Therapists by Visually Impaired Persons*, 2003Hun-Ma715, 2006Hun-Ma368 (25 May 2006) (Constitutional Court of Korea) (Official English Summary).

200 Article 82(1) of the Medical Service Act reads: 'A massage therapist shall be a visually-impaired person . . .'.

201 *Visually Impaired Massagers Case*, 2006Hun-Ma1098 (30 October 2008) (Constitutional Court of Korea); 2008Hun-Ma664 (29 July 2010) (Constitutional Court of Korea); 2011Hun-Ka39 (27 June 2013) (Constitutional Court of Korea); 2017Hun-Ka15 (28 December 2017) (Constitutional Court of Korea).

202 Since only five judges ruled against the impugned Rule in 2006 on the basis that it was disproportionate, the KCC in the 2008 massage sequel determined that its 2006 ruling on SP was not binding. See The Constitutional Court of Korea (n. 164) 509.

203 Article 20(2) of the Medical Service Act read: 'No medical person shall divulge the sex of a fetus which he/she has discovered through a diagnosis or examination of a fetus or a pregnant woman, to the pregnant woman herself or her family or other person.'

204 *Case on the Prohibition of Revealing the Sex of a Foetus*, 2004Hun-Ma1010 (31 July 2008) (Constitutional Court of Korea).

205 Ibid. (Official English Translation).

in contemporary South Korea and there was no harm in disclosing the child's sex at the later stages of the pregnancy when an abortion was virtually impossible.[206] Hence, the law was declared incompatible with the Constitution and the National Assembly was 'urged'[207] to pass remedial legislation by 31 December 2009. After this decision, the National Assembly revised the impugned law and the sex of the foetus may now be disclosed 32 weeks into the pregnancy.[208]

Even more fascinating is the KCC's decision in 2019 to declare Korea's laws against abortion incompatible with the Constitution.[209] Notably, the Mother and Child Health Act banned abortions in all stages of the woman's pregnancy, except in very limited circumstances.[210] Therefore, insofar as this prohibition applied even when the foetus was not viable, and regardless of the woman's socio-economic status, marital status and even if she was a minor, the impugned law had exceeded 'the minimum extent necessary to achieve the legislative purpose'[211] of protecting the life of the foetus. A delayed declaration of invalidity was granted and the National Assembly has been given until 31 December 2020 to pass remedial legislation.[212]

In 2014, the KCC also ruled that it was disproportionate to bar all prisoners, including probationers, from voting.[213] While the KCC accepted that the state may legitimately want to punish criminals and encourage civic behaviour, the impugned law swept too broadly as no distinction was made between the 'type, elements or degree of culpability of a specific crime'.[214] Furthermore, it was unnecessary to

206 Ibid. (Official English Translation).
207 Ibid. (Official English Translation).
208 Article 20(2) of the Medical Service Act.
209 *Case on the Crime of Abortion*, 2017Hun-Ba127 (11 April 2019) (Constitutional Court of Korea).
210 Article 14(1) of the Mother and Child Health Act read: 'A medical doctor may perform an induced abortion operation with the consent of the pregnant woman herself and her spouse ... only in the following cases: 1. Where she or her spouse suffers from any eugenic or genetic mental disability or physical disease prescribed by Presidential Decree; 2. Where she or her spouse suffers from any contagious disease prescribed by Presidential Decree; 3. Where she is impregnated by rape or quasi-rape; 4. Where pregnancy is taken place between relatives by blood or by marriage who are legally unable to marry; 5. Where the maintenance of pregnancy severely injures or is likely to injure the health of the pregnant woman for health or medical reasons.'
211 *Case on the Crime of Abortion*, 2017Hun-Ba127 (11 April 2019) (Constitutional Court of Korea) (Official English Summary).
212 As of 17 November 2020, the National Assembly has not revised this law.
213 Article 18(1)[2] of the Public Official Election Act read: 'A person falling under any of the following subparagraphs ... shall be disfranchised: 1 ... 2. A person who is sentenced to imprisonment without prison labour or a heavier punishment, but whose sentence execution has not been terminated or whose sentence execution has not been decided to be exempted.' In addition, Article 43(2) of the Criminal Act read: 'A person who is sentenced to imprisonment for a limited term or imprisonment without prison labor for a limited term shall be under suspension of qualifications as mentioned in subparagraphs 1 through 3 of the preceding paragraph until the execution of punishment is completed or remitted.' And subparagraph 2 of Article 43(1) concerns the 'Suffrage and eligibility under public Act.'
214 *Restriction on Right to Vote of Prisoners and Probationers with Suspended Sentence*, 2012Hun-Ma409, 510, 2013Hun-Ma167 (consolidated) (28 January 2014) (Constitutional Court of Korea). The Hong Kong Court

restrict the right to vote of probationers, as they were practically living normal lives.[215] Therefore, the KCC declared that it was unconstitutional to bar probationers from voting, while the government has been given until 31 December 2015 to draft a remedial legislation for other prisoners. In response to this ruling, the National Assembly revised the law and prisoners whose sentences are less than one year are now given the vote.[216]

South Korea remains one of the very few countries in the world that still requires all able-bodied men to serve in the military for a few years. No exemptions are provided on religious grounds, and Jehovah's Witnesses are regularly prosecuted for refusing to serve. In view of the relatively small number of conscientious objectors, the KCC in 2018 determined that the government's failure to provide them with an alternative to combat service 'runs against the rule of minimum restriction', especially since such a scheme would *not* have a 'significant influence to the national defense power of Korea'.[217] Furthermore, the KCC believed that a well-designed alternative scheme to combat service could include procedures to identify genuine cases and ensure equity between those in combat service and those assigned elsewhere.[218] Consequently, a Suspension Order was granted and the government has been given until 31 December 2019 to implement an alternative to combat service for conscientious objectors.[219]

## STAGE 4: BALANCING

The 'balancing' sub-test is the KCC's deployment of proportionality *stricto sensu*. When used to subvert legislation, the Court is essentially making a determination

of First Instance invalidated a comparable legislation: see *Chan Kin Sum v. Secretary of Justice* [2009] 2 HKLRD 166 (Hong Kong Court of First Instance).

215 Ibid. (Official English Translation).

216 Article 18(1)[2] of the Public Official Election Act; Article 43 (2) of the Criminal Act.

217 *Case on Conscientious Objectors*, 2011Hun-Ba379, (28 June 2018) (Constitutional Court of Korea) (Official English Summary).

218 Ibid. (Official English Summary).

219 The Military Service Act has been revised to allow conscientious objectors to military service to serve alternative duties at correctional facilities, and their duties include cooking and caring for prison inmates. This service will be for three years, in lieu of two years' military service. See Jung Da-min, 'New System of Military Service Begins' (*The Korean Times*, 30 June 2020), available at www.koreatimes.co.kr/www/nation/2020/07/205_292068.html, accessed 13 July 2020.

Notably, the TCC also confronted the same issue in 1999, but the Court herein upheld the impugned law. The TCC very curtly asserted that the law did not 'undermine the principle of proportionality bestowed in Article 23.' See J.Y. Interpretation No. 490 (1999) (Constitutional Court of Taiwan), at [1], available at http://cons.judicial.gov.tw/jcc/en-us/jep03/show?expno=490, accessed 9 May 2021. Nevertheless, the Taiwanese government voluntarily revised the Conscription Act in 2000 and included an alternative to combat service for conscientious objectors. See Chien-Chih Lin, 'Unpatriotic Heretics or Conscientious Objectors: Difficulties which Jehovah Witnesses Face in Taiwan and South Korea' (2010) 5 *National Taiwan University Law Review* 201.

that the social benefits from the law are outweighed by the burdens imposed on the individuals concerned.

In 1999, the KCC upended the government's policy of awarding military veterans with extra points when they sat for the civil service entrance examinations.[220] As all able-bodied men have to serve in the military in South Korea, this policy in substance discriminated against women and men with disabilities. The extra points would be conferred on the veteran for every civil service examination he undertook for an unlimited number of times. Central to the KCC's decision is how the adverse effects of the policy significantly outweighed the tangible benefits conferred on veterans. While a veteran would only be awarded an extra three to five percentage points per entrance examination, the Court noted that the score difference between a successful and a failed applicant was often less one percentage point. The KCC trawled through scores of data and pointed out that in the Grade 7 Administrative Examination, only 6.4 per cent of those hired did not benefit from this affirmative action. In substance, this policy was excluding women and disabled men from the civil service, and this gender imbalance would have a deleterious impact on the workforce and nation's drive towards sex equality. Therefore, the KCC determined that 'in comparing . . . the seriousness of the harm, the veterans' extra point system is seriously lacking a balance between the legal interests'.[221] This extra point system has since been abolished.

The KCC in 2002 was confronted with a tax law that required married couples to combine their annual income for the purposes of tax assessment, such that many families would be subject to a higher tax rate as a result of this aggregation.[222] In other words, married couples would pay more taxes than if they were single and taxed as individuals. While the Court accepted that the government had a legitimate aim of preventing spouses from reducing their tax liability by transferring income *inter se*, the KCC decided that this law simply failed Stage 4 of SP for its disproportionate impact on married couples:

> This [tax] disadvantage does not only concern those in the high-income group but also widely affects those in middle-income groups with asset income. The scope of disadvantage suffered by a married couple with asset income is rather large. The public interest of the society achieved through cumulative taxation for asset income, namely, prevention of tax evasion through fictitious income dispersion, realization of fair taxation in accordance with individual tax-bearing capacity, and achievement of an income redistribution effect is not as large as expected. When comparing these two competing interests, the private interest being neglected through cumulative taxation for asset income of married couples, is greater than

[220] *Constitutional Complaint Against Article 8(1) of the Support for Discharged Soldiers Act*, 98Hun-Ma363 (23 December 1999) (Constitutional Court of Korea).

[221] Ibid. (Official English Translation).

[222] *Cumulative Taxation of Income from Assets of Spouses Case*, 2001Hun-Ba82 (29 August 2002) (Constitutional Court of Korea).

> the public interest of the society achieved through such a practice, and cumulative taxation for asset income fails the balance of interest test.[223]

This KCC decision has been criticized on the basis that its primary beneficiaries were rich families who had significant savings, shares and real estate, especially since the impugned tax law had an income-retributive effect as low-income families were generally unaffected by the legislation.[224]

Like the TCC, the KCC also uses SP to assess the proportionality of statutorily imposed minimum sentences. In 2009, the KCC invalidated a penal law that required courts to impose on all persons convicted of election-related bribery a fine equivalent to 50 times the amount of the bribe they received.[225] The Court was emphatic that this law has 'lo[st] the balance between the violation of duty and the responsibility or the violation of principle of proportionality',[226] as the penal punishment imposed a 'flat 50 times administrative penalty'[227] on all offenders, without taking into account the offenders' degree of culpability, motivation, personal circumstances, or whether the bribe was eventually returned or surrendered. The law has since been revised to confer upon courts a discretion to impose a fine that ranges between 10 and 50 times the value of the bribe.[228] In the same vein, a military law which imposed the death penalty on all soldiers who murdered their military superiors was invalidated on the basis that it was 'out of proportion'[229] to impose capital punishment uniformly, and not consider the accused's motives and circumstances of the killing. The law has since been revised to allow the trial judge to sentence the offender to 'imprisonment with labour for an indefinite term',[230] in lieu of the death penalty.

Finally, in 2018, the KCC determined that Article 8 of the Act on Use and Protection of DNA Identification Information[231] was disproportionate insofar as the law did not establish a procedure by which a person could challenge the legality

223 Ibid. (Official English Translation).

224 The Constitutional Court of Korea, *Thirty Years of the Constitutional Court of Korea* (The Constitutional Court of Korea 2018) 421. The National Assembly removed this aggregation of taxable income for married couples in December 2002.

225 *Case on 50 Times Administrative Penalty Fee for Violators of Public Official Election Act*, 2007Hun-Ka22 (26 March 2009) (Constitutional Court of Korea).

226 Ibid. (Official English Translation).

227 Ibid.

228 Article 261(9) of the Public Official Election Act.

229 *Constitutional Review of Article 53 Section 1 of the Military Criminal Act*, 2006Hun-Ka13 (29 November 2007) (Constitutional Court of Korea) (Official English Translation).

230 Article 53(1) of the Military Criminal Act.

231 Article 8 of the Act on Use and Protection of DNA Identification Information read: '(1) A public prosecutor may collect DNA samples from a person ... with a warrant issued by the competent district court judge ... (2) A judicial police officer may collect DNA samples from a person ... with a warrant issued by the competent district court judge...'.

of the warrant issued by the state to collect his or her DNA sample.[232] While the KCC agreed that the issuance of such a warrant served the public interest by 'contributing to crime investigation and its prevention in the future',[233] the failure to provide procedural protections for the accused rendered their right to a fair trial nugatory and treated 'the person subject to collection of DNA samples as only subjects of [a] crime investigation'.[234] Therefore, the 'balance of interests [between the state interests and the constitutional rights] is deemed not have been reached'.[235] A Suspension Order was granted and the government has been given until 31 December 2018 to pass remedial legislation.[236]

## PART 3: HONG KONG

### DEVELOPMENT OF SP

Before the Basic Law came into force in 1997, and prior to China's resumption of sovereignty over Hong Kong, the Bill of Rights Ordinance (BORO)[237] was passed in 1991 by the colonial government to 'bring home' the rights the British government acceded to in 1976 when it ratified the International Covenant on Civil and Political Rights (ICCPR) and extended its application to Hong Kong.[238] (The passage of the BORO was, in particular, triggered by the violent suppression of the student demonstrators in Tiananmen Square over the summer of 1989.) In *Sin Yau Ming (1991)*,[239] the Court of Appeal invalidated the first law in Hong Kong for violating BORO. On the facts, statutory provisions, which presumed that the accused were drug traffickers if they were found in possession of certain amounts of prohibited drugs, were deemed to have disproportionately restricted their right to a presumption of innocence until proven guilty. While the Canadian *Oakes*[240] test was cited favourably when PA was first applied in Hong Kong,[241] PA in colonial Hong Kong lacked structure. This was a consequence of the Privy Council of Hong Kong's warning against 'follow[ing] the somewhat complex process now established in Canada',[242] such that when Hong Kong courts determined whether a legislative

232 *Case on the Procedure for the Issuance of a Warrant to Collect DNA Samples*, 2017Hun-Ma630 (30 August 2018) (Constitutional Court of Korea).

233 Ibid. (Official English Summary).

234 Ibid.

235 Ibid.

236 The National Assembly revised this provision on 21 January 2020.

237 (Cap 383).

238 See Richard Swede, 'One Territory – Three Systems? The Hong Kong Bill of Rights' (1995) 44 *International & Comparative Law Quarterly* 358.

239 *R* v. *Sin Yau-ming* [1992] 1 HKCLR 127 (Hong Kong Court of Appeal).

240 *R* v. *Oakes* [1986] 1 SCR 103.

241 *Sin Yau-ming* (n. 239).

242 *Attorney General of Hong Kong* v. *Lee Kwong-Kut* [1993] 2 HKCLR 186 (Privy Council of Hong Kong) 200.

restriction was justified, 'the tests which been identified in Canada do not need to be applied rigidly or cumulatively'.[243]

With the establishment of the Hong Kong Special Administrative Region (HKSAR) in 1997, constitutional rights enshrined in the Basic Law co-exist with statutory rights protected in BORO, which was retained post-handover.[244] Notably, neither the Basic Law nor BORO enshrines a general limitation-clause on rights. Therefore, SP in Hong Kong is largely judicially constructed.

In its first PA decision, the HKCFA in *Ng Kung Siu* (1999)[245] also retained the colonial aversion to SP. Therein, when determining the constitutionality of a statutory ban on flag desecration, the HKCFA merely assessed whether there was a legitimate aim for the law and whether the law was necessary. Specifically, proportionality was merely invoked when the Court was engaging in the necessity analysis[246] and this discussion was perfunctory. The impugned legislation was swiftly upheld on the basis that it served the goals of nation building under the 'One Country, Two Systems' constitutional model[247] and the law only imposed a 'limited restriction'[248] as only 'one mode'[249] of expression was prohibited, leaving persons with the freedom to express the same message by other means.[250] Subsequently, in *Solicitor* v. *Law Society of Hong Kong* (2003),[251] the HKCFA invoked PA to invalidate a law for the first time. An ouster clause that barred the HKCFA from hearing all appeals from the Solicitors Disciplinary Tribunal was struck down on the basis that the 'nature and extent'[252] of the blanket prohibition was not reasonably proportionate to the legitimate purpose of regulating the scope of the HKCFA's jurisdiction.[253]

A three-stage SP was finally endorsed by the HKCFA in *Leung Kwok Hung* (2005).[254] Citing the Privy Council in *De Freitas* v. *Permanent Secretary of Ministry of Agriculture, Fisheries, Lands and Housing*[255] with approval, the HKCFA formulated its proportionality test in the following terms: (1) the restriction must be *rationally connected* with one or more of the *legitimate purposes* and (2) the means used to impair the right ... must be no more than is *necessary* to accomplish

243 Ibid.
244 Po Jen Yap and Francis Chung, 'Statutory Rights and De facto Constitutional Supremacy in Hong Kong?' (2019) 17 *International Journal of Constitutional Law* 836.
245 *HKSAR* v. *Ng Kung Siu* [1999] 2 HKCFAR 442 (Hong Kong Court of Final Appeal).
246 Ibid. 461.
247 Ibid. 460.
248 Ibid. 461.
249 Ibid. 456.
250 Rehan Abeyratne, 'More Structure, More Deference?: Proportionality in Hong Kong' in Po Jen Yap (ed.), *Proportionality in Asia* (Cambridge University Press 2020) 32.
251 *Solicitor* v. *Law Society of Hong Kong* [2003] 6 HKCFAR 570 (Hong Kong Court of Final Appeal).
252 Ibid. [33].
253 Ibid. [40].
254 *Leung Kwok Hung* v. *HKSAR* [2005] 8 HKCFAR 229 (Hong Kong Court of Final Appeal).
255 [1999] 1 AC 69.

the legitimate purpose in question.[256] While framed as a two-stage analysis, this structured test encompassed the three stages of SP: the 'legitimacy', 'rational connection' and 'necessity' tests. Nevertheless, unlike *De Freitas*, the Hong Kong courts herein would not examine whether a legislative objective was 'sufficiently important'[257] to justify a rights-derogation. It would suffice if the government's purpose was legitimate. On the facts, a law which imposed a requirement on persons to notify the police prior to a public demonstration was deemed proportionate as the government had to be given time to 'take reasonable and appropriate measures to enable lawful assemblies to take place peacefully';[258] the notification requirement only applied to public demonstrations that consisted of more than 30 persons; the Police Commissioner had to act proportionately when deliberating on the notified demonstration and within tight statutory time-limits; and his discretion was subject to judicial review.[259]

Finally, in *Hysan* (2016),[260] the HKCFA added a fourth step to its SP:

> [W]here an encroaching measure has passed the three-step test, the analysis should incorporate a fourth step asking whether a reasonable balance has been struck between the societal benefits of the encroachment and the inroads made into the constitutionally protected rights of the individual, asking in particular whether pursuit of the societal interest results in an unacceptably harsh burden on the individual.[261]

Central to the HKCFA's decision to adopt this fourth step is the Supreme Court of the United Kingdom (UKSC)'s current endorsement of this four-stage SP.[262] The HKCFA's judgment in *Hysan* was replete with references to UKSC contemporary jurisprudence, and the Court also noted how *de Freitas* – the Privy Council decision which the HKCFA had relied on for its three-stage SP – has been cast aside as 'deficient in omitting reference to the fourth step'.[263] On the facts in *Hysan*, the HKCFA determined that planning restrictions imposed by the Town Planning Board on private property rights exercised by landowners/developers had to be subject to this four-step proportionality assessment.

Moreover, integrated within SP is a margin of appreciation that the HKCFA accords to the relative informational or institutional advantages the political

256 *Leung Kwok Hung* (n. 254) [36].
257 Ibid. [38].
258 Ibid. [92].
259 Ibid. [92].
260 *Hysan Development* v. *Town Planning Board* [2016] 19 HKCFAR 372 ( Hong Kong Court of Final Appeal).
261 Ibid. [135].
262 See *R (Aguilar Quila)* v. *Secretary of State for the Home Department* [2012] 1 AC 621, [45]; *Bank Mellat* v. *Her Majesty's Treasury (No. 2)* [2014] AC 700, [20] and [65]; *R (Lord Carlile of Berriew)* v. *Secretary of State for the Home Department* [2015] AC 945, [19], [98] and [148].
263 *Hysan Development* (n. 260) [66].

branches of government have over policy issues like national security[264] and resource allocation.[265] In determining how wide the margin of discretion should be, the HKCFA would examine '[t]he content and features of the impugned measure, the identity and constitutional role of its originator and any special competence possessed by such person'.[266] In *Hysan*, after noting that town planning is a polycentric exercise that involves the careful consideration of 'competing views after consultation with the public and with the parties affected with the benefit of input from relevant experts',[267] the HKCFA blunted the force of this new-found proportionality oversight by determining that if such governmental restrictions are 'unassailable on traditional judicial review grounds',[268] these limitations would 'in general only be susceptible to constitutional review if the Court is satisfied that they are manifestly without reasonable foundation'.[269]

In *Kwok Cheuk Kin*,[270] the HKCFA extended its doctrine on deference to the constitutionality of electoral restrictions. As explained by the Court, these electoral laws involve 'political or policy considerations'[271] for which the Court is 'not in a position nor is it equipped'[272] to determine their necessity. In short, the HKCFA would simply defer on 'matters of political judgment and assessment'.[273] This ground for deference will be further explained and explored in Chapter 5.

## STAGE 1: LEGITIMATE AIM

Only two laws have ever been invalidated in Hong Kong for failing to meet Stage 1 of SP and, notably, they both concern gay rights.

In *Leung* v. *Secretary for Justice* (2006),[274] the Court of Appeal (HKCA) struck down a legislative provision which required a person to be at least 21 years old before he engages in buggery. While this law ostensibly applied to both homosexual and heterosexual buggery, the Court agreed that the legislation would have a greater adverse impact on gay men[275] and would need to be justified using SP. More importantly, Chief Judge of the High Court Geoffrey Ma (as he then was) concluded that this law served no legitimate purpose:

264 Ibid. [117].
265 Ibid. [118].
266 Ibid. [114].
267 Ibid. [126].
268 Ibid. [129].
269 Ibid.
270 *Kwok Cheuk Kin* v. *Secretary for Constitutional and Mainland Affairs* [2017] 20 HKCFAR 353 (Hong Kong Court of Final Appeal).
271 Ibid. [42].
272 Ibid. [55].
273 Ibid. [55].
274 *Leung* v. *Secretary for Justice* [2006] 4 HKLRD 211 (Hong Kong Court of Appeal).
275 Ibid. [48].

> For my part, I fail to see on any basis the justification of this age limit. No evidence has been placed before us to explain why the minimum age requirement for buggery is 21 whereas as far as sexual intercourse between a man and a woman is concerned, the age of consent is only 16. There is, for example, no medical reason for this and none was suggested in the course of argument.[276]

Notably, the age of majority in Hong Kong is 18[277] and this law was impacting adults. Therefore, the CA rightly refused to allow the government to justify their conduct by merely asserting, without more, that 'homosexual and heterosexual activities were to be regarded differently'.[278]

Similarly, in *Yau Yuk Lung* (2007),[279] the HKCFA invalidated a statutory provision that criminalized homosexual buggery in public. Notably, there was no statutory equivalent that prohibited heterosexual intercourse in public, but such conduct was and remains sanctioned under the common law offence of public indecency that applies to all persons. The HKCFA was adamant that the need for the law 'cannot be established from the mere act of legislative enactment'.[280] Given that the government was unable to explain why homosexual buggery in public had to be codified as a statutory crime, while heterosexual intercourse in public was prosecuted under the common law, this law 'fail[ed] at the first stage of the justification test'.[281]

## STAGE 2: RATIONAL CONNECTION

The HKCFA has invalidated governmental rules on the basis that they fail Stage 2 of SP in three instances. But on the first occasion, this rational connection test had extraordinary bite.

In *Kong Yunming* (2013),[282] the HKCFA unanimously invalidated the government's policy, which required all recipients of the Comprehensive Social Security Assistance Scheme (CSSA) to have been a Hong Kong resident for at least seven years, on the basis that there was no rational nexus between the 7-year Rule and the government's avowed legitimate aim of ensuring the sustainability of the welfare system.

The HKCFA first found that there was no rational connection between the 7-year Rule and the avowed legitimate aim, as this Rule conflicted with the government's One Way Permit (OWP) scheme of allowing immigrants from Mainland China to

276 Ibid. [51(2)].
277 Ibid. [51(4)].
278 Ibid.
279 *Secretary for Justice* v. *Yau Yuk Lung* [2007] 10 HKCFAR 335 (Hong Kong Court of Final Appeal).
280 Ibid. [27].
281 Ibid.
282 *Kong Yunming* v. *Director of Social Welfare* [2013] 16 HKCFAR 950 (Hong Kong Court of Final Appeal).

reunite with their existing families based in Hong Kong. According to the HKCFA, the 7-year Rule was 'counter-productive'[283] as it deterred potential new arrivals who were without sufficient income to meet their basic needs in Hong Kong and this Rule therefore conflicted with the OWP policy of family union.[284] But in doing so, the HKCFA oddly disregarded another aim of the OWP: to ensure the gradual orderly admission of new arrivals and to prevent the local infrastructure in Hong Kong from being overburdened by an influx of Mainland immigration.[285]

Furthermore, the HKCFA also determined that no rational connection existed because the 7-year Rule conflicted with the governmental policy of responding to Hong Kong's ageing population problem. According to the HKCFA, only a small proportion of elderly persons who entered Hong Kong under the OWP scheme received social welfare, and hence savings to welfare expenditure from elderly new arrivals 'would be minimal and could hardly qualify as a response to the ageing population problem, aimed at ensuring the sustainability of the welfare system'.[286] Unfortunately, the HKCFA failed to fully grasp the government's argument on Hong Kong's ageing population. The 7-year Rule addressed the problems associated with Hong Kong's ageing population *not* primarily by saving on CSSA benefits that would have been given to *new elderly arrivals*. Instead, this 7-year Rule requirement allowed the government to save on CSSA benefits that would have been given to all *new adult arrivals* (young or elderly) and to use these savings to support a growing number of local elderly people in Hong Kong.[287]

Finally, the HKCFA in *Kong Yunming* also held that there was no rational connection between the 7-year Rule and the avowed legitimate aim because the Rule could only achieve modest CSSA savings. The HKCFA relied on the statistics for the fiscal year 2001–2002 as an example, and noted that if the 7-year Rule had been in effect then, the government would have saved less than HK$764 million out of a total CSSA expenditure of HK $14.4 billion that year.[288] According to the HKCFA, such a 'relatively insignificant level of savings . . . severely undermines'[289] the suggestion the 7-year Rule was rationally connected to the avowed legitimate aim of safeguarding the sustainability of the social security system. The fact that

[283] Ibid. [64].

[284] Ibid. [64]–[66].

[285] Since 1995, the OWP scheme has had a daily quota of 150 Mainland immigrants. According to the Task Force on Population Policy, whose Report was cited by the HKCFA in *Kong Yunming* (n. 282) [55], in implementing the OWP, 'a proper balance has to be struck between orderly admission of new arrivals from the Mainland, both children and spouses, and upholding family unity'.

[286] *Kong Yunming* (n. 282) [75].

[287] This is evidenced by a passage in the Task Force Report (cited again by the HKCFA in *Kong Yunming* at [70]), which states the following: 'One serious economic problem caused by an accelerated increase in the number of elderly people in the population is social security payments. The Government is committed to providing financial assistance to elderly people in need.'

[288] *Kong Yunming* (n. 282) [94]–[95].

[289] Ibid. [96].

there was a 'relatively insignificant level of savings'[290] suggests that such savings actually occurred and a rational connection can be established. In fact, one may note that in the fiscal year 2012–2013 – the fiscal year that immediately preceded the HKCFA decision of *Kong Yunming* – the HK government actually spent about HK$19 billion on CSSA.[291] Post-*Kong Yunming*, in the fiscal year 2016–2017, the CSSA expenditure has ballooned to approximately HK$ 22 billion.[292] But it is equally significant that Hong Kong's annual budget surplus was over HK$ 100 billion in the fiscal years 2016–2017[293] and 2017–2018.[294] Regardless of whether one agrees that the cost imposition of HK$ 764 million (or even HK$ 3 billion[295]) a year would be a 'relatively insignificant'[296] drain on the city's coffers, *Kong Yunming* marked a monumental decision, as the HKCFA has decisively conferred the constitutional right of social welfare on all residents who have lived in Hong Kong for at least a year – the pre-existing welfare entitlement prior to the establishment of the HKSAR.[297]

In *QT* (2018),[298] the HKCFA also upended the government's discriminatory practice of denying spousal visas to expatriates hired in Hong Kong but who were in same-sex marriages or civil unions legally registered overseas. Notably, this was achieved under Stage 2 of SP: the government had two avowed objectives but its discriminatory policy had no rational connection to the achievement of either aim. First, the government had professed it wanted to encourage foreign talent to join Hong Kong's workforce. But as pointed out by the HKCFA:

> In cases like the present, the sponsor has been granted an employment visa presumably because he or she has the talent or skills deemed needed or desirable. Such a person could be straight or gay. The Policy is, as the Director [of Immigration] has stated, aimed at encouraging such persons to join our workforce 'by giving them the choice of bringing in their dependants to live with them in Hong Kong' ... it runs wholly counter to the Director's stated aim to say: 'You can

290 Ibid.

291 Social Welfare Department, 'Social Welfare Services in Figures 2014' (2014) p. 5, available at https://web.archive.org/web/20150924112329/http://www.swd.gov.hk/doc/res_stat/swdfig2014.pdf, accessed 5 August 2019.

292 Social Welfare Department, 'Social Welfare Services in Figures 2017' (2017) p .5, available at www.swd.gov.hk/storage/asset/section/296/en/swdfig2017.pdf, accessed 5 August 2019.

293 Census and Statistics Department, 'Hong Kong Annual Digest of Statistics 2017' (October 2017) p. 245, available at www.statistics.gov.hk/pub/B10100032017AN17B0100.pdf, accessed 5 August 2019.

294 The Financial Secretary, 'The 2018–19 Budget: Appendix A: Medium Range Forecast' (March 2018) p. 7, available at www.budget.gov.hk/2018/eng/pdf/e_appendices_a.pdf, accessed 5 August 2019.

295 While the CSSA expenditure has increased by about HK$3 billion since the CFA decision of *Kong Yunming*, it is unclear how much of that sum is attributable to the removal of the 7-year residency Rule.

296 *Kong Yunming* (n. 282) [96].

297 Ibid. [44] and [186].

298 *QT* v. *Director of Immigration* [2018] HKCFA 28 (Hong Kong Court of Final Appeal).

> bring in your partner provided that he or she is straight and would be viewed as married validly under Hong Kong law.' Such a policy is counterproductive and plainly not rationally connected to advancing the 'talent' aim.[299]

The immigration policy's attempt at achieving the second avowed aim – to promote strict immigration control by drawing clear, bright administrative lines – fared no better. As observed by the HKCFA:

> But even purely at the level of convenience, [same sex couples] are just as conveniently able to produce their civil partnership certificate. Excluding them on the basis of administrative convenience is irrational. More substantively, the rationality in question is not about the convenience of drawing of bright lines but about the rationality of the demarcation. We are back to the question of why the line is drawn, not how clearly it can be drawn ... Given that the Policy cannot be justified as a measure rationally connected to the avowed 'talent' and 'immigration control' objectives, it is not saved by the 'bright line' aim.[300]

In compliance with the HKCFA decision in *QT*, the Hong Kong government now grants dependant visas to spouses of expatriates, working in Hong Kong, who are in same-sex marriages or civil unions.

Post-*QT (2018)*, the HKCFA next ruled in *Leung Chun Kwong* (2019)[301] that it was unconstitutional for the Hong Kong government to deny spousal benefits to civil servants who were in same-sex marriages legally registered overseas, and to disallow them to claim tax benefits as a family unit. While the HKCFA accepted that that it was a legitimate aim for the government to protect monogamous heterosexual marriages,[302] there was no rational connection between the impugned rules and this aim. First, the HKCFA determined that it 'cannot logically be argued that any person is encouraged to enter into an opposite-sex marriage in Hong Kong because a same-sex spouse is denied those benefits'.[303] Second, the denial of spousal benefits to same-sex married couples in the civil service undercuts the government's own published 'employment policies dedicated to the elimination of discrimination on the ground of sexual orientation'.[304] Third, the tax law simply did not 'serve the purpose of promoting traditional heterosexual monogamous marriage',[305] as polygamous marriages are recognized in Hong Kong for tax purposes.[306] Relying on both *QT* and *Leung Chun Kwong*, the HKCFI in *Ng Hon Lam* (2020) ruled that

299 Ibid. [90].
300 Ibid. [97]–[99].
301 *Leung Chun Kwong* v. *Secretary for the Civil Service* [2019] HKCFA 19 (Hong Kong Court of Final Appeal).
302 Ibid. [61].
303 Ibid. [67].
304 Ibid. [74].
305 Ibid. [75].
306 The term 'marriage' in Section 2(1) of the Inland Revenue Ordinance (Cap 112) is defined to include a man and his 'principal wife'.

the statutory denial of benefits to a person's same-sex partner who died intestate failed Stage 2 of SP as it was 'illogical to suggest that the denial of benefits under [Hong Kong's intestacy laws] to same-sex couples'[307] would encourage opposite-sex couples to marry.

## STAGE 3: NO MORE THAN NECESSARY

Most laws in Hong Kong are invalidated on the basis that they are no more than necessary to achieve the legislative goal in question. Specifically, statutory prohibitions that impose blanket or absolute prohibitions on a constitutional right rarely pass muster.

In *Kwok Hay Kwong*[308] (2006), the HKCA invalidated restrictions which *inter alia* prohibited doctors from providing basic information about their practice in newspapers, magazines, or other print media, and limiting them to signboards and directories. While the prevention of misleading advertisements was a valid concern, the Court held that 'there must be less intrusive means of dealing with the concerns ... other than a total ban'.[309] In 2008, the Medical Code was revised to allow doctors to provide basic service information about their practice in newspapers and periodicals.[310]

Similarly, like the KCC,[311] the Hong Kong Court of First Instance (HKCFI) in *Chan Kin Sum*[312] (2008) invalidated a blanket legislative ban on the prisoners' right to vote as unconstitutional. The Court acknowledged that the legislature was entitled to sanction the conduct of convicted prisoners and provide incentives for the citizenry to exercise civic responsibility.[313] Notwithstanding these legitimate aims, the Court endorsed the European Court of Human Rights Decision in *Hirst* v. *United Kingdom (No. 2)*[314] and determined that an absolute statutory prohibition was disproportionate, as all prisoners were barred from voting, regardless of the nature and severity of the offences or even the length of the custodial sentences.[315] Even prisoners on suspended sentences or released on parole were barred from voting.[316] Nevertheless, the Court was willing to suspend its declaration of invalidity

307 *Ng Hon Lam* v. *Secretary for Justice* [2020] HKCFI 2412 (Hong Kong Court of First Instance) [44].

308 *Kwok Hay Kwong* v. *Medical Council of Hong Kong* [2008] 3 HKLRD 524 (Hong Kong Court of Appeal).

309 Ibid. [47].

310 Medical Council of Hong Kong, 'Code of Professional Conduct: For the Guidance of Registered Medical Practitioners' (January 2016), available at www.mchk.org.hk/english/code/files/Code_of_Professional_Conduct_2016.pdf, accessed 5 August 2019.

311 *Restriction on Right to Vote of Prisoners and Probationers with Suspended Sentence*, 2012Hun-Ma409, 510, 2013Hun-Ma167 (consolidated) (28 January 2014) (Constitutional Court of Korea).

312 *Chan Kin Sum* v. *Secretary of Justice* [2009] 2 HKLRD 166 (Hong Kong Court of First Instance).

313 Ibid. [88].

314 [2006] 42 EHRR 849 (European Court of Human Rights).

315 *Chan Kin Sum* (n. 312) [112].

316 Ibid. [114].

for about seven months, as the learned judge considered that the legislature would 'legitimately require and deserve a reasonable period of time to work out a replacement arrangement, whatever it may be'.[317] Interestingly, in 2009, the Hong Kong Legislative Council, after deliberation, responded by repealing *all* restrictions on prisoners' right to vote, thus achieving a result that went beyond what was mandated in *Chan Kin Sum*.

In *Mok Charles* (2010),[318] the HKCFA invalidated a finality clause[319] that barred the HKCFA from hearing petitions arising from disputes over Legislative Council elections. While the HKCFA accepted that the legislature was seeking to pursue a legitimate aim – the speedy determination of an election petition – the 'absolute bar on an appeal'[320] went further than necessary to address this aim, especially since the HKCFA was statutorily empowered to resolve petitions relating to Chief Executive elections[321] and proceedings challenging the qualifications of Legislative Council members,[322] and 'no difference was given by [the government] to demonstrate the reason for this difference of approach'.[323] In compliance with *Mok Charles*, the HKCFA is now statutorily authorized to hear appeals on election petitions arising from Legislative Council elections.[324]

Back in 2006, the HKCFA in *Chan Wing Hing* (2006)[325] also invalidated a bankruptcy provision on the basis that it disproportionately restricted a bankrupt's constitutional right to travel.[326] On the facts, the impugned provision had required a bankrupt to notify his trustee of his travel itinerary prior to any trip outside of Hong Kong or the relevant period of his bankruptcy would not continue to run during the absence. The HKCFA deemed this sanction too disproportionate, as it operated irrespective of the bankrupt's reasons for non-notification and the stage of his bankruptcy, leaving the courts with no discretion to mitigate its consequences.[327] Similarly, in *Zhi Charles* (2015),[328] the HKCFA invalidated another bankruptcy provision, which provided that when a bankrupt left Hong Kong before the commencement of his bankruptcy, the relevant period of his bankruptcy would be suspended until he returned to Hong Kong and notified his trustee of his return. As this sanction imposed by the bankruptcy provision applied regardless of whether the bankrupt was willing to cooperate with his trustee or whether the bankrupt was

317 *Chan Kin Sum* v. *Secretary of Justice* [2009] HKEC 393 (Hong Kong Court of First Instance) [79].
318 *Mok Charles* v. *Tam Wai Ho* [2010] 13 HKCFAR 762 (Hong Kong Court of Final Appeal).
319 Section 67(3) of the Legislative Council Ordinance (Cap 542).
320 *Mok Charles* (n. 318) [63].
321 Section 39 of the Chief Executive Election Ordinance (Cap 569).
322 Section 73 of the Legislative Council Ordinance (Cap 542).
323 *Mok Charles* (n. 318) [68].
324 Section 70B of the Legislative Council Ordinance (Cap 542).
325 *Official Receiver* v. *Chan Wing Hing* [2006] 9 HKCFAR 545 (Hong Kong Court of Final Appeal).
326 Article 31 of the Hong Kong Basic Law.
327 *Chan Wing Hing* (n. 325) [47]–[49].
328 *Official Receiver* v. *Zhi Charles* [2015] 18 HKCFAR 467 (Hong Kong Court of Final Appeal).

unable to return because of illness, impecuniosity or incarceration,[329] the CFA held that this provision too was a disproportionate restriction on his constitutional right to travel and was therefore unconstitutional. In response to the HKCFA decisions, the Bankruptcy Ordinance now grants courts the discretion to make a 'non-commencement order', vis-à-vis a bankruptcy period, on an application made by the trustee.[330]

## STAGE 4: REASONABLE/FAIR BALANCE

While the HKCFA in *Leung Chun Kwong* (2019)[331] relied primarily on Stage 2 of SP to upend the government's policy of denying tax benefits to same-sex married couples and refusing spousal benefits to civil servants in same-sex marriages, the Court also determined that had it proceeded to consider Stage 4 of SP. The Court would *likely* have also held that the discriminatory treatment was 'not a fair balance in that it resulted in an acceptably harsh burden'[332] on same-sex married couples. But since the impugned rules already failed Stage 2 of SP, it was 'not necessary to express a concluded view'[333] on Stage 4.

Ostensibly, the HKCFA upended the discriminatory rules using Stage 2 of SP *exclusively*, but a close reading of this judgment would indicate otherwise. The lower court in *Leung Chun Kwong* had previously upheld the law *inter alia* on the basis that granting same-sex married couples the same matrimonial benefits as heterosexual married couples would dilute the *uniqueness* of traditional marriage.[334] In refuting this argument, the HKCFA responded as follows:

> [W]e are unable to accept the proposition that heterosexual marriage would be undermined by the extension of the employment and tax benefits to same-sex married couples ... Heterosexual marriage is not promoted by the differential treatment in question.[335]

However, one must note that relying on Stage 2 of SP alone would not fully refute the 'dilution' argument raised by the lower court, especially since the HKCFA had conceded that the protection of traditional marriage was a legitimate aim the government could pursue.[336] The patently discriminatory rules would certainly have served this unfortunate legislative aim of keeping heterosexual marriage exclusive and unique. In essence, what the HKCFA must have meant – even if it did not say so – is that the benefits of preventing the uniqueness of traditional marriage from

[329] Ibid. [55].
[330] See Section 30AB and Section 30AC of the Bankruptcy Ordinance (Cap 6).
[331] *Leung Chun Kwong* v. *Secretary for the Civil Service* [2019] HKCFA 19 (Hong Kong Court of Final Appeal).
[332] Ibid. [80].
[333] Ibid. [80].
[334] Ibid. [70].
[335] Ibid. [72].
[336] Ibid. [61].

being diluted are simply *outweighed* by the harms imposed on same-sex married couples who were denied equal access. But by dressing up a Stage 4 SP argument in Stage 2 garb, the CFA avoided engaging openly in policy-making, which Stage 4 would entail, and safeguarded its institutional capital by focusing on how the government had lost only because it had failed to pass a law that served its own goal.

Alec Stone Sweet has also pointed out that the Hong Kong courts have smuggled the 'balancing' Stage 4 test into the 'necessity' Stage 3 test of SP.[337] In deciding whether to accord significant deference to the lawmakers' determination of necessity or to assess on its own whether the legislative restrictions are 'of reasonable necessity',[338] the judicial *choice* on the *standard* of review in substance determines whether Hong Kong courts will 'permi[t] balancing within necessity'.[339] When the former standard of review is adopted, Stage 4 balancing is effectively jettisoned. Notably, when the HKCA invalidated a law that barred the use of facial coverings at *lawful* and authorized public assemblies, it did so by adopting the stricter 'reasonable necessity' standard of review, and the Court simply conflated its discussion of Stages 3 and 4 of SP.[340] This conflation of Stages 3 and 4 of SP is even more apparent in *Junior Police Officers Association* (2020),[341] where the HKCA treated the two concepts interchangeably when the Court declared a law disproportionate insofar as all voters were required to disclose their primary residential addresses to the public for inspection, even if individual voters could prove that unrestricted public access would pose a real risk to their safety.

## CONCLUSION

Our foregoing discussions raise several common themes that we would like to highlight herein. First, the use of SP to assess the reasonableness of rights-derogation is judicially constructed in all three East Asian democracies. The Hong Kong Basic Law does not even include a general limitation clause for rights. While the Constitutions of South Korea and Taiwan both have one, the relevant clauses do not give any guidance on the standard of review judges should adopt, let alone authorize judges to 'access social facts'[342] and *re-balance* legislative policy determinations.

337 Alec Stone Sweet, 'The Necessity of Balancing: Hong Kong's Flawed Approach to Proportionality, and Why It Matters' (2020) 50 *Hong Kong Law Journal* 541.

338 *Hysan Development* v. *Town Planning Board* [2016] 19 HKCFAR 372 (Hong Kong Court of Final Appeal) [136].

339 Stone Sweet (n. 337) 565.

340 See *Leung Kwok Hung* v. *Secretary for Justice* [2020] HKCA 192 (Hong Kong Court of Appeal) [243]–[248].

341 *Junior Police Officers Association of the Hong Kong Police Force* v. *Electoral Affairs Commission* [2020] HKCA 352 (Hong Kong Court of Appeal) [69].

342 Jamal Greene, 'Foreword: Rights as Trumps?' (2018) 132 *Harvard Law Review* 28, 63.

Second, PA in its early incarnations was all unstructured, and was first used within each jurisdiction to validate and legitimize state action.[343] But as power fragmented across the political branches of government and/or courts gained confidence over time, the judges added more structure to PA, gravitated towards a 'highly intrusive standard of review'[344] and started using SP to invalidate legislation. The fragmentation of power within the political branches of government, and the insulation of judges from political reprisal, is central to the acceptance and ascendance of SP.

In all three courts, Stage 1 of SP – the legitimacy test – is rarely used to invalidate legislative practices. But notably, where laws are invalidated under Stage 1, they usually pertain to anachronistic laws that are patriarchal[345] or heterosexist.[346] Therefore, Stage 1 of SP confers upon all three courts the opportunity to reshape the constitutional culture, and make society freer and more inclusive. Stage 2 of SP typically requires the statutory measure to have a 'rational connection'[347] to the legislative aims or for the means chosen to be 'appropriate'.[348] Generally a low bar for the government to surmount, we have also observed in exceptional circumstances where Stage 2 has extraordinary bite: Hong Kong rules limiting social welfare to Permanent Residents,[349] Taiwan legislation imposing interest payments on penalty surcharges for unpaid taxes[350] and South Korean anti-trust regulations on newspapers[351] were all invalidated for failing Stage 2. Notably these invalidated rules all pertain to socio-economic policies that traditionally attract judicial deference. Moreover, Stage 2 has also been used to advance liberal causes opposed by their governments: ending indefinite detention of undocumented migrants in Taiwan,[352] decriminalizing adultery in South Korea[353] and granting expatriates in same-sex marriages the same right to spousal visas as heterosexual married couples in Hong

343 J.Y. Interpretation No. 414 (1996) (Constitutional Court of Taiwan), available at http://cons.judicial.gov.tw/jcc/en-us/jep03/show?expno=414, accessed 9 May 2021; 88Hun-Ma1 (17 March 1989) (Constitutional Court of Korea); *HKSAR* v. *Ng Kung Siu* [1999] 2 HKCFAR 442 (Hong Kong Court of Final Appeal).

344 Stone Sweet and Mathews (n. 5) 31.

345 *Case on House Hold Head System*, 2001Hun-Ka9 (3 February 2005) (Constitutional Court of Korea).

346 *Secretary for Justice* v. *Yau Yuk Lung* [2007] 10 HKCFAR 335 (Hong Kong Court of Final Appeal).

347 *Hysan Development* v. *Town Planning Board* [2016] 19 HKCFAR 372 (Hong Kong Court of Final Appeal). J.Y. Interpretation No. 746 (2017) (Constitutional Court of Taiwan), available at http://cons.judicial.gov.tw/jcc/en-us/jep03/show?expno=746, accessed 9 May 2021.

348 *Case on School Site Acquisition Charge*, 2003Hun-Ka20 (31 March 2005) (Constitutional Court of Korea).

349 *Kong Yunming* v. *Director of Social Welfare* [2013] 16 HKCFAR 950 (Hong Kong Court of Final Appeal).

350 J.Y. Interpretation No. 746 (2017) (Constitutional Court of Taiwan), available at http://cons.judicial.gov.tw/jcc/en-us/jep03/show?expno=746, accessed 9 May 2021.

351 *The Newspaper Act Case*, 2005Hun-Ma165 (26 July 2006) (Constitutional Court of Korea).

352 J.Y. Interpretation No. 710 (2013) (Constitutional Court of Taiwan), at [3], available at http://cons.judicial.gov.tw/jcc/en-us/jep03/show?expno=710, accessed 9 May 2021.

353 *Adultery Case*, 2009Hun-Ba17 (26 February 2015) (Constitutional Court of Korea).

Kong.[354] Stage 3 of SP – the necessity test – is most frequently relied on by all three courts to subvert the legislative status quo, as it allows courts to point to tangible reasonable policy alternatives that their governments have failed to pursue, which would have been just as effective. To this end, both the South Korean[355] and Hong Kong[356] courts have ruled against the absolute prohibition of organized assemblies in the vicinity of their national legislatures, while the TCC has gone even further to exempt spontaneous and urgent assemblies in public spaces from the licensing process.[357] Insofar as the KCC has relied on Stage 3 to invalidate the virtually blanket prohibition on abortions in South Korea,[358] a South Korean woman will now be able to exercise a comparable right to her bodily autonomy vis-à-vis her counterpart in Taiwan[359] or Hong Kong.[360] Stage 4 of SP requires courts to openly debate and re-calibrate the legislative balance struck by the government, and all three courts have sparingly struck down laws on this ground. But it is notable that the KCC and the TCC have used this ground to evaluate the proportionality of statutory *minimum* sentences imposed on a variety of crimes.[361]

Yet we must also emphasize that the use of SP would *not* always lead to a convergence on substantive outcomes in all three jurisdictions.[362] As we have discussed, while the TCC has scuttled the government's plans to fingerprint all its citizens,[363] the KCC has allowed this.[364] Critics who argue that PA is not an

354 *QT* v. *Director of Immigration* [2018] HKCFA 28 (Hong Kong Court of Final Appeal).

355 *Case on the Ban on Outdoor Assemblies within 100m of the National Assembly Building*, 2013Hun-Ba322, 2016Hun-Ba354, 2017Hun-Ba360, 398, 471, 2018Hun-Ka3, 4, 9 (consolidated) (31 May 2018) (Constitutional Court of Korea).

356 In *Cheung Tak Wing* v. *Director of Immigration* [2020] HKCA 124, the Court of Appeal ruled that a Permission Scheme, which imposed a blanket ban on all public assemblies at the Forecourt of the Central Government Offices (CGO) – where the legislature is located – on weekdays and Saturdays, was constitutional. But the Court of Appeal also ruled that the government has to 'have regard to the individual circumstances of each case in the actual administration of the scheme and the enforcement of the restriction' and the exercise of such administrative discretion should also be proportionate.

357 J.Y. Interpretation No. 718 (2014) (Constitutional Court of Taiwan), at [2], available at http://cons.judicial.gov.tw/jcc/en-us/jep03/show?expno=718, accessed 9 May 2021.

358 *Case on the Crime of Abortion*, 2017Hun-Ba127 (11 April 2019) (Constitutional Court of Korea).

359 Paragraph 1, Article 9 of the Genetic Health Act.

360 Section 47A of the Offences against the Person Ordinance (Cap 212).

361 *Constitutional Review of Article 53 Section 1 of the Military Criminal Act*, 2006Hun-Ka13 (29 November 2007) (Constitutional Court of Korea); J.Y. Interpretation No. 669 (2009) (Constitutional Court of Taiwan), at [2], available at http://cons.judicial.gov.tw/jcc/en-us/jep03/show?expno=669, accessed 9 May 2021.

362 Rosalind Dixon, 'Proportionality & Comparative Constitutional Law versus Studies' (2018) 12 *Law & Ethics of Human Rights* 203, 207.

363 J.Y. Interpretation No. 603 (2005) (Constitutional Court of Taiwan), available at http://cons.judicial.gov.tw/jcc/en-us/jep03/show?expno=603, accessed 9 May 2021.

364 *Case on Putting Ten Fingerprints on Application for Issuance of Resident Registration Certificate*, 2011Hun-Ma731 (28 May 2015) (Constitutional Court of Korea).

'international tool of constitutional law'[365] because its application is 'always contingent and local'[366] have failed to grasp that the judicial deployment of SP *in itself* does not produce any policy outcomes. What SP does is to provide judges with a stable, defined, uniform, and doctrinal infrastructure to hold a government's derogation on rights to account, such that the courts have a legal basis to override legislative discretion, if they so *choose*. Furthermore, the doctrinal acceptance of SP – as opposed to a deferential standard of review – in these East Asian democracies holds the promise and increases the probability of a more rights-friendly outcome, as judges have recourse to a *heightened* standard of review to evaluate the appropriateness of state action.

Nonetheless, the judicial use of SP to subvert legislation in East Asia did not create an imperial judiciary. All three courts have also recognized that SP delineates a 'zone of proportionality',[367] such that their respective legislature, even after an original law is invalidated, can be given 'meaningful policy discretion'[368] to craft a more tailored piece of legislation on demand. This constitutional dialogue between the courts and the legislatures is best illustrated in the pair of prisoner-voting cases. While both the South Korean[369] and Hong Kong[370] courts deemed the blanket prohibition on prisoner voting incompatible with their Constitutions, neither court dictated to the lawmakers the details of an acceptable legislative sequel. In the end, the Hong Kong Legislative Council decided to allow all prisoners to vote, while the South Korean National Assembly responded by giving the vote only to prisoners sentenced to less than one year of imprisonment. In the same vein, while both the TCC[371] and the KCC[372] invalidated the massage industry monopoly granted to the visually impaired, because other deserving disabled persons were excluded from the practice, neither Constitutional Court determined how their legislatures should fix the law. The Taiwan Legislative Yuan decided to open the massage industry to everyone, while the South Korean National Assembly reinstated its original views, but this time in the form of legislation in lieu of the prior-invalidated administrative rules, and the KCC acquiesced.[373]

365 David Kenny, 'Proportionality and the Inevitability of the Local: A Comparative Localist Analysis of Canada and Ireland' (2018) 66 *American Journal of Comparative Law* 537, 537.

366 Ibid. 539.

367 Stone Sweet and Mathews (n. 5) 48.

368 Ibid.

369 *Restriction on Right to Vote of Prisoners and Probationers with Suspended Sentence*, 2012Hun-Ma409, 510, 2013Hun-Ma167 (consolidated) (28 January 2014) (Constitutional Court of Korea).

370 *Chan Kin Sum* v. *Secretary of Justice* [2009] 2 HKLRD 166 (Hong Kong Court of First Instance).

371 J.Y. Interpretation No. 649 (2008) (Constitutional Court of Taiwan), available at http://cons.judicial.gov.tw/jcc/en-us/jep03/show?expno=649, accessed 9 May 2021.

372 *Case on the Monopoly of Massage Therapists by Visually Impaired Persons*, 2003Hun-Ma715, 2006Hun-Ma368 (25 May 2006) (Constitutional Court of Korea).

373 *Visually Impaired Massagers Case*, 2006Hun-Ma1098 (30 October 2008) (Constitutional Court of Korea).

Taiwan, South Korea and Hong Kong are unique insofar as their courts are the only ones in Asia that have converged on the use of SP. The judges reason through the SP stages sequentially and deploy SP to subvert governmental action routinely. This convergence on SP in East Asia has enhanced judicial power, and correspondingly made a rights-based model of constitutional justice more effective.[374]

374 Stone Sweet and Mathews (n. 5) 51–54.

# 4

# Convergence on Innovative Constitutional Remedies

## INTRODUCTION

Where the judiciary is authorized to review the constitutionality of legislation, the standard practice is for the courts to void the law, when it is deemed unconstitutional, to the extent of the inconsistency. This is so in the West, as it is in Asia. Furthermore, judicial commitment to the separation of powers principle – a general rule observed in both civil and common law systems – would dictate that courts leave it to the legislature to introduce corrective legislation post-invalidation.

However, with the rise of the modern state, and the realist swing towards remedial discretion,[1] both common law and civil law courts have implemented innovative constitutional remedies that complement the power to declare legislative actions incompatible with their respective bills of rights. Some of the constitutional remedies are the result of specific statutory tools that empower the courts to read legislation in a rights-compatible way. In the United Kingdom, legislation must be read and given effect in a way that is compatible with the European Convention on Human Rights.[2] In the same vein, with regard to New Zealand, wherever an enactment can be given a meaning that is consistent with rights contained in its Bill of Rights Act, that meaning shall be preferred.[3] In essence, this interpretive power creates 'a practical power of law reform (in substance, a legislative power)'[4] for the judiciary. On the other hand, some remedies are the consequence of judicial innovation. For example, the Supreme Court of Canada[5] and the Federal Constitutional Court of

1 Kent Roach, 'Dialogic Remedies' (2019) 17 *International Journal of Constitutional Law* 860; Po Jen Yap, 'Remedial Discretion and Dilemmas in Asia' (2019) 69 *University of Toronto Law Journal* 84.

2 Convention for the Protection of Human Rights and Fundamental Freedoms, 4 November 1950, 213 UNTS 221 (entered into force 3 September 1953). See Human Rights Act 1998, c 42, s 3(1) (UK).

3 New Zealand Bill of Rights Act 1990, 1990/109, s 6 (NZ).

4 Philip Sales and Richard Ekins, 'Rights-Consistent Interpretation under the Human Rights Act 1998' (2011) 127 *Law Quarterly Review* 217, 224.

5 *Re Manitoba Language Rights*, [1985] 1 SCR 721, 19 DLR (4th) 1 (Supreme Court of Canada); *Carter v. Canada*, 2015 SCC 5, [2015] 1 SCR 331 (Supreme Court of Canada).

Germany[6] have increasingly suspended the immediate application of their declarations of invalidity such that the unconstitutional statute remains in place while the legislature is given time to devise remedial legislation.

In Asia, the courts in Taiwan, South Korea and Hong Kong are the *only* ones that regularly rely on *both* Remedial Interpretive powers and Suspension Orders to rectify constitutionally flawed legislation.[7] Notably, neither remedy is explicitly authorized by legislation or their Constitutions. Both remedies are completely judge-made in East Asia. The Constitutional Court of Taiwan (TCC) drew inspiration from Germany when it used both Remedial Interpretation (RI)[8] and the Suspension Order.[9] The Hong Kong Court of Final Appeal (HKCFA) expressly referenced the Supreme Court of Canada when the former first created its Suspension Order.[10] English law was cited when the HKCFA first applied RI to an impugned law.[11] When a Suspension Order – known in South Korea as a decision of incompatibility[12] or non-conformity[13] ruling – was first enforced by the Constitutional Court of Korea (KCC), the Court cited German law for this.[14]

6 BVerfGE 130, 151 (2012) (German Federal Constitutional Court); BVerfGE 141, 220 (2016) (German Federal Constitutional Court).

7 The Constitutional Court of Indonesia used to apply both constitutional remedies too, but Suspension Orders have fallen out of favour with the Court as the government routinely dragged its feet on complying with a delayed remedy. The Court now prefers to apply a Remedial Interpretation of an impugned law that provides the assurance of an immediate remedy that comes into effect when the judicial declaration is made. See Fritz Edward Siregar, 'Pragmatism and the Use of Suspension Orders by Indonesia's Constitutional Court' in Po Jen Yap (ed.) *Constitutional Remedies in Asia* (Routledge 2019) 73–74. The Constitutional Court of Thailand applied a Suspension Order for the first time in CC decision 4/2563 (2020) when it gave its Parliament one year to remedy the country's restrictive laws on abortion. But one should note that the Thai Constitutional Court is expressly authorized by Section 74 of Constitutional Court Law (Organic Act on the Constitutional Court's Procedure B.E. 2561 [2018]) to issue this delayed remedy.

8 吳庚 Wu Geng, 《憲法的解釋與適用》 *The Interpretation and Application of the Constitution*, 三民 (San Min 2004) 585.

9 Ming-Sung Kuo, 'Between Choice and Tradition: Rethinking Reme'dial Grace Periods and Unconstitutionality Management in A Comparative Light' (2019) 36 *Pacific Basin Law Journal* 157, 161.

10 *Koo Sze Yiu* v. *Chief Executive of HKSAR* [2006] 9 HKCFAR 441 (Hong Kong Court of Final Appeal).

11 *HKSAR* v. *Lam Kwong Wai* [2006] 9 HKCFAR 574 (Hong Kong Court of Final Appeal) [77]. While Hong Kong does not have any legislation that expressly authorizes the judicial use of RI, the HKCFA held that this was an 'implied power' of the Court and is an 'incident of the exercise of judicial power'. See *HKSAR* v. *Lam Kwong Wai* [2006] 9 HKCFAR 574 [73] and [78]. For a fuller discussion of the judicial use of RI in Hong Kong, see Francis Ho-Chai Chung and Jiang Zixin, 'An Alternative to Annulment – Remedial Interpretation in Hong Kong' in Po Jen Yap (ed.) *Constitutional Remedies in Asia* (Routledge 2019) 98–118.

12 Dong-Heub Lee, 'Development and Current Situation of the Constitutional Adjudication in Korea' (2012) 53(2) *Seoul Law Journal* 1.

13 The Constitutional Court of Korea, *Thirty Years of the Constitutional Court of Korea* (The Constitutional Court of Korea 2018) 125.

14 *National Assembly Candidacy Deposit Case*, 88Hun-Ka6 (8 September 1989) (Constitutional Court of Korea).

Similarly, when the KCC first used RI – known in South Korea as a decision of limited[15] or conditional[16] constitutionality/unconstitutionality – German law was relied on.[17] The judicial use of both remedial techniques in South Korea were heavily criticized by the dissenting judges as, according to the dissent, Germany had specific statutory authorization for these remedial measures,[18] while the KCC was only authorized to issue a 'decision of unconstitutionality'.[19]

With the convergence on the enforcement of these novel constitutional remedies, the three courts have intentionally expedited or delayed the legal consequences that generally follow from the judicial declaration of an unconstitutional practice, thereby blurring the traditional dichotomy between adjudication and legislation.

There is now a rich corpus of literature that explores the judicial use of these unique constitutional remedies in both mature[20] and new[21] democracies. Two recent works are particularly thought provoking and will be the subject of our discussion herein. In the first, Robert Leckey sounds a cautionary note on the courts' increased use of delayed remedies. In his view, such remedies harm individual rights-bearers, as they may be victorious in court but deprived of a remedy until legislation is passed to address their situations, if at all.[22] These harms are especially accentuated when the judiciary temporarily preserves invalid penal prohibitions, as it 'magnifi[es] differences amongst members of the litigant's class'[23] purely on the basis of whether the accused is convicted before or after the lapse of the suspended law's expiration period. In the second article, Eric Fish addresses how courts should engage in Remedial Interpretation of constitutionally problematic legislation. In essence, Fish argues that the judge should impose a remedy that would 'keep the [impugned] statute as close as possible to what the legislature desired while solving

15 The Constitutional Court of Korea, *Twenty Years of the Constitutional Court of Korea* (The Constitutional Court of Korea 2008) 101.

16 The Constitutional Court of Korea (n. 13) 125.

17 *Inheritance Tax Act Case*, 89Hun-Ma38 (21 July 1989) (Constitutional Court of Korea).

18 Article 31(2) of the Federal Constitutional Court Act (Germany) reads: '... if the Federal Constitutional Court declares a law to be compatible or incompatible with the Basic Law or if it voids the law...'.

19 See Articles 45 and 47 of the Constitutional Court Act (South Korea).

20 Sujit Choudhry and Kent Roach, 'Putting the Past Behind Us? Prospective Judicial and Legislative Constitutional Remedies' (2003) 21 *Supreme Court Law Review* (2d) 205, 219; Sales and Ekins (n. 4); John C. Jeffries Jr, 'The Right-Remedy Gap in Constitutional Law' (1999–2000) 109 *Yale Law Journal* 87; Kent Roach, 'Remedial Consensus and Dialogue under the Charter: General Declarations and Delayed Declarations of Invalidity' (2002) 35 *UBC Law Review* 211; Daryl J. Levinson, 'Rights Essentialism and Remedial Equilibration' (1999) 99 *Columbia Law Review* 857; Paul Gewirtz, 'Remedies and Resistance' (1983) 92 *Yale Law Journal* 587; Nicholas Petrie, 'Indications of Inconsistency' (2019) 78(3) *Cambridge Law Journal* 612.

21 David Landau, 'Aggressive Weak-Form Remedies' (2014) 5 *Constitutional Court Review* 244; Po Jen Yap, 'New Democracies and Novel Remedies' (2017) *Public Law* 30.

22 Robert Leckey, 'The Harms of Remedial Discretion' (2016) 14 *International Journal of Constitutional Law* 584, 591.

23 Ibid. 592.

the constitutional problem'[24] and re-interpret the law in a way that 'the enacting legislature would have preferred.'[25]

In this chapter, we make two claims. First, while Leckey's concerns about how delayed remedies harm individual rights bearers are valid, in Hong Kong, South Korea and Taiwan, the uncertainties associated with their application have been mitigated by the courts. These Asian judges are more 'experimentalist'[26] and they have created even more innovative strategies to complement the judicial use of these delayed remedies so as to coax their governments to comply with judicial rulings. Even as Suspension Orders are increasingly issued, these Asian courts have disapplied the enforcement of these offending statutes whilst remedial legislation is pending,[27] refused to shield the government from any legal liability during the suspension period,[28] adopted remedial reading-in provisos that take effect automatically if the legislature defaults upon the expiry of the suspension period[29] and even issued interim remedial readings of the law pending legislative review.[30] In short, the three courts have converged in adding significant 'bite' to their delayed declarations of invalidity, such that the government is incentivized to comply with the court's ruling, or judicial safeguards are put in place to mitigate any legislative or executive delinquency.

Our second claim addresses Fish's argument that courts should adopt a purpose preservation inquiry when re-interpreting constitutionally defective legislation, such that the court's role after striking down the unconstitutional legislation is to only impose a remedy that will best further the enacting legislature's original intended goals.[31] While Fish's arguments are valid *vis-à-vis* the American Constitution, his prescriptions are less relevant in constitutional systems where a Suspension Order is also a constitutional remedy available to courts – unlike in the United States – as we see in South Korea, Taiwan and Hong Kong.

[24] Eric S. Fish, 'Choosing Constitutional Remedies' (2016) 63 *UCLA Law Review* 322, 326.

[25] Ibid. 386.

[26] See also Charles F. Sabel and William H. Simon, 'Destabilization Rights: How Public Law Litigation Succeeds' (2004) 117 *Harvard Law Review* 1016, 1019.

[27] *Prohibition of Labor Dispute by the Public Sector Laborers Case*, 88Hun-Ma5 (11 March 1993) (Constitutional Court of Korea); *Suspension from Duty of Heads of Local Governments*, 2010Hun-Ma418 (2 September 2010) (Constitutional Court of Korea).

[28] *Koo Sze Yiu* v. *Chief Executive of the HKSAR*, [2006] HKCFA 74, [2006] 9 HKCFAR 441 (Hong Kong Court of Final Appeal).

[29] W v. *Registrar of Marriages*, [2013] HKCFA 39, [2013] 16 HKCFAR 112 (Hong Kong Court of Final Appeal); J.Y. Interpretation No. 748 (2017) (Constitutional Court of Taiwan), available at http://cons.judicial.gov.tw/jcc/en-us/jep03/show?expno=748, accessed 12 May 2021.

[30] J.Y. Interpretation No. 755 (2017) (Constitutional Court of Taiwan), available at http://cons.judicial.gov.tw/jcc/en-us/jep03/show?expno=755, accessed 12 May 2021; *Case on Search by Arrest Warrant of Dwellings other than the suspect's* [2015]Hun-Ba370 (26 April 2018) (Constitutional Court of Korea) (Official English Summary).

[31] Fish (n. 24) 325–326.

Where courts are empowered to delay their declarations of invalidity, the more relevant enquiry for judges is how to choose between a Suspension Order, which gives lawmakers time to fix the defective legislation, and an RI of the impugned law, which requires no further legislative input. A Suspension Order is most appropriate when there is a 'range of multiple constitutional options'[32] available to the legislature to rectify the defective law and the government can be trusted to deliberate and put in place a suitable replacement. But even then, there are compelling circumstances where it may be more desirable for the judiciary to rewrite the defective law on its own, while pretending to exercise restraint by upholding the impugned law,[33] so as to shore up its reputation and not drain its political capital.[34] We will explore this idea in relation to Hong Kong, South Korea and Taiwan.

Part 1 of this chapter analyses how the three Asian courts have converged in mitigating the individual harms associated with the judicial use of delayed remedies. Furthermore, this part also explores how the three courts have occasionally attenuated the force of their Suspension Orders by not imposing a fixed legislative deadline so as to ameliorate potential governmental backlash against their rulings, and this in turn fostered greater legislative compliance. Part 2 examines how the three courts have converged on the use of RI and analyses the comparative advantages of using RI and a Suspension Order. This part further explains when expedited remedies are to be preferred over delayed ones, and when RI may be necessary or desirable, even if the judicially imposed result may not be what the enacting legislature had originally intended.

## PART 1: INDIVIDUAL AND INSTITUTIONAL HARMS OF SUSPENSION ORDERS?

### IMPACT ON INDIVIDUAL RIGHTS-BEARERS

Robert Leckey argues that delayed remedies risk neglecting the victim, as successful individual claimants may receive no remedy until legislation is passed to address their situations, assuming the government complies at all.[35] These individual harms are especially accentuated when courts temporarily preserve invalid criminal

32 See Roach (n. 20) 212. While Kent Roach argues that it is the role of the legislature to select among *constitutional* options, Hamish Stewart advocates for a more robust judicial use of remedial interpretation such that courts can fix the defective law immediately on its own. For this Stewart–Roach debate, see Hamish Stewart, 'A Defence of Constitutionalized Interpretation' (2016) 36 *National Journal of Constitutional Law* 195; Kent Roach, 'Constitutionalized Interpretation, Reading Down/In and the Wisdom of *Schachter*' (2016) 36 *National Journal of Constitutional Law* 211.

33 See also Eric S. Fish, 'Constitutional Avoidance as Interpretation and as Remedy' (2015–2016) 114 *Michigan Law Review* 1275, 1315.

34 Shai Dothan, *Reputation and Judicial Tactics: A Theory of National and International Courts* (Cambridge University Press 2015).

35 Leckey (n. 22) 592.

sanctions, as distinctions drawn on the basis of whether the accused is convicted before or after the lapse of the suspended law's expiration period 'leverag[e] factual differences among members [of the litigant's class] into arbitrary and unjust effects'.[36] Leckey has raised a powerful argument against the use of Suspension Orders. Fortunately, in East Asia, the three courts have added 'bite' to their Suspension Orders such that the government is incentivized to comply or else judicial safeguards are imposed to mitigate any governmental delinquency.

In South Korea, since 1993,[37] the KCC has used a variant of this Suspension Order, which is termed a 'simple'[38] decision of non-conformity. When this 'simple' decision of non-conformity is issued, the government is prohibited from enforcing the unconstitutional legislation pending its review, and there is 'an immediate suspension of the underlying proceeding [in the lower courts] that gave rise to the constitutional challenge'.[39] In 1993, a blanket ban on all collective action by public sector employees was deemed inconsistent with the Constitution, but the KCC delayed its declaration of invalidity and gave the legislature 21 months to fix the law.[40] More significantly, the government was barred from enforcing the impugned labour provision during the suspension period. Similarly, when the KCC declared that it was disproportionate for the state to prohibit all persons with the same family names and lineal origins, regardless of the degree of consanguinity, from marrying one other, the Court enjoined all state agencies from applying this law, while granting an 18-month Suspension Order for the legislature to remedy the situation.[41] In 2010, when the KCC deemed a law that suspended elected officials from office – even when their criminal convictions were pending appeal – incompatible with the Constitution, the Court also barred lower courts, state agencies and local

36 Ibid. 593.

37 *Prohibition of Labor Dispute by the Public Sector Laborers Case*, 88Hun-Ma5 (11 March 1993) (Constitutional Court of Korea).

38 The Constitutional Court of Korea, *Twenty Years of the Constitutional Court of Korea* (The Constitutional Court of Korea 2008) 165.

39 Ibid. 166.

40 *Prohibition of Labor Dispute by the Public Sector Laborers Case*, 88Hun-Ma5 (11 March 1993) (Constitutional Court of Korea). In 1997, the National Assembly enacted the Trade Union and Labor Relations Adjustment Act (1997), in which Section 2, Article 41 narrowed the ban to public employees who are 'among the employees in important defense industries ... those primarily involved in manufacture of defense materials such as electric power and water...'. See The Constitutional Court of Korea, *The First Ten Years of The Korean Constitutional Court* (The Constitutional Court of 2001) 253–254.

41 *Case on Same Surname-Same Origin Marriage Ban*, 95Hun-Ka6 (16 July 1997) (Constitutional Court of Korea). Article 809 of the Civil Act was only amended in 2005 to prohibit marriages between blood relatives within eight degrees of consanguinity. For a detailed discussion of this litigation, see Jibong Lim, 'Judicial Intervention in Policy-Making by the Constitutional Court in Korea' in Laurent Mayali and John Yoo (eds), *Current Issues in Korean Law* (The Robbins Collection 2014) 15–48.

governments from applying the impugned provisions even as it gave the legislature over a year to revise the law.[42]

As for Hong Kong, the HKCFA has also issued Suspension Orders so that the Legislative Council is given time to pass corrective legislation. But what is unique about the Suspension Order in Hong Kong is as follows:

> The [Hong Kong] Government can, during that period of suspension, function pursuant to what has been declared unconstitutional, doing so without acting contrary to any declaration in operation. But despite such suspension, the Government is not shielded from legal liability for functioning pursuant to what has been declared unconstitutional.[43]

In *Koo Sze Yiu* (2006)[44] where the Suspension Order was first granted, the impugned law allowed the Chief Executive of the region, whenever he or she considered that public interest so required, to order the interception or disclosure to the government of any telecommunications. While the HKCFA was reluctant to hamper any legitimate covert surveillance activities,[45] which would result from an immediate invalidation of the law, the Court was equally unwilling to give the government free rein to do as it pleased during the period of reprieve. Therefore, this Suspension Order granted government officials the power to continue engaging in covert surveillance while the law was being revised, while not immunizing them from any legal liability if they abused their authority in the interim.[46]

What is even more remarkable is that in Hong Kong and Taiwan, the courts have coupled their use of a delayed declaration of invalidity with a remedial reading-in proviso that takes effect automatically, in the event of any legislative default, upon the expiry of the suspension period.

42 *Suspension from Duty of Heads of Local Governments*, 2010Hun-Ma418 (2 September 2010) (Constitutional Court of Korea). In response, the National Assembly repealed the impugned provision in 2011. The Constitutional Court of Korea, *Thirty Years of the Constitutional Court of Korea* (The Constitutional Court of Korea 2018) 359.

43 *Koo Sze Yiu v. Chief Executive of the HKSAR* [2006] 9 HKCFAR 441 (Hong Kong Court of Final Appeal) [50].

44 Ibid.

45 Notably, in 2018, the KCC decided a factually similar case. In *Case on Location Tracing Data under Protection of Communications Secrets Act*, 2012Hun-ma191 (28 June 2018) (Constitutional Court of Korea), the KCC ruled that law enforcement's statutory power to compel telecommunication providers to trace the location of any subscriber, whenever the public officials 'deem it necessary', was incompatible with the constitutional right to privacy. The law was deemed disproportionate as it applied, regardless of the gravity of the crime, to subscribers who were not even suspects of any crime, and no court order was required for this surveillance. Nevertheless, a Suspension Order for a period of 21 months was granted so that the National Assembly could deliberate on the specific details of the remedial legislation.

46 In compliance with the Suspension Order, the Interception of Communications and Surveillance Ordinance (Cap 589) was passed in 2006 to regulate the conduct of interception of communications and the use of surveillance devices by public officials.

Interpretation No. 737 (2016)[47] was the first decision in which the TCC applied this remedial measure. In this case, the accused challenged the constitutionality of various criminal procedure rules[48] that barred criminal defendants from gaining access to the prosecution's evidence against them until the investigatory stage of the proceeding was completed and the case was pending trial. The TCC agreed that this denial violated the accused's due process rights as it was 'necessary to timely inform the suspect and his counsel in appropriate manners of the reason and evidence for detention so that the right of defense can be exercised effectively'.[49] And the government was therefore given one year to revise the impugned provisions. But if the government failed to comply by the requisite deadline, the TCC ruled that criminal suspects would thereafter have access to the state's evidence against them at the investigatory stage of the criminal proceeding.[50]

This Suspension Order, coupled with a remedial interpretive 'bite', was also issued by the TCC in May 2017 when it declared that Taiwan's ban on same-sex marriage was an unconstitutional violation of a person's freedom to marry. The legislature was given two years to remedy this legislative exclusion. But, notably, the Court held that if the Taiwan Legislative Yuan defaulted after the deadline, same-sex couples would be entitled to 'apply for marriage registration to the authorities in charge of household registration ... and [they] shall be accorded the status of a legally-recognized couple and then enjoy the rights and bear the obligations arising on couples.'[51] But this decision was also dialogic, as the TCC held that it was within the government's discretion to determine whether same-sex marriage should be

47 J.Y. Interpretation No. 737 (2016) (Constitutional Court of Taiwan), available at http://cons.judicial.gov.tw/jcc/en-us/jep03/show?expno=737, accessed 12 May 2021.

48 The impugned provisions were Article 33, Paragraph 1 and Article 101, Paragraph 3 of the Code of Criminal Procedure. The former read: 'A defense attorney may examine the case file and exhibits and make copies or photographs thereof' and the latter provided 'The accused and his defense attorney shall be informed of the facts based to support the detention of an accused as specified in section I of this article. The same shall be stated in the record.'

49 J.Y. Interpretation No. 737 (2016) (Constitutional Court of Taiwan), at [7], available at http://cons.judicial.gov.tw/jcc/en-us/jep03/show?expno=737, accessed 12 May 2021.

50 Specifically, the TCC ruled that criminal suspects and their counsels should know the reasons and have access to the evidence unless 'there are facts sufficient to justify an apprehension that the suspect might destroy, forge, or alter evidence, or conspire with a co-offender or witness, etc., which jeopardizes the purpose of investigation or the life or body of others, the law may limit or forbid the suspect to access evidence relating to the motion for detention'. J.Y. Interpretation No. 737 (2016) (Constitutional Court of Taiwan), at [7], available at http://cons.judicial.gov.tw/jcc/en-us/jep03/show?expno=737, accessed 12 May 2021. Two days before the deadline, the legislature revised Article 101, Paragraph 3 of the Code of Criminal Procedure and enacted Article 33-1 of the same Code such that the accused's attorneys are now allowed to access the state's evidence against them before the defendants are formally charged in court.

51 J.Y. Interpretation No. 748 (2017) (Constitutional Court of Taiwan), at [17], available at http://cons.judicial.gov.tw/jcc/en-us/jep03/show?expno=748, accessed 12 May 2021; see also Ming-Sung Kuo and Hui-Wen Chen, 'The Brown Moment in Taiwan: Making Sense of the Law and Politics of the Taiwanese Same-Sex Marriage Case in a Comparative Light' (2017) 31 *Columbia Journal Asian Law* 72.

regulated under a separate statute, a new chapter within the pre-existing matrimonial law, or whether the pre-existing matrimonial law should simply be amended and made gender neutral. The judicial use of default rules not only incentivizes political action by allowing the legislature to have the first word on policy design when crafting remedial legislation,[52] but it also provides a baseline of protection for successful litigants if the government falters.[53]

The HKCFA also relied on this remedy when it ruled in favour of transsexual marriage in 2013. In W (2013),[54] the Court determined that the Registrar of Marriages, in applying the existing matrimonial legislation in Hong Kong that prohibited a post-operative, male-to-female transsexual from marrying in the capacity of her acquired gender, had violated her constitutional right to marriage. While the HKCFA issued a delayed declaration of invalidity that gave the Hong Kong legislature one year to reform this area of law, the Court decided at the outset that 'it is necessary in principle that remedial interpretation'[55] be given to the impugned matrimonial legislation such that a transsexual in W's situation – one who had undergone a full male-to-female sexual reassignment surgery – would be legally recognized as a woman within the statutory meaning of the pre-existing law. Upon the expiry of the 12-month suspension period and in the absence of any legislative intervention, the Court held that the post-operative male-to-female transsexual person would be automatically recognized as a woman for the purposes of marriage in Hong Kong.[56]

Remarkably, both the TCC and KCC have gone even further to issue *interim* remedial readings of the unconstitutional law during the suspension period, and the interim relief would be enforced until the revised legislation comes into effect. In response to the legislature's long-standing failure[57] to allow pre-trial detainees to challenge the conditions of their detention, the TCC in

52 Landau (n. 21) 255–258.

53 In 2019, Taiwan's Legislative Yuan enacted a same-sex marriage law that also conferred some adoption rights on same-sex couples, an issue its Constitutional Court was silent on, and the nation now formally recognizes marriage equality. Enforcement Act of Judicial Yuan Interpretation No. 748 (2019) (Taiwan), available at https://law.moj.gov.tw/LawClass/LawAll.aspx?pcode=B0000008, accessed 12 May 2021.

54 W v. *Registrar of Marriages*, [2013] HKCFA 39, [2013] 16 HKCFAR 112 (Hong Kong Court of Final Appeal).

55 Ibid. [123].

56 At the end of the suspension period, the Hong Kong Legislative Council refused to pass any remedial legislation to expressly allow transsexual persons to marry in their acquired gender, but the Registrar of Marriages, following the HKCFA ruling in W, has now permitted all post-operative male-to-female transsexuals to marry pursuant to the judicially imposed remedial interpretation of the pre-existing matrimonial legislation.

57 Back in 2007, the TCC in Interpretation No. 653 (2007) had already ruled that this practice was unconstitutional but the Court did not impose a fixed legislative deadline for the government to remedy the situation, and the government did nothing. See J.Y. Interpretation No. 653 (2007) (Constitutional Court of Taiwan), available at http://cons.judicial.gov.tw/jcc/en-us/jep03/show?expno=653, accessed 12 May 2021.

Interpretation No. 720 (2014)[58] ruled that, pending legislative reform, pre-trial detainees could invoke Article 416 of the Code of Criminal Procedure[59] to challenge the conditions of their detention.[60] In the same vein, the TCC in Interpretation No. 755 (2017)[61] also granted interim relief to inmates who were statutorily denied the right to challenge all disciplinary actions imposed on them in prison.[62] Pending legislative review, the TCC detailed the following interim measures:

> Before the revision of the aforementioned laws, if inmates . . . want to challenge the decision made by the supervisory authority, they can directly litigate in local district administrative courts . . . Such litigation shall be filed within a peremptory period of 30 days from the date they received the decision from the supervisory authority. Regulations relating to summary proceedings in the Administrative Procedure Act shall apply mutatis mutandis to these cases. . .[63]

Similarly, even though South Korea's National Assembly was given two years to devise appropriate remedial legislation after the KCC ruled that the law enforcement's statutory power to search without a warrant the premises of any person – when investigating a criminal suspect in the dwelling[64] – was incompatible with the constitutional guarantee on due process, the KCC also decided that prior to any legislative revision, the impugned statutory provision may only be applied by law enforcement when it was probable that the suspect was located in that premises and there was 'an emergency situation [which] makes it difficult to obtain a search warrant ahead of the search.'[65]

Such judicial developments are precisely the two-track remedies that Kent Roach has proposed courts use: specific relief for the successful litigants to correct the constitutional wrongs suffered (for example, exemption from the unconstitutional

58 J.Y. Interpretation No. 720 (2014) (Constitutional Court of Taiwan), available at http://cons.judicial.gov.tw/jcc/en-us/jep03/show?expno=720, accessed 12 May 2021.

59 Article 416 of the Code of Criminal Procedure provides: 'A subject of a disposition, who objects to the following disposition made by a presiding judge, commissioned judge, assigned judge, or prosecutor, may petition the concerned court to withdraw or change the disposition . . .'.

60 The TCC's RI is now enshrined in the revised Article 102 of the Detention Act (2019).

61 J.Y. Interpretation No. 755 (2017) (Constitutional Court of Taiwan), available at http://cons.judicial.gov.tw/jcc/en-us/jep03/show?expno=755, accessed 12 May 2021.

62 Article 5, Paragraph 1, Subparagraph 7 of the Enforcement Rules of the Prison Act provided: 'Grievances filed by inmates, who contest actions taken by the prison, shall be processed pursuant to the regulations stipulated below : . . .7. The supervisory authority shall have the final decision on inmates' grievances.'

63 J.Y. Interpretation No. 755 (2017) (Constitutional Court of Taiwan), at [13], available at http://cons.judicial.gov.tw/jcc/en-us/jep03/show?expno=755, accessed 12 May 2021. The TCC's RI is now enshrined in the revised Article 110 of the Prison Act (2019).

64 Article 216 of the Criminal Procedure Act read: (1) Where a prosecutor or senior judicial police officer arrests or detains a criminal suspect . . . he/she may, if necessary, take the following measures without a warrant: 1. To investigate a criminal suspect in the dwelling of another person or houses, buildings, airplanes, vessels, or vehicles which are guarded by other persons.'

65 *Case on Search by Arrest Warrant of Dwellings other than the suspect's*, 2015Hun-Ba370 (26 April 2018) (Constitutional Court of Korea) (Official English Summary).

legislation or interim injunctive relief) complemented with weaker dialogic general remedies that rely on the government's superior institutional expertise to craft a comprehensive, long-term legislation that addresses polycentric/resource allocative concerns.[66]

## INSTITUTIONAL CONCERNS OF 'WEAK' SUSPENSION ORDERS

Admittedly, in South Korea and Taiwan, their Constitutional Courts have occasionally handed down Suspension Orders that lack 'bite', insofar as these decrees do *not* impose a fixed deadline on the legislature to enact remedial legislation.

It would appear that in many of these cases, the weak delayed remedies were issued only because the courts anticipated political backlash, and the judges were further seeking to attenuate the impact of their ordinary Suspension Orders. This judicial practice is analogous to what Rosalind Dixon and Samuel Issacharoff term 'second-order' judicial deferral: courts postpone the immediacy of a judicial order to avoid a 'frontal confrontation with the political branches'.[67] This ceding of judicial ground purely to accommodate backlash may seem wholly illegitimate, as courts are supposed to adjudicate impartially, without fear or favour. But such remedies also have their institutional advantages. By attenuating the force of their Suspension Orders, the Courts can defuse governmental opposition and encourage greater compliance.

When the TCC issued its first Suspension Order in 1980, the territory was still under the Kuomintang (KMT)'s martial law rule. Specifically, in Interpretation No. 166 (1980),[68] the TCC ruled that the Act Governing the Punishment of Police Offences[69] was unconstitutional insofar as the law allowed the police to impose administrative sanctions of detention and forced labour on citizens without any court order. Interestingly, the unconstitutional legislation was not invalidated immediately. Instead, the Court only advised the legislature to introduce corrective reform 'as soon as possible'.[70] While the TCC did not provide a reason for this prudential move, it should be emphasized that Taiwan was still a police state then. Equally significant is the fact that the TCC at that time had yet to invalidate any legislation[71]

66 Roach (n. 1) 865–866; Kent Roach, 'Polycentricity and Queue Jumping in Public Law Remedies: A Two Track Response' (2016) 66(1) *University of Toronto Law Journal* 3.

67 Rosalind Dixon and Samuel Issacharoff, 'Living to Fight Another Day: Judicial Deferral in Defense of Democracy' (2016) *Wisconsin Law Review* 683, 687.

68 J.Y. Interpretation No. 166 (1980) (Constitutional Court of Taiwan), available at http://cons.judicial.gov.tw/jcc/en-us/jep03/show?expno=166, accessed 12 May 2021.

69 Act Governing the Punishment of Police Offences has been abolished in 1991. The official English translation is not available, but the original Chinese text can be found here: https://law.moj.gov.tw/LawClass/LawAll.aspx?pcode=D0080077, accessed 12 May 2021.

70 J.Y. Interpretation No. 166 (1980) (Constitutional Court of Taiwan), at [1], available at http://cons.judicial.gov.tw/jcc/en-us/jep03/show?expno=166, accessed 12 May 2021.

71 The TCC only invalidated legislation for violating the Constitution for the first time in J.Y. Interpretation No. 340 (1994), 14 years after Interpretation No. 166 (1980).

or even regulation[72] for being unconstitutional. In fact, this was the first time the Court had even deemed any act of the government unconstitutional. Where the legal culture is unaccustomed to strong-form judicial review, and the government can retaliate against confrontational judicial rulings by ousting judicial review or even the judges themselves, the TCC chose to assert itself gingerly. Not surprisingly, this advisory deadline was completely ignored by the authoritarian regime for a decade until the TCC delivered Interpretation No. 251 (1990),[73] in which the Court added a deadline for legislative compliance – 1 July 1991 – and the legislature dutifully repealed the law in June 1991. Insofar as a weak Constitutional Court was testing the political waters in 1980, and the government did not retaliate against the calibrated show of force, the Court was setting the stage for future judicial intervention, and the nation's constitutional culture was richer for it.

But one should note that even after the nation democratized in 1987, the TCC retained this 'weak-form' Suspension Order. And the Court also resorted to such orders in highly divisive, politically controversial showdowns with other branches of government. Interpretation No. 419 (1996)[74] is a case in point. In this decision, the Court had to decide whether the Vice-President of Taiwan, Lien Chan, could simultaneously serve as the nation's Premier. At that time, the KMT controlled both the presidency and the legislature, and all the Justices were appointed by President Lee Teng-hui, the very President who nominated his Vice-President as Premier. Therefore, the Justices not only had to confront a President and his legislature in lock-step, but they also had to stare down the very President who appointed all of them. One Justice even publicly disclosed later that the KMT had attempted to lobby him privately – in the middle of the TCC proceedings – to rule for the President.[75] In the face of such monumental political pressure, the TCC euphemistically ruled that 'it will not be completely in conformity with the Constitution'[76] to have the Vice-President serve simultaneously as the country's Premier because the Vice-President might act on behalf on the President on occasions and 'there is a certain check-and-balance function between the President and the Premier'.[77] Notably, the Court did not invalidate the appointment

72 The TCC only invalidated a regulatory provision for violating the Constitution for the first time in J.Y. Interpretation No. 268 (1990), 10 years after Interpretation No. 166 (1980).

73 J.Y. Interpretation No. 251 (1990) (Constitutional Court of Taiwan), available at http://cons.judicial.gov.tw/jcc/en-us/jep03/show?expno=251, accessed 12 May 2021.

74 J.Y. Interpretation No. 419 (1996) (Constitutional Court of Taiwan), available at http://cons.judicial.gov.tw/jcc/en-us/jep03/show?expno=419, accessed 12 May 2021.

75 台灣法界耆宿口述歷史, Oral History of Taiwan Senior Jurists, volume 6, 司法院 (Judicial Yuan 2011) 146.

76 J.Y. Interpretation No. 419 (1996) (Constitutional Court of Taiwan), at [1], available at http://cons.judicial.gov.tw/jcc/en-us/jep03/show?expno=419, accessed 12 May 2021.

77 See Article 49 of the Constitution of the Republic of China (Taiwan) (1947) and J.Y. Interpretation No. 419 (1996) (Constitutional Court of Taiwan), at [7], available at http://cons.judicial.gov.tw/jcc/en-us/jep03/show?expno=419, accessed 12 May 2021.

outright. But in August 1997, eight months after Interpretation No. 419 (1996), Lien Chan resigned his premiership but stayed on as Vice-President of Taiwan.

Interpretation No. 601 (2005)[78] was another landmark decision in which the TCC ruled that a governmental practice was unconstitutional, but did not impose a deadline for compliance. After the TCC foiled the KMT's plans to institute a partisan investigation into the assassination attempt on President Chen Shui-bian of the Democratic Progressive Party in 2004[79] – the KMT believed that the assassination attempt was staged by the President to gain sympathy votes prior to the election – the KMT-controlled Legislative Yuan decided to punish the Court by removing the bonuses from the TCC Justices' remuneration package. According to the legislature, the Justices only served eight-year, non-renewable terms, and hence they should not have the bonuses reserved for career judges with life tenure.[80] In response, the TCC declared that 'the definite terms for the Justices, as well as the indefinite term for [career] judges, are both designed to protect their status. It should not be inferred that the Justices are not judges simply because they hold office for a definite term'.[81] Therefore, the legislative removal of the Justices' bonuses violated the Constitution's protection of judicial independence.[82] But prudentially, the Justices also did not impose any guidelines or deadlines on how and when the legislature should compensate the TCC Justices. In the end, the legislature caved and reimbursed the Justices the following year.

But not all Suspension Orders with advisory or no deadlines for governmental compliance are met with equal success. Interpretation No. 530 (2001)[83] is a prime example of a 'weak-form' Suspension Order that remains unimplemented. The core issue in this case centred on whether Taiwan's Judicial Yuan possesses general jurisdiction over all civil, criminal and administrative matters, in addition to constitutional matters. When the Judicial Yuan was originally designed in 1947, it was heavily influenced by the United States' judicial system.[84] That is, the Judicial Yuan was supposed to be the apex court under the Constitution of the Republic of China. But this constitutional design was never implemented in practice because of vehement opposition from the Supreme Court, which existed even before the Constitution was promulgated. Therefore, the apex court in the Judicial Yuan, the

78 J.Y. Interpretation No. 601 (2005) (Constitutional Court of Taiwan), available at http://cons.judicial.gov.tw/jcc/en-us/jep03/show?expno=601, accessed 12 May 2021.

79 For a fuller discussion, see Chapter 5.

80 J.Y. Interpretation No. 601 (2005) (Constitutional Court of Taiwan), at [12], available at http://cons.judicial.gov.tw/jcc/en-us/jep03/show?expno=601, accessed 12 May 2021.

81 Ibid. [13].

82 Article 81 of the Constitution of the Republic of China (Taiwan) reads: '... No judge shall, except in accordance with law, be suspended or transferred or have his salary reduced.'

83 J.Y. Interpretation No. 530 (2001) (Constitutional Court of Taiwan), available at http://cons.judicial.gov.tw/jcc/en-us/jep03/show?expno=530, accessed 12 May 2021.

84 Wen-Chen Chang, 'Institutional Independence of the Judiciary: Taiwan's Incomplete Reform' in H. P. Lee and M. Pittard (eds), *Asia-Pacific Judiciaries: Independence, Impartiality and Integrity* (Cambridge University Press 2018) 330, 342.

Council of Grand Justices, which is referred to as the TCC after 1993,[85] only had jurisdiction over constitutional issues, and other public and private law matters were the purview of the Supreme Administrative Court and the Supreme Court. In Interpretation No. 530 (2001), the TCC revisited this thorny issue and maintained that the current institutional arrangement of the judiciary was inconsistent with the Constitution's original intent. It advised the legislature to revise related laws within two years, but the original arrangement would be left intact until legislative changes were implemented. But as any judicial reform would lead to the abolition of the Supreme Court and the Supreme Administrative Court,[86] there was firm resistance from judges of the Supreme Courts and influential academics who preferred to retain the German model of constitutional adjudication.[87] Unsurprisingly, the government has done little to implement this ruling.

In South Korea, the KCC has also occasionally issued Suspension Orders that do not impose any legislative deadline for compliance. In 2005, when the Court declared that a patriarchal law, which subordinated a woman to her father, husband (if she were married) or son (if her husband was deceased),[88] was incompatible with the Constitution, it merely asked the legislature to amend the requisite law as soon as possible.[89] On some occasions, the KCC imposed 'advisory' deadlines. In 2008, the KCC was confronted with a law[90] that prohibited doctors from disclosing the sex of a foetus to the child's family, including the mother.[91] While the legislation was declared incompatible with the Constitution, the KCC merely 'urged'[92] the National Assembly to pass remedial legislation by 31 December 2009, and the impugned law would remain force until statutory revisions were made.[93] South Korea is a modern constitutional democracy that is still steeped in Confucian

85 Article 13, Paragraph 2 of the Additional Articles of the Republic of China was passed in 1992 and it states: 'The grand justices of the Judicial Yuan shall … form a Constitutional Court to adjudicate matters relating to the dissolution of unconstitutional political parties.' Following this constitutional amendment, the Grand Justices Council Adjudication Act was revised and renamed the Constitutional Interpretation Procedure Act in 1993.

86 Yen-tu Su, 'Regime Unchanged: The Organization and Failed Reorganization of Taiwan's Judicial Yuan' in Neil Chisholm (ed.), *Judicial Reform in Taiwan: Institutionalizing Democracy and The Diffusion of Law* (Routledge 2020).

87 Chang (n. 84) 346; Su (n. 86).

88 *Case on House Hold Head System*, 2001Hun-Ka9 (3 February 2005) (Constitutional Court of Korea).

89 The law was repealed in 2005, but a child will still have to assume the father's family name, unless the couple agreed otherwise at the time of the marriage. See Article 781(1) of the Civil Act.

90 Article 20(2) of the Medical Service Act read: 'Any medical person shall not inform any pregnant woman, her family member, or any other person of the fetal gender of which he/she becomes aware through a diagnosis or examination of the fetus or the pregnant woman.'

91 *Case on the Prohibition of Revealing the Sex of a Foetus*, 2004Hun-Ma1010 (31 July 2008) (Constitutional Court of Korea).

92 Ibid. (Official English Translation).

93 In 2009, the National Assembly revised the impugned law and the sex of the foetus may now be disclosed 32 weeks into the pregnancy. See Article 20(2) of the Medical Service Act.

tradition,[94] and the KCC chose to tread carefully as it attempted to reform reactionary social mores. But this calibrated judicial show of force bore fruit, as in all these cases the National Assembly eventually passed remedial legislation to comply with these declarations, even though no fixed legislative deadlines were judicially imposed.

Where weakened Suspension Orders are issued, the judiciary is adjusting its 'remedial aspiration in the face of a resistant reality'.[95] But if the postponement or attenuation of the delayed remedies can help consolidate public support and encourage better governmental compliance in the long run, they remain valuable or even necessary remedial devices in the judicial toolkit.

## PART 2: CHOOSING BETWEEN REMEDIAL INTERPRETATION AND A SUSPENSION ORDER

In another illuminating article, Eric Fish has also examined how courts should choose a constitutional remedy when they determine that a statute violates the Constitution.[96] Specifically, Fish argues that the judges should impose an interpretive remedy that is 'most compatible with the enacting legislature's goals'[97] when resolving the constitutional problem. This purpose preservation inquiry would require the judiciary to 'look at the available evidence – the wording of the statute, its political and legal context, its legislative history, etc. – and try to decide which remedy the legislature would hypothetically have chosen'[98] when the courts adjust the statutory text to complement constitutional values.

Fish's preference for judges to provide the second-order outcome that the enacting legislature would have wanted may be most appropriate in the United States, where a Suspension Order is not available as a constitutional remedy, and the courts can only invalidate the impugned legislation outright or readjust the statutory text as best as they can. But in countries where a delayed declaration of invalidity forms part of the judicial remedial toolkit, the real choice before the courts is deciding between a Remedial Interpretation of the impugned law, a Suspension Order that gives the legislature a deadline to provide the requisite remedy or a combination of both.[99]

94 Tom Ginsburg, *Judicial Review in New Democracies* (Cambridge University Press 2003) 208; Sungmoon Kim, *Public Reason Confucianism: Democratic Perfectionism and Constitutionalism in East Asia* (Cambridge University Press 2016) 110–137.

95 Paul Gewirtz, 'Remedies and Resistance' (1983) 92 *Yale Law Journal* 587, 587.

96 Fish (n. 24).

97 Ibid. 326.

98 Ibid. 342.

99 J.Y. Interpretation No. 748 (2017) (Constitutional Court of Taiwan), available at https://cons.judicial.gov.tw/jcc/en-us/jep03/show?expno=748, accessed 12 May 2021; J.Y. Interpretation No. 755 (2017) (Constitutional Court of Taiwan), available at http://cons.judicial.gov.tw/jcc/en-us/jep03/show?expno=755, accessed 12 May 2021; *W v. Registrar of Marriages*, [2013] HKCFA 39, [2013]

## ADVANTAGES OF A SUSPENSION ORDER

The judicial use of a Suspension Order is most defensible when there is a range of constitutional options that could be implemented in light of the court's ruling,[100] such that due deference is paid to the primacy of the legislature's lawmaking role when it is given the opportunity to make the initial selection on how best to comply with the constitutional mandates among the competing alternatives available.[101]

In Interpretation No. 710 (2013),[102] the TCC ruled that it was unconstitutional for the government to indefinitely detain undocumented migrants from China, pending repatriation back to the Mainland. But the Court was also cognizant that a temporary period of detention was administratively necessary for deportation to be arranged. Therefore the Court gave the government two years to devise a new law or the original legislation would lose effect. The revised legislation now limits any administrative detention to 150 days.[103] Similarly, while the TCC in Interpretation No. 785 (2019)[104] held that the Public Functionary Service Act and the Civil Service Protection Act were unconstitutional insofar as they did not guarantee overtime pay and mandatory rest days for emergency services personnel, unlike ordinary civil servants who were statutorily given overtime pay[105] and two rest days per week,[106] the Court also left it to the legislature to determine the substantive terms of the remedial law.[107] More recently in 2020, when the TCC ruled that the statutory provision which imposed a minimum of five years imprisonment on all offenders convicted of cultivating marijuana was disproportionate,[108]

16 HKCFAR 112 (Hong Kong Court of Final Appeal); *Case on Search by Arrest Warrant of Dwellings other than the suspect's*, 2015Hun-Ba370 (26 April 2018) (Constitutional Court of Korea) (Official English Summary).

100 See Roach (n. 20) 212; Po Jen Yap, *Constitutional Dialogue in Common Law Asia* (Oxford University Press 2015) 101.

101 See Bruce Ryder, 'Suspending the Charter' (2003) 21 *Supreme Court Law Review* (2d) 267, 285.

102 J.Y. Interpretation No. 710 (2013) (Constitutional Court of Taiwan), available at http://cons.judicial.gov.tw/jcc/en-us/jep03/show?expno=710, accessed 12 May 2021.

103 Article 18-1, Paragraph 9 of Act Governing Relations between the People of the Taiwan Area and the Mainland Area.

104 J.Y. Interpretation No. 785 (2019) (Constitutional Court of Taiwan), available at http://cons.judicial.gov.tw/jcc/zh-tw/jep03/show?expno=785, accessed 12 May 2021.

105 Article 23 of the Civil Service Protection Act reads: 'Where a civil servant is required to perform duties not within regular office hours, the government agency he/she serves shall provide him/her with overtime payment, days off, reward or other equivalent compensation.'

106 Paragraph 2, Article 11 of the Public Functionary Service Act, https://law.moj.gov.tw/LawClass/LawAll.aspx?PCode=S0020038 (in Chinese), accessed 12 May 2021.

107 In this case, the TCC gave the Legislative Yuan an advisory three-year term to comply.

108 Paragraph 2, Article 12 of the Narcotics Hazard Prevention Act reads: 'Persons convicted of cultivating Cannabis with intentions to supply for manufacturing narcotics shall be punished with a minimum five-year fixed-term imprisonment, and may be fined no more than five million New Taiwan dollars.'

the Court gave the legislature one year to decide on the appropriate punishment in its legislative sequel.[109]

A Suspension Order is most desirable when there is a spectrum of reasonable options for the legislature to choose from when lawmakers deliberate on the remedial legislation. In South Korea, the KCC rightly left it to the National Assembly to recalibrate the appropriate length of time offenders should remain on the Sex Offenders Registry, after deeming a uniform 20-year rule for all cases disproportionate.[110] Similarly, the KCC justifiably allowed the legislature – in the first instance – to retweak its abortion laws after the Court deemed the virtual blanket ban on abortions in all stages of the woman's pregnancy[111] incompatible with the Constitution.[112] Equally appropriate is the KCC's decision to grant lawmakers time to devise a procedure to regulate how the state may collect DNA samples from the accused, when the original constitutional defect arose from the absence of one.[113]

Notably, while both the South Korean[114] and Hong Kong[115] courts have deemed the blanket prohibition on prisoner voting incompatible with their constitutions,

109 J.Y. Interpretation No. 790 (2020) (Constitutional Court of Taiwan), at [11], available at http://cons.judicial.gov.tw/jcc/zh-tw/jep03/show?expno=790, accessed 12 May 2021.

110 *Registration of Personal Information of Sex offenders*, 2015Hun-Ma99 (30 July 2015). The National Assembly revised the law in 2017 and the time an offender's personal information remains on the sex registry now varies according to the seriousness of the crime. See Section 1, Article 45 of the Act on Special Cases Concerning the Punishment, etc. of Sexual Crimes, which reads: 'The Minister of Justice shall retain and manage any registered information during a period according to the following classifications: 1. A person sentenced to capital punishment, imprisonment with labour for an indefinite term, imprisonment without labour for an indefiniute term, or impriusonment with or without labour for more than ten years for a seux crime which causes the registration of personal information: 30 years; 2. A person sentenced to imprisonment with or without labour for more than three years but not more than ten years for a sex crime which causes the registration of personal information: 20 years; 3. A person sentenced to imprisonment with or without labour for not more than three years for a sex crime which causes the registration of personal information or a person for whom an order to disclose information has become final and conclusive under Article 49 (1) 4 of the Act on the Protection of Children and Juveniles against Sexual Abuse; 4. A person subject to a fine for a sex crime which causes the registration of personal information: ten years.'

111 Article 14(1) of the Mother and Child Health Act read: 'A medical doctor may perform an induced abortion operation with the consent of the pregnant woman herself and her spouse ... only in the following cases: 1. Where she or her spouse suffers from any eugenic or genetic mental disability or physical disease prescribed by Presidential Decree; 2. Where she or her spouse suffers from any contagious disease prescribed by Presidential Decree; 3. Where she is impregnated by rape or quasi-rape; 4. Where pregnancy is taken place between relatives by blood or by marriage who are legally unable to marry; 5. Where the maintenance of pregnancy severely injures or is likely to injure the health of the pregnant woman for health or medical reasons.'

112 *Case on the Crime of Abortion*, 2017Hun-Ba127 (11 April 2019) (Constitutional Court of Korea) (Official English Summary). The National Assembly was given until 31 December 2020 to revise the law. As of 17 November 2020, the National Assembly has not revised this law.

113 *Case on the Procedure for the Issuance of a Warrant to Collect DNA Samples*, 2017Hun-Ma630 (30 August 2018) (Constitutional Court of Korea). The National Assembly revised this provision on 21 January 2020.

114 *Restriction on Right to Vote of Prisoners and Probationers with Suspended Sentence*, 2012Hun-Ma409 (28 January 2014) (Constitutional Court of Korea).

115 *Chan Kin Sum* v. *Secretary of Justice* [2009] 2 HKLRD 166 (Hong Kong Court of First Instance); *Chan Kin Sum* v. *Secretary for Justice* [2009] HKEC 393 (Hong Kong Court of First Instance).

they had also suspended their declaration so that their respective legislature was given time and space to devise appropriate remedial legislation. Neither court dictated to the lawmakers the details of an acceptable legislative sequel. According to the KCC, there was a 'scope of legislative discretion'[116] in determining the degree of culpability that would necessitate electoral disenfranchisement. Therefore, the 'details of granting the right to vote to prisoners [should] be decided by the legislature exercising its discretion'.[117] For Hong Kong, the Court also refused to determine at the first instance what type of voting restrictions would pass constitutional muster or 'where the cut-off line should be drawn and how it should be drawn',[118] as it is the function of the legislature and 'not the function of the courts to say what would constitute reasonable restrictions in Hong Kong'.[119] In the end, the Hong Kong Legislative Council decided to allow all prisoners to vote, while the South Korean National Assembly responded by giving the vote only to prisoners sentenced to less than one year of imprisonment.[120]

Such orders are dialogic, as the court initiates the conversation when it accepts the rights claims advanced by the litigants, but the legislature completes the conversation when it decides how best to complement and implement the judicial ruling.[121]

## ADVANTAGES OF REMEDIAL INTERPRETATION

On the other hand, an RI of an impugned law – whereby the courts read in words or read down the legal effect of statutory language, without resorting to an outright invalidation – is often defended on the basis that the legislature would prefer 'its legislative provision to have a valid, even if reduced, operation than to have no operation at all, so long as the valid operation is not fundamentally or essentially different from what it enacted'.[122] Unlike a typical canon of constitutional avoidance, which allows a court to adopt an interpretation of a statute that is constitutionally less problematic when there are 'two equally plausible'[123] readings of the legislation, an RI of the impugned law goes even further: even if the statutory text is clear, the courts will read long phrases and even sentences into the impugned statute, so as to make the defective law constitutionally compliant.

116 *Restriction on Right to Vote of Prisoners and Probationers with Suspended Sentence*, 2012Hun-Ma409, (28 January 2014) (Constitutional Court of Korea) (Official English Translation).

117 Ibid.

118 *Chan Kin Sum* [2009] 2 HKLRD 166 (Hong Kong Court of First Instance) [165].

119 Ibid.

120 Article 18(1)[2] of the Public Official Election Act; Article 43 (2) of the Criminal Act.

121 Roach (n. 1).

122 *HKSAR* v. *Lam Kwong Wai* [2006] 9 HKCFAR 574 (Hong Kong Court of Final Appeal) [77].

123 For an American example, see *Salinas* v. *United States*, 522 U.S. 52, 59–60 (1997).

In South Korea, RI – known in South Korea as a decision of limited[124] or conditional[125] constitutionality/unconstitutionality – was first applied in July 1989 when the KCC declared that a tax law, which required beneficial owners of real property to also hold the registered title,[126] was *constitutional* if it was interpreted to exempt beneficial owners who did not hold the registered title for legitimate non-tax evasion purposes.[127] Subsequently in 1991, the KCC issued its first decision of limited unconstitutionality.[128] The judicial power to award 'suitable measures to restore an injured party's reputation'[129] was deemed *unconstitutional* if it was interpreted to include a power to compel the defendant to apologize to the plaintiff. (The regulatory scope of a comparable law in Taiwan was also narrowed by the TCC.[130]) The KCC has acknowledged that in substance both 'modified'[131] rulings are the same and have equal binding force.[132]

Similar to South Korea, in Hong Kong and Taiwan, the Courts have upheld the constitutionality of impugned legislation by inserting phrases into the law to limit its regulatory scope. In *Yeung May Wan* (2005),[133] the HKCFA held that Section 50 of the Police Force Ordinance must be construed consistently with the city's constitutional guarantees against arbitrary arrest. Furthermore, the impugned statutory provision that permitted a police officer to apprehend a person 'who he reasonably believes will be charged'[134] must be read down to mean 'who he reasonably believes will be charged *on the basis of a reasonable suspicion that the arrested person is guilty of the offence to be charged*'.[135] Public order offences in Hong Kong that criminalize disorderly acts that 'prevent … the transaction of the business for [a] public gathering'[136] were judicially confined to acts which '*make it impossible in practical terms to hold or continue with the gathering; or, at least, to interrupt the gathering for*

124 The Constitutional Court of Korea (n. 38) 101.
125 Ibid. 125.
126 Article 32-2(1) of the Inheritance Tax Act (South Korea).
127 *Inheritance Tax Act Case*, 89Hun-Ma38 (21 July 1989) (Constitutional Court of Korea).
128 *Notice of Apology Case*, 89Hun-Ma160 (1 April 1991) (Constitutional Court of Korea).
129 Article 764 of the Civil Act read: 'The court may, on the application of the injured party, order the person who has impaired another's fame to take suitable measures to restore the injured party's fame, either in lieu of, or together with damages.'
130 J.Y. Interpretation No. 656 (Taiwan) (2009) (Constitutional Court of Taiwan), at [3], available at http://cons.judicial.gov.tw/jcc/en-us/jep03/show?expno=656, accessed 12 May 2021. In this decision, the TCC ruled that a judicial order for a public apology is constitutional so long as other forms of relief are 'not sufficient to warrant the restoration of the injured party's reputation', taking into account 'the severity of damage to the reputation, the identity of both parties, and the offender's economic status'; and the order does not 'induce self-humiliation to the point that human dignity is disparaged'.
131 The Constitutional Court of Korea (n. 38) 163.
132 Ibid. 224.
133 *Yeung May Wan v. HKSAR*, [2005] HKCFA 24, [2005] 8 HKCFAR 137 (Hong Kong Court of Final Appeal).
134 Section 50(1) of the Police Force Ordinance (Cap 232).
135 *Yeung May Wan* (n. 133) [66].
136 Section 17B(1) of the Public Order Act (Cap 245).

*such a duration or by using such means as substantially to impair the intended transaction of business.*'[137] In Taiwan, even though the law on criminal defamation requires the defendants to prove the truth of their statements,[138] the TCC held that the accused would equally be exculpated if they have '*reasonable grounds to believe that the statement was true at the moment of dissemination.*'[139]

Such 'strained interpretation'[140] of impugned legislative provisions in substance creates a legislative power for the judiciary, but where the requisite changes needed to the law do not require the government to deliberate over a range of complex constitutional options that implicate polycentric concerns, such piecemeal reforms writ small undertaken by the judges themselves may also be more expedient and effective, especially if there is a backlog of more important bills on the legislative agenda.

Furthermore, judges also have the strategic incentive to engage in piecemeal RI when an open invalidation of the law would trigger public disquiet or governmental backlash. By incrementally adjusting the text of the law on its own, instead of publicly deeming the legislation in question unconstitutional, the court diffuses potential political opposition, while quietly modifying the operational meaning of the flawed statute to achieve greater constitutional compliance. When the TCC was faced with the constitutionality of a statutory provision in the Child and Juvenile Sexual Transaction Prevention Act[141] that imposed strict liability on any person who publishes any information in any medium which may induce a person to engage in sexual activity, the Court was hard pressed to uphold this dragnet law because the law was intended to protect children. Therefore, of its own accord, the TCC decided to read in a new defence into the legislation: any information distributed by the accused which '*neither contains child or juvenile sexual transaction nor is intended to induce children or juveniles to engage in sexual transaction and necessary*

137 *HKSAR* v. *Chow Nok Hang* [2013] 16 HKCFAR 837 (Hong Kong Court of Final Appeal) [58].

138 Article 310, Paragraphs 3 of the Criminal Code provides that: 'A person who can prove the truth of the defamatory fact shall not be punished for the offense of defamation . . .'.

139 J.Y. Interpretation No. 509 (2000) (Constitutional Court of Taiwan), at [2], available at http://cons.judicial.gov.tw/jcc/en-us/jep03/show?expno=509, accessed 12 May 2021.

140 *HKSAR* v. *Lam Kwong Wai*, [2006] HKCFA 84, [2006] 9 HKCFAR 574 (Hong Kong Court of Final Appeal) [77]. With regard to the United Kingdom's *Human Rights Act* 1998, 1998, c 42, Aileen Kavanagh has also argued that English judges, when choosing between a declaration of incompatibility and a remedial reading of the existing law, must assess whether 'the disadvantages of a particular strained interpretation outweigh the advantages in terms of justice for the individual litigants'. See Aileen Kavanagh, *Constitutional Review under the UK Human Rights Act* (Cambridge University Press 2009) 142.

141 Although the TCC invoked RI to uphold the provision, the legislature also revised the whole Act in 2015, which incorporated the Court's ruling. The disputed provision has now been revised as Paragraph 1, Article 40 of Child and Youth Sexual Exploitation Prevention Act, which now reads: 'Any person who, by means of promotional materials, publications, broadcast, television, telecommunication, the Internet sources, or other methods, distributes, sends, publishes, or posts messages that are deemed to be sufficient to seduce, arrange, suggest, or cause a child or youth to be subjected to [sexual exploitation], shall be subject to imprisonment . . .'.

*precautionary measures have been taken to limit the recipients of such information to those who are eighteen years of age or older*' would not violate the penal statute in question.[142]

Similarly, in view of South Korea's long-standing tensions with North Korea, the KCC was understandably reluctant to openly invalidate legislation pertaining to national security. So instead, vague and overbroad penal provisions, which criminally sanctioned any person who praised or sympathized with the activities of anti-government organizations, were read down such that the law would only apply if 'national security and the basic order of free democracy'[143] were threatened.[144] In the same vein, legislation that imposed a minimum sentence of five years imprisonment on any persons who 'consult an accomplishment of purpose with an anti-government organization'[145] were deemed conditionally constitutional only if the law applied to acts that pose a grave risk to national security or the democratic fundamental order of the country.[146] Draconian laws that punish the unauthorized dissemination of all military secrets were also judicially confined to classified materials that, if disclosed, would 'pose a clear threat to national security'.[147]

Moreover, in Taiwan and Hong Kong, the Courts have also engaged in RI by adopting a statutory construction that conflicted with the plain meaning of the law, while still *claiming fidelity* to the legislature's intent. In short, RI is adopted under the guise of statutory interpretation.

In Hong Kong, an administrative by-law that imposed a blanket prohibition on signs and messages, including signs or messages on items of clothing in the

142 J.Y. Interpretation No. 623 (2007) (Constitutional Court of Taiwan), at [2], available at http://cons.judicial.gov.tw/jcc/en-us/jep03/show?expno=623, accessed 12 May 2021.

143 *Praising and Encouraging under National Security Act Case*, 89Hun-Ka113 (2 April 1990) (Constitutional Court of Korea); The Constitutional Court of Korea, *Twenty Years of the Constitutional Court of Korea* (The Constitutional Court of Korea 2008) 214. The impugned Article 7(1) of the National Security Act was revised in 1991 to reflect this judicial RI: 'Any person who praises, incites or propagates the activities of an anti-government organization, a member thereof or of the person who has received an order from it, or who acts in concert with it, or propagates or instigates a rebellion against the State, with the knowledge of the fact that it may endanger the existence and security of the State or democratic fundamental order, shall be punished by imprisonment for not more than seven years.'

144 See Ginsburg (n. 94) 236–238.

145 Article 6(2) of the National Security Act read: 'Any person who has infiltrated from or escaped to receive an order from, or consult an accomplishment of purpose with, an anti-government organization or a member thereof, shall be punished by capital punishment, imprisonment for life or imprisonment for more than five years.'

146 89Hun-Ma240 (16 January 1997) (Constitutional Court of Korea); 99Hun-Ba27 (25 April 2002) (Constitutional Court of Korea).

147 *Military Secret Leakage Case*, 89Hun-Ka104 (25 February 1992) (Constitutional Court of Korea). In 1993, the National Assembly amended the statutory definition of 'military secret' to reflect this RI: '"military secret" means a special media record or object, such as a military-related document, picture, electronic record that is not made known to the general public and, if leaked, could cause clear damage to the national security, and is thus indicated or notified as military secrets or properly protected as such.'

public/press gallery of the Hong Kong Legislative Council, was read down by the HKCFA, such that the impugned by-law would only apply to '*conduct which amounts to behaving in a disorderly manner.*'[148] According to the HKCFA, Section 12(3) of the Administrative Instructions for Regulating Admittance and Conduct of Persons (Cap 382A) was aimed at conduct which amounts to behaving in a disorderly manner and did not prohibit messages on T-shirts that were not brandished intrusively.[149] But if we examine the text of Section 12(3) closely, the by-law actually uses the word 'or' to separate each sub-clause that justifies non-admission.

In essence, according to Section 12(3):

An officer of the Council may refuse admission to a press or public gallery

(1) to any person displaying any sign, message or banner, or
(2) to any person displaying any sign or message on any item of clothing, or
(3) to any person who, in the opinion of an officer of the Council, may so display any sign, message or banner, may so display any sign or message on any item of clothing or may *otherwise behave in a disorderly manner.*

The use of the word 'or' suggests that each ground for justifying non-admission was separate and applied disjunctively. But with a sleight of hand, the HKCFA converted a separate independent sub-clause into a general limitation that restricted the operation of all the other independent clauses. In the same vein, prison rules that limited visits to 'friends' of inmates were construed by the HKCFA to include companies that deliver meals and magazines to them, such that employees of these companies were acquitted of defrauding officers of the Correctional Services Department when they had represented themselves as the inmates' friends.[150] One may note that the visitors in question did not have any pre-existing personal relationship with the inmates and had never met the inmates.[151] But in view of its 'proper construction'[152] of the prison rules, the HKCFA in essence held that a friend of a friend is a 'friend' under the prison rules. In the same vein, under the guise of statutory interpretation, the Hong Kong Court of Appeal has exempted solo demonstrators from the ostensibly blanket prohibition against public assemblies at the forecourt of the legislature on weekdays.[153]

148 *HKSAR* v. *Fong Kwok Shan Christine*, [2017] HKCFA 59, [2017] 20 HKCFAR 425 (Hong Kong Court of Final Appeal) [107].

149 Ibid.

150 *HKSAR* v. *Wan Thomas* [2018] 21 HKCFAR 214 (Hong Kong Court of Final Appeal).

151 Ibid. [19].

152 Ibid. [50].

153 *Cheung Tak Wing* v. *Director of Immigration* [2020] HKCA 124 (Hong Kong Court of Appeal) [112]–[113]. Notably, the impugned regulation provided that the forecourt of the legislature could only be made available to the public on Sundays and public days, but the Court of Appeal read solo demonstrators out of this licensing scheme altogether, such that they are not subject to the prohibition.

Even with Hong Kong's draconian National Security Law (NSL), the HKCFA has not simply capitulated to everything the government seeks. In its first substantive NSL ruling in *HKSAR* v. *Lai Chee Ying (2021)*,[154] the HKCFA had to interpret the statutory requirements for bail under the NSL. Article 42(2) of the NSL reads: 'No bail shall be granted to a criminal suspect or defendant unless the judge has sufficient grounds for believing that the criminal suspect or defendant will not continue to commit acts endangering national security.'[155] While the HKCFA accepted that the requirements for bail under the NSL are 'more stringent'[156] than the position under the ordinary criminal law where a presumption in favour of bail exists, the Court also ruled *against* the government when the former concluded that bail conditions should *not* be presumptively excluded from consideration when judges decide whether to grant bail under the NSL.[157] Therefore, lower court judges, in deciding whether to grant bail to the accused charged under the NSL, have to assess whether the preventive effect of appropriate bail conditions would suffice, instead of mechanically imposing a custodial order pending trial. And the HKCFA defended this ruling using the ordinary rules of *statutory* interpretation:

> NSL [Article] 4 and NSL [Article] 5 expressly stipulate that . . . rights, freedoms and values are to be protected and adhered to in applying the NSL. They provide the context in which NSL [Article] 42(2) must be construed and applied. As far as possible, NSL 42(2) is to be given a meaning and effect compatible with those rights, freedoms and values.[158]

Similarly, the TCC in Interpretation No. 665 (2009)[159] had to determine whether a law which allowed the state to detain a defendant charged for a serious crime before trial was constitutional. This law poses due process concerns as a defendant in Taiwan is presumed innocent until proven guilty.[160] Notably, the state was also authorized to detain a defendant pending trial if s/he was a flight-risk or if s/he could have obstructed the investigation by tampering with evidence or witnesses.[161] In short, all three grounds for pre-trial detention apply *disjunctively* – detention is

154 *HKSAR* v. *Lai Chee Ying* [2021] HKCFA 3 (Hong Kong Court of Final Appeal).

155 Article 42(2) of the Law of the People's Republic of China on Safeguarding National Security in the Hong Kong Special Administrative Region.

156 *Lai Chee Ying* (n. 154) [53(b)].

157 Ibid. [57].

158 Ibid. [42].

159 J.Y. Interpretation No. 665 (2009) (Constitutional Court of Taiwan), available at http://cons.judicial.gov.tw/jcc/en-us/jep03/show?expno=665, accessed 12 May 2021.

160 Ibid. [10].

161 Article 101, Paragraph 1 of the Code of Criminal Procedure provided: 'A defendant may be detained . . . due to the existence of one of the following circumstances. . . : (i) She has absconded, or there are facts sufficient to justify an apprehension that she may abscond; (ii) There are facts sufficient to justify an apprehension that she may destroy, forge, or alter evidence, or conspire with accomplices or witnesses or (iii) She has committed an offense punishable with the death penalty, life imprisonment, or a minimum punishment of imprisonment for no less than five years.'

authorized so long as any one condition is satisfied. In the end, the TCC upheld the constitutionality of the impugned law, but ruled that the law can apply only when 'the trial court ... has a reasonable ground to believe that the defendant is likely to escape, to destroy, forge, or alter evidence, or to conspire with accomplices or witnesses'.[162] In other words, the TCC grafted the other two preconditions onto the impugned law such that all three grounds for pre-trial detention have to now apply *conjunctively*. Notably, four Justices dissented in this case precisely because this judicial interpretation distorted the meaning of the original text.[163]

Such constitutional avoidance seeks to preserve the Court's reputation and institutional capital, as judges 'effectively re-write laws while pretending to exercise restraint'.[164] Unlike a public declaration of invalidity or an express use of RI, such judicial acts of 'passive avoidance'[165] allow the HKCFA and TCC to camouflage their judicial activism and spearhead constitutional changes by stealth.

## CONCLUSION

Naturally, there are differences in how the three East Asian courts apply these innovative remedies, which we will now explore. In Hong Kong, a Suspension Order is always accompanied with a fixed deadline for legislative compliance,[166] and occasionally the Court imposes a remedial reading-in proviso that takes effect automatically if there is no remedial law at the end of the suspension period.[167] The latter remedy also exists in Taiwan,[168] but not South Korea. Hong Kong courts tend to suspend their declaration of invalidity for a shorter period.[169] Unlike Hong Kong, the Constitutional Courts of South Korea and Taiwan have also issued Suspension Orders – albeit occasionally – that do *not* impose a deadline for legislative compliance.[170] Furthermore, in Taiwan and South Korea the

162 J.Y. Interpretation No. 665 (2009) (Constitutional Court of Taiwan), at [12], available at http://cons.judicial.gov.tw/jcc/en-us/jep03/show?expno=665, accessed 12 May 2021.

163 See dissenting opinions by Justice Tzong-Li Hsu, Justice Chen-Shan Li, Justice Tzu-Yi Lin and Justice Yu-hsiu Hsu in J.Y. Interpretation No. 665 (2009) (Constitutional Court of Taiwan).

164 Fish (n. 33) 1275, 1315.

165 Anita S. Krishnakumar, 'Passive Avoidance' (2019) 71 *Stanford Law Review* 513, 569.

166 *Koo Sze Yiu* v. *Chief Executive of HKSAR* [2006] 9 HKCFAR 441 (Hong Kong Court of Final Appeal).

167 *W* v. *Registrar of Marriages* [2013] 16 HKCFAR 112 (Hong Kong Court of Final Appeal).

168 J.Y. Interpretation No. 748 (2017) (Constitutional Court of Taiwan), available at http://cons.judicial.gov.tw/jcc/en-us/jep03/show?expno=748, accessed 12 May 2021.

169 In Hong Kong, the Hong Kong courts have yet to grant a legislative deadline that is longer than 12 months. Most legislative deadlines in Hong Kong are six months or less. In Taiwan, the average deadline is about 17 months, while in South Korea, deadlines tend to be between one and two years.

170 *Case on the House Head System*, 2001Hun-Ga9, 10, 11, 12, 13, 14, 15 and 2004Hun-Ga5 (consolidated) (3 February 2005) (Constitutional Court of Korea); J.Y. Interpretation No. 601 (2005) (Constitutional Court of Taiwan), available at http://cons.judicial.gov.tw/jcc/en-us/jep03/show?expno=601, accessed 12 May 2021.

Constitutional Courts have even issued interim remedial readings of the law pending legislative review.[171] This has not happened in Hong Kong.

Moreover, the judicial use of RI in Hong Kong appears to be on the rise, while the KCC has reduced its use of RI over the years. For Hong Kong, in view of the increased polarization and fragmentation in the legislature prior to the 2021 electoral overhaul – exacerbated by months of civil unrest following the aborted extradition bill[172] – it is the government that now regularly asks the courts to issue an RI after the law has been deemed unconstitutional, rather than leaving it to lawmakers to deliberate on a piece of remedial legislation.[173] For example, a penal provision in Hong Kong provides that 'a man who commits buggery with a man under the age of 16 … shall be … liable on conviction … to imprisonment for life',[174] while the statutory cap for heterosexual intercourse with minors is five years.[175] To remedy this discriminatory measure against gay men, the government asked the court to 'interpret' new sentencing caps into the pre-existing law: '*imprisonment for 5 years if the buggery is committed with a boy under the age of 16 but is of or above the age of 13*',[176] and the HKCFI acceded to this request. Similarly, after HKCFA ruled that it was unconstitutional to bar same-sex couples legally married overseas from claiming tax benefits in Hong Kong as a family unit,[177] it was the government who asked the Court to read the pre-existing statutory requirement of 'husband and wife'[178] as '*a married person and his or her spouse*',[179] in lieu of granting an ordinary Suspension Order for the lawmakers to amend the legislation themselves. The HKCFA agreed and it also suspended this RI for six months so that the tax authorities had time to align their administrative practices.[180] More recently, when the Hong Kong Court of Appeal declared that an electoral law was disproportionate insofar as it required all

[171] J.Y. Interpretation No. 755 (2017) (Constitutional Court of Taiwan), available at http://cons.judicial.gov.tw/jcc/en-us/jep03/show?expno=755, accessed 12 May 2021. *Case on Search by Arrest Warrant of Dwellings other than the suspect's*, 2015Hun-Ba370 (26 April 2018) (Constitutional Court of Korea) (Official English Summary).

[172] For a discussion of this saga, see Richard Cullen, *Hong Kong Constitutionalism: The British Legacy and the Chinese Future* (Routledge 2020) 131–136.

[173] *Keen Lloyd Holdings* v. *Commissioner of Customs and Excise* [2016] 2 HKLRD 1372 (Hong Kong Court of Appeal); *Yeung Chu Wing* v. *Secretary for Justice* [2019] HKCFI 1431 (Hong Kong Court of First Instance); *HKSAR* v. *Yu Lik Wai* [2019] HKCA 1093 (Hong Kong Court of Appeal); *Leung Chun Kwong* v. *Secretary for the Civil Service* [2019] HKCFA 34 (Hong Kong Court of Final Appeal).

[174] Section 118C of the Crimes Ordinance (Cap 200).

[175] Section 124 of the Crimes Ordinance (Cap 200).

[176] *Yeung Chu Wing* v. *Secretary for Justice* [2019] HKCFI 1431 (Hong Kong Court of First Instance) [34].

[177] *Leung Chun Kwong* v. *Secretary for the Civil Service* [2019] HKCFA 19 (Hong Kong Court of Final Appeal).

[178] See Section 2 of the Inland Revenue Ordinance (Cap 112).

[179] *Leung Chun Kwong* v. *Secretary for the Civil Service* [2019] HKCFA 34 (Hong Kong Court of Final Appeal) [8]–[9].

[180] Ibid. [11]. In *Ng Hon Lam* v. *Secretary for Justice* [2020] HKCFI 2412, the Hong Kong Court of First Instance also applied RI to Hong Kong intestacy laws so that same-sex spouses legally married overseas can be treated as equivalent to husbands and wives for the purpose of intestacy inheritance.

voters to disclose their primary residential addresses to the public for inspection of their authenticity, even if individual voters could prove that unrestricted public access would pose a real risk to their safety, the HKCA read-in an exception that allowed electoral candidates, political parties and members of the press access to such information for verification.[181]

On the other hand, the KCC has ratcheted *down* its use of RI, as it remains locked in a jurisdictional battle with its Supreme Court over the binding effect of the former's decisions of conditional unconstitutionality.[182] The Korean Supreme Court has regularly determined that such decisions are merely advisory and has often refused to apply these KCC precedents.[183] The KCC has even publicly lamented about the ongoing tension and expresses regret that the ordinary courts have yet to resolve this disagreement.[184] Therefore, while the KCC stands by its guns and continues to issue such 'conditional' orders, it has done so more sparingly in recent years.[185]

But we must not miss the forest for the trees. The indisputable fact remains that Hong Kong, Taiwan and South Korea are the only jurisdictions in Asia with courts that have converged on the continuous use of Suspension Orders and Remedial Interpretation when engaging in constitutional adjudication.

With regard to Suspension Orders, Hong Kong, Taiwan and South Korea have converged on using two-track remedies that provide strong individual relief for successful litigants, coupled with weak deferential judicial orders designed to allow the government to devise systemic remedies 'in a more democratic and participatory manner'[186] for the future. At the same time, the three courts have also converged on

[181] *Junior Police Officers' Association of the Hong Kong Police Force* v. *Electoral Affairs Commission* [2020] HKCA 352 (Hong Kong Court of Appeal).

[182] See The Constitutional Court of Korea (n. 42) 148–149. In *Actual Transaction Price-based Transfer Profits Tax Case*, 94Hun-Ba40 (30 November 1995) (Constitutional Court of Korea), the KCC ruled that the Income Tax rules were conditionally unconstitutional to the extent that they allowed the capital gains tax imposed on a property to be calculated using actual transaction prices that were greater than the 'tax standard value'. This decision was rejected by the Supreme Court in 95Nu11405 (9 April 1996). Notwithstanding a jurisdictional ouster clause enshrined in Article 68(1) of the Constitutional Court Act, the KCC in the *Constitutional Review of Judgements Case*, 96Hun-Ma172 (24 December 1997) (Constitutional Court of Korea) annulled this Supreme Court decision by stating that the former is not excluded from adjudicating on judgments from ordinary courts if the impugned judgments violate the fundamental rights of the people. Notably, Article 68(1) of the Constitutional Court Act (1995) provided: 'Any person who is infringed his fundamental rights guaranteed by the Constitution of the Republic of Korea due to exercise or non-exercise of the public power, *excluding judgment of the court*, may request the Constitutional Court Regulations an adjudication on constitutional petition…' (emphasis added).

[183] Supreme Court [S. Ct.], 95Nu11405, 9 April 1996, (44(1) JIP 762) (Supreme Court of Korea).

[184] The Constitutional Court of Korea, *Thirty Years of the Constitutional Court of Korea* (The Constitutional Court of Korea 2018) 148–149. See Ginsburg (n. 94) 241.

[185] Notably, since the KCC decision of 99Hun-Ba27 (25 April 2002), the Court has stopped issuing decisions of constitutional *constitutionality*. But it continues to hand down decisions of conditional *unconstitutionality*.

[186] Roach (n. 1) 877; see also Roach (n. 66).

the judicial use of RI or the 'active avoidance'[187] of a judicial declaration of invalidity that allows the impugned statute to survive, albeit in a judicially modified form.

The judicial use of remedial discretion may pose constitutional dilemmas for legal purists. But if we view governance as a 'field of partnership'[188] between the judiciary and the legislature, these innovative remedial strategies have the capacity to foster greater democratic deliberation and improve legislative and executive performance, for they conjoin the very best in statecraft and adjudication.

[187] See Neal Kumar Katyal and Thomas P. Schmidt, 'Active Avoidance: The Modern Supreme Court and Legal Change' (2015) 128 *Harvard Law Review* 2110.

[188] Philip Sales, 'Partnership and Challenge: The Courts' Role in Managing the Integration of Rights and Democracy' (2016) *Public Law* 456, 457.

# 5

# Limits on Convergence

## INTRODUCTION

There are limits to this constitutional convergence in East Asia. The three courts will *not* converge on electoral reform. There is a symbiotic relationship between a country's state of democratization and the long-term sustainability of the power that its judges can wield in generating electoral change.[1] While Taiwan and South Korea are dynamic democracies where competing political parties take turns in office, Hong Kong is a sub-unit of communist China. And China will not tolerate any judicial attempts to loosen the central government's political chokehold on the city. Therefore, the initiation of major electoral systemic changes or personnel changes adverse to China's core interests are simply off-limits to the Hong Kong courts.

Electoral competition within the polity is a defining feature that impacts the strength of its courts[2] and affects the judiciary's ability to generate systemic democratic change. The 'political-legal dynamics'[3] within a regime will often determine whether courts can succeed or fail as 'alchemists'[4] in building democracy. Courts operating in a dominant-party democracy will rarely succeed as democracy builders.[5] Similarly, in many unstable third world economies, intense political competition within that regime will only incentivize their politicians to hamper the independent performance of courts for short-term gains.[6] However, in dynamic democracies where economic development and stability are prized, their courts can

1 Po Jen Yap, *Courts and Democracies in Asia* (Cambridge University Press 2017).

2 Stephen Gardbaum, 'What Makes for More or Less Powerful Constitutional Courts?' (2018) 29 *Duke Journal of Comparative & International Law* 1, 24.

3 Theunis Roux, *The Politico-Legal Dynamics of Judicial Review: A Comparative Analysis* (Cambridge University Press 2018).

4 Tom Gerald Daly, *The Alchemists: Questioning our Faith in Courts as Democracy-Builders* (Cambridge University Press 2017). Daly is sceptical about whether courts can successfully build democracy, but his central argument rests on one national case study – Brazil. For a more contextual defence of the judicial role, see Yap (n. 1).

5 Yap (n. 1).

6 Aylin Aydin, 'Judicial Independence across Democratic Regimes: Understanding the Varying Impact of Political Competition' (2013) 47 *Law and Society Review* 105.

not only play 'a stabilizing role'[7] in fending off short-term legislative or executive assaults on long-standing institutional guardrails, they can also facilitate their nations' democratic transformation by enhancing the fairness of voting procedures and directly addressing institutional failures in the political system, including but not limited to the anti-competitive 'rules of engagement [enacted] to protect established powers from the risk of successful challenge'.[8]

In Part 1, we will examine how the Constitutional Court of Taiwan (TCC) has opened up new pathways for democratization for its nation. Part 2 continues by exploring how the Constitutional Court of Korea (KCC) has ushered into its political system a more liberal model of democratic diversity, which ordinarily would be resisted by self-serving political incumbents. In contrast, Part 3 analyses how the Hong Kong courts have yielded to Beijing's tightening political grip over the city.

## PART 1: TAIWAN

Since the lifting of martial law in 1987, Taiwan has transformed from an autocracy to a modern liberal democracy. Unlike the Ukrainian courts during the Orange Revolution (2004–2005), the TCC was not an upstream trigger of the nation's democratization.[9] Instead, the TCC served as a 'downstream democratic consolidator'[10] of the nation's democratization movement after martial law ended. And as the nation liberalized, the TCC became more assertive and successfully made both macro- and micro-systemic changes to the electoral system.[11]

In the early days, the TCC was just a handmaiden of the Kuomintang (KMT) military regime. Even though the right to vote was expressly protected in the Constitution,[12] this right was suspended in 1948 by the Temporary Provisions Effective During the Period of Communist Rebellion after civil war broke out

[7] Samuel Issacharoff, 'Judicial Review in Troubled Times: Stabilizing Democracy in a Second Best World' (2019) 1 *North Carolina Law Review* 1, 5.

[8] Samuel Issacharoff and Richard H. Pildes, 'Politics as Markets: Partisan Lockups of the Democratic Process' (1997–1998) 50 *Stanford Law Review* 643, 646.

[9] Tom Ginsburg, 'The Politics of Courts in Democratization' in Diana Kapiszewski, Gordon Silverstein, and Robert A. Kagan (eds), *Consequential Courts: Judicial Roles in Global Perspective* (Cambridge University Press 2013) 45, 49.

[10] Ibid. 50.

[11] Jiunn-rong Yeh and Wen-Chen Chang, 'An Evolving Court with Changing Functions: The Constitutional Court and Judicial Review in Taiwan' in Albert H. Y. Chen and Andrew Harding (eds), *Constitutional Courts in Asia: A Comparative Perspective* (Cambridge University Press 2018) 118–123, 138–139.

[12] Article 17 of the Constitution of the Republic of China (Taiwan) (1947) provides: 'The people shall have the right of election, recall, initiative and referendum.'

between the KMT and the Chinese communist regime.[13] Even as active hostilities ended between China and Taiwan in 1979, elections were not reinstated. Unsurprisingly, during the martial law era,[14] the TCC was firmly aligned with the KMT. In Interpretation No. 31 (1954), the TCC was asked to decide whether the first-term congressmen could continue to exercise their power in Taiwan after the expiration of their legislative term in 1951, and the Justices unanimously affirmed that national elections should be indefinitely suspended as '[the] state has been undergoing a severe calamity'.[15] Therefore, the first-term congressmen, elected in China from November 1947 to January 1948, continued to exercise their power in Taiwan for more than four decades. Since most of these representatives were KMT members, the suspension of national elections perpetuated the party-state era in which the KMT controlled all levers of political powers and obstructed any political reform that eroded its control over Taiwan.[16]

After martial law ended in 1987, the thorny issue of whether national elections in Taiwan could be suspended indefinitely arose again. This time, in the iconic Interpretation No. 261 ( 1990),[17] the TCC declared that the 'periodic election of members of Congress is a sine qua non to reflect the will of the people and implement constitutional democracy'.[18] Notably, Interpretation No. 31 (1954) was distinguished on the basis that the earlier judicial opinion did not intend to suspend national elections in Taiwan indefinitely without just cause.[19] As times have changed, the TCC exhorted the KMT government to hold elections across Taiwan 'in compliance with the spirit of the Constitution … so that the constitutional system may function properly'.[20] This landmark decision has been praised as 'the most important case'[21] the TCC has ever decided, as it paved the way for the return of legislative elections in 1992. But one should also note that this decision not only resonated with the public, it also dovetailed with the interests of the mainstream KMT party elites led by President Lee Teng-hui who were seeking to retire those geriatric legislators hindering his party reforms.[22] One former Justice who participated in Interpretation No. 261 (1990) later confirmed that the TCC had in fact

13 The Temporary Provisions were not abolished until 1991. See Temporary Provisions Effective during the Period of Communist Rebellion (1991) (Taiwan), available at https://law.moj.gov.tw/LawClass/LawAll.aspx?pcode=A0000005, accessed 15 May 2021.

14 The Martial Law in Taiwan was promulgated in 1949 and remained effective until 1987.

15 J.Y. Interpretation No. 31 (1954) (Constitutional Court of Taiwan), at [1], available at http://cons.judicial.gov.tw/jcc/en-us/jep03/show?expno=31, accessed 15 May 2021.

16 Shelley Rigger, *Politics in Taiwan: Voting for Democracy* (Routledge 1999) 55–80.

17 J.Y. Interpretation No. 261 (1990) (Constitutional Court of Taiwan), available at http://cons.judicial.gov.tw/jcc/en-us/jep03/show?expno=261, accessed 15 May 2021.

18 Ibid. [3].

19 Ibid.

20 Ibid. [5].

21 Tom Ginsburg, *Judicial Review in New Democracies: Constitutional Courts in Asian Cases* (Cambridge University Press 2003) 145.

22 Ibid. 147; Yap (n. 1) 95.

done the KMT government a favour by forcing these congressmen to retire, because the latter had become a huge political liability for the KMT.[23]

In Interpretation No. 499 (2000),[24] the TCC became even more assertive as it vetoed constitutional amendments passed by the National Assembly. In 1999, the National Assembly – by a secret ballot – used the constitutional amendment process to prolong their own legislative term for two years.[25] Most Taiwanese people were infuriated by this undemocratic constitutional revision and pressured both KMT and Democratic Progressive Party (DPP) legislators to petition the TCC for a resolution. Whether the TCC had the power to review the legality of constitutional amendments was the threshold question the TCC had to resolve. Although the Constitution does not enshrine any express limits on constitutional change, the TCC declared that 'Article 1[26] (the principle of a democratic republic), Article 2[27] (the principle of popular sovereignty), Chapter II (the protection of constitutional rights), and those providing for the separation of powers and the principle of checks and balances … constitute the foundational principles of the entire constitutional order.'[28] As such, these constitutional provisions were binding on all branches of government and could not be revised.[29] At the same time, the TCC also determined that procedurally, a constitutional amendment will also be null and void if 'a manifest and gross flaw occurs in the amendment procedures'.[30] A procedural error will be considered manifest if 'the facts of the flaw can be determined without further investigation'[31] and the error is gross when 'the facts of the flaw alone will render the procedure illegitimate'.[32]

On the facts, the TCC invoked Interpretation No. 31 (1954) and Interpretation No. 261 (1990) and ruled that the the suspension of national elections was not

23 楊與齡 Yu-Ling Yang，'大法官第二六一號解釋與我國憲政發展 (J.Y. Interpretation No. 261 and the Development of Constitutional Democracy in Taiwan)' (1998) 23 卷 3 期, 《憲政時代 *Constitutional Review*》, 19.

24 J.Y. Interpretation No. 499 (2000) (Constitutional Court of Taiwan), available at http://cons.judicial.gov.tw/jcc/en-us/jep03/show?expno=499, accessed 15 May 2021.

25 Paragraph 3, Article 1 of the Additional Articles of the Constitution of the Republic of China (Taiwan) (1999) read: '…The term of office of the Third National Assembly shall be extended to the day when the term of office of the Fourth Legislative Yuan expires…'. This would in effect prolong the term of members of the National Assembly for two years.

26 Article 1 of the Constitution of the Republic of China (Taiwan) (1947) reads: 'The Republic of China, founded on the Three Principles of the People, shall be a democratic republic of the people, to be governed by the people and for the people.'

27 Article 2 of the Constitution of the Republic of China (Taiwan) (1947) reads: 'The sovereignty of the Republic of China shall reside in the whole body of citizens.'

28 J.Y. Interpretation No. 499 (2000) (Constitutional Court of Taiwan), at [9], available at http://cons.judicial.gov.tw/jcc/en-us/jep03/show?expno=499, accessed 15 May 2021.

29 Ibid.

30 Ibid. [6].

31 Ibid.

32 Ibid.

allowed 'unless just causes exist for not holding the election'.[33] Given that no just cause existed herein, arguably as active hostilities had ended, the legislative term extension violated the principle of popular sovereignty enshrined in the Constitution. Furthermore, the TCC ruled that amendments to the Constitution must be done in an 'open and transparent'[34] manner. The use of secret ballots therefore contravened this principle. Thus, as a matter of both substance and procedure, the impugned constitutional amendments violated 'the basic norm that underpins the validity of constitutional amendments ... and [is] impermissible under the constitutional order of liberal democracy',[35] One month after this decision, the National Assembly passed a new round of constitutional reforms in April 2000, in which it became an ad hoc institution that only convened to consider constitutional amendments, territorial change, and presidential impeachment.[36] The National Assembly was eventually abolished in 2005.[37]

The TCC also removed several barriers to the citizenry's right to stand for elections. One early example is Interpretation No. 290 (1992),[38] in which the TCC had to rule on the onerous educational qualification imposed on persons who were seeking to run for public office.[39] For instance, a high school diploma was required for anyone who wanted to contest the legislative election.[40] Although the TCC upheld the impugned law in Interpretation No. 290 (1992), the Court also emphasized that with time, mass education would enhance the voters' ability to make informed choices, and restrictions based on educational qualifications should be reviewed 'in light of the examples of other democracies... The circumstances of those who have difficulty completing compulsory education should also be considered (e.g., those with physical or other disabilities ...)'.[41] Following the TCC's advice, the legislature repealed these requirements in 1994 on the ground that the Legislative Yuan should be a diverse body composed of persons with different educational and occupational backgrounds.[42]

33 Ibid. [11].

34 Ibid. [5].

35 Ibid. [12].

36 Paragraph 1, Article 1 of Additional Articles of the Constitution of the Republic of China (Taiwan) (2000), available at https://law.judicial.gov.tw/FLAW/hisdata.aspx?lsid=FL000002&ldate=20000425&lser=001, accessed 15 May 2021.

37 After the National Assembly was abolished, its power to impeach the President and Vice-President was taken over by the Constitutional Court. See Paragraph 4, Article 5 of the Additional Articles of the Constitution of the Republic of China (Taiwan) (2005). Moreover, constitutional amendments on territorial change can only be approved by a referendum by the people now. See Article 1 of the Additional Articles of the Constitution of the Republic of China (Taiwan) (2005).

38 J.Y. Interpretation No. 290 (1992) (Constitutional Court of Taiwan), at [1], available at http://cons.judicial.gov.tw/jcc/en-us/jep03/show?expno=290, accessed 15 May 2021.

39 Article 32 of Civil Servants Election and Recall Act (1991).

40 Subparagraph 1, Paragraph 1, Article 32 of the Civil Servants Election and Recall Act (1991).

41 J.Y. Interpretation No. 290 (1992) (Constitutional Court of Taiwan), at [1], available at http://cons.judicial.gov.tw/jcc/en-us/jep03/show?expno=290, accessed 15 May 2021.

42 Legislative Yuan, (1994) 83(39) *Legislative Yuan Gazette* 92-100.

In Interpretation No. 340 (1994),[43] the TCC overturned another restriction on electoral candidacy. Paragraph 2, Article 38 of the Civil Servants Election and Recall Act stipulated that 'The guarantee deposit for a party-recommended area or aboriginal candidate will be reduced by half . . .';[44] that is, an electoral candidate put forward by a political party would only need to pay half the quantum of election deposit[45] required of an independent candidate. This discriminatory measure was swiftly vetoed by the TCC. First, the TCC ruled that the impugned provision unreasonably differentiated between candidates with and without party affiliations, and this violated equal protection as enshrined in Article 7 of the Constitution.[46] Second, the TCC argued that this statutory provision was also detrimental to Taiwan's democratic development, as a person intent on running for public office would simply circumvent this differentiating measure by forming a political party; this would lead to 'smaller parties . . . mushrooming, which may not be conducive to a healthy development of party politics'.[47]

To enhance robust political debate in the legislature, the TCC has also expanded the scope of immunity granted to lawmakers for speeches made in Parliament. Even though Article 73 of the Constitution formally provides that 'no Member of the Legislative Yuan shall be held responsible outside the Yuan for opinions expressed or votes cast in the Yuan',[48] it was not uncommon for members of the opposition parties to be charged and convicted for criminally insulting government officials during legislative debates.[49] The imposition of such criminal liability would certainly have a chilling effect on parliamentary debates and obstruct a free flow of political ideas. In Interpretation No. 435 (1997), the TCC ruled that Article 73 of the Constitution seeks 'to prevent influence from other government agencies that could

43 J.Y. Interpretation No. 340 (1994) (Constitutional Court of Taiwan), available at http://cons.judicial.gov.tw/jcc/en-us/jep03/show?expno=340, accessed 15 May 2021.

44 Paragraph 2, Article 38 of the Civil Servants Election and Recall Act.

45 The quantum of deposit varied according to the type of elections. In this case, the petitioner was running for the National Assembly and was required to pay NTD 120,000 (roughly USD 4,000) as an independent.

46 Article 7 of the Constitution of the Republic of China (Taiwan) reads: 'All citizens of the Republic of China, irrespective of sex, religion, race, class, or party affiliation, shall be equal before the law.'

47 J.Y. Interpretation No. 340 (1994) (Constitutional Court of Taiwan), at [1], available at http://cons.judicial.gov.tw/jcc/en-us/jep03/show?expno=340, accessed 15 May 2021. One should note that the TCC has upheld the deposit requirement for presidential elections in Interpretation No. 468 (1998). Paragraph 1, Article 23 of the Presidential and Vice-Presidential Election and Recall Act requires presidential candidates to pay a deposit of NT$ 1,000,000 (roughly USD 30,000). The TCC upheld this provision on the basis that this provision was necessary 'to prevent the people from needlessly participating in presidential and vice presidential elections, thus wasting social resources'.

48 Article 73 of the Constitution of the Republic of China (Taiwan).

49 Paragraph 1, Article 140 of the Criminal Code reads: 'A person who offers an insult to a public official during the legal discharge of his duties or publicly offers an insult with respect to the legal discharged of such duties shall be sentenced to imprisonment for not more than six months, short-term imprisonment, or a fine of not more than one hundred yuan.'

jeopardize the exercise of legislative functions'[50] and therefore 'all statements, questioning, motions, voting and directly related conduct made in sessions or committees, such as party negotiations and statements expressed in public hearings, are thereby protected'.[51] In other words, a legislator would be granted legal immunity for what he or she said in the Legislative Yuan, so long as the speech was directly related to the exercise of his or her legislative duty. Nevertheless, the TCC also emphasized that errant legislators could still be held accountable for their speeches by the citizenry, as Article 17 of the Constitution clearly provides that the Taiwanese people have the right to recall every elected official.[52] In other words, while the legislators may be absolved of any legal liability for their speeches in Parliament, the lawmakers will remain politically accountable to the people for them.

Although the TCC is not vested with the power to monitor elections,[53] several major electoral controversies have been framed in constitutional terms and heard by the TCC. Interpretation No. 585 (2004)[54] is one such case. In the 2004 presidential election, President Chen Shui-bian won by a razor-thin margin, garnering a meagre 0.2 per cent more votes than his KMT rival. More controversially, there was an assassination attempt on President Chen and his Vice-President the day before the presidential election, and the gunman committed suicide shortly after the election. The KMT believed that the assassination attempt was staged by President Chen himself to gain sympathy votes from the public, and the KMT-controlled legislature post-election proceeded to enact the Act of the Special Commission on the Investigation of the Truth in Respect of the 319 Shooting[55] to investigate this shooting.[56] President Chen's Party, the DPP, outvoted by the KMT in the legislature, then petitioned the TCC, alleging that this law was unconstitutional as it

50 J.Y. Interpretation No. 435 (1997) (Constitutional Court of Taiwan), at [1], available at http://cons.judicial.gov.tw/jcc/en-us/jep03/show?expno=435#open_dropdown, accessed 15 May 2021.

51 Ibid.

52 Article 17 of the Constitution of the Republic of China (Taiwan) reads: 'The people shall have the right of election, recall, initiative and referendum.'

53 In Taiwan, election petitions are filed in the ordinary courts and not before the Constitutional Court. See Paragraph 1, Article 118 of the Civil Servants Election and Recall Act, which reads: 'If an election commission handles the election or recall affairs illegally ... the prosecutors, candidates, the persons recalled ... may ... file a lawsuit of invalid election or recall in the governing court ...'. Similarly, Paragraph 1, Article 102 of the Presidential and Vice-Presidential Election and Recall Act reads: 'If a government agency of election and recall handles the election or recall affairs illegally ... the prosecutors, candidates, the person recalled ... may ... file a lawsuit of invalid election or recall in the governing court against the government agency of election and recall.'

54 J.Y. Interpretation No. 585 (2004) (Constitutional Court of Taiwan), available at http://cons.judicial.gov.tw/jcc/en-us/jep03/show?expno=585, accessed 15 May 2021.

55 Act of the Special Commission on the Investigation of the Truth in Respect of the 319 Shooting (2006). The official English translation is not available, but the original provisions can be found here: https://law.moj.gov.tw/LawClass/LawAll.aspx?pcode=A0010030, accessed 15 May 2021.

56 For detailed discussion of this incident, see Wen-Chen Chang and Yi-Li Lee, 'Judicial Strategies to Resolving Presidential Election Disputes' in Po Jen Yap (ed.), *Judicial Review of Elections in Asia* (Routledge 2016) 147, 154–157.

violated the separation of powers by conferring judicial and prosecutorial power on the said Special Commission.

In Interpretation No. 585 (2004), the TCC accepted that the Legislative Yuan had the legal power to create a special commission to investigate the attempted assassination.[57] Nevertheless, the TCC ruled that the organization and the function of this special commission could not contradict the 'principles of democracy, separation of powers and checks and balances, proportionality, clarity and [certainty] of law, as well as due process of law'.[58] On this basis, the TCC invalidated various key statutory provisions in the impugned law: Article 8-II[59] and Article 13-I[60] were nullified because they granted the legislature the power to investigate criminal cases, which went 'beyond the scope of the investigation power ... and thus are contrary to the fundamental constitutional principles of separation of powers and checks and balances'.[61] Article 8-VI[62] was void because it required all government agencies to unconditionally assist this investigation, even if state secrets or prosecutorial confidentiality were involved, thereby interfering with the functions of the executive branch of government.[63] Finally, Article 13-III[64] was also struck down because it empowered the Commission to revoke judicial findings. The TCC's decision, rendered on 15 December 2004, in essence prevented the Special Commission from reopening a High Court's ruling on 4 November 2004, which decided that the assassination attempt was neither staged by President Chen nor did the gunshot

57 J.Y. Interpretation No. 585 (2004) (Constitutional Court of Taiwan), at [8], available at http://cons.judicial.gov.tw/jcc/en-us/jep03/show?expno=585, accessed 15 May 2021.

58 Ibid. [12].

59 Article 8-II of the Act of the Special Commission on the Investigation of the Truth in Respect of the 319 Shooting read: 'This Commission, in exercising the aforesaid authorities, shall have any and all powers and authorities exercisable by a prosecutor or military prosecutor pursuant to law.'

60 Article 13-I of the Act of the Special Commission on the Investigation of the Truth in Respect of the 319 Shooting read: 'In the event that the outcome of the investigation conducted by this Commission reveals any case involving criminal liabilities, the prosecutor or military prosecutor transferred pro tempore to this Commission shall sua sponte prosecute for such a case.'

61 J.Y. Interpretation No. 585 (2004) (Constitutional Court of Taiwan), at [19], available at http://cons.judicial.gov.tw/jcc/en-us/jep03/show?expno=585, accessed 15 May 2021.

62 Article 8-VI of the Act of the Special Commission on the Investigation of the Truth in Respect of the 319 Shooting read: 'This Commission and its members ... may designate any matter and request any and all agencies, groups or individuals concerned to make explanations or provide assistance ... Those so requested shall not avoid, delay or reject any relevant request on the ground of national secrets, trade secrets, investigation secrets, individual privacy or on any other ground.'

63 J.Y. Interpretation No. 585 (2004) (Constitutional Court of Taiwan), at [23], available at http://cons.judicial.gov.tw/jcc/en-us/jep03/show?expno=585, accessed 15 May 2021.

64 Article 13-III of the Act of the Special Commission on the Investigation of the Truth in Respect of the 319 Shooting read: 'In the event that the outcome of the investigation conducted by this Commission differs from the facts as determined by a court in its final and conclusive judgment, it shall be a ground for retrial.'

incident illegally interfere with the conduct of the election.[65] In essence, the TCC rendered the whole Act toothless by gutting its core provisions.

This is not to say that the TCC is partial to President Chen. The Court has made clear that the President must abide by the law, even though the Constitution confers upon him immunity from criminal prosecutions while he holds office.[66] Specifically, in Interpretation No. 627 (2007),[67] the TCC made clear the limits of this immunity. From 2006, after his re-election, President Chen Shui-bian and his wife were embroiled in a series of corruption scandals and faced allegations of money laundering.[68] Fearing that he would be treated as an accomplice to his wife's misdeeds after his presidential term ended in 2008, President Chen refused to testify in his wife's cases, asserting executive privilege and claiming presidential immunity.

At that time, all the Justices were appointed by Chen. In view of the political sensitivity of this decision, the TCC intentionally forged a unanimous decision without any concurring or dissenting opinion. First, the TCC agreed that the President had immunity while he was in office.[69] Second, this immunity did not 'extend to the evidentiary investigation and preservation ... during the investigation or trial for a criminal case involving another person',[70] though his office and residence could not be searched.[71] Third, the TCC acknowledged that the President could assert executive privilege vis-à-vis state secrets and this privilege included the 'the right to refuse to testify as to matters concerning state secrets during the criminal procedure, and ... also refuse to produce the relevant evidence'.[72] If the President insisted that his testimony in his wife's cases would undermine this executive privilege, the TCC further ruled that the Legislative Yuan could enact specific rules on how the President's right should be lawfully exercised. Before the promulgation of these special rules, the TCC created a special model of adjudication to resolve pending disputes: any disagreement between the President and the prosecution over the scope of this privilege would be adjudicated

65 Gaodeng Fayuan [High Court], Civil Division, 93 Hsuan 2 (2004); For a discussion of the High Court's decision, see Chang and Lee (n. 56), 154–157. The High Court's decision was upheld by the Supreme Court on 17 June 2015. See Yap (n. 1) 105.

66 Article 52 of the Constitution of the Republic of China (Taiwan) reads: 'The President shall not, without having been recalled, or having been relieved of his functions, be liable to criminal prosecution unless he is charged with having committed an act of rebellion or treason.'

67 J.Y. Interpretation No. 627 (2007) (Constitutional Court of Taiwan), available at http://cons.judicial.gov.tw/jcc/en-us/jep03/show?expno=627, accessed 15 May 2021.

68 John F. Copper, 'The Devolution of Taiwan's Democratic during the Chen Shui-bian Era' (2009) 18 (60) *Journal of Contemporary China* 463, 475–477.

69 J.Y. Interpretation No. 627 (2007) (Constitutional Court of Taiwan), at [6], available at http://cons.judicial.gov.tw/jcc/en-us/jep03/show?expno=627, accessed 15 May 2021.

70 Ibid. [7].

71 Ibid.

72 Ibid. [13].

by a five-judge special tribunal in the High Court.[73] In the end, Chen was arrested after his term ended in 2008; he was convicted of corruption in 2010 and sentenced to 11 years imprisonment.[74]

In 2014, the TCC was tasked to adjudicate on the constitutionality of another round of constitutional revisions in 2005 effected by Paragraph 1[75] and Paragraph 2,[76] Article 4, of the constitutional amendments. Paragraph 1, Article 4 establishes a two-vote system in legislative elections, and Paragraph 2, Article 4 stipulates a 5 per cent party-vote threshold for the allocation of seats for legislators-at-large.[77]

Prior to the 2005 amendment, lawmakers were elected via two electoral methods: the Single Non-transferrable Vote (SNTV) system for geographical district members and members representing indigenous Taiwanese; and proportional representation for legislators-at-large seats. Under Taiwan's then applicable SNTV system, each elector had only one vote, which he or she would cast in a geographical district election with multiple legislative seats, and candidates with the highest votes would be elected to those seats.[78] In addition to determining the winners in the multi-member districts, these votes in the district seats would also be used to allocate the legislators-at-large seats in proportion to the votes each political party obtained in the

73 Ibid. Specifically, the TCC ruled: 'Prior to the implementation of such law, the President should elaborate on whether the questioning and statements relating to state secrets that fall within the scope of the presidential state secrets privilege, or the production and submission of the relevant evidence, will jeopardize national interests … If the President is not satisfied with the prosecutor's or the trial court's disposition or ruling to overrule his refusal to testify or refusal to produce relevant evidence, he may raise an objection or interim appeal based on the intent of this Interpretation, and such objection or appeal should be heard by the aforesaid five-judge special tribunal at the High Court or its appropriate branch, which shall be presided over by a senior division chief judge … If the President has justified in writing that the relevant testimony or production of evidence is likely to jeopardize national interests, the prosecutor and the court should give such justification due respect. Only the prosecutor or trial judge can preside over the President's testimony and production of relevant evidence under confidential proceedings to determine if they are likely to jeopardize national interests.'

74 Zuigao Fayuan [Supreme Court], Criminal Division, 99 Tai-Shang 7078 (Taiwan) (2010).

75 Paragraph 1, Article 4 of the Additional Articles of the Constitution of the Republic of China reads: 'Beginning with the Seventh Legislative Yuan, the Legislative Yuan shall have 113 members … : 1. Seventy-three members shall be elected from the Special Municipalities, counties, and cities in the free area. At least one member shall be elected from each county and city. 2. Three members each shall be elected from among the lowland and highland aborigines in the free area. 3. A total of thirty-four members shall be elected from the nationwide constituency and among citizens residing abroad.'

76 Paragraph 2, Article 4 of the Additional Articles of the Constitution of the Republic of China reads: 'Members for the seats set forth in Subparagraph 1 of the preceding paragraph shall be elected in proportion to the population of each Special Municipality, county, or city, which shall be divided into electoral constituencies equal in number to the number of members to be elected. Members for the seats set forth in Subparagraph 3 shall be elected from the lists of political parties in proportion to the number of votes won by each party that obtains at least 5 percent of the total vote…'.

77 In Taiwan, legislators-at-large focus on national issues instead of regional/local issues. They usually have expertise in certain fields with nationwide impact, such as environmental protection, public health or international relations.

78 Jih-Wen Lin, 'Electoral System, Voter Preferences, and the Fragmentation of Party System: The East Asian Cases' (2002) 9 *Journal of Electoral Studies* 137, 139.

district elections. Since the 2005 constitutional reform, all legislative seats, except those reserved for indigenous people,[79] are generated through the Mixed Member Majoritarian (MMM) system.[80] Under Taiwan's MMM electoral system, each voter has two ballots: one vote for the preferred candidate in single-member geographical districts, and the other vote for the political party of choice. The latter, known as party votes, decides the allocation of 34 seats for legislators-at-large. These seats will be distributed proportionally to political parties that receive at least 5 per cent (roughly six hundred thousand votes) of the party votes. This 5 per cent threshold was stipulated in the Civil Servants Election and Recall Act[81] and was used to generate the party seats before the constitutional revision, and the requirement was merely enshrined in the Constitution in 2005.

A central problem with this 5 per cent threshold is the discrepancy between the number of legislative seats that a political party is eventually allocated and the proportion of votes cast in its favour. For instance, small parties may not gain any seats in the legislature, even if they garner hundreds of thousands of votes, if they do not cross the 5 per cent threshold. Two small political parties, which did not cross the 5 per cent threshold in the 2008 legislative election, thus challenged the constitutionality of these constitutional amendments. They contended that this electoral system distorted popular will, as a large number of validly cast votes were 'wasted'.

In Interpretation No. 721 (2014),[82] the TCC reaffirmed its power to review the constitutionality of constitutional amendments – as it had previously ruled in Interpretation No. 499 (2000)[83] – but on the facts, the Court herein upheld these amendments as a valid 'display of the general will of the people, and they do not contradict the principle of the democratic republic and the principle of sovereignty of and by the people'.[84] While the TCC acknowledged that there was a significant gap between the legislative seats awarded to small political parties and the votes they

79 Before 2005, two multi-member districts were reserved for indigenous Taiwanese, and each of these two districts had three seats. Each indigenous person had only one vote, which he or she would cast in either of the two reserved districts. The 2005 constitutional amendments do not change the way indigenous legislators are elected.

80 See Jih-wen Lin, 'Electoral Systems Today: The Politics of Reform in Japan and Taiwan' (2006) 17 *Journal of Democracy* 118, 124–125. Chi Huang, 'Electoral System Change and Its Effects on the Party System in Taiwan' in Christopher H. Achen and T. Y. Wang (eds), *The Taiwan Voter* (University of Michigan Press 2017) 223, 227.

81 Subparagraph 6, Paragraph 2, Article 65 of the Civil Servants Election and Recall Act (2005) read: 'The seats for legislators-at-large and overseas Chinese are allocated according to the following rules: … 6. Seats will not be allocated to political parties that do not garner 5 percent of the votes…'.

82 J.Y. Interpretation No. 721 (2014) (Constitutional Court of Taiwan), available at http://cons.judicial.gov.tw/jcc/en-us/jep03/show?expno=721, accessed 15 May 2021.

83 J.Y. Interpretation No. 499 (2000) (Constitutional Court of Taiwan), available at http://cons.judicial.gov.tw/jcc/en-us/jep03/show?expno=499, accessed 15 May 2021.

84 J.Y. Interpretation No. 721 (2014) (Constitutional Court of Taiwan), at [3], available at http://cons.judicial.gov.tw/jcc/en-us/jep03/show?expno=721, accessed 15 May 2021.

received, the TCC preached judicial restraint as this discrepancy was not grave enough to justify striking down otherwise validly passed constitutional amendments. Specifically, the TCC argued that the purpose of this 5 per cent threshold was to ensure that the 'efficiency of legislative operations and the smooth interaction between the executive branch and the Legislature is not impeded by a clustering of small parties and fragmentation of the political party system'.[85] This concern is not unjustified. For example, in the 2020 legislative election, the number of participating parties reached a record high: 19 political parties participated in that election.[86] Where intense electoral competition is now the norm in Taiwan, the TCC is more worried about the mushrooming of multiple small parties that, if elected into office, can hamper legislative efficiency and possibly paralyze the government.[87] Nevertheless, this decision is questionable on the basis that it leads to the 'wastage' of millions of votes cast in every legislative election insofar as all the votes that fall short of the 5 per cent threshold are disregarded when party-based legislators-at-large seats are divided up.[88] This system invariably favours established mainstream political parties and would entrench an oligopoly in the political market.[89]

Also troubling is the seat allocation for geographical district elections, as the disparity of voting power among individuals living in differently populated counties has become very stark. For example, the geographical district of Yilan County has a population of about 450,000 residents, while the geographical district of Matsu has a population of about 12,000 residents. Yet, both counties can return one legislator each. In particular, this electoral scheme favours the KMT, which has traditionally been popular in the sparsely populated districts (e.g. off-shore islands and aboriginal areas). But notably, this series of constitutional amendments was initiated by the DPP's President Chen Shui-bian, who wanted a more efficient governmental structure by halving the number of legislators.[90] Although the TCC upheld the constitutionality of the 2005 constitutional amendments, it avoided ruling on this issue on procedural grounds. As the petitioner, the Taiwan Constitution Association,

85 Ibid.

86 Katherine Wei, 'Record Number of Smaller Parties Seek Legislative Seats in Taiwan Election' (*Strait Times*, 9 January 2020,), available at www.straitstimes.com/asia/east-asia/record-number-of-smaller-parties-seek-legislative-seats-in-taiwan-election, accessed 14 February 2021.

87 J.Y. Interpretation No. 721 (2014) (J. Li, concurring); J.Y. Interpretation No. 721 (2014) (J. Chen, concurring).

88 See, e.g., Chun-Yuan Lin 林春元, '司法審查、選舉制度與民主代表性－從司法院釋字第721號解釋談起 Judicial Review, Electoral Systems, and Democratic Representation: The Case of J.Y. Interpretation No. 721' (2017) 20 中研院法學期刊 *Academia Sinica Law Journal* 155 (in Chinese); Wen-Sheng Hsiao 蕭文生, '百分之五政黨門檻之合憲性－司法院釋字第721號解釋評析 The Constitutionality of the Five-Percent Threshold for Political Parties' (2014) 252 台灣法學雜誌 *Taiwan Law Journal* 33.

89 J.Y. Interpretation No. 721 (2014) (J. Huang, dissenting).

90 Jean-Pierre Cabestan, 'A New Constitutional and the Prospect of Constitutional Change in Taiwan' in Steven M. Goldstein and Julian Chang (eds), *Presidential Politics in Taiwan* (EastBridge 2008) 41.

only participated in the party election and not in the geographical district election, the Court held that it had no standing to challenge the constitutionality of the seat allocation for the geographical district election.[91]

Finally, three Justices in this decision also took issue with the democratic legitimacy of the disputed constitutional provisions,[92] which were passed by members of the National Assembly elected in 2005. In that 2005 election, less than a quarter (23.36 per cent) of the electorate voted.[93] The reasons for this low turnout are beyond the scope of this book, but it would suffice to say herein that it is questionable whether these impugned amendments truly bore the imprimatur of the people.

With the end of one-party rule in Taiwan, the TCC gained political space after the nation's democratization and transformed successfully from a rubber-stamp tribunal to become one of the world's most respected constitutional courts. The Court now acts as a constitutional umpire in the political arena, as it successfully thwarts attempts by self-serving politicians to prolong their legislative terms, punish opposition lawmakers for their political speech, and disadvantage politically weak independent candidates. At the same time, the TCC has also imposed limits on presidential power, while reining-in partisan legislative attempts to interfere with executive and judicial functions.

## PART 2: SOUTH KOREA

Practically from the get-go, the KCC began to tear down systemic barriers of entry that stifled political competition. In 1989, the Court declared that a statutory provision which required independent candidates in a National Assembly election to pay a deposit of 20 million Korean won (roughly USD 16,800) – a quantum that was twice that of a party candidate – was 'non-conforming to the Constitution'[94] as the law unjustifiably placed independents at 'substantial competitive disadvantages and suppress[ed] their candidacy'.[95] This ruling of non-conformity allowed the impugned law to remain in place until the legislature passed appropriate remedial legislation.[96] But when the National Assembly proceeded by imposing a 20 million

91 A second petitioner – the Green Party – also had its constitutional petition refused, as the Court held that it had not been a party to the original lawsuit in the lower court.

92 J.Y. Interpretation No. 721 (2014) (J. Huang, dissenting); J.Y. Interpretation No. 721 (2014) (J. Li, concurring); J.Y. Interpretation No. 721 (2014) (J. Chen, concurring).

93 Central Election Commission, 'The Election of the National Assembly in 2005', available at https://db.cec.gov.tw/histQuery.jsp?voteCode=20050501R1A9&qryType=prof, accessed 14 February 2021.

94 *National Assembly Candidacy Deposit Case*, 88Hun-Ka6 (8 September 1989) (Constitutional Court of Korea) (Official English Translation of Case Summary).

95 Ibid.

96 The National Assembly reduced the deposit to 10 million won in 1997 but restored it to 20 million won in 2000. See also The Constitutional Court of Korea, *The First Ten Years of the Constitutional Court of Korea* (The Constitutional Court of Korea 2001) 174.

won deposit on all candidates, the Court decisively struck down the law in 2001. As observed by the Court:

> People of ordinary means cannot easily raise 20 million won ... and this state of affairs has not changed since the Court's decision in 1989. And a deposit requirement of 20 million won would make most people give up their political aspiration to become a member of the National Assembly ... Excessive deposit requirements would make it difficult for people of ordinary means and members of younger generations from running for the National Assembly, and this means that representatives reflecting their voices would be absent in the National Assembly.[97]

In this same decision, the KCC also invalidated the law that forfeited a candidate's election deposit if he or she failed to gain at least 20 per cent of the total valid votes cast because this statutory measure restricted 'participation of smaller political parties or newly organized parties in political affairs'.[98] The deposit required for a National Assembly candidate was subsequently reduced to 15 million Korean won (roughly USD 12,600).[99] Similarly, in 2008, the KCC determined that an election deposit of 500 million Korean won (roughly USD 420,000) for presidential candidates was excessively prohibitive and was thus incompatible with the Constitution.[100]

Even as the Constitutional Court extended the right of ordinary citizens to stand for public office, it also concurrently expanded ballot access for voters. In 2007, a blanket ban, which prohibited all Korean nationals residing abroad with no registered Korean domicile from voting in Presidential and legislative elections, was deemed incompatible with the Constitution, and the National Assembly was given 18 months to enact a more reasonable legislative response.[101] In this same case, the KCC also determined that voting in national referendums could not be limited to only those registered as residents in local districts.[102] The law now allows overseas

97 *One-Person One-Vote Case*, 2000Hun-Ma91, etc. (consolidated) (19 July 2001) (Constitutional Court of Korea). (Official English Translation). See Article 56(1) of the Public Official Election Act.

98 Ibid.

99 In 2016, the KCC upheld the election deposit of 15 million Korean won per candidate for district seats in the National Assembly election, but also determined that an election deposit of 15 million Korean won per candidate was excessive for political parties seeking to field proportional representatives in the National Assembly election. Given that such PR elections were contests between political parties and not individuals, and electoral infractions were less likely in the former contest, the KCC held that it was unnecessary to impose the same deposit quantum on PR candidates as district seats ones. See 2015Hun-Ma1160 (29 December 2016).

100 *Deposit Money in Presidential Elections Case*, 2007Hun-Ma1024 (27 November 2008) (Constitutional Court of Korea). The election deposit for presidential candidates has now been reduced to 300 million Korean won (roughly USD 252,000). See Article 56(1) of the Public Official Election Act.

101 *The Right to Vote of Nationals Residing Abroad Case*, 2004Hun-Ma644 et al. (consolidated) (28 June 2007) (Constitutional Court of Korea) (Official English Translation).

102 The National Assembly subsequently amended the law in 2009 to allow overseas Koreans to vote in national referendums, but only if they were registered as domestic residents in Korea. In *Case on*

Koreans to vote in national referendums,[103] presidential elections[104] and for proportional representatives in the National Assembly.[105]

Similarly, in 2014, a complete prohibition on prisoner voting – including those serving suspended sentences – was deemed disproportionate. As the Court observed:

> Considering the importance of the principle of popular suffrage and the right to vote, the right to vote should be restricted to the minimum extent only when it is necessary. Even though it is necessary to restrict [a] criminal's right to vote, blanket restriction on … prisoners … without considering the gravity of illegality of crimes committed by each of them, is contrary to the least restrictive requirement.'[106]

In response to this ruling, the National Assembly revised the law and prisoners whose sentences are less than one year are now given the vote.[107]

Similarly, the KCC has expanded the citizenry's right to engage in political speech. In 2011, the Court held that the statutory ban on the distribution of any material in favour of or against any political candidate six months before an election would no longer apply to the Internet. As reasoned by the Court, a complete ban on political expression in cyberspace for 180 days is no longer defensible, 'considering the reality that communication through the Internet has become common'[108] and

*Restricting Voting Right of Overseas Electors*, 2009Hun-Ma256 (24 July 2014) (Constitutional Court of Korea), the KCC held that this statutory revision was also incompatible with the Constitution but ordered the tentative application of the impugned provision, Article 14(1) of the National Referendum Act, until 31 December 2015. In April 2018, President Moon criticized the National Assembly for not revising this Act, but to no avail. See Kang Jin-Kyu, 'Constitutional Reform Derailed' (*Korea JoongAng Daily*, 24 April 2018), available at https://koreajoongangdaily.joins.com/news/article/article.aspx?aid=3047355, accessed 13 July 2021. See Association of Asian Constitutional Courts and Equivalent Institutions Secretariat for Research and Development, *Constitutional Review at AACC Members* (AACC SRD & Constitutional Court of Korea 2019) 142.

103 Article 5 of the National Referendum Act reads: 'The basis of the population as prescribed by this Act shall conform to recent demographic statistics in the census by resident registration cards pursuant to the provisions of the Resident Registration Act and the number of Korean nationals residing abroad registered in the domestic residence report register under the Act on the Immigration and Legal Status of Overseas Koreans.'

104 Article 2 of the Public Official Election Act reads: 'This Act shall apply to presidential elections…'. Article 3 of the Public Official Election Act reads: 'For the purpose of this Act, the term "elector" means a person who has the right to vote and is enrolled in the electoral register or the overseas electoral register.'

105 Article 2 of the Public Official Election Act reads: 'This Act shall apply to … elections of National Assembly members …'. Article 3 of the Public Official Election Act reads: 'For the purpose of this Act, the term "elector" means a person who has the right to vote and is enrolled in the electoral register or the overseas electoral register.'

106 *Restriction on Right to Vote of Prisoners and Probationers with Suspended Sentence*, 2012Hun-Ma409 et al. (consolidated) (28 January 2014) (Constitutional Court of Korea) (Official English Translation).

107 Article 18(1)[2] of the Public Official Election Act; Article 43(2) of the Criminal Act.

108 *Prohibition of Internet Use for Political Expression and Election Campaign*, 2007Hun-Ma1001, 2010Hun-Ba88, 2010Hun-Ma173 (consolidated) (29 December 2011) (Constitutional Court of Korea) (Official English Translation of Case Summary).

'the excessively long [period] for a fundamental right to be restricted'.[109] Similarly, a legislative prohibition which barred all private individuals – unless they were registered members of the political parties in question – from making any financial contribution to such parties was deemed incompatible with the Constitution, as the legislature should have chosen a more measured response to combat corruption in politics.[110] This decision was especially welcomed by minor political parties, which were regularly under-funded.[111]

More remarkably, the KCC has been able to reconfigure the process by which legislators are voted into the National Assembly. Like Taiwan, South Korea has adopted a mixed-member proportional representation system with single-member electoral districts and 'party' seats. Party seats in the National Assembly were previously allocated to political parties in proportion to the votes their candidates won in the district elections. But in 2001, the Constitutional Court held that this allocation of seats for the 'party' legislators – known as proportional representatives – was unconstitutional as it distorted democratic will:

> Under the present election system, allowing one vote per person, a voter's support for a particular political party is assumed through one's vote for the candidate in the electoral district. This means that an elector has no option but to express one's choice of a candidate as well as one's support for a particular political party in a single vote. This poses a serious problem when the candidate of one's choice is not from the political party that he or she supports.[112]

109 Ibid. The National Assembly has responded by amending the Public Official Election Act, in which the current Article 59 allows both voters and candidates to campaign on the Internet. Article 59 of the Public Official Election Act now reads: 'An election campaign may be allowed during the period from the commencing date of election period to the day before the election day: Provided, That the same shall not apply to any of the following cases: . . .; 2. Where a person works on an election campaign by sending text messages . . .; 3. Where a person works on an election campaign by posting a writing or video clip on an internet web-site or its bulletin board or chatting room or sending an e-mail (referring to a communication system with which computer users exchange information in the form of text, voice, images, or video clips through a network; hereinafter the same shall apply). . .'. See also The Constitutional Court of Korea, *Thirty Years of the Constitutional Court of Korea* (The Constitutional Court of Korea 2018) 313.

110 *Case Concerning Constitutional Complaint against Article 45 Section 1 of the Political Funds Act*, 2013Hun-Ba168 (23 December 2015) (Constitutional Court of Korea). The National Assembly responded by amending the Political Funds Act, which now allows a party support association to be established in the central office of a political party to collect political funds of no more than five billion won. See Article 6(1) of the Political Funds Act, which reads: 'Any of the following persons . . . may designate each one supporters' association: 1. Central Party (including any Preparatory Committee for Central Party Formation)'; Article 12, section 1, subsection 1 of the same Act reads: 'The limited amount of contributions that every supporters' association is permitted to collect each year. . . shall be as follows . . .: 1. For a supporters' association for the Central Party: five billion won including the sum of contributions collected by the supporters' association for Preparatory Committee for Central Party Formation.' See also The Constitutional Court of Korea (n. 109) 341.

111 The Constitutional Court of Korea (n. 109) 341.

112 *One-Person One-Vote Case*, 2000Hun-Ma91, etc. (consolidated) (19 July 2001) (Constitutional Court of Korea). For a more detailed discussion, see Yoojin Lim and Jungho Roh, 'Political Institutions in

Furthermore, this law disadvantages newly formed and small political parties, as electors who would otherwise want to support the new parties would vote for the major parties so as not to waste their votes. (At the time of the litigation, a political party could only gain a 'proportional representative' seat if it garnered at least 3 per cent of the total valid votes cast for all the seats in the National Assembly.[113]) Insofar as a voter has only a single ballot to determine both the district representative and the proportional representative, he or she would be less likely to vote for candidates from newly formed political parties that are less organized and have fewer resources. Therefore, the impugned electoral system also perpetuated the 'oligopoly of political parties, and hinder[ed] a new party from making its appearance in the National Assembly'.[114] Consequently, the KCC required the National Assembly to overhaul the electoral system and allow each voter to have two votes – one for his or her preferred district representative and the other for his or her preferred political party. This change was introduced in time for the subsequent 2004 National Assembly election, and currently 47 of the 300 National Assembly seats are reserved for these proportional representatives.[115] This judicially-imposed two-ballot electoral scheme has led to the rise of small political parties in the National Assembly, as voters can now 'split' their support when choosing their lawmakers.[116]

The Constitutional Court in 2014 also invalidated a statutory law that automatically de-registered political parties that did not win at least 2 per cent of the total number of valid votes cast in the National Assembly election.[117] While the KCC acknowledged that the legislature was pursuing a legitimate purpose in fostering the growth and 'development of party democracy'[118] by excluding fringe political parties that are not sufficiently electable, the Court held that the law was overbroad, as 'less restrictive means' could be used to pursue the same goals. To illustrate its point, the Court offered the following observation:

Korea' in Chung-in Moon and M. Jae Moon (eds), *Routledge Handbook of Korean Politics and Public Administration* (Routledge 2020) 21, 30.

113 Article 189(1) of the Public Official Election Act read: 'The National Election Commission shall allocate the seats of the proportional representative National Assembly members to each political party which has obtained 3/100 or more of the total valid votes in the election for a proportional representative National Assembly member or five or more seats in the general election for the local constituency National Assembly members.'

114 Ibid.

115 Article 21(1) of the Public Official Election Act.

116 See Jongcheol Kim, 'Upgrading Constitutionalism; The Ups and Downs of Constitutional Developments in South Korea since 2000' in Albert Chen (ed.), *Constitutionalism in Asia in the Early Twenty-First Century* (Cambridge University Press 2014) 83; Yeonho Lee and Yoo-Jin Lim, 'The Rise of the Labour Party in South Korea: Causes and Limits' (2006) 19(3) *The Pacific Review* 305.

117 *Case on Prohibition of Using the Name of a Political Party whose Registration has been Cancelled*, 2012Hun-Ma431, 2012Hun-Ka19 (consolidated) (28 January 2014); (Official English Translation).

118 Ibid.

> For example, the cancellation of registration, not based on the result of a single National Assembly election, can be decided depending on the result of election[s] after providing such a political party with several chances to participate in elections for a certain period of time. Also, since it is hard for newly established political parties to attain high level[s] of political support from the beginning, the cancellation of registration may be decided in combination of the number and distribution of constituencies from which candidates were recommended and the rate of votes earned in the constituencies.[119]

Specifically, the KCC was deeply concerned that the impugned law would discourage new and small parties from participating in national elections, and this in turn would 'impair political diversity and openness in [the] political process'.[120] Because the impugned provisions were nullified, small parties could nominate their own candidates in elections again.[121]

Similarly, the Constitutional Court has ameliorated the systemic problem of gerrymandering by political incumbents who manipulate the legislative reapportionment process for partisan gain.[122] Unchecked, political incumbents can always carve up or redistribute electoral constituencies such that political opposition is always 'sliced and diced' into electoral irrelevance. As such systemic problems are unlikely to be corrected by self-serving legislators themselves, the Court has taken upon itself the role of supervising this apportionment process. Therefore, in 1995, the Court held that the population ratio of the smallest electoral constituency to the largest constituency must not exceed 1:4.[123] In 2001, the Court further reduced this population ratio to 1:3.[124] Finally, in 2014, the Court imposed a 1:2 population ratio.[125] As the Court recognised in its 2014 decision, any significant deviance in population between electoral constituencies is undemocratic as it perpetuates the disparity of voting power between electorates living in different constituencies. Furthermore, this move towards equinumerosity – that all electoral districts must have equal populations – is also important, as this requirement prevents political incumbents from creating additional small electoral seats that favour them while enlarging the size of individual electoral constituencies that support the opposition, such that political insiders can gain more seats in the legislature with fewer votes.

[119] Ibid.

[120] Ibid.

[121] The Constitutional Court of Korea (n. 109) 324.

[122] Samuel Issacharoff, 'Judging Politics: The Elusive Quest for Judicial Review of Political Fairness' (1992) 71 *Texas Law Review* 1643, 1661.

[123] *Excessive Electoral District Population Disparity Case*, 95Hun-Ma224 (27 December 1995) (Constitutional Court of Korea).

[124] *National Assembly Election Redistricting Plan Case*, 2000Hun-Ma92, 2000Hun-Ma240 (consolidated) (25 October 2001) (Constitutional Court of Korea). For a more detailed discussion, see Jong Ik Chon, 'Effect of Constitutional Review on the Legislature and the Executive Branch for Last 25 Years in Korea' (2015) *Journal of Korean Law* 131, 155–156.

[125] *Case on Standard for Population Disparity allowed in Division of Electoral District*, 2012Hun-Ma190 et al. (consolidated) (30 October 2014) (Constitutional Court of Korea).

Nevertheless, this principle of equinumerosity would be insufficient without a concurrent contiguity constraint.[126] The concept of contiguity basically requires electoral seats to be made up of counties/districts that are geographically connected to each other. Without this constraint, the principle of equinumerosity would be meaningless, as political incumbents can still engineer victories by combining to their advantage equal-sized electoral seats composed of counties/districts that are all over the electoral map. The principle of contiguity exponentially shrinks the number of available electoral districting options,[127] thereby making it more difficult for political insiders to gerrymander away votes for the opposition or cobble together disparate voting blocs for themselves. To this end, the Constitutional Court has invalidated redistricting plans where electoral seats are composed of districts/counties that are not geographically contiguous.[128]

Even more fascinating is the Court's direct intervention in high-stakes political duels. In 1997, the KCC determined that individual lawmakers had legal standing to bring 'Competence disputes between State agencies'[129] against the Speaker of the National Assembly, even though the controversy at issue was *not* an inter-agency dispute.[130] On the facts, the Speaker of the National Assembly had scheduled a vote on pending legislative bills at 6 a.m. in the morning on 26 December 1996, and gave the opposition parties only 30 minutes' notice. Only lawmakers from the ruling New Korea Party were notified well ahead of the event. The proposed labour reform had stalled in the National Assembly due to filibustering by the opposition. In the end, the KCC brokered a political compromise: individual lawmakers had the *locus standi* to bring such suits, but the legislative amendments enacted under such clandestine circumstances were nevertheless still upheld because they were passed by more than half the legislators of the National Assembly in a public session open to the media and the citizenry. In this way, lawmakers could not simply ram legislation through surreptitiously if they did not carry a majority, but neither could minority lawmakers filibuster legislative bills indefinitely.

The stakes got even higher when the KCC had to decide whether a sitting President and his associates could be investigated by an independent Special

126 Daniel D. Polsby and Robert D. Popper, 'The Third Criterion: Compactness as a Procedural Safeguard against Partisan Gerrymandering' (1991) 9(2) *Yale Law and Policy Review* 301, 330.

127 Ibid.

128 *Excessive Electoral District Population Disparity Case*, 95Hun-Ma224 et al. (consolidated) (27 December 1995) (Constitutional Court of Korea).

129 See Article 111(4) of the Korean Constitution. See also Article 62(1) of the Constitutional Court Act (1995): '(1) The adjudication on jurisdictional dispute shall be classified as follows: 1. Adjudication on jurisdictional dispute between government agencies: Adjudication on jurisdictional dispute between the National Assembly, the Government, Courts and the Central Election Management Commission.'

130 *Case on Legislative Railroading*, 96Hun-Ra2 (16 July 1997) (Constitutional Court of Korea). For a more detailed discussion of this case, see Chaihark Hahm, 'Rule of Law in South Korea: Rhetoric and Implementation' in Randall Peerenboom (ed.), *Asian Discourses of Rule of Law* (Routledge 2004) 379, 399.

Prosecutor.[131] Two days before Lee Myung-bak was elected as President of South Korea, the National Assembly controlled by his political rivals – the United New Democratic Party – passed legislation in 2007 that authorized a Special Prosecutor to look into allegations of Lee's financial misconduct when he was a businessman.[132] Witnesses who were compelled by the Special Prosecutor to assist in the investigation brought a constitutional suit, arguing that the appointment of the Special Prosecutor was unconstitutional as it vested immense discretionary powers in the Special Prosecutor, to the exclusion of the country's Public Prosecutors. While the KCC invalidated a statutory provision that conferred powers on the Special Prosecutor – in lieu of the courts – to criminally sanction witnesses for non-compliance, the Court upheld the National Assembly's power to introduce 'case-specific legislation'[133] to appoint a Special Prosecutor to investigate the President's alleged past misconduct. On the facts, this decision came to naught as the Special Prosecutor succumbed to political pressure and cleared the President of all wrong-doing only four days after the latter's inauguration.[134] But this KCC decision was nevertheless instrumental in laying the constitutional foundation for the Special Prosecutor system, which brought down another corrupt President a decade later.

In 2016, a bipartisan National Assembly passed another law that authorized the appointment of an independent Special Prosecutor to investigate President Park Geun-hye's shady financial dealings through her close confidante, Cho Soon-sil. Subsequently, the National Assembly brought impeachment proceedings against President Park, and the Constitutional Court removed her from office in March 2017.[135] The Court's decision was unanimous. Specifically, the KCC determined that President Park had illegally allowed Cho to interfere in state affairs and the former had also established foundations that unlawfully pressured private conglomerates for donations to benefit Cho. In the Court's view, all these transgressions were

131 *Case on Special Prosecutor to Probe Myung-bak Lee, Presidential Candidate of Grand National Party* 2007Hun-Ma1468 (10 January 2008) (Constitutional Court of Korea).

132 Tom Ginsburg, 'The Constitutional Court and Judicialization of Korean Politics' in Andrew Harding and Penelope (Pip) Nicholson (eds), *New Courts in Asia* (Routledge 2010) 145, 149.

133 *Case on Special Prosecutor to Probe Myung-bak Lee, Presidential Candidate of Grand National Party* 2007Hun-Ma1468 (10 January 2008) (Constitutional Court of Korea).

134 Choe Sang-Hun, 'New South Korean Leader Cleared in Fraud Inquiry' (*New York Times*, 21 February 2008), available at www.nytimes.com/2008/02/21/world/asia/21iht-korea.1.10255226.html, accessed 17 February 2020. Nevertheless, President Lee was eventually charged with corruption in 2018, and was sentenced to 17 years in prison in 2020.

135 *Impeachment of the President (Park Geun-hye)*, 2016Hun-Na1 (10 March 2017) (Constitutional Court of Korea). The Korean Constitutional Court was constitutionally empowered to adjudicate over the impeachment trial of the President of the Republic. See Article 111(1)[2] of the Constitution of the Republic of Korea (1987): '(1)The Constitutional Court shall have jurisdiction over the following matters: . . . 2. Impeachment.' Article 53(1) of the Constitutional Court Act: 'Where a request for an impeachment is well-grounded, the Constitutional Court shall pronounce a decision that the respondent shall be removed from the relevant public office.'

sufficiently grave and 'overwhelmingly outweigh the national loss incurred by the removal of the President'.[136]

Previously, in 2004, in the KCC's first impeachment trial of a sitting President, the Court strategically avoided removing President Roh Moo-hyun from power after Roh's Uri party won resoundingly at the 2004 National Assembly election midway through the trial.[137] Specifically, the Court concluded that President Roh had violated electoral law on three occasions: Roh breached a statutory mandate on public officials to remain politically neutral[138] when he publicly expressed support for the Uri Party at a press conference; Roh violated his duty to abide by and protect the Constitution[139] when he criticized the National Election Commission for warning him against such partisan acts; and Roh abused his presidential authority when he grandstanded and suggested that a national referendum[140] be called to assess the public's opinion of his job performance.[141] Notably, Roh's conduct, while illegal in South Korea, would have been absolutely lawful in any other liberal democracy; and the Court would have lost significant goodwill with the public and drastically changed the course of Korean politics if it had removed a President for such minor infractions. By reflecting public opinion and restoring the President, the Court safeguarded its political capital to resolve more salient conflicts in the future.[142]

On the other hand, in 2017, when President Park was removed from office by the KCC, her approval ratings were in single digits – the lowest for any sitting President in South Korea – and she was guilty of corruption.[143] Where law and politics aligned, the KCC was presented with an opportunity to issue a unanimous, popular, and legalistic decision that enhanced the Court's legitimacy and maximized its

136 Ibid.

137 *Impeachment of the President (Roh Moo-hyun) Case*, 2004Hun-Na1 (14 May 2004) (Constitutional Court of Korea); see Wen-chen Chang, 'Strategic Judicial Responses in Politically Charged Cases: East Asian Experiences' (2010) 8(4) *International Journal of Constitutional Law* 885.

138 Article 9(1) of the Public Official Election Act reads: 'A public official or a person who is required to maintain political neutrality (including an agency and organization) shall not exercise any unreasonable influence over the election or perform any act likely to have an effect of the election result.'

139 Article 66(2) of the Constitution of the Republic of Korea reads: 'The President shall have the responsibility and duty to safeguard the independence, territorial integrity and continuity of the State and the Constitution.'

140 Article 72 of the Constitution of the Republic of Korea reads: 'The President may submit important policies relating to diplomacy, national defence, unification and other matters relating to the national destiny to a national referendum if he deems it necessary.'

141 See Youngjae Lee, 'Law, Politics, and Impeachment: The Impeachment of Roh Moo-hyun from a Comparative Constitutional Perspective' (2005) 53 *American Journal of Comparative Law* 403.

142 Yap (n. 1) 119–121.

143 For a discussion of the scandals leading to President Park's downfall, see Kun Yang, 'In the Name of Constitutional Law: Reflections on Recent Korean Constitutional Adjudication with Special Reference to President Park's Impeachment Case' (2019) 49 *Hong Kong Law Journal* 979.

power,[144] which was precisely what the Court did. The dismissal of President Park enhanced the stature of the KCC in Korean society and has been viewed as one of the Court's finest moments, as it had swiftly and decisively resolved a major political crisis for the country.[145]

But this is not to say that the KCC always lives up to its full potential as a democracy builder. No court – even one that operates in a liberal democracy – is immune from occasional falters. Notably, in 2014, the KCC dissolved the United Progressive Party (UPP) – a far-left socialist party – on the basis that the party's brand of 'progressive democracy' was a mere pretext to impose North Korean-style socialism by force.[146] But notably, as pointed out by Justice Kim Yi-su – the lone dissenting judge – the majority did so in the absence of any evidence demonstrating a 'direct connection'[147] between the party and North Korea, and the Court had merely imputed the seditious activities of a minority of members onto the entire party. Furthermore, the Court ousted all the duly elected UPP National Assembly legislators from office, as a consequence of the party's dissolution, even though the Constitution and the legislation did not expressly authorize this. It is equally unfortunate that the Court did not examine whether these five UPP lawmakers had subverted the democratic order in South Korea in any way to justify their removal from office.[148]

Furthermore, the KCC has been intransigent about upholding Article 93(1) of the Public Official Election Act, which infamously prohibits anyone from distributing any material or running any advertisement in favour of or against any political candidate six months before an election,[149] save limited campaign work undertaken by the registered election candidates and their staff[150] during the authorized campaign period – which is 120 days for National Assembly elections.[151] Despite the sweeping nature of this draconian restriction, this law has been regularly upheld by the Constitutional Court.[152] It is also significant that this campaign restriction

[144] Michael D. Gilbert and Mauricio A. Guim, 'The Active Virtues' (2021) 98 *Washington University Law Review* 857.

[145] Chaihark Hahm, 'Constitutional Court of Korea: Guardian of the Constitution or Mouthpiece of the Government' in Albert H. Y. Chen and Andrew Harding (eds), *Constitutional Courts in Asia: A Comparative Perspective* (Cambridge University Press 2018) 141, 160–163.

[146] *Dissolution of the United Progressive Party*, 2013Hun-Da1 (19 December 2014) (Constitutional Court of Korea) (Full Official English Translation).

[147] Ibid.

[148] For a close analysis of the KCC's UPP decision, see Jongcheol Kim, 'Dissolution of the United Progressive Party Case in Korea: A Critical Review with Reference to the European Court of Human Rights Case Law' (2017) 10(1) *Journal of East Asia and International Law* 139.

[149] Article 93(1) of the Public Official Election Act.

[150] See Article 60-3 of the Public Official Election Act.

[151] Article 60-2 of the Public Official Election Act.

[152] *Unlawful Distribution or Posting of Documents and Printed Materials Case*, 2011Hun-Ba17, 2012Hun-Ba391 (consolidated) (24 April 2014) (Constitutional Court of Korea); 2017Hun-Ka11 (26 July 2018) (Constitutional Court of Korea).

favours political incumbents, as a statutory exemption has been carved out to allow incumbent lawmakers to report on their parliamentary activities and 'achievements' to the electorate.[153] Consequently, incumbents are given a pretext and head start over political outsiders to campaign unofficially. But this tactical advantage conferred solely on incumbents has also been upheld by the Constitutional Court on the basis that it is 'an essential part of the job of a legislator'[154] and his or her 'political duty'[155] to brief the electorate. While the KCC in 2011 exempted the Internet from this statutory prohibition,[156] it has consistently preserved this archaic law insofar as it applies to the real world.[157]

Notwithstanding the anomalies discussed above, the KCC is one of Asia's most successful examples of a democracy builder. The Korean Constitution of 1987 instituted a system of open elections and accountable leadership. And the KCC took advantage of the country's weak party politics, asserted its authority swiftly, and went beyond the expectations of sceptics by ushering into Korea an even more liberal model of democratic diversity. The political diffusion in the legislature, coupled with a President who is constitutionally limited to one five-year term,[158] provided the Court with the 'policy' space to extend ballot access to the disenfranchised, remove political barriers of entry that were erected by incumbents to consolidate their rule, and even oust a sitting President. While the Court's record may be inconsistent – an unpopular political party was dissolved and authoritarian campaign regulations remain in force – it is indisputable that the absence of long-standing parties and long-lasting Presidents has empowered the KCC to reshape the nation's 'mega-politics'.[159]

## PART 3: HONG KONG

While China will acquiesce to the HKCFA's efforts to advance human rights protection in Hong Kong, the central government will not allow the local courts

153 Article 111 of the Public Official Election Act.

154 *Rejection Campaign by the Citizen's Alliance for the 2000 General Election Case*, 2000Hun-Ma121 (consolidated) (30 August 2001) (Constitutional Court of Korea) (Official English Translation of Case Summary).

155 Ibid.

156 *Prohibition of Internet Use for Political Expression and Election Campaign*, 2007Hun-Ma1001, 2010Hun-Ba88, 2010Hun-Ma173·191 (consolidated) (29 December 2011) (Constitutional Court of Korea) (Official English Translation of Case Summary). In *Case on Restricting Online Media from Publishing Columns, etc. Written by Candidates for Public Official Election* 2016Hun-Ma90 (28 November 2019) (Constitutional Court of Korea), the KCC also invalidated a law that barred electoral candidates from publishing in online columns within 90 days of an election.

157 *Unlawful Distribution or Posting of Documents and Printed Materials Case*, 2011Hun-Ba17, 2012Hun-Ba391 (consolidated) (24 April 2014) (Constitutional Court of Korea); 2017Hun-Ka11 (26 July 2018) (Constitutional Court of Korea).

158 Article 70 of the Constitution of the Republic of Korea.

159 Ran Hirschl, 'The Judicialization of Mega-Politics and the Rise of Political Courts' (2008) 11 *Annual Review of Political Science* 93, 94.

to unseat the city's top leaders or usher in democratic reform that threatens Beijing's rule. The Standing Committee of the National People's Congress (NPCSC) is empowered to overturn every constitutional decision handed down by the Hong Kong judiciary,[160] and the former in fact did so in the very first constitutional decision handed down by the HKCFA that it took issue with.[161] As the NPCSC's plenary power to interpret the Basic Law hangs like the sword of Damocles over Hong Kong, the HKCFA implicitly understands that its ability to generate significant changes in other areas of constitutional law is contingent on its genuflecting to Beijing on the communist regime's core concerns.

Unlike Taiwan or South Korea, the Hong Kong judiciary has steered clear of any attempts to unseat the city's Chief Executive, who is hand-picked by Beijing. In 2012, Albert Ho, a pro-democracy Chief Executive election candidate, challenged the election of Chief Executive CY Leung on the basis that Leung had violated the Elections (Corrupt and Illegal Conduct) Ordinance (Cap 554) (ECICO)[162] when he allegedly made two materially false and misleading statements prior to the election. In the first statement, CY Leung allegedly told journalists that he did not have any unauthorized building structures in his home. In the second statement, CY Leung publicly accused Henry Tang, another Chief Executive candidate, of concealing from the public the existence of illegal structures at the latter's residence. One may note that Henry Tang was a pro-Beijing candidate and he was widely tipped to be the next Chief Executive. But when local reporters revealed that Tang had unauthorized structures in his basement, the tide of public opinion turned against him; and it is believed that Beijing, in response to public opinion, influenced the delegates on the Election Committee to vote for CY Leung instead. In an interesting twist to the tale, *after* CY Leung was elected as Chief Executive, the local press uncovered that Leung too had unauthorized structures in his home. This revelation drove Albert Ho, the only pro-democracy candidate in the Chief Executive race, to lodge an election petition that CY Leung was not duly elected, in view of his alleged misrepresentations that constituted a violation of ECICO.[163] The HKCFA in *Re Ho Chun Yan Albert* (2012)[164] swiftly rejected the crux of the electoral challenge. In essence, the HKCFA decided that the first statement was

160 Article 158(1) of the Hong Kong Basic Law reads: 'The power of interpretation of this Law shall be vested in the Standing Committee of the National People's Congress.'

161 In 1999, the NPCSC issued its First Interpretation under the Hong Kong Basic Law and overruled the HKCFA's decision in *Ng Ka Ling* v. *Director of Immigration* [1999] 2 HKCFAR 4 (Hong Kong Court of Final Appeal), which exempted Mainland children born to Hong Kong Permanent Residents from obtaining the requisite immigration permits before they could acquire the right of abode in Hong Kong.

162 Section 26(2) of the ECICO.

163 Section 32(1)(a)(iv) of the CEEO reads: 'An election may be questioned only by an election petition on the ground that … the person declared by the Returning Officer … as elected was not duly elected because … he engaged in corrupt conduct or illegal conduct at the election.'

164 *Re Ho Chun Yan Albert* [2012] 15 HKCFAR 686 (Hong Kong Court of Final Appeal).

allegedly made by CY Leung *before* he had publicly declared his candidacy for Chief Executive, and the ECICO only regulated statements made by persons who had been nominated or had publicly declared their candidacy.[165] Therefore, while the first statement proved to be untrue, there was no violation of the electoral law at issue. In the Court's view, there was no legal duty on the candidate after he declared his candidacy to publicly retract any false statements he made prior to his candidacy.[166] As for the second statement, the HKCFA decided that a statement was not materially false or misleading merely because 'Mr CY Leung was susceptible to the very same attack which he was making on Mr Tang.'[167] In short, hypocrisy is not a lie. Accordingly, the HKCFA refused to grant leave to hear the substantive merits of the election dispute.

Nevertheless, the HKCFA did grant leave to hear an important *procedural* issue. Under the Chief Executive Election Ordinance (Cap 569) (CEEO), a failed candidate in the Chief Executive race has only seven days to lodge an election petition after the result is declared.[168] The lower court had found this time limit to be excessively short and applied a remedial interpretation to the electoral law so as to confer upon the Court a discretion to extend time, where necessary.[169] One must note that regardless of how the HKCFA ruled on this *procedural* issue, Leung's position was secured when the CFA refused leave to hear the *substantive* merits of the electoral dispute. By clarifying the exact terms of the appeal, the CFA made it abundantly clear to Beijing that it was not going to unseat its choice.

Subsequently, in *Leung Chun Ying* (2013)[170] the HKCFA also upheld the constitutionality of this seven-day statutory limit and thus overruled the lower court's decision to read-in a judicial discretion to extend time. In the lower court, the seven-day limit was deemed unconstitutional, as the government could not discharge its burden of justifying how this short time bar was proportionate. Notably, returns for election expenses in the Chief Executive elections do not have to be lodged until 30 days after the publication of the election result, and it would be well past the seven-day deadline before any such illegal conduct could be discovered and raised in a timely election petition.[171] But the HKCFA determined that elections involve 'political and policy considerations'[172] and a 'due margin of appreciation'[173]

165 Section 2 of the ECICO reads: '"candidate" (a) means a person who stands nominated as a candidate at an election and (b) also means a person who, at any time before the close of nominations for an election, has publicly declared an intention to stand as a candidate at the election'.

166 *Re Ho Chun Yan Albert* (n. 164) [26].

167 Ibid. [39].

168 Section 34(1) of the CEEO.

169 *Ho Chun Yan Albert* v. *Leung Chun Ying (No 1)* [2012] 5 HKLRD 149 (Court of First Instance) [125].

170 *Leung Chun Ying* v. *Ho Chun Yan Albert* [2013] 16 HKCFAR 735 (Hong Kong Court of Final Appeal).

171 Ibid. [48].

172 Ibid. [45].

173 Ibid.

must be accorded to the legislature. While the HKCFA ostensibly upheld the constitutionality of the impugned law, in perhaps the most important part of this judgment, the CFA then suggested an alternative mode of electoral redress, that is, persons who were *not* candidates in the Chief Executive election, and hence unaffected by the seven-day time bar that applied only to the election candidates, could still launch separate judicial review proceedings against the election result.[174] In other words, while the candidates themselves were time-barred after seven days, their surrogates were free to seek judicial review and challenge the validity of the election after that. There is essentially no *substantive* difference in result between (a) allowing the Court to exercise a *discretion* to extend the seven-day time bar for candidates lodging election petitions and (b) authorizing their third-party surrogates to *seek leave* to bring judicial review proceedings to litigate the very same electoral issue. But in ruling as it did, the HKCFA reached a decision that upheld the impugned law – thereby avoiding a potential conflict with the government – while preserving its oversight over electoral matters.

But as China's authoritarian impulses intensify under President Xi Jinping,[175] the Hong Kong judiciary in lockstep also increasingly toed the party line on democratic change. In 2017, the HKCFA in *Kwok Cheuk Kin* (2017)[176] announced that a 'wider'[177] margin of appreciation ought to be accorded to electoral laws. Previously, only 'due'[178] regard was required. On the facts, the HKCFA upheld a law that disqualifies a legislator from running in the by-election held to fill a vacancy consequent on that member's resignation. The law was passed in 2012 after five pro-democracy legislative councillors from different geographical constituencies – as a collective act of political protest – resigned mid-term in 2010 to trigger city-wide by-elections for their seats. Given that their re-election was virtually guaranteed, their voluntary resignation and contestation in the by-election was pure political posturing. The focus of the electoral challenge centred on whether the electoral restriction was proportionate. The Court unanimously agreed that it was legitimate for the government to deter resignations with a view to trigger by-elections,[179] especially since this (somewhat unnecessary) political exercise cost HK$ 126 million in public expenditure.[180] Furthermore, this electoral restriction was deemed proportionate, as 'some leeway should be permitted to the Legislature to determine what would be an

174 Ibid. [26], [49].

175 Cora Chan, 'Thirty Years from Tiananmen: China, Hong Kong, and the Ongoing Experiment to Preserve Liberal Values in an Authoritarian State' (2019) *International Journal of Constitutional Law* 439.

176 *Kwok Cheuk Kin* v. *Secretary for Constitutional and Mainland Affairs (2017)* [2017] 20 HKCFAR 353 (Hong Kong Court of Final Appeal).

177 Ibid. [42].

178 *Leung Chun Ying* v. *Ho Chun Yan Albert* [2013] 16 HKCFAR 735 (Hong Kong Court of Final Appeal) [45].

179 *Kwok Cheuk Kin* (n. 176) [50(4)].

180 Ibid. [9].

appropriate way of dealing with the perceived mischief'.[181] Interestingly, counsel had raised concerns that this law was overbroad, as it would also penalize legislators for changing party allegiance if they could no longer 'in good conscience continue as party member[s]'.[182] The Court was, however, unmoved by this ethical dilemma that such lawmakers would face:

> It was within [the Legislature's] political judgment or assessment to adopt this option … Certainly, the Court should not be put (nor ought it to be placed) in a position where it had to decide on political matters of this kind or have to be drawn into a political debate.[183]

Nevertheless, the HKCFA was sympathetic to one potential class of lawmakers who were caught by this overbroad electoral law: legislators who had resigned due to poor health but recovered in time for the by-election.[184] According to the Court, such ailing legislators would, pursuant to Article 79(2) of the Basic Law,[185] have a 'valid reason' to be absent from legislative meetings and could not be disqualified from office,[186] and hence would have no need to resign their office. This judicial manoeuvre extraordinarily neutralized Article 79(1) of the Basic Law, which authorized the President of the Legislative Council to disqualify a lawmaker if 'he or she loses the ability to discharge his or her duties as a result of serious illness or other reasons'.[187] It is especially noteworthy that the CFA made no mention of Article 79 (1) at all, let alone squared its reading of Article 79(2) with Article 79(1).

The HKCFA's current deference to the legislature on 'political' matters stands in sharp contrast with the Hong Kong judiciary's past practice of rigorously scrutinizing limitations on electoral rights when the invalidation of these restrictions did not risk eroding Beijing's political control over the city.[188] Previously, the Hong Kong judiciary had successfully ushered in modest changes to Hong Kong's restrictive electoral regime by extending voting rights writ small to non-indigenous villagers[189] and disenfranchised prisoners,[190] and allowing those who had been convicted of

181 Ibid. [55].
182 Ibid. [56].
183 Ibid. [57].
184 Ibid. [58].
185 Article 79 of the Hong Kong Basic Law reads: 'The President of the Legislative Council of the Hong Kong Special Administrative Region shall declare that a member of the Council is no longer qualified for the office under any of the following circumstances: … (2) When he or she, with no valid reason, is absent from meetings for three consecutive months without the consent of the President of the Legislative Council.'
186 *Kwok Cheuk Kin* (n. 176) [58].
187 Article 79 of the Hong Kong Basic Law reads: 'The President of the Legislative Council of the Hong Kong Special Administrative Region shall declare that a member of the Council is no longer qualified for the office under any of the following circumstances: (1) When he or she loses the ability to discharge his or her duties as a result of serious illness or other reasons …'.
188 Yap (n. 1) 49–55.
189 *Secretary for Justice* v. *Chan Wah* [2000] 3 HKCFAR 459 (Hong Kong Court of Final Appeal).
190 *Chan Kin Sum* v. *Secretary for Justice* [2009] 2 HKLRD 166 (Hong Kong Court of First Instance).

minor offences pending appeal to stand for elections.[191] But it is noteworthy that since the HKCFA articulated this new 'margin of appreciation' test on political matters, no electoral restriction has been invalidated by the courts again. It would appear that the HKCFA has sounded the death knell for the constitutional review of electoral law.

Perhaps even more worrying is the Hong Kong judiciary's recent participation in the active ousting of lawmakers. In August 2017, a three-member Appeals Committee of the HKCFA in *Yau Wai Ching* (2017)[192] refused to grant leave to appeal against the lower courts' decision to disqualify two lawmakers from office after they had declined to take the requisite Legislative Council (LegCo) oath at their inauguration.

The political context of this dispute can be briefly explained. In the wake of the 2014 Umbrella Movement that paralyzed the financial district in Hong Kong for 79 days, Hong Kongers thumbed their noses at Beijing by voting a slew of young pro-democracy street protestors into the LegCo in 2016. More significantly, six of the newly elected lawmakers had either openly advocated Hong Kong's independence from China or defended Hong Kong's right to democratic self-determination.[193] Less compromising and more confrontational, these newly elected lawmakers openly derided China at their swearing-in ceremony on 12 October 2016 and a pair of them (Sixtus Leung and Yau Wai-ching) even referred to China as 'Sheen-na' – a derogatory term used by the Japanese on the Chinese during the Second World War – and pledged allegiance to the 'Hong Kong nation' instead. Unsurprisingly, the President of the LegCo did not accept the validity of the pair's oaths but nevertheless allowed them to retake their oaths at the next LegCo meeting. However, before Leung and Yau could retake their oaths, the Hong Kong government swiftly went to court and sought a declaration that the pair had been disqualified from their office on 12 October 2016 when they had declined to take the requisite legislative oath and that the LegCo President was therefore disempowered from re-administering their oaths. It is also noteworthy that while the case was *sub judice* before the Court of First Instance, and only four days after the judicial review proceeding commenced, the NPCSC issued an Interpretation of article 104[194] of the

191 *Wong Hin Wai* v. *Secretary for Justice* [2012] 4 HKLRD 170 (Hong Kong Court of First Instance).

192 *Yau Wai Ching* v. *Chief Executive of the HKSAR* [2017] 20 HKCFAR 390 (Hong Kong Court of Final Appeal).

193 Gary Cheung and Jeffie Lam, 'Rise of Localists in Hong Kong Polls Set to Bring Headaches for Beijing, Analysts Say' (*South China Morning Post*, 5 September 2016), available at www.scmp.com/news/hong-kong/politics/article/2015349/rise-localists-hong-kong-polls-set-bring-headaches-beijing, accessed 1 February 2017.

194 Article 104 of the Hong Kong Basic Law reads: 'When assuming office, the Chief Executive, principal officials, members of the Executive Council and of the Legislative Council, judges of the courts at all levels and other members of the judiciary in the Hong Kong Special Administrative Region must, in accordance with law, swear to uphold the Basic Law of the Hong Kong Special Administrative Region of the People's Republic of China and swear allegiance to the Hong Kong Special Administrative Region of the People's Republic of China.'

BL, and the Interpretation *inter alia* provides that: 'If the oath taken is determined as invalid, no arrangement shall be made for retaking the oath'.[195]

Caving to the weight of this political pressure, the three-member Appeals Committee HKCFA chaired by the Chief Justice decided that the 'disqualification of [the legislators] was the automatic consequence of their declining or neglecting to take the LegCo oath',[196] and the Court refused leave as the legislators' appeal against their disqualification was simply 'not reasonably arguable'.[197] But one must note that while the NPCSC Interpretation clearly provides that legislators are disqualified if they decline to take the prescribed oath, the Interpretation is actually silent on whether the judiciary has to be the branch of government that does the disqualification.[198] Furthermore, this NPCSC Interpretation is also silent on whether it applies retrospectively to events that predated its issue.

Given that an NPCSC Interpretation is a 'legislative act',[199] the presumption against retrospectivity of legislation would arguably apply. According to this common law presumption, unless a contrary intention appears, a legislative provision is presumed not to operate retrospectively,[200] that is, to impair vested rights acquired under then-existing laws or to create a new obligation, duty or disadvantage in relation to past events,[201] regardless of whether it is 'penal in the sense of punishment'.[202] Even under Chinese socialist law, NPCSC Interpretations do not as a categorical rule apply retrospectively.[203] Nevertheless, the three-member Appeals Committee of the HKCFA simply refused leave to consider whether a presumption against retrospectivity of legislation applies to this 2016 NPCSC Interpretation. While the HKCFA has previously declared[204] that a 1999 NPCSC Interpretation applies retrospectively, it was then dealing with an Interpretation that *expressly* stated so.[205] In contrast, this 2016 Interpretation is intentionally silent on its

195 Interpretation of Article 104 of the Basic Law of the Hong Kong Special Administrative Region of the People's Republic of China by the Standing Committee of the National People's Congress (7 November 2016), available at www.elegislation.gov.hk/hk/A115!en@2016-11-07T00:00:00/longTitle?elpid=254663, accessed 17 March 2017.

196 *Yau Wai Ching* (n. 192) [36].

197 Ibid. [38].

198 See Po Jen Yap and Eric Chan, 'Legislative Oaths and Judicial Intervention in Hong Kong' (2017) 47 *Hong Kong Law Journal* 1 for a fuller discussion of the Court of Appeal's decision in this controversy.

199 Albert H. Y. Chen, 'Another Case of Conflict between the CFA and the NPC Standing Committee?' (2001) 31 *Hong Kong Law Journal* 179, 185; 王振民 Wang, Zhenmin：《中央与特别行政区关系：一种法治结构的解析》*The Central-SAR Relationship: A Legal Analysis*，清华大学出版社(Tsinghua Press 2002) 277.

200 Francis Bennion and Oliver Jones (eds), *Bennion on Statutory Interpretation* (London: Sweet and Maxwell, 6th ed., 2013) 291; *Spread Trustee Co Ltd* v. *Hutcheson* [2012] 2 AC 194 (Privy Council) [65].

201 *Yew Bon Tew* v. *Kenderaan Bas Mara* [1983] 1 AC 553 (Privy Council) 558–559.

202 *Re School Board Election for the Parish of Pulborough* [1894] 1 QB 725 (Court of Appeal) 737.

203 Yap and Chan (n. 198).

204 *Lau Kong Yung* v. *Director of Immigration* [1999] 2 HKCFAR 4 (Hong Kong Court of Final Appeal).

205 The Interpretation by the Standing Committee of the National People's Congress of Articles 22(4) and 24(2)(3) of the Basic Law of the Hong Kong Special Administrative Region of the People's

temporal effect. But the HKCFA simply deemed this legal distinction 'not reasonably arguable'.[206] Fascinatingly, six months after *Yau Wai Ching* was decided, Robert Tang – a then-Permanent Judge of the HKCFA – in an extra-judicial address at Oxford University, openly voiced his disagreement with his HKCFA brethren on this issue:

> [T]he Court of Final Appeal may if it wishes to do so reconsider the point in a full court of five judges after full argument. The 2016 Interpretation may provide a good opportunity to do so.[207]

Notably, Robert Tang PJ was not assigned by the Chief Justice to the Appeals Committee panel that decided *Yau Wai Ching*.

Furthermore, neither Article 104 of the Basic Law nor the NPCSC Interpretation displaces the common law principle of judicial non-intervention in the internal process of LegCo, which the HKCFA has previously emphasized: '[T]he courts will not intervene to rule on the regularity or irregularity of the internal processes of the legislature but will leave it to [the legislature to] determine exclusively for itself matters of this kind.'[208] Previously, in 2014, the HKCFA invoked this principle of non-intervention in the internal affairs of LegCo when it *refused* to determine whether the President of LegCo had lawfully invoked his power to terminate a legislative filibuster engineered by the pro-democracy lawmakers.[209] Then, any perceived irregularity with the internal process of the legislature was a political question for the President of LegCo alone to resolve. But now, the HKCFA held it was simply 'untenable'[210] that this principle of non-intervention would apply to another internal process of the legislature: whether the judiciary can decide whether the President of LegCo had lawfully invoked his power to grant newly elected LegCo members the opportunity to retake the requisite legislative oath after they flubbed their first attempt. It was now for the courts to adjudicate on whether

Republic of China (Adopted by the Standing Committee of the Ninth National People's Congress at its Tenth Session on 26 June 1999), available at www.elegislation.gov.hk/hk/A106!en@1999-06-26T00:00:00/longTitle?elpid=254021, accessed 17 March 2017. This 1999 NPSC Interpretation expressly provides: 'This Interpretation does not affect the right of abode in the Hong Kong Special Administrative Region granted to the litigating party in the case through the judgment made by the Court of Final Appeal of the Hong Kong Special Administrative Region on January 29, 1999. As to whether any other person conforms to the provisions of Category (3) of Paragraph 2 in Article 24 of the Basic Law of the Hong Kong Special Administrative Region, the matter shall be decided according to this Interpretation.'

206 *Yau Wai Ching* (n. 192) [36].

207 Robert Tang, 'Dr Mok Hing Yiu Memorial Lecture: One Country, Two Systems: Basic Law, Common Law and the Rule of Law', 22 February 2018 (St Hugh's College, Oxford) [47].

208 *Leung Kwok Hung* v. *President of the Legislative Council (No 1)* [2014] 17 HKCFAR 689 (Hong Kong Court of Final Appeal) [28].

209 Ibid.

210 *Yau Wai Ching* (n. 192) [24].

lawmakers had duly taken their legislative oaths and to remove any errant lawmakers 'automatical[ly]'.[211]

Admittedly, the political fates of the two lawmakers would have been sealed even if the HKCFA had punted the legality of the legislators' removal back to the legislature. But by not participating in the lawmakers' inglorious disqualification from office, the Hong Kong courts would have preserved their image as the guardian of the city's civil liberties and warded off criticisms that the judiciary had now become an enabler of the executive government's political agenda. More importantly, the Hong Kong government's victory in the lower courts had emboldened it to seek the removal of four additional pro-democracy lawmakers, who have also since been removed.[212] By unilaterally disqualifying the lawmakers, the Hong Kong judiciary has unwittingly opened the floodgates to more (unnecessary) litigation and embroiled itself in more political controversy.

Taking its cues from the HKCFA, the lower courts have gone on to allow Election Returning Officers to unilaterally bar pro-Hong Kong independence candidates from running for political office.[213] The contested legislation in question provides that a valid election nomination form must include 'a declaration to the effect that the person will uphold the Basic Law and pledge allegiance'[214] to the HKSAR. The applicant did submit such a declaration, but the Court held that this was not enough: the declarant must also be one who '*genuinely* and *truthfully* intends to uphold the Basic Law and pledge allegiance to the HKSAR.'[215] Given that the applicant was a renowned secessionist in Hong Kong, the Court agreed with the Returning Office that the nominee's declaration was insincere and thus the candidate was ineligible to run for political office. But this additional requirement was simply not included in the electoral legislation or any of the subsidiary rules. If this 'sincerity' requirement was intended, the relevant rules would have provided guidance on how the Returning Office was to determine the 'genuineness' of this intent.[216] No such statutory or administrative guidance was provided, because it was the Court that legislated so. But the Court was also cognizant that if left unfettered, it was conferring unbridled power on the Returning Officer to bar political candidates at will, and this would spell the end of democracy in Hong Kong. Therefore the Court swiftly legislated additional safeguards:

211 Ibid. [36].

212 *Chief Executive of HKSAR* v. *President of Legislative Council* [2017] 4 HKLRD 115 (Hong Kong Court of First Instance); *Secretary for Justice* v. *Leung Kwok Hung* [2019] HKCA 173 (Hong Kong Court of Appeal).

213 *Chan Ho Tin* v. *Lo Ying Ki Alan* [2018] HKCFI 345 (Hong Kong Court of First Instance).

214 Section 40(1)(b)(i) of the Legislative Council Ordinance (Cap 542).

215 Ibid. [45].

216 For a fuller discussion on the disputed electoral rules, see Po Jen Yap and Jiang Zixin, 'Electoral Disqualification, Political Allegiance, and the Courts: A "Fruitless Debate"?' (2019) 49 *Hong Kong Law Journal* 825.

> Hence, the Declaration requirement should generally be regarded as having been complied with if a candidate has submitted the nomination form with a signed Declaration. This should and can only be displaced in a plain case where, albeit on a balance of probabilities, there are cogent, clear and compelling materials which would demonstrate to an objective reasonable person that the candidate plainly cannot have that intention at the time of the nomination.[217]

On the other hand, in a subsequent electoral disqualification dispute in *Chow Ting* (2019),[218] a different judge on the CFI ruled that the abovementioned procedural safeguard imposed by his brethren should be not viewed as a 'legal requirement'[219] or there would be 'endless or fruitless debate on whether the materials are sufficiently "cogent, clear and compelling" for this purpose'.[220] Instead, the CFI in *Chow Ting* (2019) was content to just provide the candidate with a reasonable opportunity to respond to the materials that the Returning Officer intended to rely upon for any pending disqualification.

In June 2020, the NPCSC annexed a new national security legislation to Hong Kong's Basic Law.[221] Frustrated with the months of civil unrest that had rocked the city since mid-2019, and the local government's inability to pass national security law 'on its own',[222] Beijing decided to take matters into its own hands and custom-make a bespoke law for Hong Kong. Notably, the details of this law were not subject to any public consultation and were only published *after* it took effect. Secession, which includes independence advocacy;[223] subversion of state power, which includes damaging government buildings such that governmental functions can no longer be performed;[224] and collusion with foreign governments, which includes lobbying for the imposition of sanctions on Hong Kong or the People's Republic of China;[225]

217 *Chan Ho Tin* (n. 213) [79].

218 *Chow Ting* v. *Teng Yu-nan Anne* [2019] HKCFI 2135 (Hong Kong Court of First Instance). The petitioner, Agnes Chow Ting was disqualified because she was a member of the political party, Demosistō, that advocated 'democratic self-determination' for Hong Kong, which included the proposal that the future of Hong Kong be determined through a constitutionally effective referendum by the people of Hong Kong.

219 Ibid. [24].

220 Ibid.

221 The Law of the People's Republic of China on Safeguarding National Security in the Hong Kong Special Administrative Region.

222 Article 23 of the Basic Law reads: The Hong Kong Special Administrative Region shall enact laws on its own to prohibit any act of treason, secession, sedition, subversion against the Central People's Government, or theft of state secrets, to prohibit foreign political organizations or bodies from conducting political activities in the Region, and to prohibit political organizations or bodies of the Region from establishing ties with foreign political organizations or bodies.

223 Articles 20 and 21 of the Law of the People's Republic of China on Safeguarding National Security in the Hong Kong Special Administrative Region.

224 Article 22(4) of the Law of the People's Republic of China on Safeguarding National Security in the Hong Kong Special Administrative Region.

225 Article 29(4) of the Law of the People's Republic of China on Safeguarding National Security in the Hong Kong Special Administrative Region.

are all national security penal offences now. Terrorism has also been defined to include arson and the damaging of vehicular transport and traffic facilities for political ends.[226] For all four crimes, offenders face sentences of up to life imprisonment for grave violations, while short-term detentions can be imposed for minor infractions. Even non-Hong Kong residents based outside the jurisdiction are liable for prosecution if they commit any of these penal offences against Hong Kong.[227] A National Security agency established by Beijing to gather intelligence can now operate legally in Hong Kong, but must abide by local laws,[228] though these Mainland officials are not subject to local jurisdiction for acts performed in the course of duty.[229] The enforcement and prosecution decisions made under this national security law are entrusted to local officials[230] and Hong Kong courts are also empowered to adjudicate the vast majority of cases brought under this law.[231] Most local criminal law procedures and human rights safeguards continue to apply.[232] But jury trial in individual cases can be replaced with a panel of three judges,[233] and where state secrets are involved, all or part of the trial can be closed to the public, though the verdict must still be announced in open court.[234] The Chief Executive – in consultation with the Chief Justice – will decide on the list of judges who will hear these national security cases, and they will be drawn from the pool of pre-existing Hong Kong judges, but no judge can be selected if they have made any statement or behaved in any manner that endangers national security.[235] In those rare serious cases where foreign governments are involved or the Hong Kong

[226] Article 24 of the Law of the People's Republic of China on Safeguarding National Security in the Hong Kong Special Administrative Region.

[227] Article 38 of the Law of the People's Republic of China on Safeguarding National Security in the Hong Kong Special Administrative Region.

[228] Article 50 of the Law of the People's Republic of China on Safeguarding National Security in the Hong Kong Special Administrative Region.

[229] Article 60 of the Law of the People's Republic of China on Safeguarding National Security in the Hong Kong Special Administrative Region.

[230] Articles 16 and 18 of the Law of the People's Republic of China on Safeguarding National Security in the Hong Kong Special Administrative Region.

[231] Article 40 of the Law of the People's Republic of China on Safeguarding National Security in the Hong Kong Special Administrative Region.

[232] Articles 4, 5 and 41 of the Law of the People's Republic of China on Safeguarding National Security in the Hong Kong Special Administrative Region. For example, the right to trial by jury can be suspended if the Secretary for Justice so decides in individual cases. See Article 46 of the Law of the People's Republic of China on Safeguarding National Security in the Hong Kong Special Administrative Region.

[233] Article 46 of the Law of the People's Republic of China on Safeguarding National Security in the Hong Kong Special Administrative Region.

[234] Article 41 of the Law of the People's Republic of China on Safeguarding National Security in the Hong Kong Special Administrative Region.

[235] Article 44 of the Law of the People's Republic of China on Safeguarding National Security in the Hong Kong Special Administrative Region.

government is unable to enforce the law effectively, the Chinese procuratorate and courts are legally empowered to take over from local counterparts.[236] The law opens up the chilling possibility that for these exceptional cases, the offenders, if in Hong Kong, can be extradited to the Mainland to face trial. Finally, the power of interpreting this national security law lies with the NPCSC,[237] which expressly allows Mainland officials to overrule the Hong Kong judiciary's interpretation of this criminal law. It is evidently clear that Beijing is determined to subdue political strife and entrench plenary control over all sovereignty issues in Hong Kong. As of 1 May 2021, no one has been extradited to China to face trial under the National Security Law, but 54 people have been charged under this law. 47 of those persons charged were pro-democracy activists who, prior to the 2021 election revamp, had organized an informal election primary to field candidates who can win seats in the Legislative Council and subsequently block the passage of the government's budget, thereby forcing the Chief Executive's resignation.[238] But it is important to note that the Hong Kong courts have emphasized that *only* common law principles – and not Mainland Chinese legal doctrines – will be used to interpret the NSL.[239] Furthermore, Hong Kong courts have been able to compartmentalize and continue to hand down liberal rights rulings, including one on same-sex intestacy rights, even after the NSL took effect.[240] Even in its first substantive NSL ruling, the HKCFA has declared that as far as possible, the NSL 'is to be given a meaning and effect compatible with those rights, freedoms and values' [241] enshrined in the Basic Law. The actual implementation of this draconian NSL underscores how Hong Kong's continued viability as an international financial centre is indispensable to Beijing for linking the Mainland to the global economy so that China can generate capital in Hong Kong to fund its global political ambitions abroad. The intended purpose of this law is to strike fear into the hearts of Hong Kong dissidents so that they will self-censor, and not be used indiscriminately to imprison its residents, for the latter will trigger a massive capital flight from the city. In short, the real aim of this law is to deter, and not to detain.

236 Article 55 of the Law of the People's Republic of China on Safeguarding National Security in the Hong Kong Special Administrative Region.

237 Article 65 of the Law of the People's Republic of China on Safeguarding National Security in the Hong Kong Special Administrative Region.

238 Austin Ramzy and Tiffany May, 'Hong Kong Charges 47 Democracy Supporters with Violating Security Law' (*New York Times*, 28 February 2021), available at www.nytimes.com/2021/02/28/world/asia/hong-kong-security-law-arrests.html, accessed 25 May 2021.

239 *Tong Ying Kit* v. *HKSAR* [2020] HKCFI 2133 (Hong Kong Court of First Instance) [49].

240 *Ng Hon Lam* v. *Secretary for Justice* [2020] HKCFI 2412 (Hong Kong Court of First Instance). See Chapter 3.

241 *HKSAR* v. *Lai Chee Ying* [2021] HKCFA 3 (Hong Kong Court of Final Appeal) [42].

## CONCLUSION

The Constitutional Courts of Taiwan and Korea can be classed as Judicial Review regimes that observe 'democratic instrumentalism'[242] – courts operating in liberal democracies where their judges pay more attention to policy consequences and are less confined by 'semantic legal rules'.[243] In the absence of a hegemonic party in control of all levers of state power, these Courts have the policy space to make systemic innovations to political institutions and processes that enhance democratic diversity and electoral freedom. Such courts serve as institutional guardrails that stabilize the political system against temporary self-serving legislative or executive onslaughts that threaten governmental integrity,[244] and occasionally these courts can even play a transformative role to usher in a more democratic legal order.[245]

On the other hand, the Hong Kong judiciary will not converge with its East Asian counterparts on matters relating to systemic electoral reform and national security. While the HKCFA enjoys real autonomy over a gamut of constitutional law, as we have discussed in earlier chapters, its scope for independence is significantly constrained by Beijing on issues relating to democratic values. Vis-à-vis such disputes, at best, the HKCFA will be a 'passive night watchm[a]n'[246] over a democracy in stagnation or regression; and in the worst-case scenario, it becomes an enabler that clothes the authoritarian communist regime with a veneer of constitutional legitimacy.

242 Roux (n. 3) 84–85.
243 Ibid. 85.
244 Issacharoff (n. 7).
245 Ginsburg (n. 9) 50; Yap (n. 1).
246 Issacharoff (n. 7) 56.

# 6

# Conclusion

While Asia has largely stood outside the global wave of judicial review sweeping across our world,[1] this book has explained why and how three East Asian courts have remarkably bucked this Asian trend and converged as independent constraints on governmental power. Notably, the three judiciaries did not intentionally align their practices with one another. Instead, the Asian courts have deliberately adopted Western constitutional precedents, and, in doing so, these courts have *indirectly* converged on the practice of Western liberal constitutional norms.

Chapter 2 begins by examining how this 'judicialization'[2] of governance is fostered by party competition/fragmentation within that democracy *and* the operation of an independent judiciary. Party competition creates conflict between the political branches of government, which requires an independent third party – the judiciary – to mediate and resolve.[3] Political fragmentation foments gridlock, which in turn expands the space for independent judicial policy-making.[4] In such a strategic milieu, the 'zone of discretion'[5] that judges possess expands and they gain the ability to act according to their own preferences.[6] Judges become powerful as a

1 Wen-Chen Chang, 'Asian Exceptionalism?' (2019) 17 *International Journal of Constitutional Law* 31; Doreen Lustig and J. H. H. Weiler, 'Judicial Review in the Contemporary World – Retrospective and Prospective' (2018) 16 *International Journal of Constitutional Law* 315.

2 C. Neal Tate, 'Why the Expansion of Judicial Power' in C. Neal Tate and Torbjörn Vallinder (eds), *The Global Expansion of Judicial Power* (New York University Press 1995) 27, 28.

3 Martin Shapiro, *Courts* (University of Chicago Press 1981).

4 John Ferejohn, 'Judicializing Politics, Politicizing Law' (2002) 65 *Law and Contemporary Problems* 41; Tom Ginsburg, 'The Global Spread of Constitutional Review' in Keith E. Whittington, R. Daniel Kelemen and Gregory A. Caldeira (eds), *The Oxford Handbook of Law and Politics* (Oxford University Press 2010) 81, 90.

5 Alec Stone Sweet, 'Constitutions, Rights, and Judicial Power' in Daniele Caramani (ed.), *Comparative Politics* (Oxford University Press 2017) 155, 163.

6 John Ferejohn, Frances Rosenbluth and Charles Shipan, 'Comparative Judicial Politics' in Carles Boix and Susan C. Stokes (eds), *The Oxford Handbook of Comparative Politics* (Oxford University Press 2009) 727, 729.

consequence of the powers formally conferred upon them and the powers they confer upon themselves as the political branches weaken.[7]

The Constitutional Court of Taiwan (TCC) and the Hong Kong Court of Final Appeal (HKCFA) were not conceived as 'trustee courts'[8] – courts created by the Constitution in trust for the people and in defence of a rights-based democratic order. Instead, these courts were established by authoritarian governments to clothe their rule with a veneer of legitimacy and there was no intention to delegate policy control to the courts. But judicial power is not limited to what is merely conferred at the time of constitutional drafting; it can also expand as judges gain freedom to pursue their own policy agenda.[9] Taiwan and South Korea are now dynamic democracies where competing political parties routinely take turns to occupy the Presidency and rivalling political parties regularly have opportunities to appoint like-minded judges to the highest courts. This fragmentation of political power empowers their Constitutional Courts to assert their independence without risking significant political reprisals from the government of the day. On the other hand, while Hong Kong is under communist rule, the informal pro-Beijing coalition in the local legislature is splintered into multiple factions. Furthermore, the Chinese and local governments have endogenous incentives to respect local judicial authority, and the exogenous costs of attacking judicial independence in Hong Kong are also sufficiently prohibitive, such that government officials will only reverse or rebuke the courts when the State's core interests are under threat.[10] Equally important in Hong Kong is the fact that its Chief Justice exercises extraordinary autonomy over the appointment of judges, which allows the incumbent to shape the ideology of the bench, and in the particular the HKCFA, free from the control of the government. With ex ante and ex post judicial independence secured, top courts in East Asia can choose foreign law to construct an identity for their domestic polity that aligns with transnational norms, and advance a constitutional vision that is distinct from their governments. Judges speak 'the language of legal doctrine',[11] but the strategic choices they make reveal their ideological or attitudinal tilts.[12] For the Constitutional Court of Korea (KCC) and the TCC, Germany is the foreign jurisdiction most considered by both courts. As for Hong Kong, English

7 See generally Stephen Gardbaum, 'What Makes for More or Less Powerful Constitutional Courts?' (2018) 29 *Duke Journal of Comparative and International Law* 1.

8 See Alec Stone Sweet and Jud Mathews, 'Proportionality Balancing and Global Constitutionalism' (2008) 47 *Columbia Journal of Transnational Law* 72, 84; Alec Stone Sweet and Jud Mathews, *Proportionality Balancing and Constitutional Governance* (Oxford University Press 2019) 21.

9 Tom Ginsburg, *Judicial Review in New Democracies* (Cambridge University Press 2003).

10 For a general discussion on the symbiotic relationship between political fragmentation and judicial power, see Georg Vanberg, 'Constitutional Courts in Comparative Perspective: A Theoretical Assessment' (2015) 18 *Annual Review of Political Science* 167, 169.

11 Ran Hirschl, *Comparative Law Matters: The Renaissance of Comparative Constitutional Law* (Oxford University Press 2014) 42.

12 Ibid.

Commonwealth jurisprudence is most persuasive and overseas judges from the English Commonwealth are also invited to sit as Non-Permanent Judges on its highest court. By referencing or importing the constitutional practices of successful democratic regimes, local jurists can justify their choice – to the domestic audience – for reaching a similar conclusion at home.[13] The prestige of the foreign model provides the justification and the authority for the domestic adoption;[14] and this book has examined how the East Asian courts have converged on two types of 'legitimacy-generating'[15] legal transplants: Structured Proportionality and Innovative Constitutional Remedies.

Chapter 3 continues by exploring the convergence on the judicial use of Structured Proportionality (SP). Proportionality Analysis (PA) has its origins in German law, but it has diffused across Europe and beyond. Its judicial deployment is so ubiquitous that it is now a 'global, best-practice standard of rights protection'[16] and enthroned at the apex of constitutional governance. However, within Asia, *only* the courts of Taiwan, South Korea and Hong Kong apply SP – the *regular* and *routine* use of a *sequential* PA to *invalidate* legislation. SP in East Asia – as is the case in Europe – is judicially constructed: this judicial doctrinal tool authorizes courts to use a highly intrusive standard of review to evaluate legislative ends and the regulatory means by which statutory goals are pursued. With SP in its judicial arsenal, the courts in East Asia have reshaped their polity's constitutional culture, and made their societies freer and more inclusive. Patriarchal,[17] heterosexist,[18] xenophobic[19] and dogmatic[20] laws have all been judicially shredded, as the courts have used SP to pursue progressive causes opposed by their governments. But for all three courts, also embedded within SP is a 'zone of proportionality'[21] – the constitutional space

[13] Johanna Kalb, 'The Judicial Role in New Democracies: A Strategic Account of Comparative Citation' (2013) 38 *Yale Journal of International Law* 423, 440.

[14] Alan Watson, 'Aspects of Reception of Law' (1996) 44 *American Journal of Comparative Law* 335, 346, 350–351.

[15] Jonathan M. Miller, 'A Typology of Legal Transplants' (2003) 51 *American Journal of Comparative Law* 839, 854

[16] Stone Sweet and Mathews (n. 8) 7.

[17] *Case on House Hold Head System*, 2001Hun-Ka9 (3 February 2005) (Constitutional Court of Korea); *Adultery Case*, 2009Hun-Ba17 (26 February 2015) (Constitutional Court of Korea).

[18] *Secretary for Justice* v. *Yau Yuk Lung* [2007] 10 HKCFAR 335 (Hong Kong Court of Final Appeal); *QT* v. *Director of Immigration* [2018] HKCFA 28 (Hong Kong Court of Final Appeal).

[19] J.Y. Interpretation No. 710 (Taiwan) (2013) (Constitutional Court of Taiwan), at [3], available at http://cons.judicial.gov.tw/jcc/en-us/jep03/show?expno=710, accessed 15 May 2021.

[20] *Case on Conscientious Objectors*, 2011Hun-Ba379 (28 June 2018) (Constitutional Court of Korea) (Official English Summary).

[21] Aharon Barak, *Proportionality: Constitutional Rights and Their Limitations* (Cambridge University Press 2012) 417.

defined by judges for Parliament to legislate – that gives meaningful discretion to the legislature to craft a more tailored piece of legislation on remand.[22]

In Chapter 4, we proceed by analysing the East Asian convergence on two innovative constitutional remedies, specifically Suspension Orders and Remedial Interpretation. The former delays the operation of a judicial declaration of invalidity to prevent any legislative vacuum while lawmakers deliberate over remedial action; the latter expedites a remedy by allowing courts to read-in words into the impugned law such that no further action is needed by the legislature because the impugned rule continues to operate as judicially re-written. Notably, the courts in Taiwan, South Korea and Hong Kong are the *only* judiciaries in Asia that regularly rely on delayed and expedited remedies – both created in the West – to rectify constitutionally flawed legislation. While Suspension Orders may harm individual rights bearers,[23] we have shown how the East Asian courts have mitigated these harms by pairing the judicial use of this delayed remedy with novel strategies that coax or compel governmental compliance: dis-applying the enforcement of these impugned statutes while remedial legislation is pending,[24] refusing to shield the government from any legal liability during the suspension period,[25] adopting remedial reading-in provisos that take effect automatically if the legislature defaults at the end of the suspension period,[26] and even issuing interim remedial readings of the law pending legislative change.[27] These 'aggressive weak-form remedies'[28] give the legislature time and space to devise remedial action, but also impose default rules that punish legislative and executive delinquency. In contrast, Remedial Interpretation allows an impugned law to continue to operate, but in a judicially modified form. We have seen how such piecemeal, court-driven reforms may be the preferred solution for legislatures when such changes are more expedient,[29] or judges may prefer to

22 *Restriction on Right to Vote of Prisoners and Probationers with Suspended Sentence*, 2012Hun-Ma409, 510, 2013Hun-Ma167 (consolidated) (28 January 2014) (Constitutional Court of Korea); *Chan Kin Sum* v. *Secretary of Justice* [2009] 2 HKLRD 166 (Hong Kong Court of First Instance).

23 Robert Leckey, 'The Harms of Remedial Discretion' (2016) 14 *International Journal of Constitutional* Law 584.

24 *Prohibition of Labor Dispute by the Public Sector Laborers Case*, 88Hun-Ma5 (11 March 1993) (Constitutional Court of Korea); *Suspension from Duty of Heads of Local Governments*, 2010Hun-Ma418 (2 September 2010) (Constitutional Court of Korea).

25 *Koo Sze Yiu* v. *Chief Executive of the HKSAR*, [2006] HKCFA 74, [2006] 9 HKCFAR 441 (Hong Kong Court of Final Appeal).

26 *W* v. *Registrar of Marriages*, [2013] HKCFA 39, [2013] 16 HKCFAR 112 (Hong Kong Court of Final Appeal); J.Y. Interpretation No. 748 (2017) (Constitutional Court of Taiwan), available at http://cons.judicial.gov.tw/jcc/en-us/jep03/show?expno=748, accessed 15 May 2021.

27 J.Y. Interpretation No. 755 (2017) (Constitutional Court of Taiwan), available at http://cons.judicial.gov.tw/jcc/en-us/jep03/show?expno=755, accessed 15 May 2021; *Case on Search by Arrest Warrant of Dwellings other than the suspect's*, 2015Hun-Ba370 (26 April 2018) (Constitutional Court of Korea) (Official English Summary).

28 See David Landau, 'Aggressive Weak-Form Remedies' (2014) 5 *Constitutional Court Review* 244.

29 *Yeung Chu Wing* v. *Secretary for Justice* [2019] HKCFI 1431 (Hong Kong Court of First Instance); *Leung Chun Kwong* v. *Secretary for the Civil Service* [2019] HKCFA 19 (Hong Kong Court of Final

uphold a controversial law – albeit a re-written one – so as not to unnecessarily drain the court's institutional capital, especially if an open invalidation of an impugned law would cause public disquiet.[30] This convergence on the bifurcation of a rights-recognition and its remedial enforcement has created opportunities for the courts in East Asia to collaborate with their respective co-equal political branches of government, which would have been precluded if rights-implementation were under the aegis of their legislatures alone.[31]

Finally, in Chapter 5, we investigate the limits of this constitutional convergence in East Asia: electoral reform. There is a symbiotic relationship between democratization and judicial power.[32] In South Korea and Taiwan, where the institutional predicates for free and fair elections exist, their Constitutional Courts do not postpone their 'reckoning with excess power'.[33] These courts operating in dynamic democracies intervene directly in 'mega politics'[34] – matters of outright and utmost political significance that regularly define or divide whole societies – and actively address systemic failures in the electoral infrastructure. To this end, the TCC has successfully thwarted self-serving constitutional attempts to suspend elections,[35] prohibited the use of criminal sanctions against opposition lawmakers for speeches made in the legislature,[36] removed barriers of entry for electoral candidacy[37] and reined-in partisan legislative attempts to interfere with executive and judicial functions.[38] In the same vein, the KCC has invalidated prohibitive election deposits that

Appeal); J.Y. Interpretation No. 665 (2009) (Constitutional Court of Taiwan), available at http://cons.judicial.gov.tw/jcc/en-us/jep03/show?expno=665, accessed 15 May 2021; J.Y. Interpretation No. 509 (2000) (Constitutional Court of Taiwan), available at http://cons.judicial.gov.tw/jcc/en-us/jep03/show?expno=509, accessed 15 May 2020; *Inheritance Tax Act Case*, 89Hun-Ma38 (21 July 1989) (Constitutional Court of Korea).

30 J.Y. Interpretation No. 623 (Taiwan) (2007) (Constitutional Court of Taiwan), available at http://cons.judicial.gov.tw/jcc/en-us/jep03/show?expno=623, accessed 15 May 2021; *Praising and Encouraging under National Security Act Case*, 89Hun-Ka113 (2 April 1990) (Constitutional Court of Korea); *Military Secret Leakage Case*, 89Hun-Ka104 (25 February 1992) (Constitutional Court of Korea).

31 Po Jen Yap, 'New Democracies and Novel Remedies' (2017) *Public Law* 30.

32 Po Jen Yap, *Courts and Democracies in Asia* (Cambridge University Press 2017).

33 Samuel Issacharoff, 'Constitutional Courts and Consolidated Power' (2014) 62 *American Journal of Comparative Law* 585, 590.

34 Ran Hirschl, 'The Judicialization of Mega-Politics and the Rise of Political Courts' (2008) 11 *Annual Review of Political Science* 93, 94.

35 J.Y. Interpretation No. 261 (1990) (Constitutional Court of Taiwan), available at http://cons.judicial.gov.tw/jcc/en-us/jep03/show?expno=261, accessed 15 May 2021.

36 J.Y. Interpretation No. 435 (1997) (Constitutional Court of Taiwan), available at http://cons.judicial.gov.tw/jcc/en-us/jep03/show?expno=435#open_dropdown, accessed 15 May 2021.

37 J.Y. Interpretation No. 290 (1992) (Constitutional Court of Taiwan), available at http://cons.judicial.gov.tw/jcc/en-us/jep03/show?expno=290, accessed 15 May 2021.

38 J.Y. Interpretation No. 585 (2004) (Constitutional Court of Taiwan), available at http://cons.judicial.gov.tw/jcc/en-us/jep03/show?expno=585, accessed 15 May 2021.

disadvantaged small political parties,[39] expanded the electoral franchise,[40] reconfigured the voting process by which lawmakers are elected,[41] ameliorated systemic gerrymandering[42] and even removed a sitting President for corruption.[43] The KCC's removal of President Park Geun-Hye has been hailed as a 'model of procedural integrity'.[44] But one should note that while the KCC is vested with the power of constitutional review and is authorized to adjudicate over presidential impeachment, it has no jurisdiction to enforce penal legislation against specific individuals.[45] That is the purview of the ordinary courts.[46] But in this landmark decision, the KCC decided on its own that the President had violated a series of criminal laws[47] – without waiting for the ordinary courts to make this determination – and consequently removed her from office on the basis that the severity of these transgressions outweighed the national loss of a President. Nevertheless, this procedural manoeuvre saved the country from a protracted trial of the lame-duck President in the lower courts, and facilitated the swift election of a new President two months later. On the other hand, the Hong Kong judiciary is fully aware that its institutional autonomy on most human rights controversies in Hong Kong is contingent on its genuflecting to Beijing on the communist regime's core concerns in the city. As the Standing Committee of the National People's Congress is authorized to overrule every constitutional decision of the HKCFA, the courts appreciate that a collision course with China is a path fraught with peril. Accordingly, the Hong Kong courts regularly avoid the 'live wire of electoral politics'[48] and self-abnegate. The HKCFA has refused to grant leave to hear whether the Chief Executive of Hong Kong had violated electoral laws,[49] endorsed the government's tightening of rules for candidacy in by-elections[50] and even rejected hearing the appeal of pro-democracy

39 *One-Person One-Vote Case*, 2000Hun-Ma91, etc. (consolidated) (19 July 2001) (Constitutional Court of Korea); *Deposit Money in Presidential Elections Case*, 2007Hun-Ma1024 (27 November 2008) (Constitutional Court of Korea).

40 *The Right to Vote of Nationals Residing Abroad Case*, 2004Hun-Ma644 et al. (consolidated) (28 June 2007) (Constitutional Court of Korea) (Official English Translation).

41 *One-Person One-Vote Case* (n. 39).

42 *Case on Standard for Population Disparity allowed in Division of Electoral District*, 2012Hun-Ma190 et al. (consolidated) (30 October 2014) (Constitutional Court of Korea).

43 *Impeachment of the President (Park Geun-hye)*, 2016Hun-Na1 (10 March 2017) (Constitutional Court of Korea).

44 Tom Ginsburg, Aziz Huq and David Landau, 'The Uses and Abuses of Presidential Impeachment' (2021) 88 *University of Chicago Law Review* (forthcoming).

45 Article 2 of the Constitutional Court Act.

46 Jongcheol Kim, 'Courts in the Republic of Korea' in Jiunn-rong Yeh and Wen-Chen Chang (eds), *Asian Courts in Context* (Cambridge University Press 2015) 112, 113.

47 Such laws include Article 59 of the State Public Officials Act, Article 2-2 (3) of the Public Service Ethics Act, and Article 2(4a) and Article 7 of the Act on the Prevention of Corruption and the Establishment and Management of the Anti-Corruption and Civil Rights Commission.

48 Issacharoff (n. 33) 610.

49 *Re Ho Chun Yan Albert* [2012] 15 HKCFAR 686 (Hong Kong Court of Final Appeal).

50 *Kwok Cheuk Kin v. Secretary for Constitutional and Mainland Affairs (2017)* [2017] 20 HKCFAR 353 (Hong Kong Court of Final Appeal).

lawmakers disqualified from office.[51] On democratic change, or lack thereof, the HKCFA and Beijing are in lockstep.

With the rise of China, and the fragmentation of the international legal order, a new geo-political tectonic shift may be underway as globalization unfolds into an uncertain future.[52] It is beyond the scope of this book for us to navel-gaze and predict what this portends for Asia. Instead, we have focused our endeavour on exploring how three East Asian courts have to date been exceptional in profoundly altering their constitutional landscapes. These local jurists have blurred geographical boundaries, reconstructed constitutional identities and expanded our legal vistas,[53] even as they strategically manage the ineluctable tensions between institutional independence and inter-governmental interdependence. The changes the judges have effected are reified, and are not chimerical phantasms of hope. But naturally we are not making the implausible claim that the convergence will be permanent. This constitutional convergence is contingent on the political system remaining fragmented, courts staying independent, and local judges intentionally aligning their constitutional practices with Western law. So long as all three variables hold constant, this convergence will endure. After all, the resulting constitutional convergence in East Asia is simply the consequence of choices judges make in the political system they have, and not the culmination of a confluence of historical coincidences.

[51] *Yau Wai Ching* v. *Chief Executive of the HKSAR* [2017] 20 HKCFAR 390 (Hong Kong Court of Final Appeal).

[52] Stephen D. King, *Grave New World: The End of Globalization, The Return of History* (Yale University Press 2017); Harold James, *The Creation and Destruction of Value: The Globalization Cycle* (Harvard University Press 2009) 10–35.

[53] Manfred B. Steger, 'Political Ideologies in the Age of Globalization' in Michael Freeden, Lyman Tower Sargent and Marc Stears (eds), *The Oxford Handbook of Political Ideologies* (Oxford University Press 2013) 214, 228.

# Bibliography

## BOOKS AND ARTICLES


Abe, Masaki, 'The Internal Control of a Bureaucratic Judiciary: The Case of Japan' (1995) 23 *International Journal of the Sociology of Law* 303.

Abeyratne, Rehan, 'More Structure, More Deference?: Proportionality in Hong Kong' in Po Jen Yap (ed.), *Proportionality in Asia* (Cambridge, Cambridge University Press 2020) 25.

Afonso da Silva, Virgílio, 'Comparing the Incommensurable: Constitutional Principles, Balancing and Rational Decision' (2011) 31 *Oxford Journal of Legal Studies* 273.

Alarie, Benjamin and Andrew J. Green, *Commitment and Cooperation in High Courts: A Cross Country Examination of Institutional Constraints on Judges* (Oxford, Oxford University Press 2017).

Albert, Richard, *Constitutional Amendments: Making, Breaking, and Changing Constitutions* (Oxford, Oxford University Press 2019).

Albert, Richard, Xenophon Contiades and Alkmene Fotiadou (eds), *The Law and Legitimacy of Imposed Constitutions* (New York, Routledge 2018).

Aleinikoff, T. Alexander, 'Constitutional Law in the Age of Balancing' (1987) 96 *Yale Law Journal* 943.

Alexy, Robert, *A Theory of Constitutional Rights* (Oxford, Oxford University Press 2002).

Aydin, Aylin, 'Judicial Independence across Democratic Regimes: Understanding the Varying Impact of Political Competition' (2013) 47 *Law and Society Review* 105.

Barak, Aharon, *Proportionality: Constitutional Rights and their Limitations* (New York, Cambridge University Press 2012).

Barak, Aharon, 'Proportionality (2)' in Michel Rosenfeld and András Sajo (eds), *The Oxford Handbook of Comparative Constitutional Law* (Oxford, Oxford University Press 2012) 738.

Baum, Lawrence, *Judges and Their Audiences: A Perspective on Judicial Behaviour* (Princeton, Princeton University Press 2008).

Beatty, David, *The Ultimate Rule of Law* (Oxford, Oxford University Press 2005).

Bennion, Francis and Oliver Jones (eds), *Bennion on Statutory Interpretation* (London, Sweet and Maxwell, 6th ed., 2013).

Black, E. Ann and Gary F. Bell (eds), *Law and Legal Institutions of Asia* (New York, Cambridge University Press 2011).

Bomhoff, Jacco, *Balancing Constitutional Rights: The Origins and Meanings of Postwar Legal Discourse* (New York, Cambridge University Press 2013).

Brinks, Daniel M. and Abby Blass, 'Rethinking Judicial Empowerment: The New Foundations of Constitutional Justice' (2017) 15 *International Journal of Constitutional Law* 296.

Bröhmer, Jürgen, Gisela Elsner, Clauspeter Hill and Marc Spitzkatz (eds), *70 Years German Basic Law: The German Constitution and Its Court* (Berlin, Konrad-Adenauer-Stiftung e. V., 2019) 852.

Cabestan, Jean-Pierre, 'A New Constitutional and the Prospect of Constitutional Change in Taiwan' in Steven M. Goldstein and Julian Chang (eds), *Presidential Politics in Taiwan* (Norwalk, EastBridge 2008) 41.

Cahill-O'Callaghan, Rachel, *Values in the Supreme Court: Decisions, Division and Diversity* (Oxford, Hart 2020).

Chan, Cora, 'Thirty Years from Tiananmen: China, Hong Kong, and the Ongoing Experiment to Preserve Liberal Values in an Authoritarian State' (2019) *International Journal of Constitutional Law* 439.

Chan, Elaine and Rowena Kwok, 'Democratization in Turmoil? Elections in Hong Kong' (1999) 8(20) *Journal of Contemporary China* 47.

Chang, Wen-Chen, 'Strategic Judicial Responses in Politically Charged Cases: East Asian Experiences' (2010) 8(4) *International Journal of Constitutional Law* 885.

Chang, Wen-Chen, 'Institutional Independence of the Judiciary: Taiwan's Incomplete Reform' in H. P. Lee and M. Pittard (eds), *Asia-Pacific Judiciaries: Independence, Impartiality and Integrity* (New York, Cambridge University Press 2018) 330.

Chang, Wen-Chen, 'Asian Exceptionalism?' (2019) 17 *International Journal of Constitutional Law* 31.

Chang, Wen-Chen and Jiunn-Rong Yeh, 'Internationalization of Constitutional Law' in Michel Rosenfeld and András Sajó (eds), *The Oxford Handbook of Comparative Constitutional Law* (Oxford, Oxford University Press 2012) 1165.

Chang, Wen-Chen and Jiunn-Rong Yeh, 'Judges as Discursive Agent: The Use of Foreign Precedents by the Constitutional Court of Taiwan' in Tania Groppi and Marie-Claire Ponthoreau (eds), *The Use of Foreign Precedents by Constitutional Judges* (Oxford, Hart 2013) 373.

Chang, Yun-Chien and Xin Dai, 'The Limited Usefulness of the Proportionality Principle' *International Journal of Constitutional Law* (forthcoming).

Chang, Wen-Chen and Yi-Li Lee, 'Judicial Strategies to Resolving Presidential Election Disputes' in Po Jen Yap (ed.), *Judicial Review of Elections in Asia* (Oxford, Routledge 2016) 147.

Chen, Albert H. Y., 'Another Case of Conflict between the CFA and the NPC Standing Committee? (2001) 31 *Hong Kong Law Journal* 179.

Chen, Albert H. Y. (ed.), *Constitutionalism in Asia in the Early Twenty-First Century* (Cambridge, Cambridge University Press 2014).

Chen, Albert H. Y. and Andrew Harding (eds), *Constitutional Courts in Asia: A Comparative Perspective* (New York, Cambridge University Press 2018).

Chen, Albert H. Y. and P. Y. Lo, 'Hong Kong's Judiciary under One Country, Two Systems' in H. P. Lee and Marilyn Pittard (eds), *Asia Pacific Judiciaries: Independence, Impartiality and Integrity* (New York, Cambridge University Press 2018) 131.

Choi, Chongko, 'On the Reception of Western Law in Korea' (1981) 9 *Korean Journal of Comparative Law* 141.

Chon, Jong Ik, 'Effect of Constitutional Review on the Legislature and the Executive Branch for Last 25 Years in Korea' (2015) *Journal of Korean Law* 131.

Choudhry, Sujit, 'Globalization in Search of Justification: Toward a Theory of Comparative Constitutional Interpretation' (1999) 74 *Indiana Law Journal* 819.

Choudhry, Sujit, 'Migration as a New Metaphor in Comparative Constitutional Law' in Sujit Choudhry (ed.), *The Migration of Constitutional Ideas* (Cambridge, Cambridge University Press 2009) 20.

Choudhry, Sujit and Kent Roach, 'Putting the Past Behind Us? Prospective Judicial and Legislative Constitutional Remedies' (2003) 21 *Supreme Court Law Review* (2d) 205.

Chung, Francis Ho-Chai and Jiang Zixin, 'An Alternative to Annulment – Remedial Interpretation in Hong Kong' in Po Jen Yap (ed.), *Constitutional Remedies in Asia* (New York, Routledge 2019) 98.

Coan, Andrew B., 'Judicial Capacity and the Substance of Constitutional Law' (2012) 122 *Yale Law Journal* 422.

Cohen-Eliya, Moshe and Iddo Porat, *Proportionality and Constitutional Culture* (New York, Cambridge University Press 2013).

Copper, John F., 'The Devolution of Taiwan's Democracy during the Chen Shui-bian Era' (2009) 18(60) *Journal of Contemporary China* 463.

Croissant, Aurel, 'Electoral Politics in South Korea' in Aurel Croissant (ed.), *Electoral Politics in Southeast and East Asia* (Singapore, Friedrich-Ebert-Stiftung 2002) 233.

Cross, Frank B., *Decision Making in the U.S. Courts of Appeals* (Stanford, Stanford University Press 2007).

Cullen, Richard, *Hong Kong Constitutionalism: The British Legacy and the Chinese Future* (Oxford, Routledge 2020).

Dahl, Robert, 'Decision-Making in a Democracy: The Supreme Court as a National Policy-Maker' (1957) 6 *Journal of Public Law* 279.

Daly, Tom Gerald, *The Alchemists: Questioning our Faith in Courts as Democracy-Builders* (Cambridge, Cambridge University Press 2017).

Davis, D. M., 'Constitutional Borrowing: The Influence of Legal Culture and Local History in the Recognition of Comparative Influence' (2003) 1 *International Journal of Constitutional Law* 181.

Dixon, Rosalind, 'Proportionality & Comparative Constitutional Law versus Studies' (2018) 12 *Law & Ethics of Human Rights* 203.

Dixon, Rosalind and Samuel Issacharoff, 'Living to Fight Another Day: Judicial Deferral in Defense of Democracy' (2016) *Wisconsin Law Review* 683.

Dixon, Rosalind and Eric A. Posner, 'The Limits of Constitutional Convergence' (2011) 11 *Chicago Journal of International Law* 399.

Dothan, Shai, *Reputation and Judicial Tactics: A Theory of National and International Courts* (New York, Cambridge University Press 2015).

Dressel, Björn (ed.), *Judicialization of Politics in Asia* (New York, Routledge 2012).

Drezner, Daniel W., 'Globalization and Policy Convergence' (2001) 3 *International Studies Review* 53.

Duverger, Maurice, *Political Parties*, vol. 2 (London, Methuen 1954).

Elliott, Mark, Jason N. E. Varubas and Shona Wilson Stark (eds), *The Unity of Public Law?* (Oxford, Hart 2018).

Epstein, Lee and Jack Knight, *The Choices Justices Make* (Washington, D.C., CQ Press 1998).

Fallon, Richard H., '*Judicially Manageable Standards and Constitutional Meaning*' 119 (2006) *Harvard Law Review* 1275.

Fell, Dafydd, 'Social Movements in Taiwan after 2008' in Dafydd Fell (ed.), *Taiwan's Social Movements under Ma Ying-jeou* (Oxford, Routledge 2017) 1.

Fell, Dafydd, *Government and Politics in Taiwan* (New York, Routledge 2018).
Ferejohn, John, 'Judicializing Politics, Politicizing Law' (2002) 65 *Law & Contemporary Problems* 41.
Ferejohn, John, Frances Rosenbluth and Charles Shipan 'Comparative Judicial Politics' in Carles Boix and Susan C. Stokes (eds), *The Oxford Handbook of Comparative Politics* (Oxford, Oxford University Press 2009) 727.
Fish, Eric S., 'Constitutional Avoidance as Interpretation and as Remedy' (2015–2016) 114 *Michigan Law Review* 1275
Fish, Eric S., 'Choosing Constitutional Remedies' (2016) 63 *UCLA Law Review* 322.
Fong, Brian, 'Executive-Legislative Disconnection in Post-colonial Hong Kong' (2014) 1 *China Perspectives* 5.
Fong, Brian C. H., 'Executive-Legislative Disconnection in the HKSAR: Uneasy Partnership between Chief Executives and Pro-Government Parties, 1997–2016' in Brian C. H. Fong and Tai-lok Lui (eds), *Hong Kong 20 Years after the Handover: Emerging Social and Institutional Fractures After* 1997 (Cham, Palgrave Macmillan 2018) 45.
Fujita, Tokiyasu, *Saikousai kaisouroku (Memoirs of the Supreme Court)* (Tokyo, Yuhikaku Publishing 2012).
Gardbaum, Stephen, 'Political Parties, Voting Systems, and the Separation of Powers' (2017) 65 *American Journal of Comparative Law* 229.
Gardbaum, Stephen, 'What Makes for More or Less Powerful Constitutional Courts?' (2018) 29 *Duke Journal of Comparative & International Law* 1.
Garoupa, Nuno and Tom Ginsburg, *Judicial Reputation: A Comparative Theory* (Chicago, The University of Chicago Press, 2015).
Garoupa, Nuno, Veronica Grembi and Shirley Ching-ping Lin, 'Explaining Constitutional Review in New Democracies: The Case of Taiwan' (2011) 20 *Pacific Rim Law and Policy Journal* 1.
Gewirtz, Paul, 'Remedies and Resistance' (1983) 92 *Yale Law Journal* 585.
Ghai, Yash, 'Sentinels of Liberty or Sheep in Woolf's Clothing? Judicial Politics and the Hong Kong Bill of Rights' (1997) 60 *Modern Law Review* 459.
Gilbert, Michael D. and Mauricio A. Guim, 'The Active Virtues' (2021) 98 *Washington University Law Review* 857.
Ginsburg, Tom, 'Economic Analysis and the Design of Constitutional Courts' (2002) 3 *Theoretical Inquiries in Law* 49.
Ginsburg, Tom, *Judicial Review in New Democracies: Constitutional Courts in Asian Cases* (New York, Cambridge University Press 2003).
Ginsburg, Tom, 'Constitutional Courts in East Asia: Understanding Variation' (2008) 3 *Journal of Comparative Law* 80.
Ginsburg, Tom, 'The Constitutional Court and Judicialization of Korean Politics' in Andrew Harding and Penelope (Pip) Nicholson (eds), *New Courts in Asia* (Oxford, Routledge 2010) 145.
Ginsburg, Tom, 'The Global Spread of Constitutional Review' in Keith E. Whittington, R. Daniel Kelemen and Gregory A. Caldeira (eds), *The Oxford Handbook of Law and Politics* (Oxford, Oxford University Press 2010) 81.
Ginsburg, Tom, 'The Politics of Courts in Democratization' in Diana Kapiszewski, Gordon Silverstein and Robert A. Kagan (eds), *Consequential Courts: Judicial Roles in Global Perspective* (New York, Cambridge University Press 2013) 45.
Ginsburg, Tom and Tamir Moustafa (eds), *Rule by Law: The Politics of Courts in Authoritarian Regimes* (New York, Cambridge University Press 2008).

Ginsburg, Tom and Alberto Simpser (eds), *Constitutions in Authoritarian Regimes* (New York, Cambridge University Press 2014).

Ginsburg, Tom, Aziz Huq and David Landau, 'The Uses and Abuses of Presidential Impeachment' (2021) 88 *University of Chicago Law Review*.

Goderis, Benedict and Mila Versteeg, 'Transnational Constitutionalism: A Conceptual Framework' in Denis J. Galligan and Mila Versteeg (eds), *Social and Political Functions of Constitutions* (New York, Cambridge University Press 2013) 103.

Goodman, Ryan and Derek Jinks, 'How to Influence States: Socialization and International Human Rights Law' (2004) 54 *Duke Law Journal* 621.

Greene, Jamal, 'Foreword: Rights as Trumps?' (2018) 132 *Harvard Law Review* 28.

Grimm, Dieter, 'Proportionality in Canadian and German Constitutional Jurisprudence' (2007) 57 *University of Toronto Law Journal* 383.

Hahm, Chaihark, 'Rule of Law in South Korea: Rhetoric and Implementation' in Randall Peerenboom (ed.), *Asian Discourses of Rule of Law* (Oxford, Routledge 2004) 379.

Hahm, Chaihark, 'Human Rights in Korea' in Randall Peerenboom, Carole J. Peterson and Albert H. Y. Chen (eds), *Human Rights in Asia: A Comparative Legal Study of Twelve Asian Jurisdictions, France and the USA* (Oxford, Routledge 2006) 265.

Hahm, Chaihark, 'Constitutional Court of Korea: Guardian of the Constitution or Mouthpiece of the Government' in Albert H. Y. Chen and Andrew Harding (eds), *Constitutional Courts in Asia: A Comparative Perspective* (Cambridge, Cambridge University Press 2018) 141.

Haley, John O., 'The Japanese Judiciary: Maintaining Integrity, Autonomy, and the Public Trust' in Daniel H. Foote (ed.), *Law in Japan: A Turning Point* (Seattle, University of Washington Press 2008) 99.

Haley, John O., 'Constitutional Adjudication in Japan: Context, Structure, and Values' (2011) 88 *Washington Law Review* 1467.

Hasebe, Yasuo, 'The Supreme Court of Japan A Judicial Court, Not Necessarily a Constitutional Court' in Albert H. Y. Chen and Andrew Harding (eds), *Constitutional Courts in Asia: A Comparative Perspective* (New York, Cambridge University Press 2018) 289.

Hayo, Bernd and Stefan Voigt, 'Explaining De Facto Judicial Independence' (2007) 27 *International Review of Law and Economics* 269.

Heo, Uk, 'What Delays Democratic Consolidation in South Korea' (2013) 44 *Korea Observer* 569.

Heo, Uk and Seongyi Yun, 'South Korea in 2017: Presidential Impeachment and Security Volatility' (2018) 58 *Asian Survey* 65.

Hirschl, Ran, *Towards Juristocracy* (Cambridge, Harvard University Press 2004).

Hirschl, Ran, 'The Judicialization of Mega-Politics and the Rise of Political Courts' (2008) 11 *Annual Review of Political Science* 93.

Hirschl, Ran, 'The Judicialization of Politics' in Keith Whittington, R. Daniel Keleman and Gregory Caldeira (eds), *The Oxford Handbook of Law and Politics* (Oxford, Oxford University Press 2010) 119.

Hirschl, Ran, *Comparative Law Matters: The Renaissance of Comparative Constitutional Law* (Oxford, Oxford University Press 2014).

Hong, Joon Seok, 'Signaling the Turn: The Supermajority Requirement and Judicial Power on the Constitutional Court of Korea' (2019) 67 *American Journal of Comparative Law* 177.

Hsiao, Wen-Sheng 蕭文生, '百分之五政黨門檻之合憲性－司法院釋字第721號解釋評析' 'The Constitutionality of the Five-Percent Threshold for Political Parties' (2014) 252 *台灣法學雜誌 Taiwan Law Journal* 33.

Huang, Chi, 'Electoral System Change and Its Effects on the Party System in Taiwan' in Christopher H. Achen and T. Y. Wang (eds), *The Taiwan Voter* (Ann Arbor, University of Michigan Press 2017) 223.

Hwang, Jau-Yuan 黃昭元, '大法官解釋審查標準之發展 (1996~2011)：比例原則的繼受與在地化' 'Development of Standards of Review by the Constitutional Court from 1996 to 2011: Reception and Localization of the Proportionality Principle' (2013) 42 *國立臺灣大學法學論叢 National Taiwan University Law Journal* 215 (in Chinese).

Ip, Eric C., *Hybrid Constitutionalism: The Politics of Constitutional Review in the Chinese Special Administrative Regions* (New York, Cambridge University Press 2019).

Issacharoff, Samuel, 'Judging Politics: The Elusive Quest for Judicial Review of Political Fairness' (1992) 71 *Texas Law Review* 1643.

Issacharoff, Samuel, 'Constitutional Courts and Consolidated Power' (2014) 62 *American Journal of Comparative Law* 585.

Issacharoff, Samuel, 'Judicial Review in Troubled Times: Stabilizing Democracy in a Second Best World' (2019) 1 *North Carolina Law Review* 1.

Issacharoff, Samuel and Richard H. Pildes, 'Politics as Markets: Partisan Lockups of the Democratic Process' (1997–1998) 50 *Stanford Law Review* 643.

Jackson, Vicki, *Constitutional Engagement in a Transnational Era* (Oxford, Oxford University Press 2010).

Jackson, Vicki, 'Constitutional Law in an Age of Proportionality' 124 (2015) *Yale Law Journal* 3094.

Jacobsohn, Gary Jeffrey, *Constitutional Identity* (Cambridge, Harvard University Press 2010).

James, Harold, *The Creation and Destruction of Value: The Globalization Cycle* (Cambridge, Harvard University Press 2009).

Jeffries, John C. Jr, 'The Right-Remedy Gap in Constitutional Law' (1999–2000) 109 *Yale Law Journal* 87.

Jeon, Jeong-hyun, 'Political Functions and Dilemma of the Korean Constitutional Court' (2016) 47 *Korea Observer* 461.

Kalb, Johanna, 'The Judicial Role in New Democracies: A Strategic Account of Comparative Citation' (2013) 38 *Yale Journal of International Law* 423.

Kapiszewski, Diana, Gordon Silverstein and Robert A. Kagan (eds), *Consequential Courts: Judicial Roles in Global Perspective* (New York, Cambridge University Press 2013).

Katyal, Neal Kumar and Thomas P. Schmidt, 'Active Avoidance: The Modern Supreme Court and Legal Change' (2015) 128 *Harvard Law Review* 2109.

Kavanagh, Aileen, *Constitutional Review under the UK Human Rights Act* (Cambridge, Cambridge University Press 2009).

Kawagishi, Norikazu, 'Towards A More Responsive Judiciary: Courts and Judicial Power in Japan' in Jiunn-rong Yeh and Wen-Chen Chang (eds), *Asian Courts in Context* (Cambridge, Cambridge University Press 2015) 77.

Kelemen, R. Daniel, 'The Political Foundations of Judicial Independence in the European Union' (2012) 19 *Journal of European Public Policy* 43.

Kenny, David, 'Proportionality and the Inevitability of the Local: A Comparative Localist Analysis of Canada and Ireland' (2018) 66 *American Journal of Comparative Law* 537.

Keohane, Robert O., *Power and Governance in a Partially Globalized World* (New York, Routledge 2002).

Kim, Byung-Kook, 'Party Politics in South Korea's Democracy: The Crisis of Success' in Larry Diamond and Byung-Kook Kim (eds), *Consolidating Democracy in South Korea* (Boulder, Lynne Rienner Publishers 2000) 53.

Kim, Chan Jin, 'Constitutional Review in Korea' (2006) 34 *Korean Journal of International & Comparative law* 29.

Kim, Hyung-A., 'President Roh Moo-Hyun's Last Interview and the Roh Moo-Hyun Phenomenon in South Korea' (2017) 47 *Journal of Contemporary Asia* 273.

Kim, Jiyoon, 'The Party System in Korea and Identity Politics' in Larry Diamond and Gi-Wook Shin (eds), *New Challenges for Maturing Democracies in Korea and Taiwan* (Stanford, Stanford University Press 2014) 71.

Kim, Jongcheol, 'Upgrading Constitutionalism; The Ups and Downs of Constitutional Developments in South Korea since 2000' in Albert Chen (ed.), *Constitutionalism in Asia in the Early Twenty-First Century* (Cambridge, Cambridge University Press 2014) 76.

Kim, Jongcheol, 'Courts in the Republic of Korea' in Jiunn-rong Yeh and Wen-Chen Chang (eds), *Asian Courts in Context* (Cambridge, Cambridge University Press 2015) 112.

Kim, Jongcheol, 'Dissolution of the United Progressive Party Case in Korea: A Critical Review with Reference to the European Court of Human Rights Case Law' (2017) 10(1) *Journal of East Asia and International Law* 139.

Kim, Sungmoon, *Public Reason Confucianism: Democratic Perfectionism and Constitutionalism in East Asia* (New York, Cambridge University Press 2016).

Kim, Wook, 'Political Polarization: Regionalism, Ideology, and Generational Changes' in Chung-in Moon and M. Jae Moon (eds), *Routledge Handbook of Korean Politics and Public Administration* (New York, Routledge 2020) 112.

Kim, Youngmi, *The Politics of Coalition in Korea* (New York, Routledge 2011).

King, Stephen D., *Grave New World: The End of Globalization, The Return of History* (New Haven, Yale University Press 2017).

Kirk, Jeremy, 'Constitutional Guarantees, Characterization and the Concept of Proportionality' (1997) 21 *Melbourne University Law Review* 1.

Krishnakumar, Anita S., 'Passive Avoidance' (2019) 71 *Stanford Law Review* 513.

Kuo, Ming-Sung, 'Moving towards a Nominal Constitutional Court: Critical Reflections on the Shift from Judicial Activism to Constitutional Irrelevance in Taiwan's Constitutional Politics' (2016) 25 *Pacific Rim Law & Policy Journal* 597.

Kuo, Ming-Sung, 'Between Choice and Tradition: Rethinking Remedial Grace Periods and Unconstitutionality Management in A Comparative Light' (2019) 36 *Pacific Basin Law Journal* 157.

Kuo, Ming-Sung and Hui-Wen Chen, 'The Brown Moment in Taiwan: Making Sense of the Law and Politics of the Taiwanese Same-Sex Marriage Case in a Comparative Light' (2017) 31 *Columbia Journal of Asian Law* 72.

Landau, David, 'Aggressive Weak-Form Remedies' (2014) 5 *Constitutional Court Review* 244.

Lang, Andrej, 'Proportionality Analysis by the German Federal Constitutional Court' in Mordechai Kremnitzer, Talya Steiner and Andrej Lang (eds), *Proportionality in Action: Comparative and Empirical Perspectives on the Judicial Practice* (New York, Cambridge University Press 2020) 22.

Lau, Siu-kai, 'Hong Kong's Partial Democracy under Stress' in Yue-man Yeung (ed.), *New Challenges for Development and Modernisation* (Hong Kong, The Chinese University of Hong Kong Press 2002) 181.

Law, David S., 'Generic Constitutional Law' (2005) 89 *Minnesota Law Review* 652.

Law, David S., 'Globalization and the Future of Constitutional Rights' (2008) 102 *Northwestern University Law Review* 1277.

Law, David S., 'The Anatomy of a Conservative Court: Judicial Review in Japan' (2009) 87 *Texas Law Review* 1545.

Law, David S., 'Why has Judicial Review Failed in Japan?' (2011) 88 *Washington University Law Review* 1425.

Law, David S., 'Judicial Comparativism and Judicial Diplomacy' (2015) 163 *University of Pennsylvania Law Review* 927.

Law, David S. and Mila Versteeg, 'The Evolution and Ideology of Global Constitutionalism' (2011) 99 *California Law Review* 1163.

Leckey, Robert, 'The Harms of Remedial Discretion' (2016) 14 *International Journal of Constitutional Law* 584.

Lee, Dong-Heub, 'Development and Current Situation of the Constitutional Adjudication in Korea' (2012) 53(2) *Seoul Law Journal* 1.

Lee, Kang-Kook, 'The Past and Future of Constitutional Adjudication in Korea' in Laurent Mayali and John Yoo (eds), *Current Issues in Korean Law* (Berkeley, The Robbins Collection 2014) 1.

Lee, Seokmin and Fabian Duessel, 'Researching Korean Constitutional Law and the Constitutional Court of Korea' (2016) 16 *Journal of Korean Law* 265.

Lee, Yeonho and Yoo-Jin Lim, 'The Rise of the Labour Party in South Korea: Causes and Limits' (2006) 19(3) *The Pacific Review* 305.

Lee, Yoonk-yung, 'Political Parties' in Chung-in Moon and M. Jae Moon (eds), *Routledge Handbook of Korean Politics and Public Administration* (New York, Routledge 2020) 77.

Lee, Youngjae, 'Law, Politics, and Impeachment: The Impeachment of Roh Moo-hyun from a Comparative Constitutional Perspective' (2005) 53 *American Journal of Comparative Law* 403.

Levi, Margaret, 'A Model, A Method, and A Map' in Mark Irving Lichbach and Alan S. Zuckerman (eds), *Comparative Politics* (New York, Cambridge University Press 2002) 19.

Levinson, Daryl J., 'Rights Essentialism and Remedial Equilibration' (1999) 99 *Columbia Law Review* 857.

Lim, C. L., 'The Hong Kong Extradition Bill' (2020) *Law Quarterly Review* 19.

Lim, Jibong, 'Judicial Intervention in Policy-Making by the Constitutional Court in Korea' in Laurent Mayali and John Yoo (eds), *Current Issues in Korean Law* (Berkeley, The Robbins Collection 2014) 15.

Lim, Yoojin and Jungho Roh, 'Political Institutions in Korea' in Chung-in Moon and M. Jae Moon (eds), *Routledge Handbook of Korean Politics and Public Administration* (Oxford, Routledge 2020) 21.

Lin, Chien-Chih, 'Unpatriotic Heretics or Conscientious Objectors: Difficulties which Jehovah Witnesses Face in Taiwan and South Korea' (2010) 5 *National Taiwan University Law Review* 201.

Lin, Chien-Chih, 'Survival of the Fittest (?): The Endurance of the ROC Constitution and the Constitution of Japan' (2014) 62 *American Journal of Comparative Law* 775.

Lin, Chien-Chih, 'Constitutions and Courts in Chinese Authoritarian Regimes: China and Pre-Democratic Taiwan in Comparison' (2016) 14 *International Journal of Constitutional Law* 351.

Lin, Chien-Chih, 林建志, '迎接司法國的到來' 'Towards Juristocracy?' (2019) 48國立臺灣大學法學論叢 *National Taiwan University Law Journal* 873.

Lin, Chun-Yuan林春元, '司法審查、選舉制度與民主代表性－從司法院釋字第721號解釋談起' 'Judicial Review, Electoral Systems, and Democratic Representation: The Case of J.Y. Interpretation No. 721' (2017) 20 *中研院法學期刊 Academia Sinica Law Journal* 155.

Lin, Jih-Wen, 'Electoral System, Voter Preferences, and the Fragmentation of Party System: The East Asian Cases' (2002) 9 *Journal of Electoral Studies* 137.

Lin, Jih-wen, 'Electoral Systems Today: The Politics of Reform in Japan and Taiwan' (2006) 17 *Journal of Democracy* 118.

Lo, Chang-fa, 'Taiwan: External Influences mixed with Traditional Elements to Form Its Unique Legal System' in E. Ann Black and Gary F. Bell (eds), *Law and Legal Institutions of Asia* (New York, Cambridge University Press 2011) 91.

Lustig, Doreen and J. H. H. Weiler, 'Judicial Review in the Contemporary World – Retrospective and Prospective' (2018) 16 *International Journal of Constitutional Law* 315.

Ma, Ngok, *Political Development in Hong Kong: The State, Political Society and Civil Society* (Hong Kong, Hong Kong University Press 2007).

Ma, Ngok, 'From Executive Dominance to Fragmented Authority: An Institutional and Political Analysis' in Brian C. H. Fong and Tai-lok Lui (eds), *Hong Kong 20 Years after the Handover: Emerging Social and Institutional Fractures After 1997* (Cham, Palgrave Macmillan 2018) 21.

Macdonald, Roderick A. and Hoi Kong, 'Judicial Independence as a Constitutional Virtue' in Michel Rosenfeld and András Sajó (eds), *The Oxford Handbook of Comparative Constitutional Law* (Oxford, Oxford University Press 2012) 831.

Malkin, Anton and Yu-wai Vic Li, 'You Can Check in Anytime You like, but You Can Never Leave' in Ka Zeng (ed.), *Handbook on the International Political Economy of China* (Cheltenham, Edward Elgar 2019) 170.

Matsui, Shigenori, *The Constitution of Japan: A Contextual Analysis* (Oxford, Hart 2011).

Matsui, Shigenori, 'Why is the Japanese Supreme Court so Conservative?' (2011) 88 *Washington University Law Review* 1375.

Melton, James and Tom Ginsburg, 'Does De Jure Judicial Independence Really Matter? A Re-evaluation of Explanations for Judicial Independence' (2014) 2 *Journal of Law and Courts* 187.

Miller, Jonathan M., 'A Typology of Legal Transplants' (2003) 51 *American Journal of Comparative Law* 839.

Moustafa, Tamir and Tom Ginsburg, 'Introduction: The Functions of Courts in Authoritarian Politics' in Tom Ginsburg and Tamir Moustafa (eds), *Rule by Law* (New York, Cambridge University Press 2008) 1.

Nakakita, Kōji, *The Liberal Democratic Party of Japan: The Realities of Power* (Oxford, Routledge 2020).

O'Brien, David M. and Yasuo Ohkoshi, 'Stifling Judicial Independence from within: The Japanese Judiciary' in Peter H. Russell and David M. O'Brien (eds), *Judicial Independence in the Age of Democracy: Critical Perspectives from around the World* (Charlottesville, University of Virginia Press 2001) 37.

Park, Chan-Wook, 'The National Assembly in Democratized Korea' in Zheng Yongnian, Lye Liang Fook and Wilhelm Hofmeiste (eds), *Parliaments in Asia* (Oxford, Routledge 2014) 185.

Petersen, Niels, 'The German Constitutional Court and Legislative Capture' (2014) 12 *International Journal of Constitutional Law* 650.

Petersen, Niels, *Proportionality and Judicial Activism: Fundamental Rights Adjudication in Canada, Germany and South Africa* (New York, Cambridge University Press 2017).

Petrie, Nicholas, 'Indications of Inconsistency' (2019) 78(3) *Cambridge Law Journal* 612.

Polsby, Daniel D. and Robert D. Popper, 'The Third Criterion: Compactness as a Procedural Safeguard against Partisan Gerrymandering' (1991) 9(2) *Yale Law and Policy Review* 301.

Ramseyer, J. Mark and Eric B. Rasmusen, *Measuring Judicial Independence: The Political Economy of Judging in Japan* (Chicago, Chicago University Press 2003).

Reed, Steven R., 'The Liberal Democratic Party: An Explanation of Its Successes and Failures' in Robert Pekkanen (ed.), *Critical Readings on the Liberal Democratic Party in Japan* vol. 4 (Leiden, Brill 2018) 1339.

Rigger, Shelley, *Politics in Taiwan: Voting for Democracy* (London, Routledge 1999).

Roach, Kent, 'Remedial Consensus and Dialogue under the Charter: General Declarations and Delayed Declarations of Invalidity' (2002) 35 *UBC Law Review* 211.

Roach, Kent, *Supreme Court on Trial: Judicial Activism or Democratic Dialogue* (Toronto, Irwin Law 2016).

Roach, Kent, 'Constitutionalized Interpretation, Reading Down/In and the Wisdom of Schachter' (2016) 36 *National Journal of Constitutional Law* 211.

Roach, Kent, 'Polycentricity and Queue Jumping in Public Law Remedies: A Two Track Response' (2016) 66(1) *University of Toronto Law Journal* 3.

Roach, Kent, 'Dialogic Remedies' (2019) 17 *International Journal of Constitutional Law* 860.

Roux, Theunis, *The Politico-Legal Dynamics of Judicial Review: A Comparative Analysis* (New York, Cambridge University Press 2018).

Ryder, Bruce, 'Suspending the Charter' (2003) 21 *Supreme Court Law Review* (2d) 267.

Ryu, Paul Kichyun, 'The New Korean Criminal Code of October 3, 1953. An Analysis of Ideologies Embedded in It' (1957) 48 *Journal of Criminal Law, Criminology, and Police Science* 275.

Sabel, Charles F. and William H. Simon, 'Destabilization Rights: How Public Law Litigation Succeeds' (2004) 117 *Harvard Law Review* 1016.

Sales, Philip, 'Partnership and Challenge: The Courts' Role in Managing the Integration of Rights and Democracy' (2016) *Public Law* 456.

Sales, Philip and Richard Ekins, 'Rights-Consistent Interpretation under the Human Rights Act 1998' (2011) 127 *Law Quarterly Review* 217.

Saunders, Cheryl, 'Judicial Engagement' in Rosalind Dixon and Tom Ginsburg (eds), *Comparative Constitutional Law in Asia* (Northampton, Edward Elgar 2012) 80.

Saunders, Cheryl, 'Transplants in Public Law' in Mark Elliott, Jason N. E. Varubas and Shona Wilson Stark (eds), *The Unity of Public Law?* (Oxford, Hart 2018) 257.

Scheiner, Ethan, *Democracy without Competition in Japan: Opposition Failure in a One Party Dominant State* (New York, Cambridge University Press 2006).

Segal, Jeffrey A. and Harold J. Spaeth, *The Supreme Court and the Attitudinal Model Revisited* (New York, Cambridge University Press 2002).

Shaffer, Gregory, Tom Ginsburg and Terence C. Halliday (eds), *Constitution-Making and Transnational Legal Order* (New York, Cambridge University Press 2019).

Shapiro, Martin, *Courts* (Chicago, University of Chicago Press 1981).

Shapiro, Martin and Alec Stone Sweet, *On Law, Politics, and Judicialization* (Oxford, Oxford University Press 2002).

Sheng, Shing-Yuan, 盛杏湲, '立法機關與行政機關在立法過程中的影響力：一致政府與分立政府的比較' 'The Influence of the Legislative Branch and the Executive Branch in the Process of Lawmaking: A Comparison of the Unified and Divided Governments' (2003) 7(2) *台灣政治學刊 Taiwan Political Science Review* 51.

Sheng, Shing-yuan and Hsiao-chuan (Mandy) Liao, 'Issues, Political Cleavages, and Party Competition in Taiwan' in Christopher H. Achen and T. Y. Wang (eds), *The Taiwan Voter* (Ann Arbor, University of Michigan Press 2017) 98.

Shin, Yoon Jin, 'Cosmopolitanising Rights Practice: The Case of South Korea' in Takao Suami, Anne Peers, Dimitri Vanoverbeke and Mattias Kumm (eds), *Global Constitutionalism from European and East Asian Perspectives* (New York, Cambridge University Press 2018) 256.

Shin, Yoon Jin, 'Proportionality in South Korea: Contextualizing the Cosmopolitan Rights Grammar' in Po Jen Yap (ed.), *Proportionality in Asia* (Cambridge, Cambridge University Press 2020) 81.

Simmons, Beth A. and Zachary Elkins, 'The Globalization of Liberalization: Policy Diffusion in the International Political Economy' (2004) 98 *American Political Science Review* 171.

Siregar, Fritz Edward, 'Pragmatism and the Use of Suspension Orders by Indonesia's Constitutional Court' in Po Jen Yap (ed.), *Constitutional Remedies in Asia* (New York, Routledge 2019) 63.

Steger, Manfred, 'Political Ideologies in the Age of Globalization' in Michael Freeden, Lyman Tower Sargent and Marc Stears (eds), *The Oxford Handbook of Political Ideologies* (Oxford, Oxford University Press 2013) 214.

Stewart, Hamish, 'A Defence of Constitutionalized Interpretation' (2016) 36 *National Journal of Constitutional Law* 195.

Stone Sweet, Alec, *Governing with Judges: Constitutional Politics in Europe* (Oxford, Oxford University Press 2000).

Stone Sweet, Alec, 'Path Dependence, Precedent, and Judicial Power' in Martin Shapiro and Alec Stone Sweet, *On Law, Politics, and Judicialization* (Oxford, Oxford University Press 2002) 112.

Stone Sweet, Alec, 'Constitutions and Judicial Power' in Daniele Caramani (ed.), *Comparative Politics* (Oxford, Oxford University Press 2008) 217.

Stone Sweet, Alec, 'Constitutions, Rights, and Judicial Power' in Daniele Caramani (ed.), *Comparative Politics* (Oxford, Oxford University Press 2017) 155.

Stone Sweet, Alec and Jud Mathews, *Proportionality Balancing and Constitutional Governance* (Oxford, Oxford University Press 2019).

Stone Sweet, Alec, 'The Necessity of Balancing: Hong Kong's Flawed Approach to Proportionality, and Why It Matters' (2020) 50 *Hong Kong Law Journal* 541.

Stone Sweet, Alec and Jud Mathews, 'Proportionality Balancing and Global Constitutionalism' (2008) 47 *Columbia Journal of Transnational Law* 72.

Su, Yen-tu, 'Regime Unchanged: The Organization and Failed Reorganization of Taiwan's Judicial Yuan' in Neil Chisholm (ed.), *Judicial Reform in Taiwan: Institutionalizing Democracy and The Diffusion of Law* (New York, Routledge 2020) 104.

Swede, Richard, 'One Territory – Three Systems? The Hong Kong Bill of Rights' (1995) 44 *International & Comparative Law Quarterly* 358.

Tate, C. Neal, 'Why the Expansion of Judicial Power' in C. Neal Tate and Torbjorn Vallinder (eds), *The Global Expansion of Judicial Power* (New York, New York University Press 1995) 27.

Tate, C. Neal and Torbjorn Vallinder (eds), *The Global Expansion of Judicial Power* (New York, New York University Press 1997).

Thayer, James B., 'The Origin and Scope of the American Doctrine of Constitutional Law' (1893) 7 *Harvard Law Review* 129.

Tsakyrakis, Stavros, 'Proportionality: An Assault on Human Rights?' (2009) 7 *International Journal of Constitutional Law* 468.

Tsai, Chia-hung, 'Who Is Taiwan Voter?' in Christopher H. Achen and T. Y. Wang (eds), *The Taiwan Voter* (Ann Arbor, University of Michigan Press 2017) 26.

Tushnet, Mark, 'The Possibilities of Comparative Constitutional Law' (1999) 108 *Yale Law Journal* 1225.

Tushnet, Mark, 'The Inevitable Globalization of Constitutional Law' (2009) 49 *Virginia Journal of International Law* 985.

Tushnet, Mark, 'Preserving Judicial Independence in Dominant Party States' (2015) 60 *New York School Law Review* 107.

Upham, Frank K., 'Political Lackeys or Faithful Public Servants? Two Views of the Japanese Judiciary' (2005) 30 *Law & Social Inquiry* 421.

Urbina, Francisco J., 'Incommensurability and Balancing' (2015) 35 *Oxford Journal of Legal Studies* 575.

Urbina, Francisco J., *A Critique of Proportionality and Balancing* (New York, Cambridge University Press 2017).

Vanberg, Georg, 'Establishing Judicial Independence in West Germany' (2000) 32 *Comparative Politics* 333.

Vanberg, Georg, 'Constitutional Courts in Comparative Perspective: A Theoretical Assessment' (2015) 18 *Annual Review of Political Science* 167.

Wang, Zhenmin, 王振民, *中央与特别行政区关系：一种法治结构的解析 The Central-SAR Relationship: A Legal Analysis*, (北京，清华大学出版社 Beijing, Tsinghua Press 2002).

Watson, Alan, 'Aspects of Reception of Law' (1996) 44 *American Journal of Comparative Law* 335.

Webber, Grégoire, *The Negotiable Constitution* (New York, Cambridge University Press 2009).

Weinrib, Lorraine E., 'The Post-War Paradigm and American Exceptionalism' in Sujit Choudhry (ed.), *The Migration of Constitutional Ideas* (Cambridge, Cambridge University Press 2006) 84.

Weng, Yueh-sheng, 翁岳生, '台灣法治的發展' 'The Development of Rule of Law in Taiwan' (2017) 6 *馬漢寶講座論文彙編 Herbert Han-Pao Ma Distinguished Lectureship* 97.

West, James M. and Dae-Kyu Yoon, 'The Constitutional Court of the Republic of Korea: Transforming the Jurisprudence of the Vortex?' (1992) 40 *American Journal of Comparative Law* 73.

Wu, Geng, *吳庚, 憲法的解釋與適用 The Interpretation and Application of the Constitution*, (臺北，三民Taipei, San Min 2004).

Yang, Kun, 'In the Name of Constitutional Law: Reflections on Recent Korean Constitutional Adjudication with Special Reference to President Park's Impeachment Case' (2019) 49 *Hong Kong Law Journal* 979.

Yang, Yu-Ling, 楊與齡, '大法官第二六一號解釋與我國憲政發展' 'J.Y. Interpretation No. 261 and the Development of Constitutional Democracy in Taiwan' (1998) 23卷3期, 《*憲政時代 Constitutional Review*》3.

Yap, Po Jen, *Constitutional Dialogue in Common Law Asia* (Oxford, Oxford University Press 2015).

Yap, Po Jen (ed.), *Judicial Review of Elections in Asia* (Oxford, Routledge 2016).

Yap, Po Jen, 'New Democracies and Novel Remedies' (2017) *Public Law* 30.

Yap, Po Jen, *Courts and Democracies in Asia* (Cambridge, Cambridge University Press 2017).

Yap, Po Jen, 'Remedial Discretion and Dilemmas in Asia' (2019) 69 *University of Toronto Law Journal* 84.

Yap, Po Jen (ed.), *Constitutional Remedies in Asia* (Oxford, Routledge 2019).

Yap, Po Jen (ed.), *Proportionality in Asia* (Cambridge, Cambridge University Press 2020).

Yap, Po Jen, 'Proportionality in Asia: Joining the Global Choir' in Po Jen Yap (ed.), *Proportionality in Asia* (Cambridge University Press 2020) 3.

Yap, Po Jen and Eric Chan, 'Legislative Oaths and Judicial Intervention In Hong Kong' (2017) 47 *Hong Kong Law Journal* 1.

Yap, Po Jen and Francis Chung 'Statutory Rights and De facto Constitutional Supremacy in Hong Kong?' (2019) 17(3) *International Journal of Constitutional Law* 836.

Yap, Po Jen and Jiang Zixin, 'Electoral Disqualification, Political Allegiance, and the Courts: A "Fruitless Debate"?' (2019) 49 *Hong Kong Law Journal* 825.

Yap, Po Jen and Jiang Zixin, 'Remedial Discretion and the Prohibition on the Face Covering Regulation', (2020) 50 *Hong Kong Law Journal* 569.

Yeh, Jiunn-rong, 'Court-Ordered Apology: The Function of Courts in the Construction of Society, Culture and the Law' in Jiunn-rong Yeh (ed.), *The Functional Transformation of Courts: Taiwan and Korea in Comparison* (Taipei, National Taiwan University Press 2015) 21.

Yeh, Jiunn-rong, 'Politicization of Constitutional Courts in Asia: Institutional Features, Contexts and Legitimacy' in Henbning Glaser (ed.), *Constitutional Jurisprudence: Function, Impact and Challenges* (Baden-Baden, Nomos Verlagsgesellschaft 2016) 215.

Yeh, Jiunn-rong and Wen-Chen Chang, 'An Evolving Court with Changing Functions: The Constitutional Court and Judicial Review in Taiwan' in Albert H. Y. Chen and Andrew Harding (eds), *Constitutional Courts in Asia* (New York, Cambridge University Press 2018) 110.

Young, Simon and Richard Cullen, *Electing Hong Kong's Chief Executive* (Hong Kong, Hong Kong University Press 2010).

Young, Simon and Anthony Law, 'Privileged to Vote: Inequalities and Anomalies of the FC System' in Christine Loh (ed.), *Functional Constituencies: A Unique Feature of the Hong Kong Legislative Council* (Hong Kong, Hong Kong University Press 2007) 59.

Young, Simon N. M., Antonio Da Roza and Yash Ghai, 'Role of the Chief Justice' in Simon N. M. Young, Antonio Da Roza and Yash Ghai (eds), *Hong Kong's Court of Final Appeal: The Development of the Law in China's Hong Kong* (New York, Cambridge University Press 2014) 225.

## GOVERNMENT/ORGANIZATIONAL PUBLICATIONS AND SPEECHES

Association of Asian Constitutional Courts and Equivalent Institutions Secretariat for Research and Development, *Jurisdictions and Organization of AACC Members* (Seoul, AACC SRD & Constitutional Court of Korea 2018).

Association of Asian Constitutional Courts and Equivalent Institutions Secretariat for Research and Development, *Constitutional Review at AACC Members* (Seoul, AACC SRD & Constitutional Court of Korea 2019).

Census and Statistics Department, *Hong Kong Annual Digest of Statistics 2017* (October 2017).

Chief Justice Ma, Geoffrey, 'Hong Kong and the Rule of Law: Is it Tangible?' (International Bar Association Annual Conference, Seoul, 24 September 2019).

Constitutional Research Institute, Constitutional Research Institute Brochure (Seoul, The Constitutional Court of Korea 2019).

Hong Kong Judiciary, Hong Kong Judiciary Annual Report 2018.

Judicial Yuan, 司法院, Oral History of Taiwan Senior Jurists 台灣法界耆宿口述歷史, volume 6 (Taiwan, Judicial Yuan 2011).

Constitutional Court of Korea, *The First Ten Years of the Constitutional Court of Korea* (Seoul, The Constitutional Court of Korea 2001).

Constitutional Court of Korea, *Twenty Years of the Constitutional Court of Korea* (Seoul, The Constitutional Court of Korea 2008).

Constitutional Court of Korea, *Thirty Years of the Constitutional Court of Korea* (Seoul, The Constitutional Court of Korea 2018).

Legislative Yuan, *Legislative Yuan Gazette* (1994) volume 83(39) (Taipei, Legislative Yuan 1994).

Permanent Judge, Fok, Joseph, 'Judges from other Common law jurisdictions in the Hong Kong Court of Final Appeal' (International Bar Association Annual Conference, Seoul, 24 September 2019).

Permanent Judge, Tang, Robert, 'Dr Mok Hing Yiu Memorial Lecture: One Country, Two Systems: Basic Law, Common Law and the Rule of Law' (St Hugh's College, Oxford, 22 February 2018).

# Index

For EU product safety concerns, contact us at Calle de José Abascal, 56–1°, 28003 Madrid, Spain or eugpsr@cambridge.org.

www.ingramcontent.com/pod-product-compliance
Lightning Source LLC
LaVergne TN
LVHW011814200926
848484LV00005B/1188

* 9 7 8 1 1 0 8 8 3 1 1 7 8 *